OMAHA HIGH-LOW

FOR LOW-LIMIT PLAYERS

BILL BOSTON

About the Author

Bill Boston, who is also the author of *Omaha High-Low: Play to Win with the Odds*, is one of the most highly respected low-limit Omaha high-low experts in the world. He has devoted the last 25 years of his life to developing optimal winning strategies through computer simulations and real-life play.

OMAHA HIGH-LOW
FOR LOW-LIMIT PLAYERS

BILL BOSTON

CARDOZA PUBLISHING

See Free Book Offer On Page 336

Cardoza Publishing is the foremost gaming and gambling publisher in the world with a library of over 200 up-to-date and easy-to-read books and strategies. These authoritative works are written by the top experts in their fields and with more than 10 million books in print, represent the best-selling and most popular gaming books anywhere.

Library of Congress Catalog No: 2008940734
ISBN 10: 1-58042-255-1
ISBN 13: 978-1-58042-255-0

Visit our new web site (www.cardozabooks.com) or write us for a full list of books, advanced and computer strategies.

CARDOZA PUBLISHING
P.O. Box 98115, Las Vegas, NV 89193
Toll Free Phone (800) 577-WINS
email: cardozabooks@aol.com
www.cardozabooks.com

TABLE OF CONTENTS

PREFACE

By Shane Smith

You are holding in your hands the key to making money at low-limit Omaha high-low, the fastest action, most exciting low-limit poker game in the world. Bill Boston, player and statistician extraordinaire, gives you his best winning advice on beating the small games.

In his other book, *Omaha High-Low: Play to Win with the Odds*, Boston compiled the first set of scientifically tabulated charts ever published for Omaha high-low. His model was a tight $10/$20 player who was selective about the hands he played. And the book has been a huge success, especially if you want more than how-to philosophy.

But wait! Those statistics pretty much left out most of us—we're the people who regularly play in loose, high-action, fast-paced low-limit Omaha high-low in poker rooms and online sites across the country.

No more! Boston changed his computer player's profile to give us the same edge as high-limit players. This new set of stats is based on a good, aggressive, average player who calls with every hand to see the flop from every position. Sound familiar? Not to worry—although he called every flop, Mr. Computer played correctly from the flop onward.

What's the value in that? Based on the results of calling with every type of hand imaginable—great, good, marginal and bad cards—we now have a solid foundation to determine which hands are winners and which ones are losers. And why.

Digging deeper, Boston shows you how one unrelated card devalues your hand, how and why you lose when you chase, and how to adjust your play when a board card alters the value of your hand for better or worse.

If you want more than just another how-to book—if you want why-to and why-not-to, what-for, and when-to—you've found it. Here is the solid skinny, backed up by statistics, on to win at low-limit Omaha high-low poker!

❖ **1** ❖

INTRODUCTION

If you already have some experience playing low-limit Omaha high-low, but have not yet become a consistent winner, this book is for you! My sole purpose is to give you the basic tools and central concepts you need to win at this high-action, exciting poker game.

Omaha high-low is different from Texas hold'em because you are dealt four hole cards instead of two. This gives you six times as many five-card combinations to make a hand on the flop, turn and river as you do in hold'em and, therefore, an opportunity to play more hands and enjoy the action. It is common for five or more players to find hands to play, generating pots with lots of chips to divide between the winning low and high hands.

Unfortunately, many low-limit players don't understand that you must have stronger hands to become involved in the action if you want to win at Omaha high-low. They play too many hands and lose too many chips to the game.

Serious players have a good understanding of hand values and are able to win because they make good decisions based on this knowledge. In any type of poker game, hand selection is critical to your success. I ran millions of hand simulations and recorded the results of every hand you will ever play in Omaha high-low. I've compiled important hand-value charts that you can use as analytical tools to help you master hand selection and improve your game.

In this book, you'll find the hands that are profitable to play, as well as trap hands to avoid. I give you definitive reasons, backed up by statistics, why you should not play certain trap hands that other low-limit players lose a lot of chips with.

Low-limit games include $2/$4, $3/$6, $4/$8, and $5/$10 limit games. The results tabulated in this book are based on $4/$8 limits with the types of players normally found in low-limit games.

In addition to the time I've spent generating data, I've been a winning Omaha high-low player for more than 20 years. The combination of knowledge that I've gained playing my favorite game and the statistical information listed in the charts is what this book is about.

You'll learn important strategies that will show you how to win consistently at this exciting and profitable poker game. The concepts in this book, backed up by statistics and logic, will give you the skills you need to become a winning player in any low-limit Omaha high-low game you play!

❖ **2** ❖

REVIEWING THE ESSENTIALS

This book assumes that you have some experience play-ing low-limit Omaha high-low. If you play regularly, you probably don't need to read this short review. But if it's been a while since you played the game, use this brief chapter as a brush-up on the rules and sequence of play. You also may gain some pointers on certain variations in game structure, the fee the house charges you to play, and how to practice before you play in cash games.

Omaha high-low is a flop game with betting structures similar to Texas hold'em. There is a single bet preflop and again on the flop, and then the bets double on the turn and river. Some casinos and poker sites allow one bet with three raises, while others allow four raises.

Omaha high-low is a split-pot game, meaning that the pot at the end of the action will be split between the best low hand and the best high hand. If there is no qualifying low hand, the entire pot will be awarded to the best high hand. You are dealt four cards face down.

You must combine two cards from your hand with three from the five community cards to make your best five-card hand, whether it is low or high.

To qualify for low, you must use two cards from your hand and three from the board that are unpaired. The highest of the cards must be an 8 or lower. The best high hand must also be composed of two of your hole cards combined with three cards from the board. You may use one or both of the same hole cards for both low and high. The ace is played as the lowest card in the low hand, and the highest card in the high hand. You may use an ace for low and high in the same hand.

The best low hand is A-2-3-4-5, often called the "nut low," a "wheel," or a "bicycle." A wheel may also be played as a straight for high, if no other player has a hand with greater value. The ace is considered "1" when it is played as a low card, and of course "ace" when used as a high card. The worst low hand is 4-5-6-7-8, which may be played as a straight for high.

"Kill Pot" Games

Many Omaha high-low cash games in casinos are played with a "kill" or a "half-kill." If the pot meets the house requirements, the stakes for the next deal increase by 100 percent in kill games, or by 50 percent in half-kill games. Half-kill games are much more common.

For a hand to qualify for half-kill, one player must scoop the entire pot, although in some poker rooms, a player is required to win back-to-back pots. Normally, the rule is that the pot must contain ten times the small bet to qualify, which is $40 in a $4/$8 limit game. When this happens, the bets increase 50 percent on the next hand. In $4/$8 limit games, the bets rise to $6/$12. The winner of the pot is forced to post $6 on a red "kill" button, and the blinds remain $4 and $2.

The action begins with the first position to the left of the $4 big blind. To enter the hand requires a $6 bet. Action continues around the table as usual, back to the blinds, who have the option to call the extra chips to complete their bets to $6, raise, or fold their hands. In some half-kill games, the last player to act is the "killer," the player who scooped the previous pot and posted $6 on the kill button. The killer may check or raise to $12 or reraise to $24 in $4/$8 games. The first two rounds of betting are $6 limit and the last two are $12 limit.

Game rules for "kill" pots are the same as the regular limit game. If the following hand again meets the kill-pot requirements, the limits remain $6/$12 for that hand. It is not unusual to have back-to-back kill pots in Omaha high-low.

The Effects of the Rake

When you play low-limit poker in cardrooms, the house withholds a house fee, commonly called the "rake." Many cardrooms "cut" (rake) each pot 10 percent of the first $40, while some cardrooms cut the pots $5 each. For the stats in this book, the computer was set to rake each pot 10 percent from the first $30, plus a $1 "toke" (tip) for a maximum of $4 per hand.

If the casino deals 20 hands an hour, $80 to $100 per hour is removed from the game. In a tight game with little action, most or all players will have sustained a loss by the time the game is over. This is a good reason you should be selective about the game you play. Any game with mostly tight players and little action is one to avoid. That type of game usually is not profitable to play because of the casino rake.

How to Practice Before You Play

When I first started playing Omaha high-low, I sat around the kitchen table and dealt out dummy hands until I got the hang of what it took to win. Now there are many more ways to practice before you start playing in a casino.

If you are fairly new to the game and would like to gain proficiency before venturing into live action with higher limits than you are comfortable with, you may open an account with an online poker site and play Omaha high-low with free money. After gaining experience and confidence, you can transfer a small amount of cash to your account and play live action.

The advantage of playing live action online compared to playing in a walk-in casino poker room is that you may play limits as low as 2¢/4¢ compared to $4/$8. You can gain experience at reading cards for a fraction of what if would cost you in live casino action. If you misread your cards while playing at an online poker site, the computer reads them for you, which lessens the pressure on new players with limited experience.

For a few dollars, inexperienced players may enjoy the same amount of practice as they get for $500 in $4/$8 limit games, plus the dealer tips they save. In addition, if you become subjected to any disparaging remarks about how you play the game, you have an option to click on your player-name and check "block chat." For timid people who are absolutely too shy to sit at a table and play live-action poker, online poker is a great place to play and enjoy the game without feeling intimidated.

Before joining a game online, you should spend a few minutes observing different tables and select one with players who are staying for the flop with marginal hands. Find a game with several "fish" (players who play almost every hand, no matter what its value), practice what you have learned, and play the game as if you were playing for high stakes.

Further, you may enjoy playing in one of the many small tournaments that are available at online poker sites, starting at $1.10 buy-in. Most poker sites even have freeroll tournaments that cost you nothing, and give you the opportunity to win actual cash. I know several players who started with freeroll tournaments and now have sizeable accounts.

One advantage of playing Internet poker is that your cards are dealt face up and you have more time to figure out your low and high hands. After each hand is completed, the winning hands for high and low are shown in an information box for your review. If you want to be a spectator before you play online, select any game and watch the decisions that the players make.

Watching live-action games also provides great information on hand values. Your observations may also enlighten you about the types of bad decisions made by many Omaha high-low players at all limits.

In the games you play, I suggest that you record your results on low and high hands you play to get a feel for the strength of cards needed to beat the game. You may also refer to the charts in the back of this book to review hand values. This is one more tool to help improve and test your skills.

Play any game that you enjoy, regardless of limits, with all the skills you possess. The best way to become a good Omaha high-low player is to play your best with every hand that you are dealt—and always play to win!

❖ 3 ❖

READING YOUR CARDS

Omaha high-low is a hand-driven game. To be competitive at it, you must become proficient at reading your cards. The numbers change on the turn of each card, making it of utmost importance that you know whether your hand is increasing or decreasing in value as the deal progresses.

For practice, I have pictured several hands for your review. These examples show how the value of your hand can change on the turn of one card.

In the first hand, I am going to be kind and deal you good cards, the ones you like to see when you're playing a cash game or a tournament. Before reading my comments below each hand, review the hand and mentally list the cards needed to make winning low and high hands.

On the flop, review the cards to see whether you have a "nut" (best) low or high hand, or the possibility of making one. Repeat the same procedure on the turn and river.

When analyzing all possibilities, be aware of board cards as they are being dealt that may cause your hand to sink in value. Three suited cards or a board pair that doesn't help you, but may benefit another player's hand, can cause your cards to become inferior.

Practice Hand 1

YOU

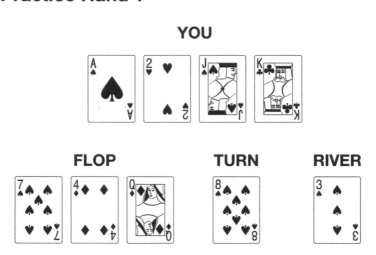

On the flop, you had a draw to the nut low (since two low cards were showing on the board). You observed two suited cards that could possibly make a diamond flush draw for another player. The 8♠ on the turn greatly improved your hand by making you the nut-low hand, and giving you a flush draw. It also made it possible for another player to make an 8-high straight for high if he had a 5-6 in his hand. The 3♠ on the river gave you the top flush, with the possibility of scooping the entire pot if no one else also had an A-2 in his hand.

In this practice hand, the 7♠ 4♦ 3♠ board cards combined with your A♠ 2♥ to make the best possible low. Your A♠ J♠ combined with the 8♠ 7♠ 3♠ to make the nut flush. This is a prime example of using the ace for low and high in the same hand.

When reading your hand, start with the highest card first and continue to the lowest. If the 7 or 8 in the board cards depicted above had been a 5, you would have made 5-4-3-2-A for low, called a "wheel" or a "bicycle," the best possible low hand in Omaha high-low.

Practice Hand 2

This is a hand that many new players misread. Your cards are suited, but the flop comes out "rainbow" (cards of three different suits).

YOU

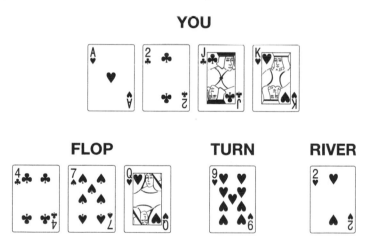

FLOP　　　　　**TURN**　　**RIVER**

The turn card is a high card, the 9♥. When a high card hits the turn in a situation like this one, some players make the mistake of concentrating only on their low draw, looking for a card that is lower than an 8 on the river. When the 2♥ is dealt on the river, counterfeiting their low draw, they sometimes overlook the nut flush they just made and throw their cards in the muck.

While playing in a $5/$10 game in Atlantic City, a player sitting to my left actually had the hand pictured above and called the turn with it. When it was checked to her on the river, she showed me her cards, turned them face down, and threw away the winning high hand. "My luck's been running real bad," she said.

If she had turned her cards face up, the dealer would have awarded her the high side of the pot. When hands are turned up on the table, "cards speak." At that time, players may assist a player or the dealer in separating winning and losing hands. But while someone is still holding his/her cards, it is improper to inform them about how to play a hand or the value of their cards, even though you are not contesting the pot. Unfortunately, winning hands are sometimes overlooked by even seasoned players and tossed into the muck.

Practice Hand 3

Now let's review an actual hand that I played against experienced players in an Omaha high-low game in a major Las Vegas poker room. I was in the big blind with the cards pictured below and will refer to my hand as "Blind Hand." The other hand belongs to "Confused." Let me add that I only played these garbage cards because nobody had raised before the flop. Otherwise, I would have mucked this hand without a second thought.

BLIND HAND

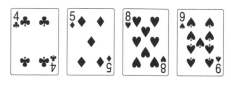

CONFUSED HAND

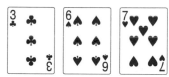

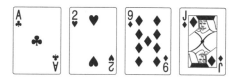

On the flop, Confused and one other player made the nut-low hand (A-2-3-6-7) and I made a 7-high straight (3-4-5-6-7). I bet and both players called. The 8♣ on the turn promoted my hand to a 9-high straight, but made it possible for another player to make a 10-high straight. Therefore, I checked. Confused bet and the other A-2-x-x called. I also called.

When the 2♠ came on the river, it "counterfeited" (duplicated) both players' A-2. However, Confused still bet, the second A-2 player folded his hand, and I called in the hope of winning the high half of the pot. I was pleased when I saw Confused's cards because I realized that I had scooped the pot (won both high and low).

How did it happen? When the 2 came on the river, my 9-high straight was still good for high and my 4-5 was promoted to the best low, as it gave me a 6-5-4-3-2 straight. With the deuce in his hand counterfeited, the best low that Confused could make was 7-6-3-2-A for the second-best low.

With both hands turned up, it was hard to convince Confused that his hand wasn't good for low. The dealer was also temporarily confused in reading the hand. Another player helped out by explaining that my cards had made a 6-low hand on the river, while poor Confused's hand had remained a 7-low. "I just can't believe that a 4-5 made the best low!" he moaned.

Some players holding the hand that I held in the blind also may have been confused in reading this hand. For example, if another player had made a 10-high straight for the best high hand, when Confused turned up his A-2, it may have appeared that the 4-5 (the 6-high straight) was no good for low. These types of hands are common in Omaha high-low; therefore, I strongly suggest turning up your cards for all to read.

Practice Hand 4

Here is another example of a player misreading his hand. During the 2007 World Series of Poker, I was playing in a $20/$40 Omaha high-low cash game when the following hand was dealt to "Joe," the player seated on my left.

JOE'S HAND

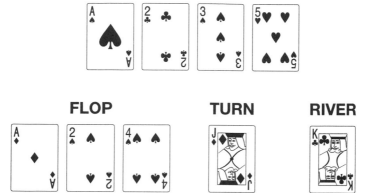

FLOP **TURN** **RIVER**

This hand was bet very aggressively on the flop and turn, and checked on the river. Joe—who had made a wheel on the flop—briefly placed his cards face up on the table and remarked, "Two pair and a flush draw on the flop and I couldn't fill up or make a flush!" With that, he immediately turned his cards facedown and threw them in the muck. Joe had been concentrating so intensely on improving his two pair or making the flush for high, he totally overlooked the wheel, which would have won both ends of the pot.

A player with three of a kind was awarded the high hand and the low was awarded to a player with A-3-6-7. By turning up your cards and letting the dealer read them, you can avoid costly mistakes like the one above.

In Chapter 3, I explain how to read the statistical charts that are such an integral part of this book. Once you know how to understand and use the stats, you'll be on your way to improving your game tremendously.

❖ 4 ❖

UNDERSTANDING THE CHARTS

When you take into consideration all four suits, there are an astounding 270,725 hand combinations possible in Omaha high-low. That's a lot of hands to wrap your mind around!

So, for the purposes of this book, "suited" means that two cards in a hand are simply of the same suit—whether it is clubs, diamonds, hearts or spades—rather than noting a specific suit. "Double-suited" means that only two suits are represented in the hand, and "non-suited" means that no cards in the hand are of the same suit. Using this method, we come up with 5,278 possible Omaha high-low hands. That's a number we can work with!

How the Statistics Were Generated

Using the hand analysis function of Wilson Software's *Turbo Omaha High-Low Split*, I ran more than 50 million hand simulations to establish the skill level of each player in Wilson's 52-player lineup. The deck was stacked and all hands were played from every position at the table 100,000 times.

After completing and recording the results of the hand simulations, I selected two tight, four average, and three loose players from Wilson's lineup. In an attempt to make the results as realistic as possible, I selected a lineup of players with eight different betting profiles similar to live action players normally found in low-limit games.

The type of player I selected from the lineup to generate the statistics in this book is an average, aggressive player with good results on all practice hands that had a profit expectation. Many results consist of 1,000,000 hand simulations, but I have reduced them down to represent 100,000 hands in order to produce consistent stats.

How Hand Values Are Calculated

Basically, hand values are calculated by dividing winning or losing amounts by the number of times a hand was dealt to a player. For a better understanding of how hand values are determined, look at the example I've inserted to illustrate a hand that was played 1,000,000 times.

OMAHA HIGH-LOW 8 OR BETTER
5,278 HANDS   9 HANDED

| HAND RANK | VALUE $4/$8 | POCKET CARDS | | HIGH % | LOW% | SCOOP % | PART OR ALL % |
		HAND	SUITED				
132	$10.09	A-A-A-2	S	3.8%	10.1%	20.6%	34.5%

The **Hand Rank** column is based on the performance of the hand compared to all 5,278 possible Omaha high-low hands. With 1 (one) being the best performer,

A-A-A-2 suited ranked 132, meaning there are only 131 hands that outperform it.

The **Value** column indicates that the hand won an average of $10.09 per hand in a $4/$8 limit game. The **Pocket Cards** column lists the hand and whether it is suited: **DS = double-suited**, **S = Suited** and **NS = non-suited**.

When a pot is split, **High** and **Low** receive one-half credit each. When one player wins the total pot, **Scoop** gets all the credit for the win. **Part or All** represents high, low and scoop totals for the hand.

To conserve space in the charts, dollar amounts were reduced to an average per-hand value as indicated above. High, low, and scoop results were converted to percentages to make the charts more meaningful.

Negative-Value Hands

After playing in many low-limit games, I realized that many people play negative-value hands that they should avoid. Therefore, to provide you with useful information about negative-value hands, I changed the calling criteria for the Computer Generated Player (the CGP). I programmed it to call a bet to see the flop with every hand dealt, from every position. After the flop, however, the CGP's betting criteria for playing a hand remained the same.

The purpose of playing these negative hands is to guide you in case you decide to play them. Some of these hands are trap hands that experienced players do not play. Many low-limit players, however, tend to gamble with negative-value hands. For example, here is a hand from the statistical charts that many low-limit players play without realizing that it is a negative-expectation hand.

HAND RANK	VALUE $4/$8	POCKET CARDS		HIGH %	LOW%	SCOOP %	PART OR ALL %
		HAND	SUITED				
3366	-$3.89	5-6-7-8	NS	5.8%	2.0%	5.1%	12.9%

Remember that the CGP calls a bet to see the flop with every hand dealt, from every position. Some hands improved enough on the flop that the CGP played them. The stats indicate that the CGP played this hand and won part or all the pot 12.9 percent of hands played, losing an average of $3.89 each time.

To keep the stats realistic, however, I want to show you that it is not profitable to venture a bet on certain types of hands. For example, an accomplished player will not enter the pot with 5-6-7-8. Look at the chart below, showing the results when the hand is played correctly.

HAND RANK	VALUE $4/$8	POCKET CARDS		HIGH %	LOW%	SCOOP %	PART OR ALL %
		HAND	SUITED				
1311	-$0.74	5-6-7-8	NS	0.5%	0.2%	0.4%	1.0%

This experienced player only lost an average of $.74 per hand because he only played it in the big blind in unraised pots, and folded it in all other positions. The only time he won with the hand, then, was when no one called the amount of the big blind, allowing him to win the pot by default.

When you compare the results of these two hands, the experienced-player hand that was never voluntarily played outranked the first example because it lost less money. After I ran the stats, this second set of results is what actually appeared in the charts, because the CGP that I assigned to play it correctly didn't play the hand except from the big blind in an uncontested pot.

After viewing several thousand such hands, I decided to program the computer player to call a bet to see the flop, and to continue with the hand only if the betting criteria were met. Don't confuse calling to see the flop with playing the hand to the river. There is a big difference in the results.

Let's look at the same hand and have the player call all bets to the river to demonstrate the difference.

HAND RANK	VALUE $4/$8	POCKET CARDS		HIGH %	LOW%	SCOOP %	PART OR ALL %
		HAND	SUITED				
5277	-$13.42	5-6-7-8	NS	7.5%	5.1%	7.4%	20.0%

Based on the results obtained by playing the hand to the river, it ranked next to the worst hand in the charts! If all hands were played to the river, there would be several hundred that would lose even more per hand.

This is a prime example of calling a bet with a marginal hand in the hope of winning part of the pot, becoming trapped with a second-best hand, and losing money to it. Such hands do win, as indicated in the first chart, but they lose far more than they win.

When you compare the results of this hand to the results that the experienced player got, you can see why you should not play negative-value hands. The 5-6-7-8 offsuit won part or all the pots 20 percent of the time—and still lost an average of $13.42 per hand!

Marginal Cards

All marginal hands were played on the flop to determine the results that you may expect if you elect to
play these types of hands. They are listed for you to
review and avoid. I have included marginal hands
because many low-limit players play far too many
marginal holdings and lose a lot of chips to the game
as the result.

Many hands show small or negative values. In no way
do I recommend playing these hands for financial gain.
I showed them because you will be dealt them. And
sometimes, you will be forced to play marginal and
negative-value hands from the blinds, making it even
more important to know this information in order to
make informed decisions on whether to call or fold
your hand under certain conditions.

If you fall into the costly habit of chasing after the flop,
your results will be much lower than the charts indicate. The charts are not based on how a professional
player would play the hand—they are based on how
the CGP, a good low-limit player, played the hand. The
amounts you win will be much less if you play your
hands improperly. It also is possible to outperform
these stats in a game packed with loose, action players.

The Impact of Game Selection on Profit

The types of players in a game influence the value of a
given hand. When few players contest a pot, less money
is won on a given hand. Therefore, a hand's value
will decrease. By replacing one or two rocks with "no
fold'em" action players, the pots will greatly increase
in size and hand values will increase accordingly.

The CGP represents live-action players quite well. Most games in which you play will vary in player skill levels, although it is possible to sit in a game full of "rocks," tight players who play only the best hands and have infinite patience in waiting for them. Tight games have little action and generate small pots. Good games have a table full of action players who create great opportunities for you to make big profits with correct play.

In other words, hand value increases in loose games because more money is bet. In tight games, it decreases because less money is bet. This is a good reason to play in games with action players.

In the lineup I used to generate the stats, five or more players saw the flop 47 percent of hands played. After viewing several hundred randomly dealt hands and how they were played, I was very satisfied with this lineup. I did not select any "no fold'em" or passive players for the lineup.

The statistical charts indicate the percentage of times that a particular hand will win high, low, or scoop the pot. These are the tools you need to master the art and science of hand selection. For consistency, the highest card of a suit is always suited with a random lower card. To simplify the stats, the ace was combined with all other cards in the deck, beginning with the lowest card and continuing until all possible hand combinations were complete.

The Value of Computer Generated Statistics

Using the computer to generate stats is a very useful tool because it is programmed to make consistent decisions based on hand value, action and position. The great things about computer players are that they don't go on tilt, become tired, drink alcohol at the table, make facial expressions, or converse. Further, their play is very consistent.

No person is going to play every hand 1,000,000 times. If you play one hand every three minutes for eight hours every day, it would take you over 9,000 years to play all 5,278 Omaha high-low hands listed in the charts 100,000 times. My point is that nobody can play enough hands to generate sufficient data with the accuracy and speed of a computer.

Generating and recording stats 1,000,000 times per hand is extremely time consuming. I believe that 100,000 times is sufficient. Nonetheless, I spent several extra weeks running 1,000,000 simulations on the most important hands that will be dealt to you. The information gained from this hard work and more than 22 years playing the game form the backbone of this book.

How Close to Reality is a Computer Game?
It is virtually impossible to play in any game that will have the hand-value consistency of a computer. Computers are programmed to call, raise or fold under certain conditions. They play marginal hands only on the button, for example, and adhere to hundreds of other criteria for playing different hands. Humans sometimes make bad plays when the pot is loaded with chips, or play marginal hands when losing in an effort to win back money—only to lose more. Computers don't fall into these expensive traps.

In casino or online games, players leave and new people join the game. Every player that joins your game will play somewhat differently from the one who left, thereby changing the stats for hand values. The statistics in this book are based on the same type of player for every hand that is played in every position. Of course, live action games will deviate from computer games, but the results in this book will give you a solid foundation to work with.

What Does It Take to Win Consistently?

It is easy for any player to win with quality starting hands. However, the true value of a hand is based on how well the hand is played and, equally important, how poorly other players perform in the same hand. To become a consistent winner requires knowledge of hand values, discipline, and practice.

To master the game, I believe that your best learning tools are hand-analysis statistics and practice. The hand-value charts I have prepared are a good reference for comparing one hand's performance against another. They are useful learning tools, and I strongly recommend that you spend time studying them.

The stats in this book are based on the results of a good average player who calls with every hand to see the flop from every position. Your results will depend on selecting cards with positive values, and then folding your hand after the flop when it becomes apparent that your cards have not improved and have no scoop potential.

After studying the material presented in the following chapters, your results actually should be superior to the charts. Why? Because you will avoid playing many of the marginal hands normally played by low-limit players.

Now let's move on to how to select good (profitable) hands to play, using the statistical charts to back up the strategies I suggest.

❖ 5 ❖

SELECTING PROFITABLE HANDS TO PLAY

Investing the first bet in any hand is like purchasing real estate. You must have a good knowledge of property values, or solicit the advice of a professional realtor. If you fail to do that, your purchase most likely will be less than a bargain.

The same applies to Omaha high-low. If you elect to play substandard starting hands, your financial rewards will be less than profitable over the long run. Therefore, you must have a good knowledge of starting hands to master this exciting game and become a consistent winner.

Selecting starting hands with good profit potential is the most important thing you can do to become a consistent winner. In many low-limit Omaha high-low games, it is not unusual for five or more players to see the flop. For this reason, the pot may be divided between several players at the showdown. This is a very important reason to play hands with scoop potential, because any hand that may only win half the pot can cost you a lot of chips over time.

Calling one small bet to see the flop is the best bargain there is in Omaha high-low when you're holding an ace with three good connecting cards. You can see seven of nine cards for $2 if you're playing $2/$4 limits, or $4 in $4/$8 games. I am not suggesting that you see the flop with any four cards; to win in the long run, it is necessary that you play cards that work together and have scoop potential. Playing cards that work together is essential: The better they fit, the greater the scoop potential they will have.

The Power of the Ace

The ace is the strongest card in the deck. If you don't hold one, two or more aces will be in the hands of other players, on average. Without an ace in your hand, it's almost like playing four cards against five for each player that is dealt one, because the ace may be played as two different cards in the same hand. It can be played as "1," representing the lowest card for low, and as "ace," the highest card in all high hands. No other card in the deck has both a low and high value.

However, the fact that you are dealt an ace is not always a valid reason to become involved in a hand. An ace should be played with good connecting cards that have high profit expectations. Of course, the ace has a greater winning potential than any card in the deck, because more cards work with it than any other card.

Here is a pictorial of all the cards that work with an ace for low, high, and scoop hands.

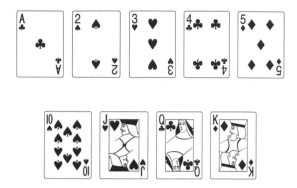

The cards pictured here represent the card ranks that work together with an ace. The ace works with 35 cards in the deck that will make the best low, highest straight, flush, full house, four of a kind, and royal flush. Combined with small connecting cards, an ace can make A-2-3-4-5 for a wheel, or the best possible nut low.

Only four ranks don't work with the ace: 6, 7, 8 and 9. Should one of these cards be the same suit as the ace, however, it may be used to make the nut-high flush.

Starting Hands

Although there are 5,278 different hands that are dealt in Omaha high-low, more than 4,000 of them have negative values and should not be played. Learning to recognize playable starting hands at a glance will greatly improve your skills in making proper decisions about which hands to play and those to avoid.

Placing hands into groups makes it easier to select hands that are profitable to play and those to avoid. I will start by listing the best hands that are dealt in Omaha high-low. Then I'll discuss less profitable hands, and finish with hands that are not profitable to play.

Listed below are 25 of the best A-A-x-x hands and 25 A-x-x-x hands, including hand values for $4/$8 limits. Hands are listed as being double-suited (DS), suited (S) or non-suited (NS). You will note that all hands listed in the chart are either double-suited or suited, and none are non-suited.

These charts show the importance of a hand being suited or double-suited, which gives it a higher probability of winning, and thus produces greater financial rewards.

THE BEST 25 A-A-X-X AND A-X-X-X HANDS

$21.68	A-A-2-2	DS	$16.54	A-2-3-K	DS
$17.98	A-A-2-2	S	$13.41	A-2-2-3	DS
$26.23	A-A-2-3	DS	$11.61	A-2-2-3	S
$22.39	A-A-2-3	S	$13.11	A-2-3-3	DS
$18.58	A-A-2-3	NS	$15.71	A-2-3-4	DS
$24.59	A-A-2-4	DS	$13.94	A-2-3-4	S
$20.12	A-A-2-4	S	$14.59	A-2-3-5	DS
$16.39	A-A-2-4	NS	$12.68	A-2-3-5	S
$22.26	A-A-2-5	DS	$12.66	A-2-3-6	DS
$18.37	A-A-2-5	S	$11.57	A-2-3-9	DS
$20.20	A-A-2-6	DS	$13.29	A-2-3-10	DS
$18.81	A-A-2-7	DS	$14.14	A-2-3-J	DS
$18.23	A-A-2-8	DS	$11.69	A-2-3-J	S
$18.06	A-A-2-9	DS	$15.05	A-2-3-Q	DS
$18.97	A-A-2-10	DS	$12.43	A-2-3-Q	S
$18.97	A-A-2-J	DS	$13.39	A-2-3-K	S
$19.00	A-A-2-Q	DS	$12.55	A-2-4-5	DS
$19.00	A-A-2-K	DS	$12.47	A-2-4-Q	DS
$18.34	A-A-3-3	DS	$13.93	A-2-4-K	DS
$21.19	A-A-3-4	DS	$11.98	A-2-5-K	DS
$17.45	A-A-3-4	S	$11.74	A-2-J-J	DS
$19.78	A-A-3-5	DS	$13.62	A-2-Q-Q	DS
$17.83	A-A-3-6	DS	$16.51	A-2-K-K	DS
$16.73	A-A-3-7	DS	$14.17	A-2-K-K	S
$17.72	A-A-4-5	DS	$12.56	A-3-K-K	DS

By comparing the hands on this chart, it is evident that any A-A hand with two good connecting cards is a superior hand to play. When a hand is suited or double-suited, the hand value greatly increases.

For example, look at the A-2-3-4 non-suited (NS) in the charts. Note that the value of the hand increases more than 25 percent when it is suited. Further, its value increases more than 50 percent when it is double-suited.

The power of the ace in Omaha high-low is remarkable—488 of the top 500 ranked hands contain an ace. That leaves only 12 "ace-less" hands that rank among the top 500. For your review, here they are:

THE 12 ACE-LESS HANDS IN THE TOP 500

HAND RANK	VALUE $4/$8	POCKET CARDS		PART OR ALL %
		HAND	SUITED	
454	$4.08	2-3-4-5	DS	22.9%
500	$3.52	2-3-Q-Q	DS	22.3%
317	$6.00	2-3-K-K	DS	25.7%
466	$3.94	2-4-K-K	DS	24.7%
486	$3.66	10-10-Q-Q	DS	18.7%
372	$5.11	10-10-K-K	DS	21.2%
387	$4.92	10-10-K-K	S	21.0%
435	$4.34	J-J-Q-Q	DS	19.0%
353	$5.37	J-J-K-K	DS	21.3%
497	$3.55	J-J-K-K	S	19.3%
329	$5.76	Q-Q-K-K	DS	21.5%
423	$4.43	Q-Q-K-K	S	19.6%

Hands with Low Cards that Connect with an Ace

For practice, look at the hand below that has good connecting cards and produces the maximum number of two-card combinations. The greater the number of card combinations in your hand, the more ways you have to win.

YOU

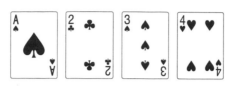

Six Two-Card Combinations
A-2, A-3, A-4, 2-3, 2-4, 3-4

$13.94	A-2-3-4	S
$10.43	A-2-3-4	NS

To demonstrate the power of an ace, let's look at a second hand without an ace for comparison. This ace-less hand produces the same number of card combinations, but has a much lower profit potential.

YOU

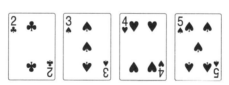

Six Ace-Less Two-Card Combinations
2-3, 2-4, 2-5, 3-4, 3-5, 4-5

$2.72	2-3-4-5	S
$1.23	2-3-4-5	NS

The basic difference between these two hands is that the first one has an ace in it, and the other hand does not. By comparing the hand values, you will discover the tremendous difference for profit potential that the hand containing the ace has compared to the other.

It is important to have an understanding of hands that have good profit potential and learn to recognize ones that do not. The majority of these negative-value hands are ace-less. With a little time studying the charts and some practice, you should be able to recognize and avoid playing the majority of bad hands that are dealt to you.

How One Card Changes the Value of a Hand

Not all hands have the same number of playable combinations, of course. By reviewing the data in the back of this book, you can see how a given hand declines in value as the number of combinations is reduced. For example, let's look at the same hand pictured above. Changing just one card illustrates how the number of possible two-card combinations and hand values decline.

If you view the list of cards that work with the ace and replace the 9 with any one of them, you will discover that the hand loses value. For practice and additional understanding of the game, give it a try.

YOU

| $10.13 | A-2-3-9 | S |
| $5.09 | A-2-3-9 | NS |

It is easy to see that the 9 does not work with any of the other three cards above; therefore, the value of the hand decreases considerably. If there are any hands you have doubts about, or would like to compare, find them on the charts for comparison. The 9 is a card you'll find in the worst hands dealt in Omaha high-low. For this reason you should only consider cards that rank 10 and higher when contesting with high hands.

The Best Omaha High-Low Hand

YOU

The best starting hand in Omaha high-low is A-A-2-3 double-suited. This hand may produce the biggest four of a kind, full house, two top flush hand possibilities and the lowest possible hand. It has counterfeit protection because it contains three low cards; and since it has two of the four aces in the deck, the possibility of another player having a hand with an A-2 is greatly reduced. With high, low and scoop potential, this hand has the best overall performance record of any hand dealt in Omaha high-low. You should be dealt this hand once in about 2,800 hands you play.

In low-limit loose games, where five or more players often see the flop, be very selective with your starting hands. As a general rule, if you are not in the blind, it is advisable that your starting hands include an A-2 or A-3 with good connecting cards, or an ace suited or double-suited with high cards. In nine-handed games, there is an 85 percent possibility that an A-2-x-x or an A-3-x-x will be dealt to one or more players.

When you are in late position and there has been a lot of action in front of you, this is normally a message that at least one player has an A-2-x-x. Therefore, it is advisable that you fold a 2-3-x-x. If you are in late position and there is little or no action, you may call with marginal hands such as A-4-5-x suited or double-suited, 2-3-4-5 or 2-3-K-K suited or double-suited.

To increase your chances of winning with marginal hands, only play them in late position. The action of the players in front of you will furnish you with information on the strength of their hands, giving you an advantage. Any hand with several players betting aggressively before the flop is one to avoid. Save your money unless you hold cards with scoop potential.

The betting habits of most low-limit players are very consistent, and their actions will provide you with meaningful information that will let you know when to call, bet, raise or fold your hand. If you observe the quality of hands that players in your game raise or check with, you should be able to easily put a player on a hand, after some practice.

Folding the Second-Best Hand

Winning money in Omaha high-low is not solely based on selecting good hands to play, but folding a second-best hand based on the betting habits of other players in the game. If you are playing $4/$8 limits and save twenty $4 bets and ten $8 bets, your chip stack will be $160 greater at the end of the game. To be a winner in any poker game, you must develop self-discipline and fold your cards when it is apparent that you are playing against a stronger hand.

It is much more profitable to fold one winning hand than to call with several losing hands. It is easy to see one more bet and become trapped with the second-best hand.

For example, the reason I suggest folding most 2-3-x-x hands in early position is because there are over 300 hands superior to the best 2-3-x-x hand, and a player holding an A-2-x-x is likely to raise behind you. In last position, you may call one bet to see the flop. If you don't improve your hand, muck it and wait for another opportunity.

If you are an action player and like to play a lot of hands, it is of utmost necessity that you develop iron-clad discipline and exercise good poker judgment. In other words, fold your hand when action dictates the necessity to do so.

Should You Raise Before the Flop?

Some people suggest raising before the flop to reduce the number of opponents and make the hand more profitable to play. I have good news: This is a misconception many players have. In low-limit Omaha high-low, when you make a raise, most players stay. In fact, you often get reraised. I suggest that you see the flop and improve your hand before becoming too aggressive with your betting.

When you are in late position, there is a table full of callers, and you are dealt an ace-deuce suited with good connecting cards, there are two good reasons not to raise before the flop. First, you don't want to run the fish out with second-best hands that will make you a lot of chips. Equally important, when there are a great number of callers in a hand, this is a good indication that an abundance of low cards could be in the hands of other players and the flop may produce high cards and make it unlikely for you to win any part of the pot.

It is not possible to know if you are going to receive a favorable flop and you don't want to build the pot for players that are playing high cards. No matter how good your starting hand, you must receive a flop that ties your hand together before becoming overly aggressive with betting.

When you raise before the flop, players that don't call are the ones with marginal hands that you want to stay in the hand and contribute more chips to your stack. You are also advertising to other players that you have a strong hand, and may not get any action after the flop.

When I am holding a strong hand in late position, I usually just call. After the turn card is dealt and the bets are doubled, I will raise because more chips are in the pot. Also, players seem to stay to the river in low-limit games once they have called three bets, thereby increasing the pot size.

In higher-limit games, I often will raise before the flop to eliminate certain players. Let me give you an example of the type of hand I might raise with in higher-limit games, but just call with in low-limit games.

YOU

The main purpose for me to raise with this hand in a higher-limit game is to drive out players holding an A-3-x-x or 2-3-x-x, which are better low hands than my A-4. Should the flop, turn or river produce a 2, I would have the winning low and possibly a scoop hand with my double-suited aces. If I hadn't raised out the player holding the A-3-x-x, he would have made the nut low and cost me no less than half the pot.

Although some writers suggest using this strategy in smaller games, it doesn't usually work in low-limit Omaha high-low, because so many players call raises before the flop. It is virtually impossible, in fact, to drive out anyone preflop.

Now let's look at a second scenario. You have a very strong starting hand with good connecting cards such as A-A-2-4 suited.

YOU

You are in first position and you raise before the flop. Your raise reduces the number of players in the pot from an average of five to three. You eliminated players with marginal hands. How do you know they had weak hands? Because players with strong hands weren't going anywhere, no matter what.

When all bets are added up for three-player and five-player pots, the total pot added up to the amounts shown below. The net profit is based on the number of players. It is clear to see how numbers affect profit potentials in a split pot.

PLAYERS	TOTAL BETS	HIGH WINS	LOW WINS	LESS BETS	NET PROFIT
3	$86	$43	$43	$28	$15
5	$112	$56	$56	$24	$32

Suppose that you are in early position and raise the bet to $8 in a $4/$8 game. If two players call, including the big blind, each player will invest a total of $28. That adds up to $84 plus the $2 forfeited by the small blind for a total of $86. With a strong hand like this—one that you are normally dealt only once a round—you invest $28 and make a profit of $15.

What if you hadn't raised? Assuming that five players were in the hand, you would have invested $24 and the pot size would have increased to $112. These results are based on the pot being split evenly between you and another player.

Of course, with your double-suited hand headed by A-A, it was possible for you to win high with a flush or full house, and either all or half of the low. This time, let's assume that you won high with the nut flush and split the low with an A-2-x-x player.

In the calculations below, you won half of the low ($22) plus the high ($43) less your bets ($28) with three players for a profit of $37. With five players, you collected half of the low ($28) plus the high ($56) less your total bets of $24. You actually bet $4 less and made more profit by not raising out two players.

PLAYERS	TOTAL BETS	HIGH WINS	LOW WINS	LESS BETS	NET PROFIT
3	$86	$43	$43	$28	$37
5	$112	$56	$56	$24	$60

You can clearly see that it is more profitable to keep as many players in a hand as possible. Having more players in a given hand makes a huge difference in the amount you may win. If you raise players who are holding marginal hands out of the pot, you win very little with your strong hands. The amounts above may increase slightly if players in your game generally call one or two bets and then fold.

Of course, no playing style works perfectly in every game. Since each game is comprised of different styles of players, you must modify the way you play to maximize your profit potential.

❖ 6 ❖

AVOIDING PROBLEM HANDS

In Omaha high-low, it is easy for any player to call to see the flop with a powerful starting hand. The problem, however, is that many low-limit players lose money because they play too many hands with negative value that should have been avoided. When calling a bet to see the flop, it is important for you to select hands that have profit potential. Otherwise, just wait for the next hand.

To give you a better understanding of hand values, let me point out that only 662 of the 5,278 hands played by low-limit players have a hand value of $2.00 or greater—and 621 of these hands contain at least one ace.

Statistics will not provide you with the absolute amount you will win or lose with any given hand. The results are based on how well a hand is played as well as the skill levels of other players in the game. The hand-value charts are good reference material and the time you spend studying them will greatly improve your knowledge of the game.

Before we discuss the hands you should play to see the flop, let me show you an easy way to eliminate many hands that you should avoid playing. Pictured below are "Problem Cards." These cards equal slightly more than half of the deck.

Problem Cards

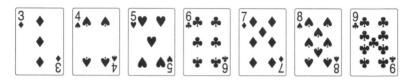

Now look at the chart below. It includes every hand with four problem cards in it that has any positive value. Note that each positive-value hand that includes problem cards is double-suited. The best hand in the group has less than $1 in hand value, and wins part of the pot or scoops it 20.2 percent of hands played. On the negative side, these hands will lose about 80 percent of the time they are played.

HANDS THAT CONTAIN FOUR PROBLEM CARDS

HAND RANK	VALUE $4/$8	POCKET CARDS		PART OR ALL %
		HAND	SUITED	
929	$0.58	3-3-4-5	DS	18.2%
907	$0.69	3-4-4-5	DS	19.3%
917	$0.63	3-4-5-5	DS	19.2%
869	$0.92	3-4-5-6	DS	20.2%
1012	$0.25	3-4-5-7	DS	19.4%

If you are dealt a hand that contains a combination of any four cards listed in the Problem Cards group, you will be holding a hand that does not rank in the top 1,000 hands unless it is double-suited. Therefore, most of the time it will be a negative-value hand that should be folded. It is easy to see that this group of cards will cost you a great number of chips if you succumb to thinking that these cards are profitable to play.

To better understand the weakness of the problem cards pictured above, we will play a commonly dealt hand and show how easy it is to become trapped.

Practice Trap Hand

YOU

FLOP

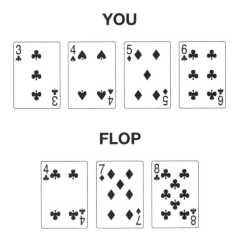

This is a good flop for the cards that you are holding—you made the nut straight by using the 5 and 6 in your hand. Now, consider the cards needed to make a possible scoop hand. Since you have the high side made, you need an A-2 to make the nut-low, which may counterfeit other players and make your hand the best for low and high. However, it's not that easy. To simplify the math, the odds are approximately 62 to 1 against being dealt those two cards.

Any time you are holding two middle cards that make a straight such as the 5-6 in the hand above, no less than five cards can kill your hand on the turn—5-6-9-10-J. Any one of these cards will make it possible for another player to make a higher straight. To give you a simple example, the 5 makes it possible for a player holding a 6-9 to make a 9-high straight. And to make things worse, if a 4, 7 or 8 pairs the board, a full house is very possible.

Here are the cards that you don't care to see after the flop when playing this hand: 4-5-6-7-8-9-10. The river card could make things worse for a player that made a 9- or 10-high straight on the turn, as he could lose to a jack- or queen-high straight on the river. And then there's the possibility that someone with a flush draw on the flop will make it on the river and beat any straight for high.

On the positive side, there are four cards in the deck that are safe, provided that you are dealt two of the four: A-2-Q-K. Any two of these cards that are not clubs will make your hand safe, and the A-2 may make your hand a scooper.

Players do win with hands similar to the one above, but they lose more than they win.

Here's the most interesting thing about this hand: After the flop, there is no single card in the deck that may be dealt on the turn that guarantees you will hold the winning hand on the river.

Playing Two-Gap Hands

YOU

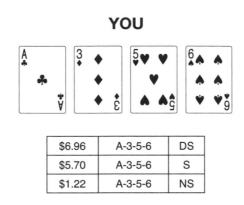

$6.96	A-3-5-6	DS
$5.70	A-3-5-6	S
$1.22	A-3-5-6	NS

The hand above is an example of a two-gap hand, meaning that two specific cards are needed to complete it, the 2 and 4, plus any other low card. It takes a "miracle" flop with odds greater than 26 to 1 to fill the gaps.

Another Two-Gap Hand

Not all two-gap hands that contain an ace are equal in value. You prefer the gaps to be away from the ace. Take a look at the next two-gap hand and you'll see what I mean.

YOU

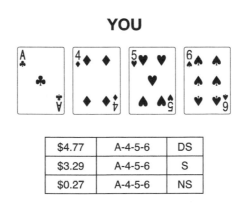

$4.77	A-4-5-6	DS
$3.29	A-4-5-6	S
$0.27	A-4-5-6	NS

The two-gap hand above looks good to many low-limit players because the 4-5-6 all work together. The problem with this hand is that the two cards needed to make a wheel are the 2 and 3. This hand is easy to become trapped with. If several low cards are dealt on the flop and you make a straight, it can easily lose to a bigger straight; and you usually are playing for half the pot. Unless this hand is suited, it is advisable to fold to any bet and save money.

One-Gap Hands

Pictured below are hands with similar cards that contain only one gap. I will insert two hands that will give you a better understanding of how hand values are affected with the reduction of gaps and a change in their proximity to the ace.

When you view these hands, you will see the difference it makes when cards work closely with an ace, and the added value of being suited or double-suited.

YOU

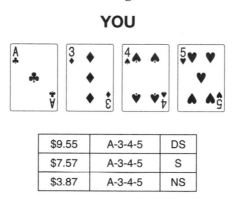

$9.55	A-3-4-5	DS
$7.57	A-3-4-5	S
$3.87	A-3-4-5	NS

The hand above is the same as in the previous example, but with one less gap. You can see the increase in hand value when one card is needed to complete a hand. Any hand containing gaps will increase in value as the gap moves away from the ace. For example, changing where the gap occurs can improve a hand's profitability.

Another One-Gap Hand

YOU

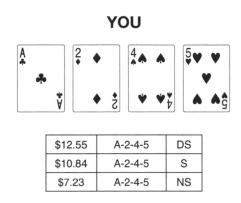

$12.55	A-2-4-5	DS
$10.84	A-2-4-5	S
$7.23	A-2-4-5	NS

No-Gap Hand

The very nice low hand pictured below has no gaps. You can see the difference in values when all cards work together without gaps.

YOU

$15.71	A-2-3-4	DS
$13.94	A-2-3-4	S
$10.43	A-2-3-4	NS

Based on the information we've just covered, it will become very easy for you to take a quick look at your cards and know whether you hold a strong hand or a problem hand. I suggest you spend time reviewing the charts for additional information.

Playing Hands with Related Cards

The better the cards in your hand fit together, the greater the win potential. Let's look at some pictorials that illustrate the importance of playing related cards and show how each card affects the value of your hand.

Each hand pictured below has four two-card combinations. And when you combine them on the river with the ten three-card combinations from the board, these hands have forty ways to make a complete hand.

The maximum number of two-card combinations a hand may produce is six, for a total of sixty possible ways to make a complete hand on the river. Each two-card combination provides ten possibilities to make hands. Every hand dealt in Omaha high-low has no less than one two-card combination.

Practice Hand 1

YOU

Hand Rank: 95

Practice Hand 2

YOU

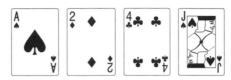

Hand Rank: 171

Practice Hand 3

YOU

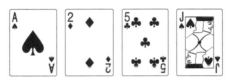

Hand Rank: 251

Practice Hand 4

YOU

Hand Rank: 430

You can readily see how one card affects the value of a hand. The better the cards fit, the higher the hand value and the greater the financial rewards.

Note that there is only one card that is different in all of the hands above—but the hand values are drastically different! It is differences such as these that many low-limit Omaha high-low players overlook. For that reason, they play weaker hands with the same strategy they play their strong hands. Understanding these important hand-value differences, you can play your best game every time.

Now let's look at some practice hands that illustrate how the value of a hand declines when it does not contain an ace. When playing any hand without an ace, remember that there are more than 300 hands superior to the one you hold. Therefore, when the action dictates that some of those hands are out against you, your best decision is to fold and save money.

By observing other players and remembering the hands they raise with, you will gain much-needed information with which to make informed decisions.

Practice Hand 5

YOU

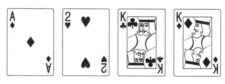

Hand Rank: 52

Practice Hand 6

YOU

Hand Rank: 532

These last two hands are good examples of how the value of a hand changes with and without an ace. Many low-limit players consider these hands nearly equal in value and make the mistake of playing both of them with the same aggressiveness.

To give you a better perspective on such hands, I've inserted a chart with the value of both hands. It's hard for me not to keep reminding you of the importance of selecting hands to play that have an ace. My motto is, "Don't bet without one."

52	$14.17	A-2-K-K	S	32.5%
532	$3.25	2-3-K-K	S	23.6%

Playing Connectors

Playing connectors in Omaha high-low is an important part of the game. However, if you don't play connecting cards with scoop potential, you lose money. Since one card can make such a big difference in how well a hand performs in Omaha high-low, having a good knowledge of the value of connecting cards is essential to your success.

Not all connectors are to be treated equally. In fact, the four connectors pictured below are involved in more losing hands than any other cards in the deck. I refer to these cards as "trap connectors" because they have little chance of winning low and a very small chance of winning high or scooping the pot. Omaha high-low hands that win you money are the ones with scoop potential.

Trap Connectors

It is very important to recognize and avoid playing hands that will cause you to become trapped and lose money. Such hands may look very promising on the flop, only to become second-best hands on the turn or river. The hand below is a prime example of such a hand. Looking at its stats, you will readily see why it's a trap hand.

Practice Hand

YOU

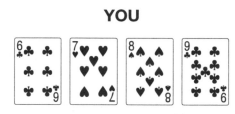

RANK	VALUE	HIGH	LOW	SCOOP	WIN %
2090	-$2.27	6.6%	1.4%	6.8%	14.9%

If you fold this hand without calling a bet in any position, your loss per hand will average less than $1. In other words, you only lose the $6 posted in the big and small blinds (in a $4/$8 limit game) and fold in the other seven positions.

Middle cards have very little chance of winning any part of a low hand, and usually lose to higher hands when played for the high side of the pot. In fact, the 7, 8 and 9 are the worst cards in the deck. They are included in more losing hands than any other cards played. Most hands containing two or more of these cards should be folded.

When combined in the same hand, 6-7-8-9 are the worst four connecting cards that you can be dealt. When playing the blind, you actually save money by folding these and similar trap hands that have negative value. You might want to build your own list of trap hands based on the charts in the back of this book so that you can avoid playing them.

For now, let's move forward to playing good cards that give us the fewest problems and the most winning possibilities. The next chapter focuses on playing your best hands in the best way possible on the flop to increase your chances of progressing to the river in winning shape.

❖ **7** ❖

PLAYING A-2 HANDS
FOR PROFIT

On the Flop and Beyond

Every hand dealt in Omaha high-low will increase or decrease in value on the flop. If your hand does not improve, it is most probable that the flop has improved the hands of other players. The flop is the time to assess your winning possibilities and exercise good poker judgment before you proceed with a hand.

Since so many winning Omaha high-low hands contain an A-2, this chapter is devoted to the skill and art of playing your A-2 hands for profit. Even strong hands with an A-2 can cost you money rather than earn you money if you don't play them correctly.

Many low-limit Omaha high-low players raise before the flop with any A-2 hand. In fact, players probably raise more with this hand than any other holding. However, I do not recommend this play. I strongly suggest that you see the flop before betting aggressively with an A-2. Before the flop, there is only a 7 percent probability that the hand will flop three cards lower than an 8 to make a low hand. Further, 35 percent of hands dealt will not produce a low.

Playing A-2 with Connecting Cards

Any A-2 hand without good backup cards lives a dangerous life, because it becomes counterfeited 25 percent of the time. For an A-2 to have the greatest winning possibility, it must be combined with cards that give it scoop potential. When the A-2 is combined with two good auxiliary cards, the hand will have a much greater possibility of winning low, high or scooping the pot.

An A-2 should be dealt to you 6.4 percent of hands dealt, or once in about every 16 hands. You'll be dealt an A-2-3-x once in about every 100 hands. In nine-handed games, there is a 58 percent chance that one or more players will be dealt an A-2-x-x on the same deal, and an 85 percent possibility that one or more players will be dealt an A-2-x-x or an A-3-x-x. This is a good reason not to play hands such as 2-3-x-x if the action is heavy in front of you. Nut hands are the ones that win the big pots in Omaha high-low.

Listed below is a group of cards that represent the best auxiliary cards for an A-2. The cards are listed in the order that produces the best winning results. Only four cards are not included among the desirable auxiliary cards—I'll show them to you next.

An A-2 hand containing any two of the auxiliary cards below is a strong hand. If the hand is suited or double-suited, its value greatly improves. A-A-2-x hands are the most profitable of all.

Desirable Auxiliary Cards

Several A-2 hands with connecting cards are listed in the chart below to illustrate how each card affects hand values. When any of these hands are suited or double-suited, hand values greatly increase.

A-2 HAND VALUES

HAND RANK	VALUE $4/$8	POCKET CARDS		PART OR ALL %
		HAND	SUITED	
25	$16.54	A-2-3-K	DS	35.1%
65	$13.39	A-2-3-K	S	33.0%
149	$9.57	A-2-3-K	NS	29.7%
105	$11.35	A-2-4-J	DS	30.8%
171	$8.96	A-2-4-J	S	29.3%
421	$4.48	A-2-4-J	NS	26.4%
78	$12.47	A-2-4-Q	DS	31.9%
147	$9.62	A-2-4-Q	S	30.2%
386	$4.92	A-2-4-Q	NS	27.1%
58	$13.93	A-2-4-K	DS	33.5%
118	$10.85	A-2-4-K	S	31.2%
254	$6.96	A-2-4-K	NS	27.9%
138	$9.81	A-2-10-J	DS	28.9%
203	$7.96	A-2-10-J	S	27.5%
480	$3.73	A-2-10-J	NS	25.0%
133	$9.92	A-2-10-Q	DS	29.0%
222	$7.59	A-2-10-Q	S	27.3%
487	$3.66	A-2-10-Q	NS	24.5%
127	$10.29	A-2-10-K	DS	29.4%
237	$7.33	A-2-10-K	S	27.2%
513	$3.40	A-2-10-K	NS	24.7%
62	$13.62	A-2-Q-Q	DS	30.9%
102	$11.41	A-2-Q-Q	S	29.1%
242	$7.16	A-2-Q-Q	NS	26.3%
104	$11.38	A-2-Q-K	DS	30.4%
165	$9.07	A-2-Q-K	S	28.0%
26	$16.51	A-2-K-K	DS	34.3%
52	$14.17	A-2-K-K	S	32.5%
162	$9.27	A-2-K-K	NS	30.0%
25	$16.54	A-2-3-K	DS	35.1%
65	$13.39	A-2-3-K	S	33.0%
149	$9.57	A-2-3-K	NS	29.7%

Any A-2 hand containing a 3 for backup protection reduces the hand from becoming counterfeited by at least 50 percent. Further, the hand can use that extra low card to make a wheel for low and increase its scoop potential.

The only four cards in the deck that do not coordinate with A-2 to produce scoop possibilities are 9, 8, 7 and 6. I strongly suggest that you remember them when you're dealt an A-2.

Undesirable Auxiliary Cards

YOU

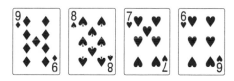

Combine an A-2 with any two undesirable auxiliary cards and you will have a weak hand, especially if the cards are not suited or double-suited. To better understand the difference in hand values, compare the results in this chart with those in the Desirable Auxiliary Cards chart.

A-2 HANDS WITH UNDESIRABLE AUXILIARY CARDS

HAND RANK	VALUE $4/$8	POCKET CARDS	
		HAND	SUITED
282	$6.55	A-2-6-7	DS
370	$5.16	A-2-6-7	S
825	$1.13	A-2-6-7	NS
327	$5.77	A-2-7-9	DS
419	$4.49	A-2-7-9	S
958	$0.45	A-2-7-9	NS
306	$6.24	A-2-8-9	DS
895	$0.76	A-2-8-9	NS

The A-2 hands above are good examples of how the hand plunges in value when a 6, 7, 8 or 9 is included in it. Looking at the charts, you can see that A-2 hands with any two face cards have a better hand rank and hand value than any A-2 hand combined with any two bad cards.

For practice, we will play several hands with the A-2-7-8. First, we'll replace the 7 with a good auxiliary card, and then we'll replace both the 7 and the 8 with better cards.

Practice Hand 1: Weak Auxiliary Cards

YOU

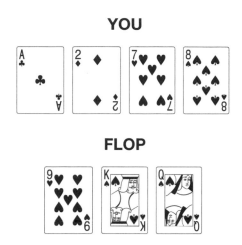

FLOP

The pot was raised before the flop and the practice hand called. He then folded on the flop, losing $8. This is a good example of why two high cards are better performers than the 7 and 8. Had the 7 and 8 been two face cards, the hand may have had a draw to an ace-high straight.

Let's try again and hope for a better flop.

FLOP

Before dealing the next two cards, let's discuss the hand's possibilities. To win half of the pot, we need one of the following low cards: 3, 4, 7 or 8. This possibility may look good to a novice, but I will apply numbers that will give you some real facts.

I ran 100,000 simulations with this hand, with the following results:

Before the Flop

YOU

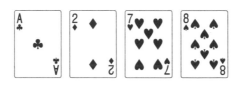

WIN HIGH	WIN LOW	SCOOP	HAND VALUE
4%	8%	6%	$0

On The Flop

FLOP

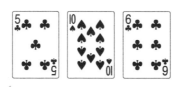

The flop has two low suited cards and one high card. The two low cards increased the hand value to $15. At this point in the game, there is an 11 percent chance to scoop the pot and 16 percent chance to win the low.

WIN HIGH	WIN LOW	SCOOP	HAND VALUE
5%	16%	11%	$15

On The Turn

FLOP   TURN

On the turn, the board is double-suited with a pair that makes a full house possible for other players. Any time the board pairs when you are on a flush draw, I suggest folding if there is heavy action in front of you, unless you also have a low hand that could win part of the pot.

WIN HIGH	WIN LOW	SCOOP	HAND VALUE
2%	12%	5%	-$2

The bad news for players drawing for low is that they may face heavy action from players drawing for flushes or full houses. They also can get into real trouble playing for a draw to a small straight.

You have to improve this type of hand on the turn because you face a 25 percent possibility of becoming counterfeited on the river. The player called a double bet to see the river. When a face card was dealt, he lost $42 on the hand. There was a 12 percent chance of winning part or all of the low, but it didn't happen.

The percentages indicate the weakness of the hand. If you add them up, you have about a 19 percent possibility of winning part of the pot. However, the big problem with this type of hand is that you only have a 5 percent chance to scoop the pot. In other terms, the odds of scooping are 19 to 1 against.

The Importance of Scoop Potential

To be a winner in Omaha high-low, you must play hands with good scoop potential; this type of hand just doesn't qualify. You may occasionally win with these hands, but you will lose more than you win over time.

Practice Hand 2: Replacing the 7 with a Good Card

Let's replace the 7 with a 3 and play a hand.

YOU

Before The Flop

WIN HIGH	WIN LOW	SCOOP	HAND VALUE
4%	13%	8%	$5

On The Flop

FLOP

This flop gives us hope to win low and should we be lucky enough to catch a 4, we would make a wheel. The turn card is important because it will increase or decrease the hand value.

WIN HIGH	WIN LOW	SCOOP	HAND VALUE
2%	25%	4%	$7

On The Turn

FLOP   **TURN**

WIN HIGH	WIN LOW	SCOOP	HAND VALUE
4	34%	7%	$18

On The River

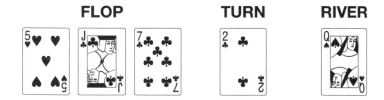

FLOP   **TURN**   **RIVER**

This shows the importance of having backup cards to provide counterfeit protection; however, there is no 100 percent guarantee that the hand will not become counterfeited. With one card to come, the hand has a chance of being counterfeited. On the positive side, there is an 8 percent probability of being dealt a 4 for a wheel for a possible scoop of the pot. The river card didn't kill the hand and it won $23 for low.

Practice Hand 3: Replacing the 7-8 with Good Cards

We will really upgrade the A-2 hand by replacing the 7 with a 3, and the 8 with a king that is suited with the ace. Remember that we are looking at randomly dealt flops.

YOU

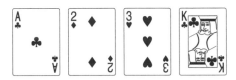

Before The Flop

WIN HIGH	WIN LOW	SCOOP	HAND VALUE
5%	13%	15%	$13

On The Flop

FLOP

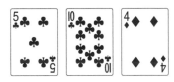

WIN HIGH	WIN LOW	SCOOP	HAND VALUE
8%	15%	33%	$49

On The Turn

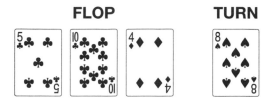

FLOP			TURN

WIN HIGH	WIN LOW	SCOOP	HAND VALUE
7%	28%	22%	$44

On The River

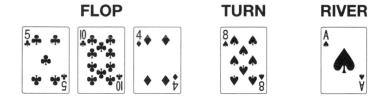

FLOP   **TURN**   **RIVER**

The flop made this a good multiway hand because it has low and high possibilities. Should an A, 2, 3 or 6 be dealt, the hand would make a wheel or a 6-high straight. It also could make a flush.

I will deal the next card and record the results.

When the 8♠ was dealt on the turn, the hand's value was slightly reduced because no wheel or flush card was dealt. On the positive side, the hand was certain to win all or part of the low because it became 100 percent counterfeit proof.

The river card produced the A♠, making a wheel. The hand scooped the pot and won $72. Without the 3 in the hand as a backup card, the ace on the river would have counterfeited the ace in the hand, and it would have won nothing. This is an example of playing hands with good connecting cards.

Playing the Best Hand in Omaha High-Low

The best starting hand in Omaha high-low is A-A-2-3 double-suited. This hand may produce the biggest four of a kind, full house, two top flush possibilities, and the lowest possible hand. The 3 is a good auxiliary card that reduces this hand becoming counterfeited by 50 percent. Further, holding two aces greatly reduces the possibility of another player having an A-2 hand.

The hand has high, low and scoop potential, and has the best overall performance of any hand dealt in Omaha high-low, winning approximately 45 percent of hands played. You may expect to be dealt this hand once every 2,820 hands you play.

For practice, we will play the hand with several different flop, turn, and river cards to illustrate the change in hand value.

Practice Hand 4: The Best Omaha High-Low Hand

YOU

Before The Flop

WIN HIGH	WIN LOW	SCOOP	HAND VALUE
5%	11%	28%	$26

On The Flop

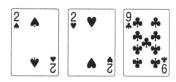

Four players called to see the flop. After the flop, an early position player bet and A-A-2-3 raised. All other players folded and A-A-2-3 scooped the $39 pot. The results may have been different had another player held a deuce or, worse yet, a 2-9 or 9-9 for a full house.

Betting on the flop was the correct decision. Had the hand been checked and the board produced a card that made another player three of a kind for a bigger full house, there is a good chance that A-A-2-3 would have lost everything.

We will try another flop and hope for some action.

On The Flop

FLOP

WIN HIGH	WIN LOW	SCOOP	HAND VALUE
8%	15%	33%	$49

On The Turn

FLOP   TURN

WIN HIGH	WIN LOW	SCOOP	HAND VALUE
13%	9%	56%	$66

On The River

FLOP   TURN   RIVER

WIN HIGH	WIN LOW	SCOOP	HAND VALUE
14%	7%	65%	$77

Let's analyze this flop to determine our expectations for the A-A-2-3 double-suited. There are 20 cards (4, 5, 6, 7, 8) times four that would make a low with two cards to come. Six cards would make a full house and one would make four of a kind, for a total of 27 cards. Plus, runner-runner clubs would make a flush. More than half the deck can improve the hand!

On the turn, the hand's value increased from $26 before the flop to $49. Before the river card is dealt, this hand is expected to scoop the pot 50 percent of the time. We need to see a club on the river, or the board needs to pair to win high. We just hope no 2 or 3 will be dealt to counterfeit the low end of the hand. The K♣ on the river made the A-A-2-3 double-suited a scooper. It won $77.

The charts show that the A-A-2-3 double-suited is expected to win 45 percent of hands played. Unfortunately, it wins nothing the other 55 percent of the time.

Another A-A-2-3 Example

Now let's examine an A-A-2-3 hand that was dealt to me in a $10/$20 game in a Las Vegas casino, along with the results.

MY HAND

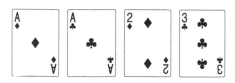

In this hand, I was in last position when A-A-2-3 double-suited was dealt to me. A player in early position bet $10, several players called, and I raised the bet to

$20. Three players called. This was the first time I had raised before the flop in quite some time. Normally I wait and see the flop before becoming very aggressive, but the game had several loose, action players that called a lot of bets.

The player in the blind was very aggressive and played a lot of hands, so I wasn't surprised to see him call. And I must admit that I was quite pleased to have the other players call my raise.

I mentioned earlier that there is no hand profitable to play that contains a 5, 6, 7, 8 or 9. The big blind's hand pictured below clearly fits into this group of bad cards. The only hand I will play that contains a 4 is 4-5-K-K double-suited.

BIG BLIND'S HAND

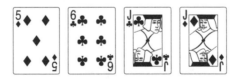

The flop, turn and river cards are illustrated below.

FLOP   TURN   RIVER

After the flop, things improved for the big blind. He flopped an open-ended straight draw and a flush draw. The flop counterfeited my ace, but I was happy because it gave me trip aces, the nut low and the nut flush draw. Further, if the board paired, I would make a full house.

Here are the numbers for both hands after the flop, turn and river. Notice the high potential earn for my hand.

Blind Hand: Flop

WIN HIGH	WIN LOW	SCOOP	HAND VALUE
4%	6%	4%	-$83

A-A-2-3 (DS): Flop

WIN HIGH	WIN LOW	SCOOP	HAND VALUE
17%	9%	47%	$179

Blind Hand: Turn

WIN HIGH	WIN LOW	SCOOP	HAND VALUE
5%	4%	3%	-$86

A-A-2-3 (DS): Turn

WIN HIGH	WIN LOW	SCOOP	HAND VALUE
14%	11%	51%	$193

On the flop, the hand was checked around to me and I bet $10. All players called. After the turn, the big blind bet his trip jacks, I raised, and the other two players folded. Any time that you make three of a kind and there are overcards on the table, you must use caution because a bigger three of a kind may be in another player's hand. It is easy to become trapped with a smaller set of trips or an inferior full house and lose a lot of money in this game.

The 3 on the river double-counterfeited my hand, meaning that I no longer had the nut-low hand. My best low hand was 7-4-3-2-A. My best high hand was A-A-A-J-7.

The big blind scooped the pot. He made a 7-high straight for the best high hand, and a 6-5-4-3-A for low. The end result was that I sustained an $80 loss holding the best hand possible in Omaha high-low!

On the river, the number of possible five-card hand combinations increases from 24 to 60 for each player. Unless your hand is counterfeit proof for the low on the turn, or unbeatable for high, there is always the possibility of losing on the river, even with the best hand dealt in Omaha high-low.

The Worst Possible A-2-x-x Hand

Now let's look at the worst A-2-x-x hand possible: the A-2-2-2 non-suited. The reason this hand is the worst of all A-2-x-x hands is because it has fewer ways to improve than the other A-2-x-x hands. The upside to the hand is that if you should make the nut low, there is a 90 percent chance that you will hold the only nut low hand. The downside is that you are normally playing for only one-half the pot because there is about a 95 percent chance that the hand will not win high or scoop the pot. Further, there is only a 10 percent chance of winning low.

First, let's examine the A-2-2-2 non-suited and then look at the A-2-2-2 suited. You will see how the hand value changes on the flop and turn. Before the flop, this hand has a negative value of $2, meaning that it loses an average of $2 per hand after being played 100,000 times.

The problem with any one-way hand is that you are playing for only half the pot. You can make a wheel with the hand, but the odds are more than 100 to 1 against.

Look at the hand and flop pictured below.

A-2-2-2 Non-Suited

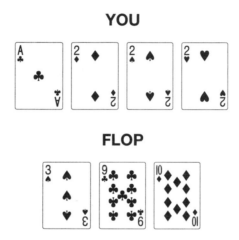

A big mistake that many low-limit players make is continuing to play their low-draw hands after a flop similar to the one above. Essentially, they are hoping to catch runner-runner low cards and win half of the pot.

An experienced player will fold this hand after the flop, but many low-limit players will continue to play and hope to become lucky. There is about an 11 percent chance that this hand will win part of the low. If you are playing any hand for low only and need two low cards after the flop to win low, you are going to lose about 89 percent of all hands you play. Your average loss per hand will be $23.

A-2-2-2 Suited

When a hand is suited and you receive a flop similar to the one above, this hand is profitable to play to the river. With two suited cards and a low draw on the flop, the hand value is $50. It is necessary for the hand to make a low or flush on the turn or the hand's value will decrease as much as 75 percent.

It is very important to know that all hand values decrease drastically on the turn if they don't improve. If you remember this fact and apply it to your game, it will be worth the price of this book many times over.

Chasing with A-2-x-x

Chasing with an A-2-x-x is one of the most costly mistakes made by Omaha high-low players. Pictured below is a commonly dealt hand along with a flop that many players chase.

CHASING HAND

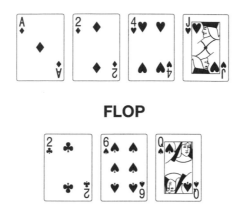

FLOP

Before the flop, this hand is very profitable to play, even against strong action. However, the hand has a negative value of $7 after the flop, and should be folded to any bet. For the hand to have a chance to win the nut low, a 3 must be dealt on the board. There is only a 16 percent possibility of that happening with two cards to come.

The good news is that you will win low with this flop approximately 20 percent of hands played. The bad news is that if you don't catch the 3, you will lose an average of $12 per hand played.

You will lose money if you chase after the flop with these types of cards. Using good discipline and folding your hand when it is apparent that it has negative value will help you become a consistent winner.

❖ 8 ❖

PLAYING THE TURN

On the turn, the possible five-card combinations increase from 6 to 24, and the hand values of each player in the game either increases or decreases.

In Omaha high-low, it is impossible to be dealt four cards that cannot produce either a straight, a full house or a flush. This is one reason that many Omaha high-low players lose money. It is so easy for them to find hands that look good and call a bet to see the flop. They often become trapped because they simply don't understand hand values.

Here is some simple math for your consideration: With five players in the game on the turn, five-card hand combinations for these players increase from 30 to 120 ways (6 to 24 ways multiplied by 5) to make hands. Compare that with a total of 20 ways in Texas hold'em. Those extra 90 hand possibilities on the turn are a valid reason why your hand usually must improve to have a winning expectation.

After the turn card is dealt, bets double. For you to contest the pot, your hand should have scoop potential. If not, it is most probable that one or more players in the game holds a hand that can scoop the pot on the river. At this point, you have only invested two small bets. Unless the turn card improves your hand to scoop potential, I suggest that you fold. For example, if your cards become counterfeited for low on the turn—and you can win only half the pot by drawing—you should save your bets and wait for the next hand.

The practice hand below is one that has good positive hand value when played over time. Like all other hands, however, it needs good cards on the flop and turn to have maximum profit expectations.

Practice Hand A

The A-2-Q-J double-suited had nut-low and nut-flush potential on the flop. But the 2♠ on the turn counterfeited the hand's low draw, turning it into a one-way hand. It had little chance of winning low, and to win any part of the pot for high, a club had to be dealt on the river that didn't pair the board. The hand became very marginal on the turn. In a situation like this, I would fold to any bet.

To demonstrate typical live-action results when the hand was played out, I allowed the computer to continue with the deal.

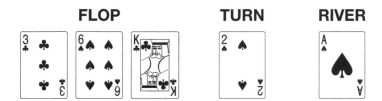

When the A♠ was dealt on the river, the hand's only possible win was two pair for high. It could not win low because both the ace and deuce were counterfeited. On this particular deal, the hand lost $24.

The information below represents the results on all possible deals when the hand did not improve on the turn.

Hand Value Before the Flop

WIN HIGH	WIN LOW	SCOOP	HAND VALUE
8%	6%	15%	$11

Hand Value On the Flop

WIN HIGH	WIN LOW	SCOOP	HAND VALUE
9%	15%	21%	$27

Hand Value On the Turn

WIN HIGH	WIN LOW	SCOOP	HAND VALUE
10%	5%	5%	-$15

The value of any hand that has two-way win possibilities on the flop takes a drastic drop in value if the turn card changes it to a one-way hand. It instantly goes from being very profitable to play to becoming a costly mistake to continue. I suggest that you exercise good discipline and fold these types of hands to save money.

How Hand Value Changes with a Different Turn Card

To illustrate how the value of a hand changes on the turn, I will picture the same hand below and change the turn card to show the new values for the hand. This time, a 4♠ is the turn card.

Practice Hand A

Unless the hand is counterfeited on the river, it will win part or all of the low. If a 5 or a club is dealt on the river, the hand may scoop the entire pot. The 4♠ is a favorable turn card. There is now a 9.1 percent chance of making a wheel and a 20.5 percent chance of making a flush. The odds are about 6.5 to 1 against the hand becoming counterfeited, making it profitable to continue to the river. New hand values are shown below.

Hand Value on the Turn

WIN HIGH	WIN LOW	SCOOP	HAND VALUE
18%	31%	13%	$25

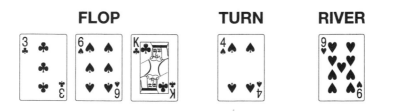

The computer dealt the 9♥ on the river. The hand won $43 for the low side of the pot. I was hoping for a club to make the nut flush for high, although the odds were about 4 to 1 against it.

These values are based on $4/$8 limit games with each hand being played an average of 100,000 hands. The charts indicate that hands in Omaha high-low have a higher mortality rate than in hold'em and other games that are played with seven or fewer cards. There are six times the number of hand combinations in Omaha high and high-low as there are in hold'em, therefore it takes stronger hands to win most pots. Further, getting counterfeited for low is not a factor in other games.

Never become disappointed when you fold a hand that would have won, because you should fold many such hands if you are to play the game successfully. Show me a player that never folds a winning hand and I will show you a player that contributes generously to the game.

The Danger in Chasing

Regardless of hand value, continuing with any hand that does not improve on the flop or on the turn is putting your chips at risk. Chasing after the turn is one of the costly mistakes that Omaha high-low players make. Practice Hand B is a common example that costs many players a lot of chips when they chase after the turn.

Practice Hand B

YOU

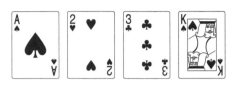

Hand Value on the Turn

FLOP   **TURN**

After the turn, some players continue to call bets with hands similar to the one above. They hope to catch a miracle card and win part of the pot, only to wind up losing a lot of chips. Similar hands with this type of flop and turn do win occasionally, but they lose more often than they win and cost a lot of chips.

Hand Value

BEFORE THE FLOP	AFTER THE FLOP	AFTER THE TURN
$13.39	$15.04	-$14.57

When three cards that work together are showing on the board, such as 2-3-4, they provide many ways to make a wheel or a 6-high straight. Most likely, one or more players contesting the pot made one or both of those hands when the turn card was dealt.

Should You Play for Half the Pot?

Low-limit players often play hands such as Practice Hand C aggressively because the hand is double-suited with all face cards. But look what happened on the turn with this one-way hand.

Practice Hand C

YOU

FLOP   TURN

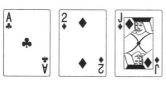

The turn card made a low hand possible. To continue would be playing for one-half or one-fourth of the pot. There are only nine cards in the deck that will make this hand a straight. Three of these cards are diamonds that may make a flush for another player and trap the straight. That leaves only six safe cards to make a high straight.

BEFORE THE FLOP	AFTER THE FLOP	AFTER THE TURN
$3.17	-$3.38	-$16.31

Hand Performance Overall

WIN HIGH	WIN LOW	SCOOP
6%	0%	4%

The numbers were based on two suited cards coming out on the flop. You may think that the hand would be much stronger without the suited board cards to be concerned about. Here are the results without a flush possibility on the flop.

Hand Value After the Turn

WIN HIGH	WIN LOW	SCOOP	HAND VALUE
8%	0%	5%	-$12.12

It doesn't matter what cards you are drawing for, the same numbers apply to all hands. You may see a lot of flops and call one additional bet to see the turn if your hand has scoop potential. If you neither make nor improve your hand, fold it and save money.

In summary, after the turn card is dealt, you must make sound decisions to be successful in Omaha high-low, or any other poker game that is a flop game. You will gain a lot of useful information by observing hands that scoop the money. The one important aspect of the game that you must learn if you are to be a successful player is self-discipline.

Now, let's assume that our hands have improved and we're ready to take a look at the river card, the subject of the next chapter.

❖ **9** ❖

PLAYING THE RIVER

Many players believe that playing the river is a no-brainer: You either have a hand, or you don't. That's close to the truth, but not entirely factual. In low-limit games, you often will be playing against several players with marginal to substandard hands that are stone dead — until they catch a magic card on the river!

Recall that the number of five-card combinations increases on the river from 24 to 60, giving every player at the table an additional 36 five-card combinations with which to beat you. One card can make a big difference in this game, which reinforces the importance of playing hands with four good connecting cards. It is possible for a hand with four cards working together to have twice the number of ways to make a winning hand as hands that have only three cards that work together.

Many hand values can and will change with the dealing of the river card — the most anticipated card on the board. When five-card combinations increase from 24 to 60, it's a new game — and not always favorable for your previously best hand. If you have the nut high and a low hand, put all the pressure possible on other players, as most of them will call one more bet in the hope of winning part of the pot. And some will call to protect their bets. This is not a game in which you call to protect your bets and it definitely is not a bluffing game (except in rare situations).

It is possible to have a double-nut hand on the turn with scoop potential and end up with garbage on the river! Some call it rotten luck. If you hold a hand on the turn that can be beaten, the river card brings many additional hand combinations to help accomplish that possibility, which is another reason to play quality hands. The greater the number of strong hand possibilities you have on the turn, the fewer hands you will lose on the river, and the more you will win.

Start with good hands and you will have less to consider at the river. For example: Did the straight get beaten by a flush? Did the board pair for a full-house possibility against your flush? Did your low get counterfeited? We know that a straight is subject to lose more than 50 percent of times played, and a flush will lose to a full house about 25 percent of the time. On the bright side, straights and flushes do win their share of pots.

You probably have made many flushes on the river and beaten a straight, or made a full house to beat the nut flush and scoop the pot. Or maybe an opponent with A-2-x-x got counterfeited on the river and you won low with an A-3-x-x. When you luck out, it is because you're so skillful, right? But when things are reversed, you wonder how a player could stay with such bad cards! It's all a part of the game and nothing is going to change except, hopefully, your level of skill.

Why You Lose on the River

"Without the river there would be no fish," you've heard players say. I contend that the river is where the fish get caught. Unfortunately, at some time or other, we all have been the fish that got hooked. Frustrating, wasn't it?

To better understand why you lose on the river, compare Omaha high-low with Texas hold'em. After you are dealt the first card in hold'em, there are only three cards in the deck that can make you a pocket pair, and you have one chance of being dealt that card. In Omaha, you have three chances to pair your first card, two chances to pair your second card, and one chance to pair your third card. In other words, there are nine cards in the deck that can make you a pocket pair, meaning that your chances of making a pair are nine times greater in Omaha high-low than in hold'em.

Your odds of being dealt pocket aces are greatly improved when the first card dealt to you is an ace. You have three chances of being dealt another ace, whereas if the third card is an ace, you have only one chance of being dealt the second ace.

The high number of pairs that are dealt in Omaha high-low is the reason why flushes become weak when the board pairs. Be on the lookout for any card that will beat you. If it comes on the river and there is action in front of you, I recommend that you release your hand and save yourself some money.

At the river, you either make a hand and stay, or you fold—it's as simple as that. The top players have no problem in releasing second-best hands, but it is very difficult for many low-limit players to lay them down.

When your hand gets demoted to the second-best possible hand, it usually is smart to release your cards and save your money for the next playable hand. To be a consistent winner, you must muck many hands that look good to a novice.

Avoiding Costly Mistakes on the River

Omaha high-low players make several costly mistakes on the river. One of them is betting a flush when a full house is possible. Some players make a big flush on the river with a card that also pairs the board, only to lose to a full house.

Another mistake is calling or making a bet with a straight when a flush is possible. Be aware of runner-runner flush cards on the turn and river that may demote your straight to the second-best high hand. Players with big flush cards usually muck their hands when fewer than two suited cards came on the flop. But players with other types of draws may backdoor a flush when they catch two running suited cards on the turn and river. Small flushes, in fact, generally win only when you make them on the river with runner-runner board cards.

Playing marginal hands will cost any weak player a lot of chips at the end. Loose players become trapped with second-best hands and often are playing a "dead" hand (one with no way to win). These players will contribute to your stack. Recognize them and take advantage of the opportunity while it lasts. Nut hands are the ones that win most of the pots. Half of the pots will be scoopers. Occasionally, a hand will win with virtually nothing (one pair, for example); however, the pot usually will be small with little profit.

If your hand becomes marginal on the river and you can only win low, save money by checking if you are first to act. Your check may save you from having to call a raise that costs you money in the event that you and another player must share the low end of the pot, in which case you will win only one-fourth of the pot.

When staying for the river card, you should have a made hand or a good drawing hand with multiple outs that give you scoop possibilities. Many players do stay with only a straight draw and catch the winning card, but I consider this to be a bad play that can be very costly over time.

There isn't much we need to know about hands that can't possibly lose. All you need to do is bet or raise your winners—and hope that everybody stays with you.

One type of hand you do not want to get caught with on the river is a marginal hand. The next chapter gives you important data on marginal cards, as well as advice about when and how to play them.

❖ 10 ❖

PLAYING MARGINAL HANDS

Never become disappointed when you fold marginal cards that would have won. You will lose more in the long run by playing them. Players who win with such hands are only collecting a down payment on future losses. Keep in mind that if you fold negative hands without investing a bet, you lose nothing.

Of course, it is possible to be in the blind with a garbage hand that you would never play, get no callers, and win the pot by default. And sometimes, nobody raises before the flop, you receive a magical flop that defies all odds, and end up scooping the pot.

Below is a chart that I have compiled that classifies hands into categories based on their hand values (win rates). For the purposes of this book, I will use the hand values listed below to place hands into each category, starting with premium hands. Note that I consider any hand that doesn't have an ace to be marginal.

The number of hands in each category is listed to give you a better understanding of the statistics.

To save you from doing the math, approximately 80 percent of the 5,278 hands shown in the charts have a negative value!

HAND CLASSIFICATIONS

Premium:	$10 and greater	=	131 hands
Intermediate:	$4 to $9.99	=	332 hands
Marginal:	$2 to $3.99	=	197 hands
Very Weak:	$ .0 to $1.99	=	410 hands

Negative Value Hands = 4,207
Total Hands = 5,278

You will be dealt a lot of marginal hands, but to make things simpler, I've selected a small group of them that are close in value. Based on the types of hands selected for the list, it should be easy for you to compare them with similar hands. Hand values are listed to indicate the strength (or the lack of strength) of each hand.

To repeat, hand value is the average amount that a hand is expected to win or lose over time when played properly. You should not become involved in a hand with marginal cards when there is heavy action, which usually means that other players are holding powerful hands.

MARGINAL HANDS CHART

HAND VALUE	HAND	SUIT
$2.53	A-10-J-Q	S
$2.27	A-10-J-K	S
$1.88	A-10-Q-K	S
$1.96	A-J-J-Q	DS
$2.33	A-J-Q-Q	DS
$2.07	A-J-Q-K	S
$2.41	A-J-K-K	S
$2.10	A-Q-K-K	S
$1.82	2-2-3-4	S
$2.33	2-2-3-5	DS
$1.91	2-3-3-4	S
$2.46	2-3-3-5	DS
$2.00	2-3-4-4	S
$2.08	2-3-4-7	DS
$2.38	2-3-4-K	DS
$1.96	2-3-J-J	DS

A big pot does not justify calling one or more bets with a marginal hand. To become involved in any action, you need to play four cards that work together and have the possibility of making a nut hand with a favorable flop. Many marginal hands do not have this possibility. Of course, when luck comes into play, some marginal cards will scoop the pot, though most will not.

Omaha high-low requires the discipline to lay down a hand when it doesn't improve or it is evident that it is inferior to other hands. Marginal hands require more skill to play profitably than premium or intermediate hands, because they have fewer ways to win and more ways to lose.

The hand listed below is a typical marginal hand selected from the group of hands above to illustrate why these types of hands are marginal. To illustrate how hand values change, I show the hand's value before the flop, after the flop, on the turn and on the river.

Marginal Hand

YOU

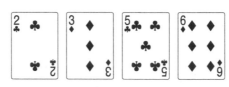

HAND VALUE	HIGH	LOW	SCOOP	TOTAL WIN %
$2.99	4.2%	7.4%	9.3%	21%

These results are based on playing the hand 1,000,000 times for high, low, scoop, and total win percentages before the flop. After the flop these numbers increase or decrease in each category.

For this hand to win any part of the pot on the flop, an ace with two random low cards must be dealt. The chances of this happening are only 3 percent, or 32.5 to 1 against. There is an 18 percent possibility that an ace will be dealt on the flop, but making a low hand requires that two more low cards also appear on the board. Remembering these numbers can greatly improve your game, because you may apply them to all similar hands.

To show how the numbers change after the flop, look at this sample flop and note the hand values for comparison.

Practice Flop 1

FLOP

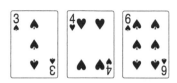

HAND VALUE	HIGH	LOW	SCOOP	TOTAL WIN %
$12.79	17.0%	8.1%	17%	42.1%

After the flop, this type of hand looks very good to many low-limit players. It is a hand that could turn into a monster, but it also has many ways to lose. It is possible for another player to have a better low and a 7-high straight for a better high.

For hand comparisons, look at a flop that contains an ace with good connecting cards.

Practice Flop 2

FLOP

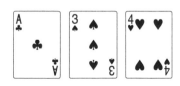

HAND VALUE	HIGH	LOW	SCOOP	TOTAL WIN %
$57	9%	17%	49%	76%

This hand turned into a monster on the flop, and players holding an A-2 without low backup cards got smashed. This scenario will occur often, both for and against you, if you are an avid Omaha high-low player.

Suppose that you hold small suited cards and three cards flop that make you a flush. If there is heavy action, it is most likely that your hand is beaten, unless you also have the nut low. Once again, you can see how powerful the ace is in this type of situation. Of course, it is always possible that an opponent is betting on a low hand. This is a good reason to monitor players who play low cards aggressively.

Play Marginal Hands from Late Position Only

You will be dealt many marginal hands in Omaha high-low that are less than premium quality. If you only play them in late position, they will be much more profitable than if you play them from earlier positions. The benefit of last position is that there is minimal risk of being raised and having to call additional bets by players holding superior hands. Anytime you limp into the pot in early position, you are subject to being raised and must call additional bets or forfeit the money you have put in the pot. You know the players who bet aggressively when they are dealt good hands, and you know to stay out of the action when they act in front of you.

Pot size alone is not enough reason to become involved in action. It is much more profitable to call a bet with a marginal hand when several players limp in the pot, because the potential reward justifies the risk. However, if there is strong action in front of you, and you are holding marginal cards, exercise good judgment. It is usually best to muck your hand because you have been put on notice that you are up against a strong hand. You don't want to flop a second-best hand and lose a stack of chips.

When a Marginal Hand Becomes a Monster

On the flop, marginal hands may become monsters and premium hands can easily become marginal hands. Look at the premium hand pictured below, which has a hand value of $17.48. The marginal hand from the list above has a hand value of only $1.82, which represents less than one-ninth the value of the premium hand.

Premium Hand

YOU

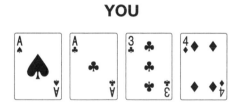

Marginal Hand

YOU

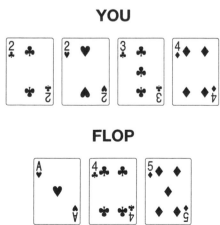

FLOP

Notice how these hands reversed in value after the flop! No doubt this unfortunate occurrence has happened to you (and other players at your table). Before the flop, the premium hand was very superior in value, but after the flop, the marginal hand became strong and profitable to play. Although a marginal hand can be profitable if you can see the flop cheaply, if your hand does not improve, it is time to muck it and save money.

The most common problem for many low-limit players is that they fail to recognize the trap that is created with such a flop. By not looking for ways the hand can lose, they contribute a lot of chips to the game without knowing the error they have committed. They blame it all on bad luck.

It is very easy to establish your own list of playable hands based on past results, but to master hand values, you need to have a good knowledge of hands that are premium, marginal, or negative in value. If you have a friend who plays Omaha high-low, compare your assessment of the hands that each of you likes to play and those you believe should be avoided.

How to Recognize Marginal Hands

Allow me to show you how to eliminate over 2,750 of the 5,278 hands dealt in Omaha high-low the easy way. If the lowest card in your hand is a 3, 4, 5, 6, 7, 8, or 9, there are only 29 hands of the 2,786 hands in this group that have a hand value of $1 or more.

To save you time researching the charts, I listed all 29 hands with Hand Rank and Hand Value for your review.

29 LOW CARD HANDS OF 3 TO 9 WITH A VALUE HIGHER THAN $1

HAND RANK	VALUE $4/$8	POCKET CARDS	
		HAND	SUITED
519	$3.36	3-4-K-K	DS
733	$1.44	3-4-Q-Q	DS
787	$1.22	3-4-K-K	S
587	$2.58	3-5-K-K	DS
806	$1.17	3-6-Q-Q	DS
798	$1.19	3-6-K-K	DS
569	$2.88	4-5-K-K	DS
779	$1.26	4-6-K-K	DS
707	$1.62	5-6-K-K	DS
776	$1.27	6-7-K-K	DS
855	$1.04	7-7-K-K	DS
775	$1.27	7-8-K-K	DS
783	$1.23	7-10-K-K	DS
771	$1.28	8-8-K-K	DS
794	$1.20	8-10-J-Q	DS
743	$1.40	8-10-K-K	DS
858	$1.01	8-J-K-K	DS
820	$1.14	9-9-10-10	DS
822	$1.13	9-9-J-J	DS
732	$1.44	9-9-Q-Q	DS
578	$2.75	9-9-K-K	DS
781	$1.25	9-9-K-K	S
700	$1.70	9-10-J-Q	DS
731	$1.44	9-10-J-K	DS
818	$1.14	9-10-Q-K	DS
708	$1.61	9-10-K-K	DS
827	$1.12	9-J-Q-K	DS
745	$1.39	9-J-K-K	DS
838	$1.10	9-Q-K-K	DS

Note that you will not find a non-suited hand on this chart. If you study these charts and apply the knowledge to your game, you will fold many hands that other players lose a lot of money with.

Your "poker assistant"—your good judgment—is always there to help you save bets and win money. It really dislikes losing! Your intuition may not always be correct, but the dollars you save will be greater than your losses if you heed it. Listen to it and be a winner.

The next chapter gives you valuable information and winning strategies for playing high cards in Omaha high-low.

❖ 11 ❖

PLAYING HIGH CARDS

Some players believe that any four random high cards ranked 9 and higher are playable. However, more than 50 percent of hands dealt with four cards ranking 9 and higher have a negative value. Therefore, I suggest that you avoid most high hands unless you are in the blind or in late position and no one has raised in front of you. The most profitable high-card hand to play is two aces, suited or double-suited, accompanied by face cards.

The most profitable high hand to play containing all high cards is A-A-K-K double-suited. Many Omaha high-low players prefer four unpaired cards in sequence because the hand has more possibilities of making straights. Is this good or bad?

Let's take a look at how the two hands compare in action. To illustrate the difference in hand strengths, two high hands in different suits are pictured to make them as equal as possible before the flop.

High Hands Compared

PLAYER HAND 1

Hand Rank: 481

PLAYER HAND 2

Hand Rank: 199

BIG BLIND

Hand Rank: 4,033

EARLY POSITION PLAYER

Hand Rank: 203

FLOP	TURN	RIVER

What makes Player Hand 2 superior to all other high card hands is that it is impossible to deal any three high cards that will not improve the hand to three of a kind, a straight, or a full house. Any four high cards will make the hand a nut straight or full house. That is not the case with Player Hand 1.

Before the flop, Early Position raised and Player Hand 1, Player Hand 2 and Big Blind called to see the flop.

On the flop, Big Blind made the "idiot end" (low end) of a straight and bet $4. Player Hand 2 raised and was called by the other players. Early Position made a nut straight, Player Hand 1 made three pair and Player Hand 2 made three of a kind.

The turn gave Player Hand 1 a full house and Player Hand 2 a bigger full house. After the river card, Big Blind bet, Early Position called, and Player Hand 1 raised. Player Hand 2 reraised and Early Position folded. Big Blind called. Player Hand 2 scooped the pot.

Best High-Card Hands in Omaha
The chart below includes the best high-card hands dealt in Omaha high-low, plus several negative-value hands that you should avoid.

27 HIGH HANDS WITH CARDS 10 OR HIGHER

HAND RANK	VALUE $4/$8	POCKET CARDS		PART OR ALL %
		HAND	SUITED	
2802	-$3.23	A-A-A-K	S	21.1%
213	$7.75	A-A-10-10	DS	28.7%
290	$6.42	A-A-10-J	DS	27.8%
319	$5.94	A-A-10-Q	DS	27.3%
1011	$0.25	A-A-10-Q	NS	22.3%
354	$5.37	A-A-10-K	DS	27.0%
1121	-$0.20	A-A-10-K	NS	21.9%
207	$7.88	A-A-J-J	DS	28.7%
966	$0.42	A-A-J-Q	NS	22.3%
358	$5.31	A-A-J-K	DS	27.1%
1100	-$0.10	A-A-J-K	NS	21.7%
205	$7.91	A-A-Q-Q	DS	28.7%
339	$5.63	A-A-Q-K	DS	27.2%
1051	$0.09	A-A-Q-K	NS	22.1%
199	$8.05	A-A-K-K	DS	28.7%
2162	-$2.38	A-10-10-K	NS	13.6%
515	$3.39	A-10-J-K	DS	20.4%
1091	-$0.08	A-10-J-K	NS	15.6%
1758	-$1.71	A-10-Q-Q	NS	15.5%
469	$3.89	A-10-K-K	DS	23.0%
1852	-$1.86	A-J-J-K	NS	15.8%
481	$3.72	A-J-Q-K	DS	20.4%
979	$0.37	A-J-Q-K	NS	15.2%
455	$4.07	A-J-K-K	DS	23.0%
1203	-$0.46	A-J-K-K	NS	18.3%
499	$3.54	A-Q-Q-K	DS	22.7%
1496	-$1.15	A-Q-Q-K	NS	15.3%

High-Card Hands Are One-Way Hands

If you study the chart above, you will know when to call or fold most similar high hands that will be dealt to you.

When playing high cards, always keep in mind that you are playing a one-way hand. There are many hands with an ace that should not be played. An example of such a hand is A-9-10-J suited or non-suited.

Most hands containing four random high cards seldom win big pots. Unless the hand has an ace and is suited or double-suited, it is a weak hand to play. Here is the type of high hand that many low-limit players lose a lot of chips with.

PRACTICE HAND

YOU

FLOP   **TURN**   **RIVER**

Hand Value

BEFORE THE FLOP	AFTER THE FLOP	AFTER THE TURN	ON THE RIVER
$2.14	-$2.34	-$15.78	-$19.37

To win with four sequential high cards, you need a flop that contains an ace and two other cards that make a straight. Flops similar to the one above produce low hands and are not profitable to play when you have cards similar to this practice hand.

When the board consists of all high cards and there is heavy action, if you are holding a hand similar to the practice hand, you usually are playing for half of the pot or playing a dead hand. Playing hands with big pairs are the most profitable high hands to play because you usually either flop a strong hand with good potential, or you miss the flop completely and can fold the hand after only investing one small bet.

Be selective with high cards that you elect to play, and don't worry about throwing away a winning hand if your four high cards are not suited or do not contain a big pair. Two pair such as 3-3-K-K is not normally profitable to play, because a 3 may be dealt on the flop making you a small three of a kind, costing you a bundle of chips to a bigger three of a kind. Although they are strong in hold'em, small trips are often losers in Omaha high-low.

The chart below includes the best ace-less high hands dealt in Omaha high-low. There are very few non-suited high hands that are profitable to play. You must always keep in mind when playing ace-less high cards, that you seldom scoop big pots and risk many chips for small rewards.

THE BEST ACE-LESS HIGH HANDS IN OMAHA HIGH-LOW

HAND RANK	VALUE $4/$8	POCKET CARDS		PART OR ALL %
		HAND	SUITED	
329	$5.76	Q-Q-K-K	DS	21.5%
353	$5.37	J-J-K-K	DS	21.3%
372	$5.11	10-10-K-K	DS	21.2%
423	$4.43	Q-Q-K-K	S	19.6%
435	$4.34	J-J-Q-Q	DS	19.0%
486	$3.66	10-10-Q-Q	DS	18.7%
497	$3.55	J-J-K-K	S	19.3%
525	$3.32	10-10-J-J	DS	17.1%
540	$3.17	10-J-Q-K	DS	17.6%
830	$1.11	10-J-Q-K	NS	14.6%
562	$2.97	J-Q-K-K	DS	19.6%
564	$2.93	10-Q-K-K	DS	19.7%
579	$2.75	J-J-Q-Q	S	17.4%
601	$2.50	Q-Q-K-K	NS	17.5%
699	$1.70	9-10-J-Q	DS	16.2%
1079	-$.03	9-10-J-Q	NS	14.0%
1041	$0.12	9-10-K-K	S	17.4%
1025	$0.18	9-10-Q-K	S	15.2%
780	$1.25	9-9-K-K	S	17.8%

After examining the hands above, note that you should avoid playing many high hands that are dealt to you. The logic you apply to hands containing an ace may be applied to all high hands. It is possible to win with the high hands on this chart, but most pots will be small because these cards lose most often to higher hands with an ace. Even the best high hand without an ace is weak to play. These hands win most often when an ace is dealt on the flop because they need an ace to make the high straight or flush.

Now, let's proceed to one of the most important skills in Omaha high-low: Learning how to eliminate your mistakes. As you've probably heard, he who makes the fewest mistakes makes the most money.

❖ 12 ❖

ELIMINATING MISTAKES

Even with all the knowledge currently available on how to play poker, many low-limit Omaha high-low players are still making the same costly mistakes as in past years.

Playing Trap Hands

Playing trap hands is one of the biggest mistakes made by low-limit Omaha high-low players. Many of these hands contain cards such as the 4-5-6-7 pictured here.

YOU

This hand looks very promising to some players, but it is a major trap hand. Recognizing and avoiding possible trap hands is important to your profit picture. Any time you play middle cards such as these, you most often become trapped in the middle for low, make the second-best high, and lose both ways.

It is imperative that you exercise good poker judgment and muck these hands unless you are in the blind and there are no additional bets to call. You must beat high odds to win even half the pot should you elect to play trap hands, thus making another mistake—playing hands that do not have scoop potential.

You might win with some substandard hands, but in the long run, your losses will be much greater than your winnings. Some players almost jump out of their seats when a card hits on the river that would have given them a winning hand if they hadn't folded their marginal cards. Don't get into this habit. Instead, remind yourself that you played the hand properly. Feel good about your decision, because you are going to win more and lose less over time.

Chasing After the Flop

Many hands with high profit expectations can become very costly to play after the flop. Since the value of a hand improves or decreases after the flop, it is important to play according to the changing conditions.

Hands similar to the A-2-3-4 pictured below are very profitable to play if you receive a favorable flop. If not, you will save money by folding your cards and waiting for another hand to play.

Practice Hand

YOU

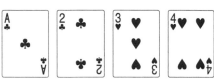

An A-2-3-4 double-suited should be dealt to you once in about 1,050 hands. It is a great hand because all cards work together for a possible nut low, wheel, 6-high straight, 7-high straight, and nut flush. Further, it has maximum protection against becoming counterfeited on the low end. This hand has approximately twice the value of the best ace-less hand dealt in Omaha high-low.

On the downside, however, a bad flop can make it very costly to play. The flop pictured below is typical of flops that kill even the best starting hands. With only one low card on the flop and no cards in your suit, runner-runner low cards are necessary to win any part of the pot. You should fold the hand to any bet.

FLOP

Chasing after the flop with low hands is a common mistake that is very costly to many players. The main reason that you should fold the hand to any bet, of course, is that you missed the flop. Your hole cards don't work together with the board cards. Yet, novice players often continue with similar hands and lose money.

We have discussed all of the ways that A-2-3-4 can win. Now let's discuss the number of ways the hand can lose, which is equally important. If any one of the cards pictured below shows up on the turn or river, it will kill the practice hand.

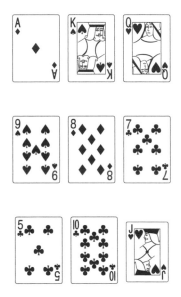

With any of these cards on the board, it is possible for another player to make a straight, flush or full house by the river. You can easily see how important it is for your hole cards to mesh with the board cards on the flop. No hand is profitable to play if you have to chase with it.

Not Controlling Your Emotions

Allowing your emotions to get out of control at the poker table usually leads to letting your game get out of control. In split games such as Omaha high-low where so much depends on the river card, it can be especially irksome when your low gets counterfeited or your flush loses to a full house. It's tough to take bad beats in any hand, but it's just a part of the game.

Some big-bet poker players seem especially prone to losing their composure. About twenty years ago, I was playing in a no-limit tournament when a newly crowned world poker champion arrived late for the game. He took his place in a seat that had been empty for about forty-five minutes. On his first hand he was dealt Q-Q and made a sizeable bet. Everybody folded around to me, and I called with K-K. I thought that he had a strong hand and didn't want to raise into pocket aces and possibly lose most of my chips.

The flop came K-Q-3 in different suits, making trips for both of us. He immediately pushed his remaining chips into the middle and I called. He had lost his entire stack in less than five minutes and became quite irate. After saying several unkind words, he threw his cards toward the dealer and stalked out of the poker room.

I believe all players should show the same respect to the dealer and other players as they expect to receive.

Playing Too Many Hands
Playing too many hands is a common mistake made by poker players of all limits. This bad habit actually ties in with maintaining your self-control. When they are losing too much money, many players become overly aggressive and play too many hands. In their attempt to get lucky and win back their money, they often go broke.

To make a small point, I played in a $4/$8 game in which two players had been playing all night long. One was down $1,300. We knew the amount that this player had lost because his friend would announce the amount after each visit he made to the ATM machine. He always came back with $100, but since he seldom folded, the $100 didn't last long.

Not Setting Limits for Losing or Winning

To become successful in business or poker, it is necessary to set goals; when they are met, it is time to quit. Before sitting in a game, set a limit you can afford to lose and a winning amount that meets your financial goal.

Not Knowing When to Leave a Game

It is important to know when to leave a game. Your decision should be based on three basic factors: time played, win or loss amount, and type of game you are playing. If there is little action in the game it is time to quit. Many games may have good action when you join them, but as players go broke or quit and new ones enter the game, action slows. When this happens, it may become unprofitable to stay. Quit and move to another table or wait for another day. Fortunately, in poker there will always be another game!

Not Limiting Your Time at the Table

Playing too many hours in one session is another major problem. After a person becomes fatigued, it seems as if he plays hands he normally would fold. (Five hours is about my limit.)

Drinking While Playing

Drinking too much can be very costly when you're playing poker, whether you're in a casino or playing online. Some players can drink moderately and play the game very well, while others lose all respect for their bankroll.

I was playing in a higher-limit game a few years ago alongside a highly respected and famous athlete. After a few hours of heavy drinking, he began betting aggressively on almost every hand dealt to him. Losing the desire to play with a drunk, even though he was donating money to the game like it had no value, I sat out. Out of curiosity, I stayed on the rail and observed the game for a while. After the athlete had lost $500,000 against his credit line, the casino closed the game.

Three Mistakes to Avoid

I have a friend that I call "Texas Ron" because he lives near Dallas. Ron plays poker four or five days a week, but he makes three mistakes that we often discuss.

Playing frequently isn't bad, of course, except that Ron plays for about 24 hours in every session without sleep. That's mistake number one. He drinks some type of energy drink at the tables and claims it keeps him alert.

My friend and I disagree about his playing habits. He sometimes builds his stack up $500 or $800, and then stays until it goes down to $200 or less before he leaves the game. And that's where he makes mistake number two.

Advertising his hand is mistake number three for Texas Ron. He likes to be a nice guy at the tables, and will tell any player that he personally knows when he makes a strong hand. They have no reason to doubt him because he will show his cards if they fold theirs.

I have suggested to Ron that if he advertises his hand when it is strong, astute players will know his cards are weak when he is silent. They will bet against him in those instances and win the hand without further action. I strongly suggest that players don't converse a lot at the poker table. Of course, I know that's hard to do in a friendly hometown casino game. But still I think you should be there to win, not to be "Mr. Nice Guy."

Playing Shorthanded Games

I received a phone call from Texas Ron while I was writing this book. "How do you play in a six-handed Omaha high-low game and make a profit?" he wanted to know.

"Go home or go broke!" was the best answer I could think of. Quit the game and save your money. If you cannot find a full table of players, go home and wait for another day.

Playing at a table with six players is normally losing poker. The three main problems are:

1. Fewer players are contesting the pot and you win less with the few premium hands you are dealt;

2. You ante fifty percent more often in six-handed games than in games with nine or ten players;

3. The house cuts the pot $80 to $100 per hour. Your share would be $15 per hour based on a $90 rake compared to $10 in a nine-handed game. A dealer can deal many additional hands per hour to six people because there is less action and the pots are much smaller.

I recommend that you play only nine or ten-handed Omaha high-low, because short-handed, low-limit poker is usually a losing situation. Texas Ron must have been reading my mind while I was writing on this subject; he left the short game soon after we talked. He is one of the few players I know who admits when he sustains a loss. It is good to report that Texas Ron went on a winning streak after that.

❖ 13 ❖

USING THE STATISTICAL CHARTS TO IMPROVE YOUR GAME

These statistical charts are based on the results of an average, aggressive, low-limit Omaha high-low player who usually gets good results on sample hands that have a profit expectation. That is, he's a pretty good player in the small $2/$4 through $5/$10 games.

I programmed the Computer Generated Player (CGP) to call a bet to see the flop with every hand dealt, from every position. By looking at every flop, the CGP provides us with valuable information about negative-value hands. I then programmed the CGP to play solid Omaha high-low after the flop. Some marginal hands improved enough on the flop that the CGP played them through the turn or river. Otherwise, he folded.

Using the player profiles in Wilson Software's *Turbo Omaha High-Low Split*, I selected two tight, four average, and three loose players from the Wilson lineup. By doing this, I attempted to make the results as realistic as possible. My goal was to emulate real conditions and situations in low-limit, nine-handed Omaha high-low games to produce statistics that are as reliable as possible.

Many results consist of 1,000,000 hand simulations, though some reflect 100,000 simulations. In order to produce consistent stats and make them easier to read, I have reduced all of them down to represent 100,000 hands.

I find these charts immensely helpful to me in selecting starting hands, and in deciding whether to continue with a hand past the flop. My ultimate goal in generating these stats is to give you a set of important tools you need to master and make money at my favorite poker game, Omaha high-low.

The **Hand Rank** column is based on the performance of the hand compared to all 5,278 possible Omaha high-low hands. With 1 (one) being the best performer, A-A-A-2 suited ranked 132, meaning there are only 131 hands that outperform it.

The **Value** column indicates that the hand won an average of $10.09 per hand in a $4/$8 limit game. The **Pocket Cards** column lists the hand and whether it is suited: **DS = double-suited, S = suited** and **NS = non-suited**.

When a pot is split, **High** and **Low** receive one-half credit each. When one player wins the total pot, **Scoop** gets all the credit for the win. **Part or All** represents high, low and scoop totals for the hand.

To conserve space in the charts, dollar amounts were reduced to an average per-hand value as indicated above. High, low, and scoop results were converted to percentages to make the charts more meaningful.

To provide you with useful information about negative-value hands, I changed the calling criteria for the Computer Generated Player (the "CGP"). I programmed him/her to call a bet to see the flop with every hand dealt, from every position. After the flop, however, the CGP's betting criteria for playing a hand remained the same. Some hands improved enough on the flop that the CGP played them.

STATISTICAL CHARTS

To generate these stats, I selected a nine-handed, $4/$8 Omaha high-low game with two tight, four average, and three loose players. The Computer Generated Player (CGP) was programmed to call a bet to see every flop, but play solid strategy after the flop.

Hand Rank: The hand's relative value compared to the best Omaha hand.

Value $4/$8: The average win or loss expectation of an average, aggressive player on every hand.

Hand: Your four pocket cards.

Suited: DS = double suited, S = suited, NS = non-suited. *Suited* indicates that the highest pocket card held is of the same suit as another pocket card. *Double suited* indicates that the two highest pocket cards are matched with other pocket cards of the same suit, for example A♥ K♦ 5♦ 2♥. *Non-suited* means none of the cards are of the same suit.

High %: The percentage of the time that these cards will win only the high portion of the pot.

Low %: The percentage of the time that these cards will win only the low portion of the pot.

Scoop %: The percentage of the time that these cards will win both the high and low portions of the pot.

Win Part or All %: The percentage of the time that these cards will win some portion of the pot: high, low, or all of it.

OMAHA HIGH-LOW 8 OR BETTER
5,278 HANDS   9 HANDED

HAND RANK	VALUE $4/$8	POCKET CARDS HAND	SUITED	HIGH %	LOW %	SCOOP %	PART OR ALL %
5272	-$10	A-A-A-A	NS	2.3%	0.0%	12.6%	14.8%
131	$10	A-A-A-2	S	3.8%	10.1%	20.6%	34.5%
302	$6	A-A-A-2	NS	3.6%	11.1%	17.6%	32.2%
210	$8	A-A-A-3	S	3.9%	9.2%	20.4%	33.5%
473	$4	A-A-A-3	NS	3.5%	9.8%	17.5%	30.8%
340	$6	A-A-A-4	S	4.2%	7.4%	19.7%	31.3%
856	$1	A-A-A-4	NS	3.5%	8.0%	16.3%	27.8%
555	$3	A-A-A-5	S	4.2%	6.0%	18.9%	29.1%
1426	-$1	A-A-A-5	NS	3.6%	6.2%	15.6%	25.4%
1105	-$0	A-A-A-6	S	4.2%	5.0%	16.9%	26.0%
2988	-$3	A-A-A-6	NS	3.5%	5.0%	14.3%	22.8%
1902	-$2	A-A-A-7	S	4.2%	3.3%	15.2%	22.7%
4332	-$5	A-A-A-7	NS	3.6%	3.4%	13.5%	20.5%
2516	-$3	A-A-A-8	S	4.7%	2.6%	15.2%	22.4%
4660	-$6	A-A-A-8	NS	3.8%	2.5%	13.0%	19.2%
4322	-$5	A-A-A-9	S	5.1%	0.0%	13.2%	18.3%
5096	-$8	A-A-A-9	NS	4.1%	0.0%	11.9%	16.0%
3409	-$4	A-A-A-10	S	5.5%	0.0%	14.8%	20.3%
4853	-$6	A-A-A-10	NS	4.2%	0.0%	13.1%	17.3%
3313	-$4	A-A-A-J	S	5.4%	0.0%	14.3%	19.7%
4822	-$6	A-A-A-J	NS	4.3%	0.0%	13.0%	17.3%
3207	-$4	A-A-A-Q	S	5.5%	0.0%	14.3%	19.7%
4826	-$6	A-A-A-Q	NS	4.2%	0.0%	13.0%	17.3%
2802	-$3	A-A-A-K	S	5.8%	0.0%	15.3%	21.1%
4709	-$6	A-A-A-K	NS	4.3%	0.0%	13.1%	17.4%
5	$22	A-A-2-2	DS	6.7%	9.2%	26.2%	42.0%
20	$18	A-A-2-2	S	5.6%	10.7%	27.2%	43.4%
51	$14	A-A-2-2	NS	6.4%	10.7%	20.6%	37.7%
1	$26	A-A-2-3	DS	5.9%	11.4%	28.1%	45.3%
3	$22	A-A-2-3	S	5.0%	12.2%	25.4%	42.7%

OMAHA HIGH-LOW 8 OR BETTER
5,278 HANDS   9 HANDED

HAND RANK	VALUE $4/$8	POCKET CARDS HAND	SUITED	HIGH %	LOW %	SCOOP %	PART OR ALL %
15	$19	A-A-2-3	NS	4.9%	13.1%	22.8%	40.7%
2	$25	A-A-2-4	DS	5.7%	10.6%	27.4%	43.7%
8	$20	A-A-2-4	S	5.3%	11.3%	24.7%	41.4%
27	$16	A-A-2-4	NS	5.2%	12.1%	22.1%	39.3%
4	$22	A-A-2-5	DS	5.9%	9.8%	26.5%	42.2%
16	$18	A-A-2-5	S	5.6%	10.3%	24.3%	40.2%
45	$15	A-A-2-5	NS	5.3%	11.1%	21.4%	37.8%
7	$20	A-A-2-6	DS	6.1%	9.5%	24.9%	40.4%
28	$16	A-A-2-6	S	5.7%	10.0%	22.4%	38.1%
79	$12	A-A-2-6	NS	5.4%	10.7%	19.8%	35.9%
14	$19	A-A-2-7	DS	6.3%	8.9%	24.0%	39.2%
44	$15	A-A-2-7	S	5.8%	9.7%	21.6%	37.1%
111	$11	A-A-2-7	NS	5.5%	10.0%	19.0%	34.6%
18	$18	A-A-2-8	DS	6.6%	8.8%	23.4%	38.9%
50	$14	A-A-2-8	S	6.1%	9.2%	20.9%	36.2%
158	$9	A-A-2-8	NS	5.8%	9.8%	18.4%	34.1%
19	$18	A-A-2-9	DS	7.0%	8.8%	22.0%	37.9%
55	$14	A-A-2-9	S	6.5%	9.2%	20.2%	35.9%
164	$9	A-A-2-9	NS	6.1%	10.0%	17.6%	33.7%
13	$19	A-A-2-10	DS	7.4%	8.7%	23.3%	39.3%
41	$15	A-A-2-10	S	6.7%	9.2%	21.1%	37.0%
94	$12	A-A-2-10	NS	6.3%	9.9%	18.6%	34.8%
12	$19	A-A-2-J	DS	7.4%	8.7%	23.3%	39.3%
40	$15	A-A-2-J	S	6.7%	9.2%	21.2%	37.1%
93	$12	A-A-2-J	NS	6.4%	9.8%	18.7%	34.9%
11	$19	A-A-2-Q	DS	7.4%	8.6%	23.3%	39.3%
39	$15	A-A-2-Q	S	6.8%	9.2%	21.1%	37.1%
91	$12	A-A-2-Q	NS	6.4%	9.8%	18.7%	34.9%
10	$19	A-A-2-K	DS	7.4%	8.7%	23.3%	39.4%
37	$15	A-A-2-K	S	6.8%	9.1%	21.2%	37.1%

OMAHA HIGH-LOW 8 OR BETTER
5,278 HANDS   9 HANDED

| HAND RANK | VALUE $4/$8 | POCKET CARDS | | HIGH % | LOW % | SCOOP % | PART OR ALL % |
		HAND	SUITED				
89	$12	A-A-2-K	NS	6.5%	9.8%	18.7%	35.1%
17	$18	A-A-3-3	DS	6.5%	9.9%	23.4%	39.9%
46	$15	A-A-3-3	S	7.0%	8.1%	22.9%	38.1%
132	$10	A-A-3-3	NS	6.8%	8.7%	20.6%	36.1%
6	$21	A-A-3-4	DS	6.1%	9.2%	26.7%	42.0%
23	$17	A-A-3-4	S	5.8%	9.9%	24.3%	40.0%
61	$14	A-A-3-4	NS	5.5%	10.4%	21.9%	37.8%
9	$20	A-A-3-5	DS	6.4%	8.4%	26.0%	40.9%
29	$16	A-A-3-5	S	6.0%	8.9%	23.8%	38.7%
84	$12	A-A-3-5	NS	5.7%	9.4%	21.4%	36.5%
21	$18	A-A-3-6	DS	6.7%	8.0%	24.6%	39.3%
56	$14	A-A-3-6	S	6.1%	8.5%	22.2%	36.8%
170	$9	A-A-3-6	NS	5.8%	9.1%	20.0%	34.8%
24	$17	A-A-3-7	DS	6.9%	7.5%	23.7%	38.2%
72	$13	A-A-3-7	S	6.3%	7.9%	21.5%	35.7%
198	$8	A-A-3-7	NS	5.9%	8.4%	19.0%	33.3%
38	$15	A-A-3-8	DS	6.9%	7.4%	22.9%	37.2%
98	$12	A-A-3-8	S	6.3%	7.8%	20.6%	34.7%
258	$7	A-A-3-8	NS	6.0%	8.3%	18.0%	32.3%
48	$15	A-A-3-9	DS	7.5%	7.2%	21.9%	36.6%
121	$11	A-A-3-9	S	6.7%	7.6%	19.7%	34.0%
297	$6	A-A-3-9	NS	6.3%	8.2%	17.5%	32.0%
33	$16	A-A-3-10	DS	7.7%	7.2%	22.7%	37.6%
82	$12	A-A-3-10	S	7.0%	7.6%	20.7%	35.3%
212	$8	A-A-3-10	NS	6.6%	8.2%	18.4%	33.2%
31	$16	A-A-3-J	DS	7.7%	7.2%	22.7%	37.7%
81	$12	A-A-3-J	S	7.0%	7.6%	20.7%	35.3%
197	$8	A-A-3-J	NS	6.4%	8.1%	18.8%	33.3%

OMAHA HIGH-LOW 8 OR BETTER
5,278 HANDS   9 HANDED

HAND RANK	VALUE $4/$8	POCKET CARDS		HIGH %	LOW %	SCOOP %	PART OR ALL %
		HAND	SUITED				
32	$16	A-A-3-Q	DS	7.7%	7.2%	22.7%	37.7%
85	$12	A-A-3-Q	S	7.3%	7.8%	20.5%	35.5%
225	$8	A-A-3-Q	NS	6.6%	8.3%	18.3%	33.2%
36	$16	A-A-3-K	DS	7.8%	7.2%	22.7%	37.6%
77	$12	A-A-3-K	S	7.0%	7.6%	20.8%	35.5%
192	$8	A-A-3-K	NS	6.5%	8.2%	18.6%	33.3%
34	$16	A-A-4-4	DS	7.9%	5.9%	24.4%	38.2%
86	$12	A-A-4-4	S	7.5%	6.3%	22.1%	35.9%
231	$7	A-A-4-4	NS	7.1%	6.7%	19.8%	33.6%
22	$18	A-A-4-5	DS	5.1%	12.1%	22.1%	39.3%
54	$14	A-A-4-5	S	6.6%	7.5%	23.2%	37.2%
157	$9	A-A-4-5	NS	6.2%	7.9%	20.7%	34.8%
30	$16	A-A-4-6	DS	7.2%	6.7%	24.0%	37.8%
87	$12	A-A-4-6	S	6.7%	7.1%	21.7%	35.4%
233	$7	A-A-4-6	NS	6.1%	7.4%	19.2%	32.7%
43	$15	A-A-4-7	DS	7.4%	6.1%	23.3%	36.8%
112	$11	A-A-4-7	S	6.8%	6.4%	21.1%	34.3%
284	$7	A-A-4-7	NS	6.4%	6.8%	18.7%	31.8%
60	$14	A-A-4-8	DS	7.5%	6.0%	22.3%	35.8%
141	$10	A-A-4-8	S	6.8%	6.4%	20.1%	33.3%
350	$5	A-A-4-8	NS	6.4%	6.7%	17.6%	30.6%
90	$12	A-A-4-9	DS	7.8%	5.7%	21.1%	34.6%
201	$8	A-A-4-9	S	6.8%	6.0%	19.0%	31.9%
490	$4	A-A-4-9	NS	6.3%	6.3%	16.9%	29.5%
68	$13	A-A-4-10	DS	8.0%	5.7%	21.8%	35.5%
140	$10	A-A-4-10	S	7.2%	6.0%	19.9%	33.0%
345	$5	A-A-4-10	NS	6.5%	6.3%	17.9%	30.8%
70	$13	A-A-4-J	DS	8.0%	5.7%	21.8%	35.5%

OMAHA HIGH-LOW 8 OR BETTER
5,278 HANDS   9 HANDED

HAND RANK	VALUE $4/$8	POCKET CARDS		HIGH %	LOW %	SCOOP %	PART OR ALL %
		HAND	SUITED				
150	$10	A-A-4-J	S	7.2%	5.8%	20.0%	33.0%
355	$5	A-A-4-J	NS	6.6%	6.3%	17.8%	30.7%
69	$13	A-A-4-Q	DS	8.0%	5.7%	21.9%	35.6%
152	$10	A-A-4-Q	S	7.1%	6.1%	19.9%	33.1%
328	$6	A-A-4-Q	NS	6.5%	6.3%	17.8%	30.6%
66	$13	A-A-4-K	DS	8.1%	5.7%	21.9%	35.6%
137	$10	A-A-4-K	S	7.2%	5.9%	20.2%	33.3%
321	$6	A-A-4-K	NS	6.7%	6.3%	17.9%	30.8%
59	$14	A-A-5-5	DS	8.4%	4.5%	23.4%	36.3%
143	$10	A-A-5-5	S	7.8%	4.8%	21.1%	33.7%
347	$5	A-A-5-5	NS	7.3%	4.9%	18.9%	31.2%
49	$14	A-A-5-6	DS	7.6%	5.5%	23.3%	36.4%
153	$10	A-A-5-6	S	7.0%	5.8%	21.2%	34.0%
315	$6	A-A-5-6	NS	6.5%	6.0%	18.7%	31.2%
63	$13	A-A-5-7	DS	7.8%	4.9%	22.7%	35.5%
174	$9	A-A-5-7	S	7.2%	5.1%	20.6%	32.9%
357	$5	A-A-5-7	NS	6.6%	5.4%	18.6%	30.7%
83	$12	A-A-5-8	DS	8.0%	4.8%	21.7%	34.5%
209	$8	A-A-5-8	S	7.3%	5.0%	19.8%	32.1%
453	$4	A-A-5-8	NS	6.7%	5.2%	17.5%	29.4%
139	$10	A-A-5-9	DS	8.3%	4.4%	20.4%	33.2%
333	$6	A-A-5-9	S	7.4%	4.6%	18.4%	30.4%
625	$2	A-A-5-9	NS	6.6%	4.8%	16.4%	27.8%
107	$11	A-A-5-10	DS	8.2%	4.4%	21.0%	33.6%
269	$7	A-A-5-10	S	7.2%	4.6%	19.2%	31.0%
530	$3	A-A-5-10	NS	6.6%	4.7%	17.0%	28.3%
110	$11	A-A-5-J	DS	8.2%	4.4%	20.9%	33.6%
259	$7	A-A-5-J	S	7.3%	4.5%	19.1%	30.9%

OMAHA HIGH-LOW 8 OR BETTER 5,278 HANDS 9 HANDED							
		POCKET CARDS					
HAND RANK	VALUE $4/$8	HAND	SUITED	HIGH %	LOW %	SCOOP %	PART OR ALL %
475	$4	A-A-5-J	NS	6.6%	4.7%	16.9%	28.2%
108	$11	A-A-5-Q	DS	8.3%	4.4%	21.0%	33.6%
262	$7	A-A-5-Q	S	7.3%	4.6%	19.1%	30.9%
493	$4	A-A-5-Q	NS	6.5%	4.7%	17.0%	28.2%
106	$11	A-A-5-K	DS	8.3%	4.4%	21.1%	33.7%
243	$7	A-A-5-K	S	7.4%	4.6%	19.3%	31.2%
479	$4	A-A-5-K	NS	6.6%	4.7%	17.2%	28.5%
115	$11	A-A-6-6	DS	8.5%	3.7%	21.6%	33.8%
308	$6	A-A-6-6	S	7.7%	3.8%	19.7%	31.2%
620	$2	A-A-6-6	NS	6.9%	4.0%	17.3%	28.2%
103	$11	A-A-6-7	DS	8.1%	4.1%	21.5%	33.7%
274	$7	A-A-6-7	S	7.4%	4.2%	19.4%	31.0%
682	$2	A-A-6-7	NS	5.7%	4.2%	15.0%	24.9%
129	$10	A-A-6-8	DS	8.2%	4.0%	20.6%	32.7%
341	$6	A-A-6-8	S	7.3%	4.2%	18.4%	29.9%
656	$2	A-A-6-8	NS	6.6%	4.3%	16.5%	27.4%
202	$8	A-A-6-9	DS	8.7%	3.6%	19.1%	31.4%
464	$4	A-A-6-9	S	7.5%	3.7%	17.2%	28.4%
1399	-$1	A-A-6-9	NS	5.8%	3.6%	13.0%	22.3%
172	$9	A-A-6-10	DS	8.5%	3.5%	19.9%	32.0%
380	$5	A-A-6-10	S	7.5%	3.6%	18.0%	29.1%
1055	$0	A-A-6-10	NS	5.6%	3.4%	13.9%	22.9%
188	$8	A-A-6-J	DS	8.1%	3.5%	19.5%	31.1%
436	$4	A-A-6-J	S	7.0%	3.6%	17.8%	28.4%
1200	-$0	A-A-6-J	NS	5.6%	3.4%	13.7%	22.6%
193	$8	A-A-6-Q	DS	8.3%	3.5%	19.6%	31.4%
434	$4	A-A-6-Q	S	7.1%	3.6%	17.7%	28.5%
847	$1	A-A-6-Q	NS	6.2%	3.5%	15.9%	25.7%

OMAHA HIGH-LOW 8 OR BETTER
5,278 HANDS   9 HANDED

| HAND RANK | VALUE $4/$8 | POCKET CARDS | | HIGH % | LOW % | SCOOP % | PART OR ALL % |
		HAND	SUITED				
184	$8	A-A-6-K	DS	8.2%	3.5%	19.5%	31.3%
420	$4	A-A-6-K	S	7.2%	3.6%	18.0%	28.7%
832	$1	A-A-6-K	NS	6.4%	3.6%	15.8%	25.8%
142	$10	A-A-7-7	DS	8.9%	2.5%	20.6%	32.0%
365	$5	A-A-7-7	S	8.2%	2.5%	18.5%	29.2%
709	$2	A-A-7-7	NS	7.2%	2.6%	16.6%	26.3%
166	$9	A-A-7-8	DS	8.7%	3.0%	19.7%	31.3%
402	$5	A-A-7-8	S	7.8%	2.9%	17.8%	28.6%
1113	-$0	A-A-7-8	NS	6.0%	2.8%	13.8%	22.5%
266	$7	A-A-7-9	DS	9.2%	2.4%	18.5%	30.1%
547	$3	A-A-7-9	S	8.1%	2.4%	16.8%	27.3%
1561	-$1	A-A-7-9	NS	6.2%	2.2%	12.8%	21.2%
187	$8	A-A-7-10	DS	8.9%	2.4%	19.5%	30.8%
425	$4	A-A-7-10	S	7.8%	2.4%	17.6%	27.8%
1047	$0	A-A-7-10	NS	6.1%	2.2%	14.6%	22.8%
223	$8	A-A-7-J	DS	8.6%	2.4%	19.0%	30.0%
477	$4	A-A-7-J	S	7.5%	2.4%	17.4%	27.2%
1183	-$0	A-A-7-J	NS	5.6%	2.1%	13.7%	21.5%
267	$7	A-A-7-Q	DS	8.6%	2.3%	18.9%	29.8%
539	$3	A-A-7-Q	S	7.3%	2.4%	17.2%	26.9%
1415	-$1	A-A-7-Q	NS	5.7%	2.1%	13.1%	20.9%
256	$7	A-A-7-K	DS	8.6%	2.4%	18.7%	29.7%
510	$3	A-A-7-K	S	7.3%	2.4%	17.2%	26.9%
1279	-$1	A-A-7-K	NS	5.7%	2.1%	13.7%	21.6%
185	$8	A-A-8-8	DS	9.3%	1.8%	20.2%	31.3%
399	$5	A-A-8-8	S	8.2%	1.9%	18.2%	28.3%
752	$1	A-A-8-8	NS	7.4%	1.9%	16.6%	25.9%
276	$7	A-A-8-9	DS	9.6%	1.7%	18.0%	29.4%

OMAHA HIGH-LOW 8 OR BETTER
5,278 HANDS 9 HANDED

| HAND RANK | VALUE $4/$8 | POCKET CARDS | | HIGH % | LOW % | SCOOP % | PART OR ALL % |
		HAND	SUITED				
580	$3	A-A-8-9	S	8.5%	1.8%	16.5%	26.8%
1538	-$1	A-A-8-9	NS	6.6%	1.6%	12.8%	21.0%
221	$8	A-A-8-10	DS	9.4%	1.7%	18.7%	29.9%
431	$4	A-A-8-10	S	8.2%	1.7%	17.5%	27.5%
1017	$0	A-A-8-10	NS	6.6%	1.6%	14.7%	22.9%
268	$7	A-A-8-J	DS	9.1%	1.7%	18.5%	29.4%
491	$4	A-A-8-J	S	7.8%	1.8%	17.4%	27.0%
1071	-$0	A-A-8-J	NS	6.0%	1.7%	14.7%	22.3%
295	$6	A-A-8-Q	DS	8.9%	1.7%	18.4%	29.0%
541	$3	A-A-8-Q	S	7.6%	1.7%	17.0%	26.4%
1392	-$1	A-A-8-Q	NS	5.7%	1.5%	13.5%	20.7%
324	$6	A-A-8-K	DS	9.0%	1.7%	18.0%	28.6%
583	$3	A-A-8-K	S	7.7%	1.8%	16.6%	26.1%
1465	-$1	A-A-8-K	NS	6.0%	1.6%	13.6%	21.1%
311	$6	A-A-9-9	DS	9.7%	0.0%	17.7%	27.5%
560	$3	A-A-9-9	S	8.3%	0.0%	16.6%	24.9%
1127	-$0	A-A-9-9	NS	6.7%	0.0%	14.9%	21.5%
381	$5	A-A-9-10	DS	10.0%	0.0%	16.7%	26.7%
692	$2	A-A-9-10	S	9.1%	0.0%	15.5%	24.6%
1512	-$1	A-A-9-10	NS	7.8%	0.0%	14.2%	22.0%
395	$5	A-A-9-J	DS	10.0%	0.0%	16.8%	26.8%
786	$1	A-A-9-J	S	8.6%	0.0%	15.4%	24.0%
1590	-$1	A-A-9-J	NS	7.1%	0.0%	14.2%	21.4%
449	$4	A-A-9-Q	DS	9.7%	0.0%	16.6%	26.2%
902	$1	A-A-9-Q	S	8.1%	0.0%	15.2%	23.3%
1792	-$2	A-A-9-Q	NS	6.7%	0.0%	14.1%	20.9%
474	$4	A-A-9-K	DS	9.5%	0.0%	16.5%	26.0%
961	$0	A-A-9-K	S	8.0%	0.0%	15.1%	23.2%

OMAHA HIGH-LOW 8 OR BETTER
5,278 HANDS   9 HANDED

| HAND RANK | VALUE $4/$8 | POCKET CARDS | | HIGH % | LOW % | SCOOP % | PART OR ALL % |
		HAND	SUITED				
1990	-$2	A-A-9-K	NS	6.4%	0.0%	13.6%	20.0%
213	$8	A-A-10-10	DS	10.0%	0.0%	18.8%	28.7%
391	$5	A-A-10-10	S	8.8%	0.0%	17.6%	26.3%
670	$2	A-A-10-10	NS	7.1%	0.0%	16.3%	23.4%
290	$6	A-A-10-J	DS	10.2%	0.0%	17.5%	27.8%
489	$4	A-A-10-J	S	8.8%	0.0%	16.7%	25.5%
931	$1	A-A-10-J	NS	7.4%	0.0%	15.3%	22.8%
319	$6	A-A-10-Q	DS	9.9%	0.0%	17.4%	27.3%
522	$3	A-A-10-Q	S	9.4%	0.0%	16.4%	25.9%
1011	$0	A-A-10-Q	NS	7.0%	0.0%	15.3%	22.3%
354	$5	A-A-10-K	DS	9.7%	0.0%	17.2%	27.0%
596	$3	A-A-10-K	S	8.3%	0.0%	16.2%	24.5%
1121	-$0	A-A-10-K	NS	6.8%	0.0%	15.1%	21.9%
207	$8	A-A-J-J	DS	10.0%	0.0%	18.7%	28.7%
385	$5	A-A-J-J	S	8.6%	0.0%	17.5%	26.0%
637	$2	A-A-J-J	NS	7.1%	0.0%	16.0%	23.1%
313	$6	A-A-J-Q	DS	9.9%	0.0%	17.6%	27.5%
526	$3	A-A-J-Q	S	8.1%	0.0%	16.0%	24.1%
966	$0	A-A-J-Q	NS	6.9%	0.0%	15.4%	22.3%
358	$5	A-A-J-K	DS	9.9%	0.0%	17.2%	27.1%
571	$3	A-A-J-K	S	8.1%	0.0%	16.3%	24.4%
1100	-$0	A-A-J-K	NS	6.7%	0.0%	15.0%	21.7%
205	$8	A-A-Q-Q	DS	10.0%	0.0%	18.7%	28.7%
361	$5	A-A-Q-Q	S	8.6%	0.0%	17.4%	26.0%
575	$3	A-A-Q-Q	NS	7.2%	0.0%	16.2%	23.4%
339	$6	A-A-Q-K	DS	9.8%	0.0%	17.4%	27.2%
544	$3	A-A-Q-K	S	8.3%	0.0%	16.2%	24.5%
1051	$0	A-A-Q-K	NS	6.9%	0.0%	15.2%	22.1%

		POCKET CARDS					
HAND RANK	VALUE $4/$8	HAND	SUITED	HIGH %	LOW %	SCOOP %	PART OR ALL %
199	$8	A-A-K-K	DS	10.1%	0.0%	18.6%	28.7%
359	$5	A-A-K-K	S	8.7%	0.0%	17.3%	26.0%
557	$3	A-A-K-K	NS	7.3%	0.0%	16.1%	23.4%
660	$2	A-2-2-2	S	2.3%	10.6%	7.1%	20.0%
1541	-$1	A-2-2-2	NS	1.9%	11.2%	3.2%	16.3%
64	$13	A-2-2-3	DS	3.7%	12.6%	13.9%	30.2%
96	$12	A-2-2-3	S	3.6%	12.8%	12.2%	28.6%
208	$8	A-2-2-3	NS	3.3%	13.4%	8.5%	25.2%
99	$11	A-2-2-4	DS	4.0%	11.7%	13.3%	29.1%
135	$10	A-2-2-4	S	3.9%	12.1%	11.0%	26.9%
346	$5	A-2-2-4	NS	3.5%	12.4%	8.4%	24.3%
126	$10	A-2-2-5	DS	4.2%	10.7%	12.6%	27.5%
195	$8	A-2-2-5	S	4.0%	10.9%	11.3%	26.2%
432	$4	A-2-2-5	NS	3.6%	11.3%	7.7%	22.6%
216	$8	A-2-2-6	DS	4.4%	10.3%	11.3%	26.0%
314	$6	A-2-2-6	S	4.2%	10.5%	9.0%	23.7%
699	$2	A-2-2-6	NS	3.8%	10.8%	6.3%	20.9%
279	$7	A-2-2-7	DS	4.4%	9.6%	10.6%	24.7%
415	$5	A-2-2-7	S	4.2%	9.7%	9.3%	23.3%
901	$1	A-2-2-7	NS	3.7%	10.1%	5.7%	19.5%
323	$6	A-2-2-8	DS	4.9%	9.3%	10.5%	24.7%
439	$4	A-2-2-8	S	4.6%	9.4%	9.1%	23.1%
995	$0	A-2-2-8	NS	3.6%	8.9%	4.9%	17.4%
349	$5	A-2-2-9	DS	5.1%	9.3%	10.6%	25.0%
482	$4	A-2-2-9	S	4.8%	9.5%	9.2%	23.4%
1157	-$0	A-2-2-9	NS	4.1%	9.7%	5.3%	19.0%
257	$7	A-2-2-10	DS	5.5%	9.3%	11.9%	26.7%
393	$5	A-2-2-10	S	5.0%	9.6%	10.4%	25.0%

OMAHA HIGH-LOW 8 OR BETTER
5,278 HANDS   9 HANDED

OMAHA HIGH-LOW 8 OR BETTER
5,278 HANDS   9 HANDED

HAND RANK	VALUE $4/$8	POCKET CARDS		HIGH %	LOW %	SCOOP %	PART OR ALL %
		HAND	SUITED				
851	$1	A-2-2-10	NS	4.6%	10.2%	6.8%	21.6%
235	$7	A-2-2-J	DS	5.7%	9.3%	12.4%	27.4%
348	$5	A-2-2-J	S	5.2%	9.8%	10.6%	25.6%
813	$1	A-2-2-J	NS	4.3%	9.6%	6.7%	20.6%
196	$8	A-2-2-Q	DS	5.8%	9.3%	13.0%	28.1%
318	$6	A-2-2-Q	S	5.4%	9.8%	11.3%	26.4%
720	$2	A-2-2-Q	NS	4.5%	9.7%	7.0%	21.2%
144	$10	A-2-2-K	DS	6.2%	9.4%	14.0%	29.7%
278	$7	A-2-2-K	S	5.8%	9.7%	12.0%	27.4%
585	$3	A-2-2-K	NS	5.3%	10.2%	8.9%	24.4%
71	$13	A-2-3-3	DS	3.9%	12.3%	13.8%	30.1%
101	$11	A-2-3-3	S	3.8%	12.6%	12.3%	28.7%
246	$7	A-2-3-3	NS	3.5%	13.1%	8.9%	25.4%
35	$16	A-2-3-4	DS	3.7%	13.4%	14.7%	31.8%
57	$14	A-2-3-4	S	3.6%	13.5%	13.2%	30.4%
125	$10	A-2-3-4	NS	3.2%	14.1%	9.8%	27.2%
47	$15	A-2-3-5	DS	3.8%	12.8%	14.3%	30.9%
73	$13	A-2-3-5	S	3.8%	12.9%	12.8%	29.5%
182	$8	A-2-3-5	NS	3.4%	13.3%	9.7%	26.4%
74	$13	A-2-3-6	DS	4.1%	12.6%	12.9%	29.6%
116	$11	A-2-3-6	S	4.0%	12.9%	11.3%	28.1%
241	$7	A-2-3-6	NS	3.4%	13.3%	7.9%	24.6%
100	$11	A-2-3-7	DS	4.0%	12.2%	12.4%	28.7%
148	$10	A-2-3-7	S	3.8%	12.2%	11.1%	27.1%
322	$6	A-2-3-7	NS	3.4%	12.8%	8.0%	24.1%
109	$11	A-2-3-8	DS	4.2%	12.0%	12.3%	28.5%
173	$9	A-2-3-8	S	3.9%	12.1%	10.9%	27.0%
379	$5	A-2-3-8	NS	3.5%	12.6%	7.7%	23.8%

OMAHA HIGH-LOW 8 OR BETTER
5,278 HANDS   9 HANDED

HAND RANK	VALUE $4/$8	POCKET CARDS		HIGH %	LOW %	SCOOP %	PART OR ALL %
		HAND	SUITED				
97	$12	A-2-3-9	DS	4.2%	12.9%	12.7%	29.8%
130	$10	A-2-3-9	S	3.8%	13.3%	10.8%	27.9%
376	$5	A-2-3-9	NS	3.4%	13.6%	8.0%	25.0%
67	$13	A-2-3-10	DS	4.6%	13.1%	14.0%	31.8%
113	$11	A-2-3-10	S	4.3%	13.5%	12.5%	30.2%
300	$6	A-2-3-10	NS	3.9%	14.1%	9.3%	27.2%
53	$14	A-2-3-J	DS	4.8%	13.1%	14.8%	32.6%
95	$12	A-2-3-J	S	4.6%	13.4%	13.0%	30.9%
250	$7	A-2-3-J	NS	4.0%	13.9%	10.1%	27.9%
42	$15	A-2-3-Q	DS	4.9%	13.0%	15.6%	33.5%
80	$12	A-2-3-Q	S	4.8%	13.3%	13.7%	31.8%
204	$8	A-2-3-Q	NS	4.1%	13.9%	10.7%	28.7%
25	$17	A-2-3-K	DS	5.2%	12.9%	17.0%	35.1%
65	$13	A-2-3-K	S	5.0%	13.3%	14.7%	33.0%
149	$10	A-2-3-K	NS	4.3%	13.9%	11.4%	29.7%
122	$11	A-2-4-4	DS	4.3%	10.7%	13.5%	28.5%
169	$9	A-2-4-4	S	4.1%	10.9%	12.0%	27.0%
410	$5	A-2-4-4	NS	3.7%	11.2%	9.0%	23.8%
76	$13	A-2-4-5	DS	4.3%	11.3%	14.2%	29.8%
119	$11	A-2-4-5	S	4.1%	11.5%	12.7%	28.3%
240	$7	A-2-4-5	NS	3.7%	11.9%	9.5%	25.0%
117	$11	A-2-4-6	DS	4.5%	11.2%	12.7%	28.4%
160	$9	A-2-4-6	S	4.3%	11.2%	11.6%	27.1%
378	$5	A-2-4-6	NS	3.9%	11.6%	8.5%	24.0%
145	$10	A-2-4-7	DS	4.5%	10.9%	12.2%	27.6%
194	$8	A-2-4-7	S	4.2%	10.9%	11.2%	26.2%
459	$4	A-2-4-7	NS	3.8%	11.1%	8.2%	23.0%
159	$9	A-2-4-8	DS	4.6%	10.4%	12.3%	27.4%

OMAHA HIGH-LOW 8 OR BETTER
5,278 HANDS 9 HANDED

HAND RANK	VALUE $4/$8	POCKET CARDS		HIGH %	LOW %	SCOOP %	PART OR ALL %
		HAND	SUITED				
217	$8	A-2-4-8	S	4.3%	10.5%	11.0%	25.8%
495	$4	A-2-4-8	NS	4.0%	11.0%	7.9%	22.9%
177	$9	A-2-4-9	DS	4.3%	11.4%	12.3%	28.1%
271	$7	A-2-4-9	S	3.8%	11.8%	11.1%	26.7%
593	$3	A-2-4-9	NS	3.3%	12.2%	7.8%	23.3%
123	$11	A-2-4-10	DS	4.7%	11.8%	13.5%	30.0%
183	$8	A-2-4-10	S	4.4%	12.0%	12.3%	28.7%
478	$4	A-2-4-10	NS	3.8%	12.5%	8.9%	25.3%
105	$11	A-2-4-J	DS	4.9%	11.7%	14.2%	30.8%
171	$9	A-2-4-J	S	4.5%	12.1%	12.6%	29.3%
421	$4	A-2-4-J	NS	4.0%	12.6%	9.8%	26.4%
78	$12	A-2-4-Q	DS	5.1%	11.6%	15.2%	31.9%
147	$10	A-2-4-Q	S	4.7%	12.1%	13.5%	30.2%
386	$5	A-2-4-Q	NS	4.2%	12.5%	10.4%	27.1%
58	$14	A-2-4-K	DS	5.5%	11.5%	16.4%	33.5%
118	$11	A-2-4-K	S	5.0%	11.9%	14.4%	31.2%
254	$7	A-2-4-K	NS	4.4%	12.5%	11.0%	27.9%
168	$9	A-2-5-5	DS	4.4%	9.0%	13.1%	26.5%
244	$7	A-2-5-5	S	4.1%	9.0%	11.5%	24.6%
534	$3	A-2-5-5	NS	3.5%	9.3%	8.6%	21.4%
155	$9	A-2-5-6	DS	4.7%	10.0%	12.5%	27.2%
190	$8	A-2-5-6	S	4.5%	9.9%	11.5%	25.9%
458	$4	A-2-5-6	NS	4.1%	10.3%	8.4%	22.8%
179	$9	A-2-5-7	DS	4.7%	9.5%	12.6%	26.8%
253	$7	A-2-5-7	S	4.4%	9.5%	11.5%	25.3%
543	$3	A-2-5-7	NS	3.9%	9.8%	8.2%	21.9%
186	$8	A-2-5-8	DS	4.9%	9.3%	12.5%	26.7%
249	$7	A-2-5-8	S	4.7%	9.3%	11.0%	24.9%

		POCKET CARDS					
HAND RANK	VALUE $4/$8	HAND	SUITED	HIGH %	LOW %	SCOOP %	PART OR ALL %
570	$3	A-2-5-8	NS	4.1%	9.6%	8.1%	21.8%
191	$8	A-2-5-9	DS	4.7%	10.0%	12.3%	26.9%
298	$6	A-2-5-9	S	4.1%	9.9%	10.9%	24.9%
643	$2	A-2-5-9	NS	3.6%	10.4%	8.2%	22.2%
178	$9	A-2-5-10	DS	4.8%	10.3%	12.8%	28.0%
286	$7	A-2-5-10	S	4.2%	10.5%	11.8%	26.5%
638	$2	A-2-5-10	NS	3.7%	10.9%	8.6%	23.2%
161	$9	A-2-5-J	DS	4.9%	10.3%	13.6%	28.8%
251	$7	A-2-5-J	S	4.4%	10.4%	12.2%	27.0%
572	$3	A-2-5-J	NS	3.9%	10.9%	9.3%	24.0%
124	$10	A-2-5-Q	DS	5.1%	10.2%	14.5%	29.8%
214	$8	A-2-5-Q	S	4.5%	10.5%	13.0%	28.0%
520	$3	A-2-5-Q	NS	4.1%	10.7%	9.9%	24.8%
88	$12	A-2-5-K	DS	5.5%	10.1%	15.8%	31.5%
167	$9	A-2-5-K	S	5.2%	10.5%	13.7%	29.3%
396	$5	A-2-5-K	NS	4.4%	10.8%	10.9%	26.2%
247	$7	A-2-6-6	DS	4.5%	8.1%	11.8%	24.4%
371	$5	A-2-6-6	S	4.1%	8.1%	9.9%	22.0%
711	$2	A-2-6-6	NS	3.6%	8.2%	7.4%	19.2%
282	$7	A-2-6-7	DS	4.9%	9.0%	10.9%	24.8%
370	$5	A-2-6-7	S	4.5%	8.9%	10.1%	23.5%
825	$1	A-2-6-7	NS	3.3%	8.1%	5.9%	17.3%
264	$7	A-2-6-8	DS	5.0%	8.7%	11.1%	24.8%
356	$5	A-2-6-8	S	4.7%	8.6%	10.1%	23.5%
805	$1	A-2-6-8	NS	3.6%	7.9%	5.8%	17.4%
307	$6	A-2-6-9	DS	5.0%	9.2%	11.1%	25.3%
401	$5	A-2-6-9	S	4.3%	9.2%	9.9%	23.5%
864	$1	A-2-6-9	NS	3.7%	9.5%	6.9%	20.1%

OMAHA HIGH-LOW 8 OR BETTER
5,278 HANDS   9 HANDED

OMAHA HIGH-LOW 8 OR BETTER
5,278 HANDS   9 HANDED

HAND RANK	VALUE $4/$8	POCKET CARDS		HIGH %	LOW %	SCOOP %	PART OR ALL %
		HAND	SUITED				
273	$7	A-2-6-10	DS	4.9%	9.5%	11.9%	26.2%
362	$5	A-2-6-10	S	4.4%	9.7%	10.7%	24.9%
862	$1	A-2-6-10	NS	3.8%	10.0%	7.5%	21.4%
283	$7	A-2-6-J	DS	4.8%	9.6%	11.9%	26.3%
405	$5	A-2-6-J	S	4.3%	9.8%	10.5%	24.5%
937	$1	A-2-6-J	NS	3.7%	10.1%	7.4%	21.2%
230	$7	A-2-6-Q	DS	5.0%	9.6%	12.8%	27.4%
360	$5	A-2-6-Q	S	4.5%	9.8%	11.2%	25.6%
774	$1	A-2-6-Q	NS	3.9%	10.1%	8.1%	22.1%
156	$9	A-2-6-K	DS	5.5%	9.5%	14.1%	29.2%
310	$6	A-2-6-K	S	4.8%	9.6%	12.0%	26.5%
680	$2	A-2-6-K	NS	3.7%	9.3%	8.1%	21.2%
287	$6	A-2-7-7	DS	4.5%	7.3%	11.1%	22.9%
456	$4	A-2-7-7	S	4.0%	7.2%	9.9%	21.1%
906	$1	A-2-7-7	NS	3.4%	7.3%	7.0%	17.8%
280	$7	A-2-7-8	DS	5.3%	8.0%	11.6%	24.9%
389	$5	A-2-7-8	S	4.9%	7.9%	10.5%	23.2%
756	$1	A-2-7-8	NS	4.2%	8.2%	7.1%	19.5%
327	$6	A-2-7-9	DS	5.1%	8.3%	11.4%	24.8%
419	$4	A-2-7-9	S	4.5%	8.4%	10.3%	23.2%
958	$0	A-2-7-9	NS	3.9%	8.6%	7.0%	19.5%
263	$7	A-2-7-10	DS	5.1%	8.8%	12.1%	26.0%
409	$5	A-2-7-10	S	4.6%	8.9%	10.9%	24.4%
898	$1	A-2-7-10	NS	4.0%	9.1%	7.9%	21.0%
305	$6	A-2-7-J	DS	5.1%	8.9%	12.0%	25.9%
437	$4	A-2-7-J	S	4.4%	8.9%	10.8%	24.2%
993	$0	A-2-7-J	NS	3.8%	9.3%	7.9%	21.0%
304	$6	A-2-7-Q	DS	5.3%	8.9%	12.1%	26.3%

OMAHA HIGH-LOW 8 OR BETTER
5,278 HANDS 9 HANDED

HAND RANK	VALUE $4/$8	POCKET CARDS		HIGH %	LOW %	SCOOP %	PART OR ALL %
		HAND	SUITED				
441	$4	A-2-7-Q	S	4.5%	8.9%	10.6%	23.9%
960	$0	A-2-7-Q	NS	3.7%	9.2%	7.5%	20.4%
200	$8	A-2-7-K	DS	5.6%	8.8%	13.5%	27.8%
377	$5	A-2-7-K	S	4.8%	8.8%	11.5%	25.1%
843	$1	A-2-7-K	NS	4.2%	9.2%	8.7%	22.1%
294	$6	A-2-8-8	DS	4.8%	6.9%	11.1%	22.8%
446	$4	A-2-8-8	S	4.1%	6.8%	9.8%	20.7%
918	$1	A-2-8-8	NS	3.6%	7.0%	7.1%	17.7%
306	$6	A-2-8-9	DS	5.4%	8.0%	11.7%	25.1%
384	$5	A-2-8-9	S	4.8%	8.1%	10.7%	23.6%
895	$1	A-2-8-9	NS	4.2%	8.3%	7.7%	20.2%
218	$8	A-2-8-10	DS	5.6%	8.5%	12.7%	26.8%
336	$6	A-2-8-10	S	5.0%	8.5%	11.6%	25.1%
766	$1	A-2-8-10	NS	3.8%	8.1%	7.8%	19.8%
248	$7	A-2-8-J	DS	5.5%	8.6%	12.6%	26.8%
373	$5	A-2-8-J	S	4.9%	8.6%	11.4%	24.9%
793	$1	A-2-8-J	NS	4.2%	9.0%	8.7%	21.9%
252	$7	A-2-8-Q	DS	5.6%	8.6%	12.7%	26.9%
388	$5	A-2-8-Q	S	4.9%	8.6%	11.3%	24.8%
883	$1	A-2-8-Q	NS	4.2%	9.1%	8.5%	21.8%
228	$8	A-2-8-K	DS	5.8%	8.4%	13.1%	27.3%
369	$5	A-2-8-K	S	5.1%	8.5%	11.6%	25.2%
876	$1	A-2-8-K	NS	4.4%	8.9%	8.6%	21.8%
181	$9	A-2-9-9	DS	4.6%	7.8%	12.3%	24.7%
272	$7	A-2-9-9	S	3.7%	7.8%	11.0%	22.5%
552	$3	A-2-9-9	NS	3.0%	8.2%	8.7%	20.0%
245	$7	A-2-9-10	DS	5.7%	7.9%	12.3%	25.9%
337	$6	A-2-9-10	S	4.9%	7.9%	11.4%	24.2%

OMAHA HIGH-LOW 8 OR BETTER
5,278 HANDS   9 HANDED

| HAND RANK | VALUE $4/$8 | POCKET CARDS | | HIGH % | LOW % | SCOOP % | PART OR ALL % |
		HAND	SUITED				
780	$1	A-2-9-10	NS	3.8%	7.7%	7.5%	19.0%
277	$7	A-2-9-J	DS	5.6%	8.2%	12.1%	25.8%
368	$5	A-2-9-J	S	4.8%	8.4%	11.4%	24.5%
848	$1	A-2-9-J	NS	3.6%	8.0%	7.6%	19.1%
265	$7	A-2-9-Q	DS	5.6%	8.4%	12.3%	26.4%
383	$5	A-2-9-Q	S	4.6%	8.5%	11.2%	24.3%
865	$1	A-2-9-Q	NS	3.9%	9.0%	8.4%	21.3%
232	$7	A-2-9-K	DS	5.8%	8.4%	12.9%	27.1%
397	$5	A-2-9-K	S	4.7%	8.6%	11.4%	24.6%
888	$1	A-2-9-K	NS	4.0%	9.0%	8.5%	21.6%
134	$10	A-2-10-10	DS	5.0%	7.9%	14.1%	26.9%
180	$9	A-2-10-10	S	4.1%	8.0%	12.9%	25.0%
422	$4	A-2-10-10	NS	3.5%	8.4%	10.2%	22.1%
138	$10	A-2-10-J	DS	6.2%	8.4%	14.4%	28.9%
203	$8	A-2-10-J	S	5.3%	8.5%	13.7%	27.5%
480	$4	A-2-10-J	NS	5.2%	9.0%	10.8%	25.0%
133	$10	A-2-10-Q	DS	6.2%	8.5%	14.3%	29.0%
222	$8	A-2-10-Q	S	5.3%	8.7%	13.3%	27.3%
487	$4	A-2-10-Q	NS	4.6%	9.2%	10.7%	24.5%
127	$10	A-2-10-K	DS	6.3%	8.5%	14.6%	29.4%
237	$7	A-2-10-K	S	5.2%	8.7%	13.2%	27.2%
513	$3	A-2-10-K	NS	4.8%	9.3%	10.7%	24.7%
92	$12	A-2-J-J	DS	5.3%	8.0%	15.3%	28.6%
154	$9	A-2-J-J	S	4.4%	8.1%	14.1%	26.6%
343	$6	A-2-J-J	NS	3.7%	8.6%	11.6%	23.9%
120	$11	A-2-J-Q	DS	6.2%	8.5%	14.8%	29.5%
206	$8	A-2-J-Q	S	5.3%	8.8%	13.7%	27.8%
457	$4	A-2-J-Q	NS	4.8%	9.1%	11.1%	25.0%

OMAHA HIGH-LOW 8 OR BETTER
5,278 HANDS   9 HANDED

HAND RANK	VALUE $4/$8	POCKET CARDS HAND	POCKET CARDS SUITED	HIGH %	LOW %	SCOOP %	PART OR ALL %
114	$11	A-2-J-K	DS	6.5%	8.5%	15.0%	30.0%
227	$8	A-2-J-K	S	5.8%	8.9%	13.3%	27.9%
467	$4	A-2-J-K	NS	4.8%	9.3%	11.0%	25.1%
62	$14	A-2-Q-Q	DS	5.7%	8.1%	17.1%	30.9%
102	$11	A-2-Q-Q	S	5.1%	8.3%	15.7%	29.1%
242	$7	A-2-Q-Q	NS	4.1%	8.6%	13.6%	26.3%
104	$11	A-2-Q-K	DS	6.5%	8.5%	15.4%	30.4%
165	$9	A-2-Q-K	S	5.8%	8.9%	13.3%	28.0%
417	$5	A-2-Q-K	NS	4.9%	9.2%	11.5%	25.6%
26	$17	A-2-K-K	DS	6.4%	8.0%	19.9%	34.3%
52	$14	A-2-K-K	S	5.7%	8.3%	18.4%	32.5%
162	$9	A-2-K-K	NS	4.7%	8.7%	16.5%	30.0%
2139	-$2	A-3-3-3	S	2.6%	7.9%	7.1%	17.6%
3865	-$4	A-3-3-3	NS	2.0%	8.1%	3.6%	13.8%
215	$8	A-3-3-4	DS	4.5%	9.2%	13.4%	27.1%
291	$6	A-3-3-4	S	4.3%	9.3%	12.1%	25.6%
615	$2	A-3-3-4	NS	3.8%	9.7%	9.0%	22.5%
281	$7	A-3-3-5	DS	4.7%	8.4%	12.9%	26.0%
367	$5	A-3-3-5	S	4.6%	8.5%	11.6%	24.7%
760	$1	A-3-3-5	NS	4.1%	8.7%	8.6%	21.4%
438	$4	A-3-3-6	DS	5.0%	8.0%	11.2%	24.2%
550	$3	A-3-3-6	S	4.7%	8.2%	10.0%	22.9%
1307	-$1	A-3-3-6	NS	4.2%	8.4%	7.0%	19.5%
507	$3	A-3-3-7	DS	5.2%	7.5%	11.0%	23.7%
668	$2	A-3-3-7	S	4.9%	7.5%	9.5%	22.0%
1863	-$2	A-3-3-7	NS	4.2%	7.7%	6.3%	18.2%
636	$2	A-3-3-8	DS	5.1%	7.2%	10.3%	22.7%
890	$1	A-3-3-8	S	4.8%	7.3%	8.9%	21.0%

OMAHA HIGH-LOW 8 OR BETTER
5,278 HANDS   9 HANDED

HAND RANK	VALUE $4/$8	POCKET CARDS HAND	SUITED	HIGH %	LOW %	SCOOP %	PART OR ALL %
2555	-$3	A-3-3-8	NS	4.1%	7.6%	5.7%	17.4%
702	$2	A-3-3-9	DS	5.4%	7.0%	10.4%	22.8%
1027	$0	A-3-3-9	S	4.9%	7.3%	8.9%	21.0%
2947	-$3	A-3-3-9	NS	4.1%	7.5%	5.8%	17.4%
558	$3	A-3-3-10	DS	5.8%	7.2%	11.4%	24.4%
717	$2	A-3-3-10	S	5.4%	7.2%	10.2%	22.8%
2408	-$3	A-3-3-10	NS	4.5%	7.7%	6.7%	18.9%
501	$4	A-3-3-J	DS	6.0%	7.0%	12.0%	25.0%
688	$2	A-3-3-J	S	5.5%	7.3%	10.4%	23.2%
1951	-$2	A-3-3-J	NS	4.6%	7.7%	7.4%	19.7%
444	$4	A-3-3-Q	DS	6.3%	7.1%	12.5%	26.0%
613	$2	A-3-3-Q	S	5.8%	7.4%	11.3%	24.4%
1762	-$2	A-3-3-Q	NS	4.9%	7.8%	7.9%	20.5%
316	$6	A-3-3-K	DS	6.6%	7.3%	13.8%	27.7%
542	$3	A-3-3-K	S	6.0%	7.3%	11.9%	25.2%
1494	-$1	A-3-3-K	NS	5.3%	7.7%	8.9%	22.0%
236	$7	A-3-4-4	DS	4.8%	9.0%	13.2%	27.0%
338	$6	A-3-4-4	S	4.5%	9.2%	11.7%	25.4%
606	$2	A-3-4-4	NS	4.0%	9.4%	9.0%	22.5%
151	$10	A-3-4-5	DS	4.6%	9.6%	13.4%	27.6%
226	$8	A-3-4-5	S	4.5%	9.7%	12.4%	26.6%
470	$4	A-3-4-5	NS	3.9%	10.0%	9.3%	23.2%
189	$8	A-3-4-6	DS	4.9%	9.5%	12.1%	26.4%
309	$6	A-3-4-6	S	4.7%	9.6%	11.1%	25.4%
603	$2	A-3-4-6	NS	4.1%	9.8%	7.9%	21.8%
238	$7	A-3-4-7	DS	5.1%	9.0%	12.1%	26.2%
344	$5	A-3-4-7	S	4.9%	9.0%	11.1%	24.9%
716	$2	A-3-4-7	NS	4.3%	9.1%	8.1%	21.5%

OMAHA HIGH-LOW 8 OR BETTER
5,278 HANDS   9 HANDED

HAND RANK	VALUE $4/$8	POCKET CARDS		HIGH %	LOW %	SCOOP %	PART OR ALL %
		HAND	SUITED				
325	$6	A-3-4-8	DS	4.8%	8.9%	11.8%	25.6%
424	$4	A-3-4-8	S	4.6%	8.9%	10.5%	24.0%
987	$0	A-3-4-8	NS	4.0%	9.2%	7.5%	20.7%
335	$6	A-3-4-9	DS	4.7%	9.5%	12.1%	26.3%
445	$4	A-3-4-9	S	4.4%	9.6%	10.8%	24.8%
1187	-$0	A-3-4-9	NS	3.7%	9.9%	7.8%	21.4%
239	$7	A-3-4-10	DS	5.2%	9.6%	13.5%	28.4%
364	$5	A-3-4-10	S	4.8%	9.7%	12.1%	26.5%
829	$1	A-3-4-10	NS	4.1%	10.2%	9.3%	23.7%
219	$8	A-3-4-J	DS	5.3%	9.5%	14.1%	28.9%
320	$6	A-3-4-J	S	5.0%	9.9%	12.7%	27.5%
746	$1	A-3-4-J	NS	4.4%	10.2%	9.7%	24.2%
176	$9	A-3-4-Q	DS	5.6%	9.6%	15.1%	30.3%
260	$7	A-3-4-Q	S	5.2%	9.8%	13.4%	28.4%
617	$2	A-3-4-Q	NS	4.6%	10.3%	10.4%	25.3%
128	$10	A-3-4-K	DS	6.0%	9.4%	16.3%	31.8%
211	$8	A-3-4-K	S	5.4%	9.8%	14.0%	29.3%
537	$3	A-3-4-K	NS	4.9%	10.1%	11.7%	26.7%
301	$6	A-3-5-5	DS	4.9%	7.5%	12.8%	25.3%
414	$5	A-3-5-5	S	4.6%	7.6%	11.2%	23.4%
833	$1	A-3-5-5	NS	4.0%	7.7%	8.7%	20.5%
255	$7	A-3-5-6	DS	5.3%	8.5%	12.3%	26.0%
334	$6	A-3-5-6	S	4.9%	8.5%	10.8%	24.2%
788	$1	A-3-5-6	NS	4.5%	8.6%	8.2%	21.3%
293	$6	A-3-5-7	DS	5.5%	7.9%	12.1%	25.5%
394	$5	A-3-5-7	S	5.1%	7.9%	11.0%	24.0%
846	$1	A-3-5-7	NS	4.6%	5.1%	8.2%	17.9%
375	$5	A-3-5-8	DS	5.2%	7.8%	11.6%	24.5%

OMAHA HIGH-LOW 8 OR BETTER
5,278 HANDS   9 HANDED

HAND RANK	VALUE $4/$8	POCKET CARDS HAND	SUITED	HIGH %	LOW %	SCOOP %	PART OR ALL %
494	$4	A-3-5-8	S	4.9%	7.8%	10.2%	22.9%
1149	-$0	A-3-5-8	NS	4.3%	8.1%	7.8%	20.2%
366	$5	A-3-5-9	DS	5.1%	8.2%	11.9%	25.2%
514	$3	A-3-5-9	S	4.7%	8.1%	10.6%	23.5%
1201	-$0	A-3-5-9	NS	4.0%	8.3%	8.1%	20.4%
332	$6	A-3-5-10	DS	5.2%	8.4%	12.9%	26.5%
468	$4	A-3-5-10	S	4.7%	8.5%	11.6%	24.8%
1134	-$0	A-3-5-10	NS	4.1%	8.8%	8.8%	21.7%
275	$7	A-3-5-J	DS	5.3%	8.4%	13.6%	27.3%
430	$4	A-3-5-J	S	5.0%	8.4%	12.1%	25.5%
997	$0	A-3-5-J	NS	4.2%	8.8%	9.4%	22.5%
234	$7	A-3-5-Q	DS	5.6%	8.3%	14.5%	28.4%
392	$5	A-3-5-Q	S	5.1%	8.4%	12.8%	26.3%
800	$1	A-3-5-Q	NS	4.5%	8.7%	10.3%	23.5%
175	$9	A-3-5-K	DS	6.0%	8.2%	15.6%	29.9%
292	$6	A-3-5-K	S	5.4%	8.4%	13.7%	27.5%
649	$2	A-3-5-K	NS	4.8%	8.7%	11.1%	24.6%
408	$5	A-3-6-6	DS	5.1%	6.8%	11.2%	23.0%
559	$3	A-3-6-6	S	4.6%	6.7%	9.6%	21.0%
1352	-$1	A-3-6-6	NS	4.1%	6.8%	7.0%	17.8%
403	$5	A-3-6-7	DS	5.7%	7.5%	10.8%	24.0%
548	$3	A-3-6-7	S	5.2%	7.3%	10.0%	22.6%
1248	-$1	A-3-6-7	NS	4.7%	7.7%	6.9%	19.3%
496	$4	A-3-6-8	DS	5.4%	7.4%	10.2%	23.0%
611	$2	A-3-6-8	S	5.1%	7.3%	9.3%	21.7%
1540	-$1	A-3-6-8	NS	3.7%	6.7%	5.3%	15.7%
498	$4	A-3-6-9	DS	5.4%	7.4%	10.8%	23.6%
646	$2	A-3-6-9	S	4.8%	7.5%	9.5%	21.8%

OMAHA HIGH-LOW 8 OR BETTER
5,278 HANDS 9 HANDED

| HAND RANK | VALUE $4/$8 | POCKET CARDS | | HIGH % | LOW % | SCOOP % | PART OR ALL % |
		HAND	SUITED				
1729	-$2	A-3-6-9	NS	4.2%	7.8%	6.6%	18.6%
463	$4	A-3-6-10	DS	5.5%	7.8%	11.6%	24.9%
588	$3	A-3-6-10	S	5.0%	7.8%	10.4%	23.2%
1618	-$1	A-3-6-10	NS	4.3%	8.1%	7.6%	20.1%
462	$4	A-3-6-J	DS	5.5%	7.7%	11.6%	24.9%
621	$2	A-3-6-J	S	4.8%	7.8%	10.4%	23.0%
1835	-$2	A-3-6-J	NS	4.1%	8.1%	7.5%	19.7%
382	$5	A-3-6-Q	DS	5.7%	7.7%	12.6%	26.1%
545	$3	A-3-6-Q	S	5.0%	7.8%	11.1%	23.9%
1364	-$1	A-3-6-Q	NS	4.3%	8.1%	8.4%	20.8%
299	$6	A-3-6-K	DS	6.1%	7.7%	13.8%	27.5%
485	$4	A-3-6-K	S	5.4%	7.8%	11.9%	25.1%
1114	-$0	A-3-6-K	NS	4.6%	8.1%	9.2%	21.9%
450	$4	A-3-7-7	DS	5.2%	5.9%	11.0%	22.1%
622	$2	A-3-7-7	S	4.6%	5.9%	9.5%	20.0%
1587	-$1	A-3-7-7	NS	4.1%	5.9%	6.7%	16.6%
533	$3	A-3-7-8	DS	5.6%	6.7%	10.7%	23.0%
652	$2	A-3-7-8	S	5.3%	6.6%	9.6%	21.5%
1782	-$2	A-3-7-8	NS	4.4%	6.7%	6.6%	17.8%
546	$3	A-3-7-9	DS	5.7%	6.7%	10.8%	23.2%
675	$2	A-3-7-9	S	5.2%	6.7%	9.8%	21.7%
1808	-$2	A-3-7-9	NS	4.3%	6.9%	6.7%	17.9%
440	$4	A-3-7-10	DS	5.8%	7.0%	11.9%	24.6%
586	$3	A-3-7-10	S	5.2%	7.1%	10.8%	23.1%
1644	-$1	A-3-7-10	NS	4.5%	7.3%	7.6%	19.3%
442	$4	A-3-7-J	DS	5.7%	7.1%	12.1%	25.0%
653	$2	A-3-7-J	S	5.1%	7.0%	10.8%	22.8%
1825	-$2	A-3-7-J	NS	4.2%	7.4%	7.8%	19.3%

OMAHA HIGH-LOW 8 OR BETTER
5,278 HANDS   9 HANDED

| HAND RANK | VALUE $4/$8 | POCKET CARDS | | HIGH % | LOW % | SCOOP % | PART OR ALL % |
		HAND	SUITED				
471	$4	A-3-7-Q	DS	5.8%	7.0%	12.1%	24.9%
673	$2	A-3-7-Q	S	5.1%	7.0%	10.6%	22.7%
1486	-$1	A-3-7-Q	NS	4.4%	7.1%	8.6%	20.2%
352	$5	A-3-7-K	DS	6.2%	7.0%	13.3%	26.5%
573	$3	A-3-7-K	S	5.4%	7.1%	11.4%	23.9%
1451	-$1	A-3-7-K	NS	4.6%	7.2%	8.6%	20.4%
576	$3	A-3-8-8	DS	5.1%	5.6%	10.6%	21.3%
758	$1	A-3-8-8	S	4.6%	5.4%	9.3%	19.3%
2063	-$2	A-3-8-8	NS	3.8%	5.6%	6.5%	16.0%
597	$3	A-3-8-9	DS	5.8%	6.6%	10.7%	23.1%
767	$1	A-3-8-9	S	5.1%	6.5%	10.0%	21.6%
2204	-$2	A-3-8-9	NS	4.3%	6.8%	6.8%	17.9%
448	$4	A-3-8-10	DS	5.9%	6.9%	12.0%	24.8%
601	$3	A-3-8-10	S	5.3%	6.8%	11.2%	23.3%
1699	-$2	A-3-8-10	NS	4.3%	7.1%	8.1%	19.5%
483	$4	A-3-8-J	DS	5.8%	6.9%	12.1%	24.8%
666	$2	A-3-8-J	S	5.0%	7.0%	11.0%	23.0%
1941	-$2	A-3-8-J	NS	4.2%	7.1%	8.0%	19.4%
492	$4	A-3-8-Q	DS	5.8%	7.0%	12.3%	25.0%
687	$2	A-3-8-Q	S	5.0%	7.0%	11.1%	23.1%
1957	-$2	A-3-8-Q	NS	3.5%	6.3%	6.9%	16.7%
447	$4	A-3-8-K	DS	6.1%	6.8%	12.7%	25.6%
690	$2	A-3-8-K	S	5.3%	6.7%	10.9%	23.0%
2044	-$2	A-3-8-K	NS	4.3%	6.9%	8.1%	19.3%
351	$5	A-3-9-9	DS	4.8%	5.9%	12.0%	22.7%
565	$3	A-3-9-9	S	3.9%	5.9%	10.6%	20.5%
1151	-$0	A-3-9-9	NS	2.8%	5.7%	7.5%	16.1%
538	$3	A-3-9-10	DS	6.0%	6.2%	11.5%	23.7%

		POCKET CARDS					
HAND RANK	VALUE $4/$8	HAND	SUITED	HIGH %	LOW %	SCOOP %	PART OR ALL %
644	$2	A-3-9-10	S	5.1%	6.2%	10.8%	22.2%
1804	-$2	A-3-9-10	NS	4.3%	6.6%	7.8%	18.6%
529	$3	A-3-9-J	DS	5.9%	6.3%	11.9%	24.0%
689	$2	A-3-9-J	S	5.0%	6.3%	10.9%	22.3%
2072	-$2	A-3-9-J	NS	4.0%	6.7%	7.8%	18.5%
531	$3	A-3-9-Q	DS	5.7%	6.4%	12.1%	24.3%
751	$1	A-3-9-Q	S	4.8%	6.6%	11.0%	22.4%
2193	-$2	A-3-9-Q	NS	3.8%	6.9%	7.9%	18.5%
508	$3	A-3-9-K	DS	6.0%	6.5%	12.5%	24.9%
759	$1	A-3-9-K	S	4.8%	6.5%	11.2%	22.5%
2286	-$3	A-3-9-K	NS	3.8%	6.9%	8.1%	18.8%
288	$6	A-3-10-10	DS	5.3%	6.0%	13.6%	25.0%
428	$4	A-3-10-10	S	4.4%	6.2%	12.5%	23.0%
867	$1	A-3-10-10	NS	3.6%	6.4%	10.0%	20.0%
331	$6	A-3-10-J	DS	6.4%	6.5%	13.7%	26.5%
411	$5	A-3-10-J	S	5.5%	6.6%	13.1%	25.2%
934	$1	A-3-10-J	NS	4.8%	7.0%	10.6%	22.4%
326	$6	A-3-10-Q	DS	6.4%	6.6%	13.9%	27.0%
451	$4	A-3-10-Q	S	5.5%	6.7%	13.0%	25.2%
984	$0	A-3-10-Q	NS	4.7%	7.1%	10.6%	22.4%
289	$6	A-3-10-K	DS	6.7%	6.5%	14.2%	27.4%
472	$4	A-3-10-K	S	5.5%	6.7%	13.1%	25.3%
1065	$0	A-3-10-K	NS	4.7%	7.1%	10.5%	22.3%
220	$8	A-3-J-J	DS	5.7%	6.1%	14.8%	26.6%
342	$6	A-3-J-J	S	4.6%	6.3%	13.7%	24.6%
667	$2	A-3-J-J	NS	3.8%	6.5%	11.5%	21.7%
303	$6	A-3-J-Q	DS	6.4%	6.6%	14.5%	27.5%
406	$5	A-3-J-Q	S	5.5%	6.7%	13.5%	25.8%

OMAHA HIGH-LOW 8 OR BETTER
5,278 HANDS   9 HANDED

| HAND RANK | VALUE $4/$8 | POCKET CARDS | | HIGH % | LOW % | SCOOP % | PART OR ALL % |
		HAND	SUITED				
1003	$0	A-3-J-Q	NS	4.0%	6.3%	9.2%	19.4%
261	$7	A-3-J-K	DS	6.7%	6.7%	14.6%	28.0%
426	$4	A-3-J-K	S	5.6%	6.7%	13.4%	25.7%
924	$1	A-3-J-K	NS	4.8%	7.1%	11.0%	22.9%
163	$9	A-3-Q-Q	DS	6.0%	6.3%	16.5%	28.8%
296	$6	A-3-Q-Q	S	5.0%	6.3%	15.1%	26.4%
524	$3	A-3-Q-Q	NS	4.2%	6.6%	13.3%	24.1%
224	$8	A-3-Q-K	DS	6.8%	6.5%	15.2%	28.5%
398	$5	A-3-Q-K	S	5.7%	6.7%	13.7%	26.2%
809	$1	A-3-Q-K	NS	5.0%	7.1%	11.4%	23.5%
75	$13	A-3-K-K	DS	6.7%	6.3%	19.2%	32.2%
136	$10	A-3-K-K	S	5.8%	6.3%	17.9%	30.0%
330	$6	A-3-K-K	NS	4.9%	6.7%	16.3%	27.9%
3873	-$5	A-4-4-4	S	2.8%	5.2%	6.9%	14.9%
5024	-$7	A-4-4-4	NS	2.1%	5.3%	3.5%	10.9%
400	$5	A-4-4-5	DS	5.3%	6.3%	12.6%	24.2%
528	$3	A-4-4-5	S	5.0%	6.4%	11.3%	22.8%
1148	-$0	A-4-4-5	NS	4.3%	6.5%	8.6%	19.4%
567	$3	A-4-4-6	DS	5.4%	6.1%	11.2%	22.7%
706	$2	A-4-4-6	S	5.2%	6.1%	10.0%	21.3%
1919	-$2	A-4-4-6	NS	4.4%	6.4%	6.7%	17.5%
647	$2	A-4-4-7	DS	5.7%	5.5%	10.6%	21.9%
916	$1	A-4-4-7	S	5.4%	5.6%	9.3%	20.3%
2431	-$3	A-4-4-7	NS	4.6%	5.6%	6.1%	16.4%
814	$1	A-4-4-8	DS	5.7%	5.3%	10.0%	21.0%
1309	-$1	A-4-4-8	S	5.2%	5.4%	8.4%	19.0%
3490	-$4	A-4-4-8	NS	4.5%	5.4%	5.5%	15.4%
1176	-$0	A-4-4-9	DS	5.5%	4.8%	9.9%	20.2%

OMAHA HIGH-LOW 8 OR BETTER
5,278 HANDS   9 HANDED

HAND RANK	VALUE $4/$8	POCKET CARDS		HIGH %	LOW %	SCOOP %	PART OR ALL %
		HAND	SUITED				
1923	-$2	A-4-4-9	S	5.0%	4.8%	8.6%	18.4%
4295	-$5	A-4-4-9	NS	4.0%	5.0%	5.5%	14.5%
881	$1	A-4-4-10	DS	5.9%	5.0%	10.9%	21.7%
1430	-$1	A-4-4-10	S	5.3%	5.0%	9.5%	19.8%
3723	-$4	A-4-4-10	NS	4.5%	5.1%	6.5%	16.0%
796	$1	A-4-4-J	DS	6.1%	4.9%	11.4%	22.4%
1099	-$0	A-4-4-J	S	5.5%	5.0%	10.2%	20.7%
3378	-$4	A-4-4-J	NS	4.6%	5.2%	7.0%	16.7%
645	$2	A-4-4-Q	DS	6.4%	4.9%	12.1%	23.4%
1002	$0	A-4-4-Q	S	5.8%	4.9%	10.7%	21.4%
2952	-$3	A-4-4-Q	NS	4.8%	5.2%	7.6%	17.6%
517	$3	A-4-4-K	DS	6.8%	5.0%	13.1%	24.9%
859	$1	A-4-4-K	S	6.1%	5.0%	11.3%	22.4%
2290	-$3	A-4-4-K	NS	4.4%	4.6%	7.4%	16.4%
407	$5	A-4-5-5	DS	5.5%	6.3%	12.4%	24.2%
551	$3	A-4-5-5	S	5.1%	6.4%	11.0%	22.4%
1178	-$0	A-4-5-5	NS	4.5%	6.4%	8.4%	19.4%
363	$5	A-4-5-6	DS	5.6%	7.1%	11.7%	24.3%
516	$3	A-4-5-6	S	5.4%	7.1%	10.7%	23.2%
1124	-$0	A-4-5-6	NS	4.7%	7.2%	7.6%	19.5%
404	$5	A-4-5-7	DS	6.0%	6.5%	11.9%	24.4%
574	$3	A-4-5-7	S	5.6%	6.5%	10.6%	22.7%
1313	-$1	A-4-5-7	NS	5.1%	6.6%	8.1%	19.7%
511	$3	A-4-5-8	DS	5.8%	6.3%	11.3%	23.3%
639	$2	A-4-5-8	S	5.5%	6.4%	10.0%	21.8%
1537	-$1	A-4-5-8	NS	4.2%	6.0%	6.7%	16.9%
582	$3	A-4-5-9	DS	5.2%	6.4%	11.6%	23.2%
772	$1	A-4-5-9	S	4.8%	6.5%	10.4%	21.7%

		POCKET CARDS					
HAND RANK	VALUE $4/$8	HAND	SUITED	HIGH %	LOW %	SCOOP %	PART OR ALL %
1929	-$2	A-4-5-9	NS	3.4%	6.0%	6.5%	15.9%
484	$4	A-4-5-10	DS	5.5%	6.6%	12.6%	24.8%
658	$2	A-4-5-10	S	5.0%	6.7%	11.5%	23.3%
1669	-$2	A-4-5-10	NS	3.9%	6.5%	7.8%	18.2%
418	$4	A-4-5-J	DS	5.7%	6.6%	13.2%	25.5%
584	$3	A-4-5-J	S	5.3%	6.7%	12.0%	24.0%
1471	-$1	A-4-5-J	NS	4.2%	6.5%	8.3%	18.9%
374	$5	A-4-5-Q	DS	6.0%	6.5%	13.9%	26.4%
527	$3	A-4-5-Q	S	5.5%	6.8%	12.5%	24.7%
1219	-$1	A-4-5-Q	NS	4.2%	6.4%	9.0%	19.6%
270	$7	A-4-5-K	DS	6.5%	6.6%	15.1%	28.2%
460	$4	A-4-5-K	S	5.8%	6.7%	13.2%	25.8%
959	$0	A-4-5-K	NS	5.1%	6.8%	10.9%	22.8%
549	$3	A-4-6-6	DS	5.6%	5.6%	11.0%	22.1%
723	$1	A-4-6-6	S	5.2%	5.6%	9.3%	20.1%
1931	-$2	A-4-6-6	NS	4.5%	5.5%	6.8%	16.8%
556	$3	A-4-6-7	DS	6.3%	6.2%	10.6%	23.1%
672	$2	A-4-6-7	S	6.0%	6.2%	9.5%	21.7%
1965	-$2	A-4-6-7	NS	5.0%	6.3%	6.5%	17.8%
607	$2	A-4-6-8	DS	6.2%	6.0%	10.3%	22.5%
860	$1	A-4-6-8	S	5.7%	6.0%	9.1%	20.8%
2257	-$3	A-4-6-8	NS	4.9%	6.1%	6.0%	17.1%
801	$1	A-4-6-9	DS	5.6%	6.0%	9.9%	21.6%
1110	-$0	A-4-6-9	S	5.1%	6.0%	9.0%	20.0%
2945	-$3	A-4-6-9	NS	4.1%	6.1%	6.0%	16.2%
612	$2	A-4-6-10	DS	6.0%	6.2%	11.1%	23.3%
828	$1	A-4-6-10	S	5.4%	6.2%	10.3%	22.0%
2486	-$3	A-4-6-10	NS	4.4%	6.4%	7.1%	18.0%

OMAHA HIGH-LOW 8 OR BETTER
5,278 HANDS   9 HANDED

OMAHA HIGH-LOW 8 OR BETTER
5,278 HANDS   9 HANDED

| HAND RANK | VALUE $4/$8 | POCKET CARDS | | HIGH % | LOW % | SCOOP % | PART OR ALL % |
		HAND	SUITED				
624	$2	A-4-6-J	DS	5.8%	6.1%	11.5%	23.4%
913	$1	A-4-6-J	S	5.5%	6.2%	9.9%	21.6%
2601	-$3	A-4-6-J	NS	4.3%	6.2%	7.1%	17.7%
504	$3	A-4-6-Q	DS	6.1%	6.1%	12.3%	24.5%
762	$1	A-4-6-Q	S	5.4%	6.2%	10.7%	22.4%
2060	-$2	A-4-6-Q	NS	4.5%	6.3%	7.8%	18.6%
413	$5	A-4-6-K	DS	6.5%	6.1%	13.3%	26.0%
629	$2	A-4-6-K	S	5.8%	6.1%	11.6%	23.5%
1673	-$2	A-4-6-K	NS	5.0%	6.2%	8.9%	20.1%
631	$2	A-4-7-7	DS	5.8%	4.8%	10.4%	21.0%
803	$1	A-4-7-7	S	5.4%	4.8%	9.3%	19.6%
2108	-$2	A-4-7-7	NS	4.4%	4.7%	6.4%	15.5%
655	$2	A-4-7-8	DS	6.3%	5.4%	10.4%	22.1%
912	$1	A-4-7-8	S	5.9%	5.3%	9.3%	20.5%
2805	-$3	A-4-7-8	NS	5.0%	5.4%	6.3%	16.8%
808	$1	A-4-7-9	DS	6.0%	5.3%	10.2%	21.5%
1255	-$1	A-4-7-9	S	5.5%	5.3%	8.7%	19.4%
3370	-$4	A-4-7-9	NS	4.3%	5.3%	6.2%	15.8%
623	$2	A-4-7-10	DS	6.3%	5.5%	11.2%	23.1%
849	$1	A-4-7-10	S	5.8%	5.5%	10.5%	21.8%
2436	-$3	A-4-7-10	NS	4.8%	5.6%	7.4%	17.8%
633	$2	A-4-7-J	DS	6.2%	5.4%	11.6%	23.2%
884	$1	A-4-7-J	S	5.5%	5.5%	10.5%	21.6%
2676	-$3	A-4-7-J	NS	4.6%	5.6%	7.6%	17.8%
600	$3	A-4-7-Q	DS	6.2%	5.3%	11.9%	23.4%
947	$0	A-4-7-Q	S	5.8%	5.5%	10.2%	21.4%
2769	-$3	A-4-7-Q	NS	4.5%	5.4%	7.3%	17.2%
465	$4	A-4-7-K	DS	6.8%	5.4%	13.0%	25.2%

OMAHA HIGH-LOW 8 OR BETTER
5,278 HANDS   9 HANDED

HAND RANK	VALUE $4/$8	POCKET CARDS		HIGH %	LOW %	SCOOP %	PART OR ALL %
		HAND	SUITED				
738	$1	A-4-7-K	S	5.8%	5.4%	11.3%	22.5%
2157	-$2	A-4-7-K	NS	4.8%	5.5%	8.4%	18.7%
715	$2	A-4-8-8	DS	5.8%	4.4%	10.2%	20.4%
1015	$0	A-4-8-8	S	5.2%	4.4%	8.9%	18.4%
2831	-$3	A-4-8-8	NS	4.2%	4.3%	6.1%	14.7%
939	$1	A-4-8-9	DS	5.8%	5.1%	10.2%	21.2%
1483	-$1	A-4-8-9	S	5.3%	5.1%	9.2%	19.5%
3846	-$4	A-4-8-9	NS	4.3%	5.0%	6.5%	15.8%
616	$2	A-4-8-10	DS	6.3%	5.2%	11.6%	23.1%
823	$1	A-4-8-10	S	5.8%	5.3%	10.9%	22.0%
2363	-$3	A-4-8-10	NS	4.7%	5.4%	8.1%	18.2%
610	$2	A-4-8-J	DS	6.2%	5.2%	11.9%	23.3%
962	$0	A-4-8-J	S	5.8%	5.3%	10.5%	21.6%
2758	-$3	A-4-8-J	NS	4.5%	5.4%	8.0%	17.9%
641	$2	A-4-8-Q	DS	6.2%	5.2%	12.0%	23.4%
981	$0	A-4-8-Q	S	5.5%	5.2%	10.7%	21.5%
2974	-$3	A-4-8-Q	NS	4.4%	5.3%	7.9%	17.6%
568	$3	A-4-8-K	DS	6.7%	5.0%	12.4%	24.1%
1034	$0	A-4-8-K	S	5.7%	5.1%	10.6%	21.4%
2773	-$3	A-4-8-K	NS	4.7%	5.1%	8.0%	17.8%
678	$2	A-4-9-9	DS	4.8%	4.3%	11.0%	20.2%
896	$1	A-4-9-9	S	3.9%	4.3%	9.9%	18.1%
2026	-$2	A-4-9-9	NS	2.9%	4.3%	7.6%	14.8%
802	$1	A-4-9-10	DS	6.0%	4.5%	11.0%	21.6%
1131	-$0	A-4-9-10	S	5.3%	4.6%	10.1%	19.9%
3213	-$4	A-4-9-10	NS	4.2%	4.6%	7.3%	16.2%
840	$1	A-4-9-J	DS	5.8%	4.5%	11.1%	21.4%
1195	-$0	A-4-9-J	S	5.3%	4.6%	10.0%	19.9%

		POCKET CARDS					
HAND RANK	VALUE $4/$8	HAND	SUITED	HIGH %	LOW %	SCOOP %	PART OR ALL %
3289	-$4	A-4-9-J	NS	3.9%	4.5%	7.5%	15.9%
837	$1	A-4-9-Q	DS	5.8%	4.4%	11.4%	21.5%
1236	-$1	A-4-9-Q	S	4.8%	4.4%	10.4%	19.6%
3384	-$4	A-4-9-Q	NS	3.7%	4.5%	7.5%	15.8%
725	$1	A-4-9-K	DS	6.0%	4.4%	11.8%	22.2%
1164	-$0	A-4-9-K	S	4.9%	4.5%	10.5%	19.9%
3444	-$4	A-4-9-K	NS	3.7%	4.4%	7.7%	15.8%
536	$3	A-4-10-10	DS	5.3%	4.5%	12.7%	22.4%
663	$2	A-4-10-10	S	4.4%	4.4%	11.7%	20.5%
1472	-$1	A-4-10-10	NS	3.4%	4.6%	9.6%	17.6%
502	$4	A-4-10-J	DS	6.5%	4.6%	12.8%	23.9%
632	$2	A-4-10-J	S	5.7%	4.7%	12.3%	22.7%
1574	-$1	A-4-10-J	NS	4.6%	4.9%	9.7%	19.2%
506	$3	A-4-10-Q	DS	6.3%	4.6%	13.3%	24.1%
662	$2	A-4-10-Q	S	5.4%	4.6%	12.4%	22.5%
1696	-$2	A-4-10-Q	NS	4.3%	4.8%	9.7%	18.9%
461	$4	A-4-10-K	DS	6.6%	4.6%	13.6%	24.7%
679	$2	A-4-10-K	S	5.5%	4.6%	12.1%	22.1%
1629	-$1	A-4-10-K	NS	4.4%	4.7%	9.9%	19.0%
390	$5	A-4-J-J	DS	5.7%	4.6%	14.2%	24.4%
590	$3	A-4-J-J	S	4.7%	4.5%	12.7%	21.9%
1271	-$1	A-4-J-J	NS	3.8%	4.7%	10.7%	19.2%
476	$4	A-4-J-Q	DS	6.5%	4.6%	13.3%	24.4%
605	$2	A-4-J-Q	S	5.5%	4.6%	12.6%	22.7%
1477	-$1	A-4-J-Q	NS	4.4%	4.8%	10.3%	19.5%
443	$4	A-4-J-K	DS	6.6%	4.6%	13.8%	24.9%
594	$3	A-4-J-K	S	5.5%	4.6%	12.7%	22.8%
1576	-$1	A-4-J-K	NS	4.5%	4.8%	10.1%	19.4%

OMAHA HIGH-LOW 8 OR BETTER
5,278 HANDS   9 HANDED

OMAHA HIGH-LOW 8 OR BETTER
5,278 HANDS   9 HANDED

HAND RANK	VALUE $4/$8	POCKET CARDS		HIGH %	LOW %	SCOOP %	PART OR ALL %
		HAND	SUITED				
312	$6	A-4-Q-Q	DS	6.2%	4.7%	15.8%	26.6%
452	$4	A-4-Q-Q	S	5.1%	4.7%	14.6%	24.4%
874	$1	A-4-Q-Q	NS	4.2%	4.9%	12.6%	21.7%
412	$5	A-4-Q-K	DS	6.7%	4.5%	14.2%	25.4%
566	$3	A-4-Q-K	S	5.6%	4.6%	13.0%	23.2%
1285	-$1	A-4-Q-K	NS	4.7%	4.7%	10.9%	20.3%
146	$10	A-4-K-K	DS	6.9%	4.7%	18.6%	30.3%
285	$7	A-4-K-K	S	6.2%	4.8%	17.1%	28.1%
518	$3	A-4-K-K	NS	5.1%	5.0%	15.6%	25.7%
3833	-$4	A-5-5-5	S	2.8%	3.0%	6.0%	11.8%
4864	-$6	A-5-5-5	NS	2.0%	2.9%	3.4%	8.3%
669	$2	A-5-5-6	DS	5.9%	4.6%	10.9%	21.4%
1088	-$0	A-5-5-6	S	4.8%	4.2%	8.8%	17.8%
1959	-$2	A-5-5-6	NS	3.7%	3.6%	5.6%	12.9%
763	$1	A-5-5-7	DS	6.1%	4.1%	10.5%	20.7%
1508	-$1	A-5-5-7	S	4.7%	3.4%	7.3%	15.4%
2994	-$3	A-5-5-7	NS	3.7%	3.0%	5.2%	11.9%
1046	$0	A-5-5-8	DS	6.0%	3.8%	9.8%	19.6%
1491	-$1	A-5-5-8	S	5.6%	3.8%	8.6%	18.1%
3176	-$4	A-5-5-8	NS	3.8%	2.9%	4.9%	11.6%
1575	-$1	A-5-5-9	DS	5.9%	3.2%	9.4%	18.5%
2252	-$3	A-5-5-9	S	5.4%	3.2%	8.3%	16.9%
4135	-$5	A-5-5-9	NS	3.5%	2.1%	4.6%	10.1%
1258	-$1	A-5-5-10	DS	5.9%	3.2%	10.2%	19.3%
1865	-$2	A-5-5-10	S	5.2%	3.1%	9.2%	17.5%
3792	-$4	A-5-5-10	NS	3.6%	2.3%	5.2%	11.1%
1115	-$0	A-5-5-J	DS	6.1%	3.2%	10.7%	19.9%
1653	-$2	A-5-5-J	S	5.5%	3.2%	9.5%	18.3%

HAND RANK	VALUE $4/$8	POCKET CARDS		HIGH %	LOW %	SCOOP %	PART OR ALL %
		HAND	SUITED				
3500	-$4	A-5-5-J	NS	3.6%	2.4%	5.0%	11.0%
927	$1	A-5-5-Q	DS	6.3%	3.2%	11.3%	20.8%
1434	-$1	A-5-5-Q	S	4.8%	2.7%	8.6%	16.0%
3342	-$4	A-5-5-Q	NS	3.9%	2.2%	5.6%	11.8%
701	$2	A-5-5-K	DS	6.8%	3.3%	12.3%	22.4%
1146	-$0	A-5-5-K	S	6.0%	3.2%	10.8%	20.0%
2733	-$3	A-5-5-K	NS	4.8%	3.1%	8.0%	15.9%
693	$2	A-5-6-6	DS	6.0%	4.6%	10.5%	21.0%
965	$0	A-5-6-6	S	5.5%	4.6%	9.0%	19.0%
1996	-$2	A-5-6-6	NS	3.7%	3.6%	5.6%	12.9%
677	$2	A-5-6-7	DS	6.4%	4.9%	10.4%	21.8%
905	$1	A-5-6-7	S	6.1%	4.9%	9.1%	20.2%
2400	-$3	A-5-6-7	NS	4.5%	4.1%	5.2%	13.7%
722	$1	A-5-6-8	DS	6.4%	4.8%	9.9%	21.2%
1080	-$0	A-5-6-8	S	6.0%	4.8%	8.8%	19.5%
3013	-$3	A-5-6-8	NS	4.2%	3.7%	4.9%	12.7%
938	$1	A-5-6-9	DS	5.9%	4.6%	9.7%	20.3%
1263	-$1	A-5-6-9	S	5.1%	4.2%	7.8%	17.1%
3485	-$4	A-5-6-9	NS	4.4%	4.4%	5.9%	14.7%
844	$1	A-5-6-10	DS	5.8%	4.7%	10.7%	21.2%
1284	-$1	A-5-6-10	S	5.0%	4.6%	8.5%	18.1%
3276	-$4	A-5-6-10	NS	4.3%	4.5%	6.7%	15.5%
797	$1	A-5-6-J	DS	6.0%	4.6%	11.2%	21.8%
1104	-$0	A-5-6-J	S	5.0%	4.4%	9.0%	18.3%
2618	-$3	A-5-6-J	NS	3.6%	3.9%	5.7%	13.2%
640	$2	A-5-6-Q	DS	6.2%	4.6%	12.0%	22.8%
1029	$0	A-5-6-Q	S	5.0%	4.3%	9.5%	18.8%
2558	-$3	A-5-6-Q	NS	3.7%	3.6%	6.3%	13.5%

OMAHA HIGH-LOW 8 OR BETTER
5,278 HANDS   9 HANDED

OMAHA HIGH-LOW 8 OR BETTER 5,278 HANDS 9 HANDED							
HAND RANK	VALUE $4/$8	POCKET CARDS		HIGH %	LOW %	SCOOP %	PART OR ALL %
		HAND	SUITED				
523	$3	A-5-6-K	DS	6.7%	4.7%	13.1%	24.5%
819	$1	A-5-6-K	S	6.0%	4.6%	11.4%	21.9%
1970	-$2	A-5-6-K	NS	4.0%	3.8%	7.2%	15.0%
739	$1	A-5-7-7	DS	6.3%	3.8%	10.1%	20.1%
1076	-$0	A-5-7-7	S	5.6%	3.7%	9.0%	18.3%
2577	-$3	A-5-7-7	NS	4.7%	3.9%	6.3%	14.9%
790	$1	A-5-7-8	DS	6.7%	4.1%	10.2%	21.0%
1068	$0	A-5-7-8	S	6.4%	4.1%	9.2%	19.7%
3301	-$4	A-5-7-8	NS	4.4%	3.2%	4.9%	12.5%
991	$0	A-5-7-9	DS	6.2%	3.9%	9.6%	19.8%
1314	-$1	A-5-7-9	S	5.3%	3.6%	8.1%	17.0%
3348	-$4	A-5-7-9	NS	3.8%	2.8%	5.1%	11.7%
816	$1	A-5-7-10	DS	6.2%	4.0%	11.1%	21.4%
1193	-$0	A-5-7-10	S	5.7%	4.1%	9.9%	19.7%
3178	-$4	A-5-7-10	NS	3.8%	3.1%	5.7%	12.6%
747	$1	A-5-7-J	DS	6.4%	4.1%	11.4%	21.9%
1145	-$0	A-5-7-J	S	5.2%	3.7%	9.4%	18.3%
2905	-$3	A-5-7-J	NS	3.9%	3.3%	6.1%	13.2%
714	$2	A-5-7-Q	DS	6.5%	3.9%	11.6%	21.9%
1143	-$0	A-5-7-Q	S	4.8%	3.4%	8.7%	16.8%
2870	-$3	A-5-7-Q	NS	4.0%	3.1%	6.0%	13.1%
563	$3	A-5-7-K	DS	7.0%	4.0%	12.6%	23.6%
986	$0	A-5-7-K	S	6.1%	3.8%	11.0%	20.9%
2484	-$3	A-5-7-K	NS	4.1%	3.0%	6.6%	13.6%
880	$1	A-5-8-8	DS	6.2%	3.5%	9.9%	19.5%
1349	-$1	A-5-8-8	S	5.6%	3.4%	8.5%	17.4%
2789	-$3	A-5-8-8	NS	3.7%	2.6%	4.8%	11.2%
1109	-$0	A-5-8-9	DS	6.4%	3.7%	9.9%	20.0%

		POCKET CARDS					
OMAHA HIGH-LOW 8 OR BETTER							
5,278 HANDS 9 HANDED							
HAND RANK	VALUE $4/$8	HAND	SUITED	HIGH %	LOW %	SCOOP %	PART OR ALL %
1523	-$1	A-5-8-9	S	5.3%	3.4%	8.1%	16.7%
3879	-$5	A-5-8-9	NS	4.0%	3.0%	4.9%	11.9%
854	$1	A-5-8-10	DS	6.3%	3.3%	10.9%	20.6%
1135	-$0	A-5-8-10	S	5.8%	3.8%	10.2%	19.8%
2727	-$3	A-5-8-10	NS	3.7%	3.1%	6.6%	13.4%
729	$1	A-5-8-J	DS	6.4%	3.9%	11.6%	21.9%
1278	-$1	A-5-8-J	S	5.1%	3.2%	8.7%	17.0%
3293	-$4	A-5-8-J	NS	3.8%	3.1%	6.2%	13.1%
744	$1	A-5-8-Q	DS	6.4%	3.8%	11.7%	21.9%
1266	-$1	A-5-8-Q	S	5.2%	3.4%	9.4%	18.0%
3470	-$4	A-5-8-Q	NS	3.7%	3.1%	6.0%	12.9%
704	$2	A-5-8-K	DS	6.9%	3.7%	12.0%	22.6%
1194	-$0	A-5-8-K	S	5.9%	3.6%	10.5%	20.0%
3513	-$4	A-5-8-K	NS	3.9%	2.7%	5.7%	12.3%
899	$1	A-5-9-9	DS	5.2%	3.0%	10.4%	18.6%
1163	-$0	A-5-9-9	S	4.3%	2.8%	9.4%	16.5%
2820	-$3	A-5-9-9	NS	3.1%	2.9%	7.0%	13.0%
1227	-$1	A-5-9-10	DS	6.0%	3.0%	10.2%	19.2%
1750	-$2	A-5-9-10	S	4.7%	2.8%	8.2%	15.7%
3921	-$5	A-5-9-10	NS	3.6%	2.5%	5.5%	11.6%
1086	-$0	A-5-9-J	DS	6.2%	3.0%	10.6%	19.9%
1595	-$1	A-5-9-J	S	4.8%	2.7%	8.7%	16.2%
3174	-$4	A-5-9-J	NS	3.6%	2.6%	6.3%	12.4%
1085	-$0	A-5-9-Q	DS	6.0%	3.0%	10.9%	19.9%
1530	-$1	A-5-9-Q	S	4.6%	2.7%	8.5%	15.8%
3557	-$4	A-5-9-Q	NS	3.9%	2.8%	7.4%	14.0%
915	$1	A-5-9-K	DS	6.3%	3.0%	11.3%	20.6%
1572	-$1	A-5-9-K	S	4.5%	2.6%	9.0%	16.2%

OMAHA HIGH-LOW 8 OR BETTER
5,278 HANDS   9 HANDED

HAND RANK	VALUE $4/$8	POCKET CARDS		HIGH %	LOW %	SCOOP %	PART OR ALL %
		HAND	SUITED				
3684	-$4	A-5-9-K	NS	3.0%	2.3%	6.1%	11.4%
691	$2	A-5-10-10	DS	5.3%	3.1%	12.0%	20.4%
982	$0	A-5-10-10	S	4.7%	3.1%	10.9%	18.7%
2254	-$3	A-5-10-10	NS	2.8%	2.7%	7.4%	12.8%
661	$2	A-5-10-J	DS	6.3%	3.0%	12.3%	21.6%
875	$1	A-5-10-J	S	5.4%	3.0%	11.6%	20.0%
2320	-$3	A-5-10-J	NS	3.8%	2.6%	7.7%	14.1%
657	$2	A-5-10-Q	DS	6.2%	3.0%	12.3%	21.4%
935	$1	A-5-10-Q	S	5.5%	2.9%	11.4%	19.8%
2365	-$3	A-5-10-Q	NS	3.6%	2.6%	7.6%	13.8%
635	$2	A-5-10-K	DS	6.3%	2.9%	12.7%	21.9%
980	$0	A-5-10-K	S	5.4%	2.8%	11.3%	19.5%
2682	-$3	A-5-10-K	NS	3.5%	2.3%	7.4%	13.2%
599	$3	A-5-J-J	DS	5.7%	3.3%	12.9%	22.0%
834	$1	A-5-J-J	S	5.0%	3.2%	12.1%	20.3%
1914	-$2	A-5-J-J	NS	3.0%	2.8%	8.6%	14.4%
589	$3	A-5-J-Q	DS	6.3%	2.9%	13.0%	22.2%
770	$1	A-5-J-Q	S	5.3%	2.9%	12.0%	20.2%
1867	-$2	A-5-J-Q	NS	3.9%	2.5%	8.2%	14.6%
577	$3	A-5-J-K	DS	6.4%	2.9%	13.0%	22.3%
817	$1	A-5-J-K	S	5.3%	2.8%	11.8%	20.0%
2006	-$2	A-5-J-K	NS	3.7%	2.5%	7.4%	13.6%
429	$4	A-5-Q-Q	DS	6.2%	3.4%	15.3%	24.9%
654	$2	A-5-Q-Q	S	5.1%	3.3%	13.7%	22.1%
1459	-$1	A-5-Q-Q	NS	3.4%	3.0%	10.2%	16.6%
512	$3	A-5-Q-K	DS	6.5%	2.9%	13.7%	23.1%
696	$2	A-5-Q-K	S	5.5%	2.8%	12.3%	20.6%
1616	-$1	A-5-Q-K	NS	4.1%	2.4%	8.1%	14.6%

		POCKET CARDS					
HAND RANK	VALUE $4/$8	HAND	SUITED	HIGH %	LOW %	SCOOP %	PART OR ALL %
		OMAHA HIGH-LOW 8 OR BETTER 5,278 HANDS 9 HANDED					
229	$7	A-5-K-K	DS	7.1%	3.4%	17.7%	28.2%
416	$5	A-5-K-K	S	5.8%	3.4%	16.5%	25.7%
694	$2	A-5-K-K	NS	4.8%	3.6%	15.0%	23.3%
4832	-$6	A-6-6-6	S	2.7%	2.0%	4.6%	9.3%
5061	-$8	A-6-6-6	NS	1.8%	1.7%	2.1%	5.6%
1159	-$0	A-6-6-7	DS	6.3%	3.1%	9.6%	19.0%
1534	-$1	A-6-6-7	S	5.5%	2.8%	7.5%	15.8%
3851	-$4	A-6-6-7	NS	3.5%	2.2%	4.3%	10.0%
1567	-$1	A-6-6-8	DS	6.3%	2.9%	8.8%	18.1%
1964	-$2	A-6-6-8	S	5.3%	2.6%	7.1%	15.0%
3896	-$5	A-6-6-8	NS	4.7%	2.6%	5.0%	12.4%
2262	-$3	A-6-6-9	DS	6.3%	2.2%	8.0%	16.6%
3194	-$4	A-6-6-9	S	5.6%	2.1%	6.6%	14.4%
4932	-$7	A-6-6-9	NS	4.5%	2.0%	4.5%	11.0%
1871	-$2	A-6-6-10	DS	6.2%	2.2%	9.2%	17.6%
2377	-$3	A-6-6-10	S	5.1%	2.0%	7.4%	14.5%
4402	-$5	A-6-6-10	NS	3.3%	1.3%	4.4%	9.0%
1915	-$2	A-6-6-J	DS	6.0%	2.2%	9.2%	17.5%
2503	-$3	A-6-6-J	S	4.9%	2.0%	7.5%	14.4%
4431	-$5	A-6-6-J	NS	3.4%	1.1%	4.5%	9.0%
1414	-$1	A-6-6-Q	DS	6.2%	2.3%	10.2%	18.6%
2405	-$3	A-6-6-Q	S	5.0%	2.0%	7.7%	14.7%
3959	-$5	A-6-6-Q	NS	3.5%	1.3%	4.7%	9.4%
1032	$0	A-6-6-K	DS	6.9%	2.3%	11.2%	20.4%
2029	-$2	A-6-6-K	S	5.8%	2.2%	9.3%	17.4%
4191	-$5	A-6-6-K	NS	3.8%	1.3%	5.0%	10.2%
1117	-$0	A-6-7-7	DS	6.4%	3.1%	9.4%	18.8%
1548	-$1	A-6-7-7	S	5.3%	2.7%	7.4%	15.4%

OMAHA HIGH-LOW 8 OR BETTER
5,278 HANDS   9 HANDED

| HAND RANK | VALUE $4/$8 | POCKET CARDS | | HIGH % | LOW % | SCOOP % | PART OR ALL % |
		HAND	SUITED				
3382	-$4	A-6-7-7	NS	3.9%	2.1%	4.7%	10.7%
999	$0	A-6-7-8	DS	6.9%	3.2%	9.5%	19.6%
1535	-$1	A-6-7-8	S	5.4%	2.6%	6.9%	14.9%
3786	-$4	A-6-7-8	NS	4.4%	2.3%	4.4%	11.1%
1243	-$1	A-6-7-9	DS	6.7%	3.0%	9.1%	18.8%
1679	-$2	A-6-7-9	S	5.1%	2.5%	6.8%	14.4%
3393	-$4	A-6-7-9	NS	4.3%	2.2%	4.6%	11.1%
1078	-$0	A-6-7-10	DS	6.7%	3.1%	10.2%	20.0%
1505	-$1	A-6-7-10	S	5.1%	2.6%	7.6%	15.2%
3483	-$4	A-6-7-10	NS	4.0%	2.2%	5.5%	11.7%
1191	-$0	A-6-7-J	DS	5.7%	2.8%	9.3%	17.8%
1693	-$2	A-6-7-J	S	4.8%	2.5%	7.7%	14.9%
3676	-$4	A-6-7-J	NS	3.9%	2.2%	5.2%	11.3%
1063	$0	A-6-7-Q	DS	6.0%	2.7%	9.7%	18.4%
1579	-$1	A-6-7-Q	S	4.9%	2.5%	7.7%	15.1%
3988	-$5	A-6-7-Q	NS	3.8%	2.1%	5.4%	11.3%
695	$2	A-6-7-K	DS	7.2%	3.1%	12.0%	22.3%
1460	-$1	A-6-7-K	S	5.2%	2.5%	8.7%	16.3%
3387	-$4	A-6-7-K	NS	4.0%	2.5%	5.9%	12.4%
1166	-$0	A-6-8-8	DS	6.4%	2.8%	9.5%	18.7%
2023	-$2	A-6-8-8	S	5.8%	2.6%	8.0%	16.3%
3515	-$4	A-6-8-8	NS	4.7%	2.4%	5.6%	12.7%
1514	-$1	A-6-8-9	DS	6.6%	2.7%	9.1%	18.5%
2066	-$2	A-6-8-9	S	5.1%	2.2%	6.7%	14.0%
4429	-$5	A-6-8-9	NS	4.5%	2.0%	4.6%	11.1%
1094	-$0	A-6-8-10	DS	6.6%	2.8%	10.2%	19.6%
1498	-$1	A-6-8-10	S	5.1%	2.4%	7.9%	15.4%
3889	-$5	A-6-8-10	NS	4.8%	2.5%	7.1%	14.3%

OMAHA HIGH-LOW 8 OR BETTER
5,278 HANDS   9 HANDED

| HAND RANK | VALUE $4/$8 | POCKET CARDS | | HIGH % | LOW % | SCOOP % | PART OR ALL % |
		HAND	SUITED				
1247	-$1	A-6-8-J	DS	6.4%	2.7%	10.2%	19.4%
1754	-$2	A-6-8-J	S	4.8%	2.3%	7.7%	14.8%
4088	-$5	A-6-8-J	NS	3.7%	2.0%	5.4%	11.1%
1084	-$0	A-6-8-Q	DS	6.0%	2.5%	9.9%	18.4%
1849	-$2	A-6-8-Q	S	4.9%	2.3%	8.3%	15.5%
3951	-$5	A-6-8-Q	NS	3.9%	2.1%	5.9%	11.9%
977	$0	A-6-8-K	DS	7.0%	2.7%	11.2%	20.8%
1717	-$2	A-6-8-K	S	5.1%	2.3%	8.3%	15.7%
4018	-$5	A-6-8-K	NS	3.9%	1.9%	5.6%	11.3%
1330	-$1	A-6-9-9	DS	5.5%	2.1%	9.7%	17.3%
1768	-$2	A-6-9-9	S	4.8%	2.1%	8.7%	15.6%
3146	-$4	A-6-9-9	NS	3.3%	1.9%	6.5%	11.8%
1612	-$1	A-6-9-10	DS	6.5%	2.1%	9.4%	18.0%
2357	-$3	A-6-9-10	S	4.8%	1.6%	7.2%	13.6%
4138	-$5	A-6-9-10	NS	4.0%	1.4%	5.1%	10.4%
1748	-$2	A-6-9-J	DS	6.1%	2.1%	9.5%	17.7%
2349	-$3	A-6-9-J	S	4.5%	1.6%	7.0%	13.1%
4181	-$5	A-6-9-J	NS	3.5%	1.4%	5.3%	10.2%
1543	-$1	A-6-9-Q	DS	6.4%	2.0%	10.0%	18.5%
2134	-$2	A-6-9-Q	S	4.4%	1.6%	7.5%	13.5%
4333	-$5	A-6-9-Q	NS	3.5%	1.4%	5.2%	10.1%
1395	-$1	A-6-9-K	DS	6.6%	2.0%	10.4%	19.0%
2358	-$3	A-6-9-K	S	4.7%	1.6%	7.4%	13.7%
4240	-$5	A-6-9-K	NS	3.5%	1.4%	5.5%	10.4%
1077	-$0	A-6-10-10	DS	5.5%	2.3%	11.0%	18.8%
1602	-$1	A-6-10-10	S	4.6%	2.2%	9.9%	16.8%
2908	-$3	A-6-10-10	NS	2.8%	1.7%	6.6%	11.1%
1056	$0	A-6-10-J	DS	6.2%	2.0%	11.0%	19.1%

OMAHA HIGH-LOW 8 OR BETTER
5,278 HANDS   9 HANDED

| HAND RANK | VALUE $4/$8 | POCKET CARDS | | HIGH % | LOW % | SCOOP % | PART OR ALL % |
		HAND	SUITED				
1672	-$2	A-6-10-J	S	5.0%	1.8%	9.1%	15.9%
3554	-$4	A-6-10-J	NS	3.4%	1.4%	6.7%	11.5%
891	$1	A-6-10-Q	DS	6.4%	2.0%	11.5%	19.9%
1390	-$1	A-6-10-Q	S	5.7%	1.9%	10.2%	17.9%
3246	-$4	A-6-10-Q	NS	4.2%	1.8%	8.4%	14.4%
824	$1	A-6-10-K	DS	6.6%	2.0%	12.0%	20.7%
1872	-$2	A-6-10-K	S	5.1%	1.9%	9.3%	16.3%
2813	-$3	A-6-10-K	NS	3.7%	1.3%	7.2%	12.2%
1019	$0	A-6-J-J	DS	5.5%	2.4%	11.8%	19.8%
1655	-$2	A-6-J-J	S	4.7%	2.1%	10.3%	17.1%
3198	-$4	A-6-J-J	NS	2.9%	1.9%	7.6%	12.5%
928	$1	A-6-J-Q	DS	6.1%	2.0%	11.4%	19.5%
1398	-$1	A-6-J-Q	S	4.3%	1.6%	9.1%	15.1%
2662	-$3	A-6-J-Q	NS	3.6%	1.4%	7.1%	12.0%
852	$1	A-6-J-K	DS	6.3%	2.0%	11.8%	20.1%
1396	-$1	A-6-J-K	S	5.4%	1.8%	9.6%	16.8%
2670	-$3	A-6-J-K	NS	3.7%	1.4%	6.5%	11.6%
686	$2	A-6-Q-Q	DS	6.1%	2.4%	13.8%	22.3%
1089	-$0	A-6-Q-Q	S	4.8%	2.4%	12.5%	19.7%
3025	-$3	A-6-Q-Q	NS	3.4%	2.5%	9.1%	15.0%
1053	$0	A-6-Q-K	DS	4.9%	2.4%	12.7%	20.0%
1522	-$1	A-6-Q-K	S	4.7%	1.6%	10.0%	16.3%
2767	-$3	A-6-Q-K	NS	3.6%	1.3%	6.7%	11.6%
427	$4	A-6-K-K	DS	6.9%	2.7%	16.6%	26.3%
697	$2	A-6-K-K	S	6.0%	2.8%	15.1%	23.9%
1288	-$1	A-6-K-K	NS	4.3%	2.6%	13.9%	20.8%
4869	-$6	A-7-7-7	S	2.5%	1.0%	3.6%	7.1%
5067	-$8	A-7-7-7	NS	1.9%	1.0%	2.1%	4.9%

OMAHA HIGH-LOW 8 OR BETTER
5,278 HANDS   9 HANDED

| HAND RANK | VALUE $4/$8 | POCKET CARDS | | HIGH % | LOW % | SCOOP % | PART OR ALL % |
		HAND	SUITED				
1359	-$1	A-7-7-8	DS	6.7%	2.1%	9.2%	18.0%
1946	-$2	A-7-7-8	S	5.7%	1.8%	7.3%	14.8%
4377	-$5	A-7-7-8	NS	5.1%	1.8%	5.5%	12.4%
2160	-$2	A-7-7-9	DS	6.8%	1.4%	8.5%	16.7%
2775	-$3	A-7-7-9	S	5.5%	1.2%	6.8%	13.5%
4176	-$5	A-7-7-9	NS	5.0%	1.2%	5.0%	11.2%
1593	-$1	A-7-7-10	DS	6.7%	1.5%	9.5%	17.7%
2574	-$3	A-7-7-10	S	6.2%	1.4%	8.2%	15.9%
4314	-$5	A-7-7-10	NS	4.8%	1.2%	6.1%	12.1%
1632	-$1	A-7-7-J	DS	6.4%	1.5%	9.8%	17.6%
2506	-$3	A-7-7-J	S	5.4%	1.2%	7.2%	13.8%
3995	-$5	A-7-7-J	NS	4.5%	1.2%	6.1%	11.9%
1767	-$2	A-7-7-Q	DS	6.5%	1.5%	9.6%	17.6%
2638	-$3	A-7-7-Q	S	5.2%	1.2%	7.2%	13.7%
3979	-$5	A-7-7-Q	NS	4.5%	1.2%	5.9%	11.6%
1208	-$0	A-7-7-K	DS	7.1%	1.5%	10.6%	19.3%
2444	-$3	A-7-7-K	S	6.2%	1.4%	8.6%	16.1%
3636	-$4	A-7-7-K	NS	4.0%	0.9%	5.1%	10.0%
1245	-$1	A-7-8-8	DS	6.8%	2.0%	9.4%	18.1%
1898	-$2	A-7-8-8	S	6.2%	2.0%	8.3%	16.5%
3615	-$4	A-7-8-8	NS	5.1%	1.7%	5.6%	12.4%
1360	-$1	A-7-8-9	DS	7.2%	1.8%	9.1%	18.1%
2016	-$2	A-7-8-9	S	5.6%	1.5%	6.7%	13.8%
3556	-$4	A-7-8-9	NS	5.3%	1.5%	6.0%	12.8%
1001	$0	A-7-8-10	DS	7.2%	2.1%	10.2%	19.4%
1784	-$2	A-7-8-10	S	5.4%	1.7%	7.6%	14.7%
3120	-$4	A-7-8-10	NS	4.5%	1.4%	6.1%	12.0%
1048	$0	A-7-8-J	DS	7.0%	2.0%	10.4%	19.3%

OMAHA HIGH-LOW 8 OR BETTER
5,278 HANDS   9 HANDED

| HAND RANK | VALUE $4/$8 | POCKET CARDS | | HIGH % | LOW % | SCOOP % | PART OR ALL % |
		HAND	SUITED				
1614	-$1	A-7-8-J	S	5.4%	1.7%	7.8%	14.9%
3074	-$4	A-7-8-J	NS	4.8%	1.8%	7.4%	14.0%
1240	-$1	A-7-8-Q	DS	6.2%	1.8%	9.3%	17.4%
1740	-$2	A-7-8-Q	S	5.3%	1.6%	7.9%	14.8%
3481	-$4	A-7-8-Q	NS	4.9%	1.7%	7.1%	13.7%
932	$1	A-7-8-K	DS	7.4%	2.1%	11.2%	20.6%
1705	-$2	A-7-8-K	S	5.6%	1.6%	8.1%	15.3%
3239	-$4	A-7-8-K	NS	5.1%	1.8%	7.7%	14.6%
1350	-$1	A-7-9-9	DS	5.9%	1.3%	9.7%	17.0%
1704	-$2	A-7-9-9	S	5.1%	1.3%	8.6%	14.9%
3116	-$4	A-7-9-9	NS	3.6%	1.1%	6.7%	11.5%
1320	-$1	A-7-9-10	DS	7.1%	1.3%	9.6%	18.0%
1870	-$2	A-7-9-10	S	5.8%	1.1%	7.9%	14.7%
3269	-$4	A-7-9-10	NS	5.0%	1.0%	6.6%	12.7%
1473	-$1	A-7-9-J	DS	6.8%	1.3%	9.7%	17.8%
1924	-$2	A-7-9-J	S	5.1%	1.0%	7.4%	13.6%
3540	-$4	A-7-9-J	NS	4.6%	1.0%	6.7%	12.3%
1785	-$2	A-7-9-Q	DS	6.6%	1.2%	9.5%	17.4%
2338	-$3	A-7-9-Q	S	5.6%	1.2%	8.3%	15.1%
3812	-$4	A-7-9-Q	NS	4.3%	1.0%	6.4%	11.7%
1261	-$1	A-7-9-K	DS	7.2%	1.3%	10.4%	18.9%
2095	-$2	A-7-9-K	S	6.1%	1.1%	8.8%	16.0%
3510	-$4	A-7-9-K	NS	4.5%	1.1%	7.1%	12.7%
1059	$0	A-7-10-10	DS	5.8%	1.4%	11.1%	18.3%
1347	-$1	A-7-10-10	S	5.2%	1.4%	10.4%	17.1%
2633	-$3	A-7-10-10	NS	3.3%	1.0%	7.0%	11.3%
863	$1	A-7-10-J	DS	6.7%	1.3%	11.3%	19.3%
1184	-$0	A-7-10-J	S	5.6%	1.2%	9.4%	16.1%

HAND RANK	VALUE $4/$8	POCKET CARDS		HIGH %	LOW %	SCOOP %	PART OR ALL %
		HAND	SUITED				
OMAHA HIGH-LOW 8 OR BETTER							
5,278 HANDS 9 HANDED							
2304	-$3	A-7-10-J	NS	4.3%	1.0%	7.6%	12.8%
811	$1	A-7-10-Q	DS	6.1%	1.6%	13.3%	21.0%
1388	-$1	A-7-10-Q	S	5.4%	1.2%	9.2%	15.7%
2448	-$3	A-7-10-Q	NS	3.9%	1.0%	7.2%	12.1%
724	$1	A-7-10-K	DS	7.1%	1.3%	11.9%	20.3%
1253	-$1	A-7-10-K	S	6.2%	1.3%	10.8%	18.3%
2492	-$3	A-7-10-K	NS	4.6%	1.1%	9.0%	14.7%
910	$1	A-7-J-J	DS	5.8%	1.5%	12.1%	19.4%
1277	-$1	A-7-J-J	S	5.2%	1.4%	11.2%	17.9%
3050	-$3	A-7-J-J	NS	3.1%	1.2%	7.7%	11.9%
1039	$0	A-7-J-Q	DS	6.3%	1.2%	11.1%	18.6%
1450	-$1	A-7-J-Q	S	4.6%	1.0%	8.6%	14.3%
3054	-$4	A-7-J-Q	NS	3.6%	0.7%	6.7%	11.0%
748	$1	A-7-J-K	DS	6.8%	1.4%	12.0%	20.2%
1304	-$1	A-7-J-K	S	5.2%	1.0%	9.6%	15.9%
2641	-$3	A-7-J-K	NS	3.8%	0.8%	7.3%	11.9%
799	$1	A-7-Q-Q	DS	6.1%	1.6%	13.4%	21.1%
1230	-$1	A-7-Q-Q	S	5.3%	1.5%	12.1%	19.0%
3419	-$4	A-7-Q-Q	NS	3.3%	1.6%	8.8%	13.7%
778	$1	A-7-Q-K	DS	6.6%	1.3%	11.9%	19.8%
1192	-$0	A-7-Q-K	S	4.9%	1.0%	9.7%	15.6%
2391	-$3	A-7-Q-K	NS	3.7%	0.9%	6.7%	11.3%
488	$4	A-7-K-K	DS	7.1%	1.6%	15.9%	24.7%
698	$2	A-7-K-K	S	5.6%	1.6%	15.0%	22.2%
1545	-$1	A-7-K-K	NS	2.7%	1.1%	8.8%	12.5%
4938	-$7	A-8-8-8	S	2.7%	0.6%	3.7%	7.0%
5097	-$8	A-8-8-8	NS	2.0%	0.6%	2.1%	4.8%
2039	-$2	A-8-8-9	DS	7.4%	1.0%	8.9%	17.3%

OMAHA HIGH-LOW 8 OR BETTER
5,278 HANDS   9 HANDED

| HAND RANK | VALUE $4/$8 | POCKET CARDS | | HIGH % | LOW % | SCOOP % | PART OR ALL % |
		HAND	SUITED				
3262	-$4	A-8-8-9	S	6.8%	0.9%	7.5%	15.3%
4266	-$5	A-8-8-9	NS	5.4%	0.8%	5.5%	11.8%
1376	-$1	A-8-8-10	DS	7.2%	1.0%	10.0%	18.3%
1848	-$2	A-8-8-10	S	6.7%	1.1%	9.4%	17.1%
3551	-$4	A-8-8-10	NS	5.3%	0.9%	6.9%	13.1%
1429	-$1	A-8-8-J	DS	7.0%	1.0%	10.2%	18.2%
2180	-$2	A-8-8-J	S	6.3%	1.1%	9.3%	16.6%
3506	-$4	A-8-8-J	NS	5.1%	0.9%	7.1%	13.0%
1571	-$1	A-8-8-Q	DS	7.1%	1.1%	10.0%	18.2%
2324	-$3	A-8-8-Q	S	6.1%	1.0%	9.3%	16.4%
3616	-$4	A-8-8-Q	NS	4.9%	0.9%	6.9%	12.7%
1374	-$1	A-8-8-K	DS	7.4%	1.0%	10.5%	19.0%
2330	-$3	A-8-8-K	S	6.4%	0.9%	9.1%	16.5%
3942	-$5	A-8-8-K	NS	5.0%	0.8%	6.6%	12.4%
1551	-$1	A-8-9-9	DS	6.2%	0.9%	9.8%	16.9%
1806	-$2	A-8-9-9	S	5.4%	0.9%	9.0%	15.2%
3407	-$4	A-8-9-9	NS	3.8%	0.7%	7.0%	11.6%
1231	-$1	A-8-9-10	DS	7.4%	0.9%	9.8%	18.0%
1582	-$1	A-8-9-10	S	6.8%	0.8%	8.9%	16.5%
2836	-$3	A-8-9-10	NS	5.4%	0.8%	7.4%	13.6%
1241	-$1	A-8-9-J	DS	7.3%	0.9%	10.0%	18.2%
1667	-$2	A-8-9-J	S	5.6%	0.8%	8.7%	15.1%
2898	-$3	A-8-9-J	NS	5.5%	0.7%	7.2%	13.5%
1435	-$1	A-8-9-Q	DS	7.3%	0.9%	9.8%	18.0%
1805	-$2	A-8-9-Q	S	6.3%	0.8%	8.9%	16.0%
3324	-$4	A-8-9-Q	NS	4.7%	0.7%	7.4%	12.8%
1528	-$1	A-8-9-K	DS	7.3%	0.9%	10.0%	18.3%
1887	-$2	A-8-9-K	S	5.2%	0.7%	7.8%	13.7%

OMAHA HIGH-LOW 8 OR BETTER 5,278 HANDS 9 HANDED							
		POCKET CARDS					
HAND RANK	VALUE $4/$8	HAND	SUITED	HIGH %	LOW %	SCOOP %	PART OR ALL %
3570	-$4	A-8-9-K	NS	4.7%	0.8%	7.0%	12.5%
973	$0	A-8-10-10	DS	6.2%	1.0%	11.5%	18.6%
1280	-$1	A-8-10-10	S	5.3%	0.9%	10.7%	17.0%
2573	-$3	A-8-10-10	NS	3.5%	0.8%	7.5%	11.8%
710	$2	A-8-10-J	DS	7.2%	1.0%	11.9%	20.0%
914	$1	A-8-10-J	S	6.3%	0.9%	11.2%	18.5%
2176	-$2	A-8-10-J	NS	4.6%	0.8%	8.0%	13.4%
782	$1	A-8-10-Q	DS	7.2%	1.0%	11.6%	19.8%
1045	$0	A-8-10-Q	S	5.6%	0.8%	10.3%	16.7%
2206	-$2	A-8-10-Q	NS	4.5%	0.6%	7.9%	13.0%
815	$1	A-8-10-K	DS	7.4%	1.0%	11.8%	20.2%
1217	-$1	A-8-10-K	S	5.7%	0.9%	11.1%	17.8%
2873	-$3	A-8-10-K	NS	4.3%	0.7%	7.0%	12.0%
857	$1	A-8-J-J	DS	6.1%	1.0%	12.5%	19.6%
1087	-$0	A-8-J-J	S	5.1%	0.9%	11.3%	17.3%
2017	-$2	A-8-J-J	NS	3.7%	0.9%	9.7%	14.3%
773	$1	A-8-J-Q	DS	6.8%	0.9%	11.7%	19.4%
1050	$0	A-8-J-Q	S	5.3%	0.8%	10.5%	16.6%
1949	-$2	A-8-J-Q	NS	4.0%	0.8%	7.9%	12.6%
853	$1	A-8-J-K	DS	7.1%	0.9%	11.7%	19.7%
1552	-$1	A-8-J-K	S	5.7%	0.8%	10.5%	17.0%
2288	-$3	A-8-J-K	NS	3.8%	0.7%	7.5%	12.0%
726	$1	A-8-Q-Q	DS	6.4%	1.1%	13.6%	21.0%
1137	-$0	A-8-Q-Q	S	5.1%	1.1%	12.8%	19.0%
2491	-$3	A-8-Q-Q	NS	3.8%	1.0%	10.8%	15.5%
904	$1	A-8-Q-K	DS	6.9%	0.9%	11.5%	19.4%
1332	-$1	A-8-Q-K	S	5.2%	0.8%	9.3%	15.3%
2927	-$3	A-8-Q-K	NS	3.8%	0.7%	6.8%	11.2%

		POCKET CARDS					
HAND RANK	**VALUE $4/$8**	**HAND**	**SUITED**	**HIGH %**	**LOW %**	**SCOOP %**	**PART OR ALL %**
592	$3	A-8-K-K	DS	7.4%	1.2%	15.3%	23.9%
821	$1	A-8-K-K	S	5.9%	1.1%	14.5%	21.6%
1677	-$2	A-8-K-K	NS	4.4%	1.1%	13.0%	18.6%
4584	-$6	A-9-9-9	S	2.6%	0.0%	4.3%	6.9%
4942	-$7	A-9-9-9	NS	1.1%	0.0%	2.6%	3.7%
1316	-$1	A-9-9-10	DS	6.4%	0.0%	9.6%	16.0%
1706	-$2	A-9-9-10	S	5.8%	0.0%	9.2%	15.0%
3399	-$4	A-9-9-10	NS	3.7%	0.0%	6.2%	9.9%
1358	-$1	A-9-9-J	DS	6.0%	0.0%	9.8%	15.8%
1680	-$2	A-9-9-J	S	5.3%	0.0%	9.3%	14.6%
3664	-$4	A-9-9-J	NS	3.2%	0.0%	6.1%	9.3%
1306	-$1	A-9-9-Q	DS	6.0%	0.0%	10.0%	16.0%
1702	-$2	A-9-9-Q	S	4.4%	0.0%	8.0%	12.4%
2878	-$3	A-9-9-Q	NS	3.2%	0.0%	7.4%	10.6%
1317	-$1	A-9-9-K	DS	6.4%	0.0%	10.4%	16.7%
2001	-$2	A-9-9-K	S	4.9%	0.0%	9.3%	14.2%
2785	-$3	A-9-9-K	NS	3.4%	0.0%	7.5%	10.9%
1329	-$1	A-9-10-10	DS	6.4%	0.0%	9.9%	16.3%
1878	-$2	A-9-10-10	S	5.7%	0.0%	8.8%	14.5%
2672	-$3	A-9-10-10	NS	4.1%	0.0%	7.5%	11.5%
835	$1	A-9-10-J	DS	7.3%	0.0%	11.0%	18.3%
1518	-$1	A-9-10-J	S	6.7%	0.0%	10.0%	16.8%
2327	-$3	A-9-10-J	NS	4.6%	0.0%	7.2%	11.8%
871	$1	A-9-10-Q	DS	7.1%	0.0%	11.1%	18.2%
1232	-$1	A-9-10-Q	S	6.7%	0.0%	10.0%	16.8%
2011	-$2	A-9-10-Q	NS	4.4%	0.0%	7.9%	12.3%
882	$1	A-9-10-K	DS	7.6%	0.0%	11.3%	18.9%
1242	-$1	A-9-10-K	S	6.0%	0.0%	10.7%	16.7%

OMAHA HIGH-LOW 8 OR BETTER
5,278 HANDS 9 HANDED

| HAND RANK | VALUE $4/$8 | POCKET CARDS | | HIGH % | LOW % | SCOOP % | PART OR ALL % |
		HAND	SUITED				
2476	-$3	A-9-10-K	NS	4.6%	0.0%	8.8%	13.4%
1182	-$0	A-9-J-J	DS	6.2%	0.0%	10.8%	17.1%
1666	-$2	A-9-J-J	S	5.4%	0.0%	10.1%	15.5%
2381	-$3	A-9-J-J	NS	4.6%	0.0%	8.8%	13.4%
870	$1	A-9-J-Q	DS	6.5%	0.0%	11.1%	17.7%
1116	-$0	A-9-J-Q	S	5.8%	0.0%	10.5%	16.3%
2003	-$2	A-9-J-Q	NS	3.5%	0.0%	8.0%	11.5%
886	$1	A-9-J-K	DS	7.1%	0.0%	11.6%	18.6%
1092	-$0	A-9-J-K	S	5.5%	0.0%	11.1%	16.7%
2281	-$3	A-9-J-K	NS	3.7%	0.0%	7.2%	11.0%
1016	$0	A-9-Q-Q	DS	6.5%	0.0%	12.2%	18.7%
1355	-$1	A-9-Q-Q	S	5.2%	0.0%	11.4%	16.6%
2609	-$3	A-9-Q-Q	NS	3.8%	0.0%	9.6%	13.4%
900	$1	A-9-Q-K	DS	6.8%	0.0%	11.6%	18.4%
1172	-$0	A-9-Q-K	S	5.4%	0.0%	11.0%	16.4%
1799	-$2	A-9-Q-K	NS	3.6%	0.0%	8.8%	12.4%
721	$1	A-9-K-K	DS	7.5%	0.0%	14.2%	21.7%
1128	-$0	A-9-K-K	S	6.2%	0.0%	13.2%	19.4%
2071	-$2	A-9-K-K	NS	4.2%	0.0%	12.2%	16.4%
4482	-$5	A-10-10-10	S	3.1%	0.0%	5.6%	8.7%
5168	-$9	A-10-10-10	NS	1.5%	0.0%	3.9%	5.4%
757	$1	A-10-10-J	DS	6.8%	0.0%	11.8%	18.6%
989	$0	A-10-10-J	S	5.7%	0.0%	11.0%	16.7%
2037	-$2	A-10-10-J	NS	4.2%	0.0%	9.6%	13.8%
750	$1	A-10-10-Q	DS	6.6%	0.0%	12.2%	18.8%
1052	$0	A-10-10-Q	S	5.4%	0.0%	11.1%	16.5%

OMAHA HIGH-LOW 8 OR BETTER
5,278 HANDS   9 HANDED

HAND RANK	VALUE $4/$8	POCKET CARDS HAND	POCKET CARDS SUITED	HIGH %	LOW %	SCOOP %	PART OR ALL %
2088	-$2	A-10-10-Q	NS	3.9%	0.0%	9.8%	13.7%
730	$1	A-10-10-K	DS	7.1%	0.0%	12.2%	19.3%
1207	-$0	A-10-10-K	S	5.5%	0.0%	11.0%	16.5%
2162	-$2	A-10-10-K	NS	3.9%	0.0%	9.7%	13.6%
685	$2	A-10-J-J	DS	6.5%	0.0%	13.0%	19.5%
955	$0	A-10-J-J	S	5.9%	0.0%	11.5%	17.5%
1801	-$2	A-10-J-J	NS	4.1%	0.0%	9.8%	13.9%
509	$3	A-10-J-Q	DS	7.0%	0.0%	12.7%	19.7%
598	$3	A-10-J-Q	S	6.3%	0.0%	12.2%	18.5%
952	$0	A-10-J-Q	NS	4.6%	0.0%	10.7%	15.3%
515	$3	A-10-J-K	DS	7.6%	0.0%	12.8%	20.4%
630	$2	A-10-J-K	S	6.2%	0.0%	12.1%	18.3%
1091	-$0	A-10-J-K	NS	4.7%	0.0%	10.9%	15.6%
626	$2	A-10-Q-Q	DS	6.9%	0.0%	13.4%	20.3%
868	$1	A-10-Q-Q	S	6.0%	0.0%	12.7%	18.7%
1758	-$2	A-10-Q-Q	NS	4.2%	0.0%	11.3%	15.5%
521	$3	A-10-Q-K	DS	7.2%	0.0%	12.8%	20.0%
674	$2	A-10-Q-K	S	5.8%	0.0%	12.1%	17.8%
1044	$0	A-10-Q-K	NS	4.2%	0.0%	10.7%	14.9%
469	$4	A-10-K-K	DS	7.9%	0.0%	15.1%	23.0%
719	$2	A-10-K-K	S	6.4%	0.0%	14.3%	20.7%
1276	-$1	A-10-K-K	NS	4.8%	0.0%	13.4%	18.2%
4504	-$6	A-J-J-J	S	3.5%	0.0%	6.6%	10.0%
4985	-$7	A-J-J-J	NS	1.8%	0.0%	5.0%	6.8%
664	$2	A-J-J-Q	DS	6.9%	0.0%	13.2%	20.1%
936	$1	A-J-J-Q	S	5.9%	0.0%	12.2%	18.1%
1733	-$2	A-J-J-Q	NS	3.7%	0.0%	9.5%	13.2%
676	$2	A-J-J-K	DS	7.4%	0.0%	13.3%	20.8%

OMAHA HIGH-LOW 8 OR BETTER
5,278 HANDS   9 HANDED

| HAND RANK | VALUE $4/$8 | POCKET CARDS | | HIGH % | LOW % | SCOOP % | PART OR ALL % |
		HAND	SUITED				
1018	$0	A-J-J-K	S	5.9%	0.0%	12.3%	18.2%
1852	-$2	A-J-J-K	NS	4.3%	0.0%	11.5%	15.8%
618	$2	A-J-Q-Q	DS	6.9%	0.0%	13.5%	20.4%
807	$1	A-J-Q-Q	S	6.1%	0.0%	12.8%	18.8%
1694	-$2	A-J-Q-Q	NS	4.3%	0.0%	11.3%	15.5%
481	$4	A-J-Q-K	DS	7.4%	0.0%	13.0%	20.4%
651	$2	A-J-Q-K	S	6.0%	0.0%	12.2%	18.2%
979	$0	A-J-Q-K	NS	4.4%	0.0%	10.9%	15.2%
455	$4	A-J-K-K	DS	7.9%	0.0%	15.1%	23.0%
609	$2	A-J-K-K	S	6.4%	0.0%	14.5%	20.8%
1203	-$0	A-J-K-K	NS	4.8%	0.0%	13.5%	18.3%
4777	-$6	A-Q-Q-Q	S	3.6%	0.0%	7.7%	11.3%
5221	-$9	A-Q-Q-Q	NS	2.2%	0.0%	6.7%	8.9%
499	$4	A-Q-Q-K	DS	7.9%	0.0%	14.8%	22.7%
712	$2	A-Q-Q-K	S	6.7%	0.0%	14.2%	20.8%
1496	-$1	A-Q-Q-K	NS	4.1%	0.0%	11.2%	15.3%
433	$4	A-Q-K-K	DS	8.0%	0.0%	15.2%	23.2%
648	$2	A-Q-K-K	S	6.6%	0.0%	14.4%	21.1%
1246	-$1	A-Q-K-K	NS	4.2%	0.0%	12.0%	16.2%
4158	-$5	A-K-K-K	S	4.5%	0.0%	10.5%	14.9%
5109	-$8	A-K-K-K	NS	2.9%	0.0%	8.6%	11.5%
5111	-$8	2-2-2-2	NS	0.0%	0.0%	0.0%	0.0%
3057	-$4	2-2-2-3	S	1.7%	6.1%	4.2%	12.0%
3876	-$5	2-2-2-3	NS	1.5%	6.2%	2.9%	10.6%
3751	-$4	2-2-2-4	S	1.8%	5.5%	4.1%	11.4%
4265	-$5	2-2-2-4	NS	1.5%	5.4%	2.9%	9.8%
4448	-$5	2-2-2-5	S	1.8%	3.9%	3.9%	9.6%
4734	-$6	2-2-2-5	NS	1.5%	3.6%	2.8%	8.0%

OMAHA HIGH-LOW 8 OR BETTER
5,278 HANDS   9 HANDED

HAND RANK	VALUE $4/$8	POCKET CARDS HAND	POCKET CARDS SUITED	HIGH %	LOW %	SCOOP %	PART OR ALL %
5012	-$7	2-2-2-6	S	1.7%	2.6%	2.9%	7.2%
5080	-$8	2-2-2-6	NS	1.4%	2.4%	1.7%	5.5%
5153	-$8	2-2-2-7	S	1.5%	1.6%	2.3%	5.4%
5229	-$9	2-2-2-7	NS	1.2%	1.3%	1.2%	3.8%
5223	-$9	2-2-2-8	S	1.7%	1.1%	2.2%	4.9%
5251	-$9	2-2-2-8	NS	1.3%	0.9%	1.2%	3.4%
5098	-$8	2-2-2-9	S	1.5%	0.0%	2.0%	3.5%
5125	-$8	2-2-2-9	NS	1.1%	0.0%	1.2%	2.3%
5093	-$8	2-2-2-10	S	1.5%	0.0%	1.9%	3.4%
5127	-$8	2-2-2-10	NS	1.0%	0.0%	1.2%	2.3%
5107	-$8	2-2-2-J	S	1.5%	0.0%	2.2%	3.7%
5112	-$8	2-2-2-J	NS	1.1%	0.0%	2.2%	3.3%
5122	-$8	2-2-2-Q	S	1.7%	0.0%	2.5%	4.2%
5162	-$9	2-2-2-Q	NS	1.1%	0.0%	1.4%	2.5%
5105	-$8	2-2-2-K	S	2.1%	0.0%	3.2%	5.2%
5186	-$9	2-2-2-K	NS	1.2%	0.0%	1.6%	2.8%
713	$2	2-2-3-3	DS	4.8%	6.2%	9.3%	20.3%
963	$0	2-2-3-3	S	4.6%	6.2%	8.0%	18.7%
1268	-$1	2-2-3-3	NS	4.3%	6.2%	6.8%	17.3%
505	$3	2-2-3-4	DS	3.6%	7.8%	9.8%	21.2%
681	$2	2-2-3-4	S	3.4%	7.9%	8.7%	20.0%
942	$1	2-2-3-4	NS	3.2%	7.9%	7.3%	18.5%
619	$2	2-2-3-5	DS	3.8%	7.1%	9.8%	20.7%
841	$1	2-2-3-5	S	3.6%	7.1%	8.4%	19.1%
1024	$0	2-2-3-5	NS	3.2%	7.1%	7.1%	17.4%
866	$1	2-2-3-6	DS	3.8%	6.6%	8.3%	18.7%
1138	-$0	2-2-3-6	S	3.5%	6.7%	7.0%	17.2%
1521	-$1	2-2-3-6	NS	3.3%	6.6%	5.7%	15.6%

OMAHA HIGH-LOW 8 OR BETTER
5,278 HANDS   9 HANDED

| HAND RANK | VALUE $4/$8 | POCKET CARDS | | HIGH % | LOW % | SCOOP % | PART OR ALL % |
		HAND	SUITED				
1102	-$0	2-2-3-7	DS	3.7%	6.2%	7.5%	17.4%
1645	-$1	2-2-3-7	S	3.4%	6.1%	6.3%	15.8%
2152	-$2	2-2-3-7	NS	3.2%	5.9%	5.2%	14.2%
1507	-$1	2-2-3-8	DS	3.8%	5.8%	7.2%	16.7%
1917	-$2	2-2-3-8	S	3.5%	5.8%	6.0%	15.3%
2591	-$3	2-2-3-8	NS	3.2%	5.8%	4.9%	13.9%
1604	-$1	2-2-3-9	DS	3.8%	5.6%	7.0%	16.4%
2242	-$3	2-2-3-9	S	3.6%	5.6%	5.8%	14.9%
2934	-$3	2-2-3-9	NS	3.0%	5.7%	4.7%	13.4%
1630	-$1	2-2-3-10	DS	3.7%	5.6%	7.3%	16.6%
2147	-$2	2-2-3-10	S	3.5%	5.7%	6.0%	15.2%
3043	-$3	2-2-3-10	NS	3.1%	5.7%	4.7%	13.5%
1368	-$1	2-2-3-J	DS	3.9%	5.7%	7.6%	17.3%
1971	-$2	2-2-3-J	S	3.7%	5.6%	6.3%	15.6%
2887	-$3	2-2-3-J	NS	3.2%	5.7%	4.8%	13.7%
1292	-$1	2-2-3-Q	DS	4.0%	5.6%	8.0%	17.5%
1742	-$2	2-2-3-Q	S	3.7%	5.7%	6.8%	16.2%
2892	-$3	2-2-3-Q	NS	3.2%	5.7%	5.1%	14.1%
1156	-$0	2-2-3-K	DS	4.1%	5.7%	8.6%	18.5%
1554	-$1	2-2-3-K	S	3.9%	5.8%	7.5%	17.2%
2881	-$3	2-2-3-K	NS	3.3%	5.8%	5.3%	14.3%
1020	$0	2-2-4-4	DS	5.0%	5.1%	9.2%	19.3%
1305	-$1	2-2-4-4	S	4.7%	5.2%	7.9%	17.8%
1770	-$2	2-2-4-4	NS	4.4%	5.1%	6.7%	16.3%
684	$2	2-2-4-5	DS	4.3%	6.7%	9.9%	20.8%
996	$0	2-2-4-5	S	3.9%	6.5%	8.3%	18.7%
1319	-$1	2-2-4-5	NS	3.6%	6.5%	7.0%	17.1%
1006	$0	2-2-4-6	DS	4.2%	5.9%	8.4%	18.6%

OMAHA HIGH-LOW 8 OR BETTER
5,278 HANDS   9 HANDED

| HAND RANK | VALUE $4/$8 | POCKET CARDS | | HIGH % | LOW % | SCOOP % | PART OR ALL % |
		HAND	SUITED				
1380	-$1	2-2-4-6	S	3.9%	5.9%	7.1%	17.0%
1841	-$2	2-2-4-6	NS	3.6%	5.8%	6.0%	15.4%
1411	-$1	2-2-4-7	DS	4.2%	5.3%	7.5%	17.0%
2086	-$2	2-2-4-7	S	3.8%	5.2%	6.3%	15.4%
2704	-$3	2-2-4-7	NS	3.5%	5.2%	5.3%	14.0%
1726	-$2	2-2-4-8	DS	4.2%	5.2%	7.3%	16.7%
2294	-$3	2-2-4-8	S	3.9%	5.1%	6.3%	15.3%
3344	-$4	2-2-4-8	NS	3.5%	4.9%	4.9%	13.3%
2195	-$2	2-2-4-9	DS	3.8%	4.7%	7.0%	15.6%
2955	-$3	2-2-4-9	S	3.5%	4.6%	5.9%	14.1%
3746	-$4	2-2-4-9	NS	3.1%	4.7%	4.6%	12.4%
2164	-$2	2-2-4-10	DS	3.9%	4.8%	7.1%	15.9%
2931	-$3	2-2-4-10	S	3.6%	4.7%	5.9%	14.3%
3582	-$4	2-2-4-10	NS	3.1%	4.7%	4.9%	12.7%
1947	-$2	2-2-4-J	DS	4.0%	4.8%	7.4%	16.2%
2615	-$3	2-2-4-J	S	3.7%	4.8%	6.3%	14.8%
3712	-$4	2-2-4-J	NS	3.2%	4.8%	4.8%	12.7%
1969	-$2	2-2-4-Q	DS	4.1%	4.7%	7.7%	16.5%
2544	-$3	2-2-4-Q	S	3.8%	4.8%	6.6%	15.2%
3688	-$4	2-2-4-Q	NS	3.2%	4.8%	5.1%	13.0%
1581	-$1	2-2-4-K	DS	4.3%	4.8%	8.5%	17.6%
2241	-$3	2-2-4-K	S	3.9%	4.9%	7.3%	16.1%
3685	-$4	2-2-4-K	NS	3.2%	4.9%	5.3%	13.5%
1407	-$1	2-2-5-5	DS	5.1%	3.5%	8.7%	17.3%
1800	-$2	2-2-5-5	S	4.8%	3.4%	7.6%	15.8%
2318	-$3	2-2-5-5	NS	4.5%	3.4%	6.7%	14.5%
1155	-$0	2-2-5-6	DS	4.5%	4.7%	8.6%	17.8%
1678	-$2	2-2-5-6	S	4.1%	4.7%	7.3%	16.1%

OMAHA HIGH-LOW 8 OR BETTER
5,278 HANDS   9 HANDED

HAND RANK	VALUE $4/$8	POCKET CARDS		HIGH %	LOW %	SCOOP %	PART OR ALL %
		HAND	SUITED				
2274	-$3	2-2-5-6	NS	3.8%	4.6%	6.1%	14.5%
1862	-$2	2-2-5-7	DS	4.3%	4.2%	7.6%	16.0%
2612	-$3	2-2-5-7	S	4.0%	4.1%	6.3%	14.4%
3294	-$4	2-2-5-7	NS	3.7%	4.0%	5.3%	12.9%
2042	-$2	2-2-5-8	DS	4.5%	3.9%	7.5%	15.9%
2848	-$3	2-2-5-8	S	4.1%	3.9%	6.2%	14.3%
3455	-$4	2-2-5-8	NS	3.8%	3.7%	5.3%	12.8%
2598	-$3	2-2-5-9	DS	4.3%	3.5%	6.9%	14.8%
3418	-$4	2-2-5-9	S	3.9%	3.4%	5.8%	13.1%
4144	-$5	2-2-5-9	NS	3.4%	3.4%	4.7%	11.6%
2987	-$3	2-2-5-10	DS	3.8%	3.3%	6.9%	14.0%
3693	-$4	2-2-5-10	S	3.5%	3.3%	5.6%	12.4%
4225	-$5	2-2-5-10	NS	3.1%	3.2%	4.6%	10.9%
2973	-$3	2-2-5-J	DS	3.9%	3.4%	7.0%	14.4%
3672	-$4	2-2-5-J	S	3.6%	3.2%	5.9%	12.8%
4262	-$5	2-2-5-J	NS	3.1%	3.2%	4.8%	11.1%
2479	-$3	2-2-5-Q	DS	4.1%	3.3%	7.5%	14.9%
3337	-$4	2-2-5-Q	S	3.7%	3.3%	6.4%	13.4%
4360	-$5	2-2-5-Q	NS	3.1%	3.1%	4.8%	11.1%
2303	-$3	2-2-5-K	DS	4.2%	3.6%	8.1%	15.9%
2855	-$3	2-2-5-K	S	4.0%	3.5%	7.0%	14.6%
4293	-$5	2-2-5-K	NS	3.2%	3.3%	5.2%	11.7%
2507	-$3	2-2-6-6	DS	5.0%	2.5%	7.4%	14.9%
3086	-$4	2-2-6-6	S	4.7%	2.3%	6.4%	13.4%
3748	-$4	2-2-6-6	NS	4.4%	2.2%	5.3%	11.8%
2800	-$3	2-2-6-7	DS	4.5%	3.2%	6.8%	14.6%
3807	-$4	2-2-6-7	S	4.1%	3.1%	5.7%	12.9%
4452	-$5	2-2-6-7	NS	3.7%	3.0%	4.5%	11.2%

OMAHA HIGH-LOW 8 OR BETTER
5,278 HANDS   9 HANDED

| HAND RANK | VALUE $4/$8 | POCKET CARDS | | HIGH % | LOW % | SCOOP % | PART OR ALL % |
		HAND	SUITED				
3186	-$4	2-2-6-8	DS	4.5%	2.9%	6.6%	14.1%
3764	-$4	2-2-6-8	S	4.3%	2.9%	5.6%	12.8%
4424	-$5	2-2-6-8	NS	3.9%	2.7%	4.5%	11.1%
3834	-$4	2-2-6-9	DS	4.4%	2.5%	6.1%	13.0%
4388	-$5	2-2-6-9	S	4.0%	2.4%	5.1%	11.5%
4762	-$6	2-2-6-9	NS	3.6%	2.3%	4.0%	9.9%
4050	-$5	2-2-6-10	DS	4.1%	2.5%	6.0%	12.5%
4543	-$6	2-2-6-10	S	3.7%	2.3%	4.8%	10.8%
4895	-$7	2-2-6-10	NS	3.2%	2.1%	3.6%	9.0%
4218	-$5	2-2-6-J	DS	3.8%	2.3%	6.0%	12.1%
4648	-$6	2-2-6-J	S	3.4%	2.2%	4.8%	10.4%
4961	-$7	2-2-6-J	NS	2.9%	2.0%	3.7%	8.6%
4024	-$5	2-2-6-Q	DS	4.0%	2.4%	6.3%	12.7%
4459	-$5	2-2-6-Q	S	3.7%	2.2%	5.2%	11.1%
4927	-$7	2-2-6-Q	NS	3.0%	2.1%	3.7%	8.8%
3608	-$4	2-2-6-K	DS	4.2%	2.5%	7.0%	13.7%
4351	-$5	2-2-6-K	S	3.9%	2.3%	5.8%	12.0%
4922	-$7	2-2-6-K	NS	3.0%	2.1%	4.0%	9.1%
3505	-$4	2-2-7-7	DS	4.8%	1.6%	6.9%	13.3%
4014	-$5	2-2-7-7	S	4.6%	1.4%	5.8%	11.8%
4513	-$6	2-2-7-7	NS	4.0%	1.3%	4.8%	10.1%
4174	-$5	2-2-7-8	DS	4.5%	2.1%	6.3%	13.0%
4489	-$6	2-2-7-8	S	4.3%	2.0%	5.3%	11.6%
4847	-$6	2-2-7-8	NS	3.8%	1.8%	4.5%	10.1%
4549	-$6	2-2-7-9	DS	4.5%	1.6%	5.6%	11.7%
4824	-$6	2-2-7-9	S	4.0%	1.5%	4.8%	10.2%
5013	-$7	2-2-7-9	NS	3.6%	1.3%	3.7%	8.6%
4562	-$6	2-2-7-10	DS	4.1%	1.6%	5.6%	11.3%

OMAHA HIGH-LOW 8 OR BETTER
5,278 HANDS   9 HANDED

| HAND RANK | VALUE $4/$8 | POCKET CARDS | | HIGH % | LOW % | SCOOP % | PART OR ALL % |
		HAND	SUITED				
4868	-$6	2-2-7-10	S	3.6%	1.4%	4.8%	9.8%
5004	-$7	2-2-7-10	NS	3.2%	1.2%	3.8%	8.1%
4692	-$6	2-2-7-J	DS	3.7%	1.5%	5.6%	10.8%
4921	-$7	2-2-7-J	S	3.3%	1.3%	4.7%	9.3%
5035	-$7	2-2-7-J	NS	2.8%	1.2%	3.7%	7.7%
4624	-$6	2-2-7-Q	DS	3.8%	1.5%	5.7%	11.0%
4878	-$6	2-2-7-Q	S	3.4%	1.4%	4.8%	9.5%
5068	-$8	2-2-7-Q	NS	2.7%	1.2%	3.3%	7.2%
4548	-$6	2-2-7-K	DS	4.1%	1.6%	6.3%	12.0%
4835	-$6	2-2-7-K	S	3.7%	1.5%	5.1%	10.3%
5056	-$8	2-2-7-K	NS	2.8%	1.2%	3.5%	7.5%
3816	-$4	2-2-8-8	DS	5.1%	1.1%	6.7%	12.9%
4192	-$5	2-2-8-8	S	4.8%	1.0%	5.7%	11.5%
4506	-$6	2-2-8-8	NS	4.3%	0.9%	4.8%	10.0%
4750	-$6	2-2-8-9	DS	4.8%	1.2%	5.8%	11.8%
4946	-$7	2-2-8-9	S	4.3%	1.0%	4.9%	10.3%
5049	-$8	2-2-8-9	NS	3.9%	0.9%	4.1%	8.9%
4528	-$6	2-2-8-10	DS	4.4%	1.1%	6.1%	11.6%
4896	-$7	2-2-8-10	S	4.0%	1.0%	5.3%	10.3%
4975	-$7	2-2-8-10	NS	3.3%	0.9%	4.5%	8.7%
4615	-$6	2-2-8-J	DS	4.1%	1.1%	6.1%	11.4%
4899	-$7	2-2-8-J	S	3.7%	1.0%	5.3%	9.9%
5038	-$7	2-2-8-J	NS	3.0%	0.9%	4.2%	8.1%
4786	-$6	2-2-8-Q	DS	4.1%	1.1%	5.8%	11.0%
4917	-$7	2-2-8-Q	S	3.7%	1.0%	5.1%	9.8%
5081	-$8	2-2-8-Q	NS	2.9%	0.9%	3.8%	7.6%
4688	-$6	2-2-8-K	DS	4.3%	1.2%	6.1%	11.6%
4923	-$7	2-2-8-K	S	3.9%	1.1%	5.1%	10.0%

OMAHA HIGH-LOW 8 OR BETTER
5,278 HANDS   9 HANDED

| HAND RANK | VALUE $4/$8 | POCKET CARDS | | HIGH % | LOW % | SCOOP % | PART OR ALL % |
		HAND	SUITED				
5078	-$8	2-2-8-K	NS	2.9%	0.9%	3.7%	7.4%
2922	-$3	2-2-9-9	DS	4.1%	0.0%	7.0%	11.1%
3203	-$4	2-2-9-9	S	3.7%	0.0%	6.2%	9.9%
3742	-$4	2-2-9-9	NS	3.2%	0.0%	5.2%	8.4%
4488	-$6	2-2-9-10	DS	4.3%	0.0%	5.9%	10.2%
4719	-$6	2-2-9-10	S	4.0%	0.0%	5.0%	9.0%
4940	-$7	2-2-9-10	NS	3.4%	0.0%	4.2%	7.6%
4520	-$6	2-2-9-J	DS	3.9%	0.0%	5.9%	9.8%
4749	-$6	2-2-9-J	S	3.5%	0.0%	5.2%	8.7%
4919	-$7	2-2-9-J	NS	3.0%	0.0%	4.3%	7.4%
4503	-$6	2-2-9-Q	DS	3.8%	0.0%	6.0%	9.8%
4776	-$6	2-2-9-Q	S	3.3%	0.0%	5.3%	8.6%
4968	-$7	2-2-9-Q	NS	2.7%	0.0%	4.2%	6.8%
4525	-$6	2-2-9-K	DS	4.0%	0.0%	6.2%	10.2%
4807	-$6	2-2-9-K	S	3.6%	0.0%	5.4%	9.0%
4952	-$7	2-2-9-K	NS	2.5%	0.0%	4.1%	6.6%
3007	-$3	2-2-10-10	DS	4.4%	0.0%	7.5%	11.9%
3468	-$4	2-2-10-10	S	3.9%	0.0%	6.7%	10.6%
3868	-$5	2-2-10-10	NS	3.4%	0.0%	6.0%	9.3%
3697	-$4	2-2-10-J	DS	4.5%	0.0%	6.8%	11.2%
4243	-$5	2-2-10-J	S	4.0%	0.0%	6.0%	10.0%
4590	-$6	2-2-10-J	NS	3.5%	0.0%	5.3%	8.8%
3822	-$4	2-2-10-Q	DS	4.2%	0.0%	7.0%	11.2%
4401	-$5	2-2-10-Q	S	3.7%	0.0%	6.1%	9.9%
4626	-$6	2-2-10-Q	NS	3.1%	0.0%	5.3%	8.4%
3943	-$5	2-2-10-K	DS	4.5%	0.0%	6.9%	11.4%
4302	-$5	2-2-10-K	S	4.0%	0.0%	6.4%	10.3%
4802	-$6	2-2-10-K	NS	2.9%	0.0%	5.0%	7.9%

194

OMAHA HIGH-LOW 8 OR BETTER
5,278 HANDS   9 HANDED

HAND RANK	VALUE $4/$8	POCKET CARDS		HIGH %	LOW %	SCOOP %	PART OR ALL %
		HAND	SUITED				
2488	-$3	2-2-J-J	DS	4.7%	0.0%	8.4%	13.1%
3283	-$4	2-2-J-J	S	4.2%	0.0%	7.4%	11.6%
3710	-$4	2-2-J-J	NS	3.7%	0.0%	6.8%	10.5%
3394	-$4	2-2-J-Q	DS	4.3%	0.0%	7.4%	11.7%
4095	-$5	2-2-J-Q	S	3.9%	0.0%	6.6%	10.5%
4614	-$6	2-2-J-Q	NS	3.2%	0.0%	5.5%	8.7%
3839	-$4	2-2-J-K	DS	4.5%	0.0%	7.3%	11.8%
4406	-$5	2-2-J-K	S	4.0%	0.0%	6.5%	10.5%
4764	-$6	2-2-J-K	NS	3.0%	0.0%	5.2%	8.2%
2101	-$2	2-2-Q-Q	DS	5.4%	0.0%	10.3%	15.8%
3088	-$4	2-2-Q-Q	S	4.6%	0.0%	9.1%	13.7%
3790	-$4	2-2-Q-Q	NS	4.0%	0.0%	8.0%	12.0%
3287	-$4	2-2-Q-K	DS	4.7%	0.0%	7.9%	12.7%
4079	-$5	2-2-Q-K	S	4.0%	0.0%	6.9%	10.9%
4622	-$6	2-2-Q-K	NS	3.2%	0.0%	5.6%	8.7%
1334	-$1	2-2-K-K	DS	6.6%	0.0%	12.9%	19.6%
2546	-$3	2-2-K-K	S	5.3%	0.0%	11.3%	16.7%
3502	-$4	2-2-K-K	NS	4.4%	0.0%	10.1%	14.5%
2979	-$3	2-3-3-3	S	1.8%	6.1%	4.2%	12.1%
3670	-$4	2-3-3-3	NS	1.5%	4.8%	3.3%	9.7%
503	$3	2-3-3-4	DS	3.8%	7.8%	10.3%	21.9%
671	$2	2-3-3-4	S	3.5%	7.9%	8.7%	20.1%
897	$1	2-3-3-4	NS	3.3%	7.9%	7.5%	18.7%
604	$2	2-3-3-5	DS	3.9%	7.1%	9.9%	20.8%
785	$1	2-3-3-5	S	3.6%	7.3%	8.4%	19.2%
971	$0	2-3-3-5	NS	3.4%	7.2%	7.0%	17.6%
850	$1	2-3-3-6	DS	3.9%	6.6%	8.3%	18.8%
1140	-$0	2-3-3-6	S	3.4%	6.5%	7.0%	16.9%

OMAHA HIGH-LOW 8 OR BETTER
5,278 HANDS   9 HANDED

HAND RANK	VALUE $4/$8	POCKET CARDS HAND	POCKET CARDS SUITED	HIGH %	LOW %	SCOOP %	PART OR ALL %
1470	-$1	2-3-3-6	NS	3.3%	6.6%	5.9%	15.8%
1165	-$0	2-3-3-7	DS	3.7%	6.2%	7.6%	17.5%
1647	-$1	2-3-3-7	S	3.4%	6.0%	6.1%	15.4%
2271	-$3	2-3-3-7	NS	3.1%	6.0%	4.9%	14.0%
1381	-$1	2-3-3-8	DS	3.8%	5.8%	7.2%	16.8%
1968	-$2	2-3-3-8	S	3.4%	5.8%	5.8%	14.8%
2830	-$3	2-3-3-8	NS	3.2%	5.7%	4.8%	14.5%
1539	-$1	2-3-3-9	DS	3.8%	5.5%	7.1%	16.3%
2225	-$2	2-3-3-9	S	3.4%	5.5%	5.7%	14.2%
3039	-$3	2-3-3-9	NS	3.1%	5.6%	4.5%	14.5%
1519	-$1	2-3-3-10	DS	3.8%	5.6%	7.3%	16.7%
2012	-$2	2-3-3-10	S	3.5%	5.6%	6.0%	14.8%
2977	-$3	2-3-3-10	NS	3.1%	5.6%	4.8%	14.3%
1445	-$1	2-3-3-J	DS	3.9%	5.6%	7.6%	16.9%
1866	-$2	2-3-3-J	S	3.6%	5.6%	6.2%	15.1%
2703	-$3	2-3-3-J	NS	3.2%	5.6%	5.0%	14.6%
1351	-$1	2-3-3-Q	DS	4.0%	5.6%	8.0%	17.3%
1780	-$2	2-3-3-Q	S	3.7%	5.6%	6.5%	15.6%
2880	-$3	2-3-3-Q	NS	3.0%	5.7%	5.2%	15.1%
1118	-$0	2-3-3-K	DS	4.3%	5.8%	8.8%	18.4%
1625	-$1	2-3-3-K	S	3.8%	5.7%	7.1%	16.3%
2827	-$3	2-3-3-K	NS	3.2%	5.7%	5.4%	15.0%
554	$3	2-3-4-4	DS	4.0%	7.7%	10.0%	21.1%
659	$2	2-3-4-4	S	3.7%	7.7%	9.0%	20.3%
903	$1	2-3-4-4	NS	3.4%	7.7%	7.5%	18.7%
454	$4	2-3-4-5	DS	4.0%	8.1%	10.8%	22.9%
581	$3	2-3-4-5	S	3.7%	8.2%	9.4%	21.3%
784	$1	2-3-4-5	NS	3.4%	8.2%	8.2%	19.8%

OMAHA HIGH-LOW 8 OR BETTER
5,278 HANDS   9 HANDED

| HAND RANK | VALUE $4/$8 | POCKET CARDS | | HIGH % | LOW % | SCOOP % | PART OR ALL % |
		HAND	SUITED				
535	$3	2-3-4-6	DS	4.2%	8.0%	9.5%	21.7%
703	$2	2-3-4-6	S	3.8%	8.0%	8.1%	19.9%
950	$0	2-3-4-6	NS	3.5%	8.0%	6.9%	18.5%
650	$2	2-3-4-7	DS	3.8%	7.7%	8.9%	20.4%
953	$0	2-3-4-7	S	3.4%	7.7%	7.4%	18.6%
1290	-$1	2-3-4-7	NS	2.5%	6.5%	5.1%	14.2%
826	$1	2-3-4-8	DS	3.6%	7.5%	8.5%	19.7%
1111	-$0	2-3-4-8	S	3.3%	7.6%	7.3%	18.3%
1492	-$1	2-3-4-8	NS	2.4%	6.4%	4.8%	13.6%
873	$1	2-3-4-9	DS	3.3%	7.9%	8.8%	20.1%
1126	-$0	2-3-4-9	S	2.7%	7.3%	6.9%	16.8%
1573	-$1	2-3-4-9	NS	2.1%	6.8%	5.2%	14.1%
792	$1	2-3-4-10	DS	3.5%	7.9%	9.3%	20.7%
1129	-$0	2-3-4-10	S	2.8%	7.4%	7.0%	17.1%
1520	-$1	2-3-4-10	NS	2.2%	7.1%	5.3%	14.6%
764	$1	2-3-4-J	DS	3.6%	7.8%	9.5%	20.9%
1096	-$0	2-3-4-J	S	2.9%	7.3%	7.3%	17.4%
1577	-$1	2-3-4-J	NS	2.2%	6.9%	5.4%	14.6%
705	$2	2-3-4-Q	DS	3.7%	7.9%	9.7%	21.3%
940	$1	2-3-4-Q	S	3.4%	8.0%	8.6%	19.9%
1356	-$1	2-3-4-Q	NS	2.4%	7.0%	5.9%	15.2%
614	$2	2-3-4-K	DS	3.8%	7.9%	10.5%	22.2%
795	$1	2-3-4-K	S	3.7%	8.0%	9.5%	21.1%
1389	-$1	2-3-4-K	NS	2.5%	7.0%	6.0%	15.5%
591	$3	2-3-5-5	DS	4.0%	6.7%	10.0%	20.7%
755	$1	2-3-5-5	S	3.7%	6.6%	8.9%	19.3%
994	$0	2-3-5-5	NS	3.1%	6.2%	6.7%	16.0%
561	$3	2-3-5-6	DS	4.2%	7.4%	9.3%	21.0%

OMAHA HIGH-LOW 8 OR BETTER
5,278 HANDS   9 HANDED

HAND RANK	VALUE $4/$8	POCKET CARDS		HIGH %	LOW %	SCOOP %	PART OR ALL %
		HAND	SUITED				
737	$1	2-3-5-6	S	4.2%	7.4%	8.4%	19.9%
1036	$0	2-3-5-6	NS	3.8%	7.4%	7.2%	18.3%
740	$1	2-3-5-7	DS	4.1%	7.0%	9.0%	20.1%
1067	$0	2-3-5-7	S	3.8%	7.0%	7.8%	18.5%
1272	-$1	2-3-5-7	NS	2.8%	5.9%	5.3%	14.0%
887	$1	2-3-5-8	DS	3.9%	6.8%	8.5%	19.3%
1167	-$0	2-3-5-8	S	3.7%	6.9%	7.6%	18.2%
1495	-$1	2-3-5-8	NS	2.7%	5.8%	5.2%	13.7%
894	$1	2-3-5-9	DS	3.7%	7.1%	8.9%	19.6%
1212	-$0	2-3-5-9	S	3.0%	6.5%	7.0%	16.4%
1611	-$1	2-3-5-9	NS	2.5%	6.1%	5.4%	14.0%
1090	-$0	2-3-5-10	DS	3.4%	7.0%	8.9%	19.3%
1362	-$1	2-3-5-10	S	2.8%	6.3%	6.9%	16.0%
1689	-$2	2-3-5-10	NS	2.3%	6.1%	5.3%	13.6%
948	$0	2-3-5-J	DS	3.5%	7.0%	9.1%	19.6%
1252	-$1	2-3-5-J	S	3.2%	7.0%	7.8%	18.0%
1958	-$2	2-3-5-J	NS	2.7%	6.9%	6.4%	15.9%
861	$1	2-3-5-Q	DS	3.6%	7.0%	9.6%	20.2%
1160	-$0	2-3-5-Q	S	3.0%	6.4%	7.5%	16.9%
1756	-$2	2-3-5-Q	NS	2.4%	5.7%	5.5%	13.6%
683	$2	2-3-5-K	DS	3.8%	7.0%	10.6%	21.5%
1035	$0	2-3-5-K	S	3.6%	7.0%	9.1%	19.6%
1449	-$1	2-3-5-K	NS	2.5%	5.9%	6.4%	14.9%
845	$1	2-3-6-6	DS	4.0%	5.6%	8.4%	18.1%
1037	$0	2-3-6-6	S	3.1%	4.8%	6.1%	14.1%
1269	-$1	2-3-6-6	NS	2.7%	4.6%	5.2%	12.5%
1081	-$0	2-3-6-7	DS	3.4%	5.6%	6.2%	15.2%
1453	-$1	2-3-6-7	S	3.0%	5.4%	5.0%	13.4%

OMAHA HIGH-LOW 8 OR BETTER
5,278 HANDS   9 HANDED

| HAND RANK | VALUE $4/$8 | POCKET CARDS | | HIGH % | LOW % | SCOOP % | PART OR ALL % |
		HAND	SUITED				
1819	-$2	2-3-6-7	NS	2.8%	5.4%	4.1%	12.3%
1153	-$0	2-3-6-8	DS	3.3%	5.4%	6.3%	14.9%
1648	-$1	2-3-6-8	S	2.9%	5.0%	5.0%	12.9%
2150	-$2	2-3-6-8	NS	2.8%	5.0%	4.0%	11.8%
1112	-$0	2-3-6-9	DS	3.3%	5.6%	6.4%	15.3%
1897	-$2	2-3-6-9	S	3.0%	5.2%	4.7%	12.9%
2332	-$3	2-3-6-9	NS	2.5%	5.2%	4.1%	11.9%
1423	-$1	2-3-6-10	DS	2.9%	5.4%	6.2%	14.6%
1906	-$2	2-3-6-10	S	2.5%	5.1%	4.7%	12.3%
2382	-$3	2-3-6-10	NS	2.3%	5.1%	4.0%	11.5%
1370	-$1	2-3-6-J	DS	2.8%	5.4%	6.2%	14.4%
2104	-$2	2-3-6-J	S	2.3%	5.1%	4.7%	12.1%
2453	-$3	2-3-6-J	NS	2.2%	5.0%	3.8%	10.9%
1239	-$1	2-3-6-Q	DS	2.9%	5.4%	6.7%	15.0%
1860	-$2	2-3-6-Q	S	2.8%	5.1%	6.0%	13.9%
2765	-$3	2-3-6-Q	NS	2.7%	5.2%	5.1%	13.0%
1070	$0	2-3-6-K	DS	3.4%	5.8%	7.8%	17.0%
1379	-$1	2-3-6-K	S	2.9%	5.6%	6.3%	14.8%
2698	-$3	2-3-6-K	NS	2.8%	5.6%	5.4%	13.8%
1025	$0	2-3-7-7	DS	3.9%	5.0%	7.8%	16.7%
1427	-$1	2-3-7-7	S	3.5%	4.8%	6.7%	15.0%
2096	-$2	2-3-7-7	NS	3.2%	4.8%	5.3%	13.2%
1515	-$1	2-3-7-8	DS	3.7%	5.6%	7.5%	16.8%
2097	-$2	2-3-7-8	S	3.4%	5.6%	6.3%	15.3%
3095	-$4	2-3-7-8	NS	3.1%	5.5%	5.1%	13.7%
1448	-$1	2-3-7-9	DS	3.8%	5.7%	7.4%	16.9%
2127	-$2	2-3-7-9	S	3.4%	5.7%	6.3%	15.4%
2986	-$3	2-3-7-9	NS	3.1%	5.7%	5.1%	13.8%

OMAHA HIGH-LOW 8 OR BETTER
5,278 HANDS   9 HANDED

| HAND RANK | VALUE $4/$8 | POCKET CARDS | | HIGH % | LOW % | SCOOP % | PART OR ALL % |
		HAND	SUITED				
1695	-$2	2-3-7-10	DS	3.5%	5.7%	7.3%	16.4%
2409	-$3	2-3-7-10	S	3.1%	5.7%	6.0%	14.8%
3412	-$4	2-3-7-10	NS	2.7%	5.7%	4.9%	13.3%
1881	-$2	2-3-7-J	DS	3.1%	5.6%	7.3%	15.9%
2740	-$3	2-3-7-J	S	2.8%	5.5%	5.9%	14.2%
3565	-$4	2-3-7-J	NS	2.4%	5.6%	4.7%	12.7%
2007	-$2	2-3-7-Q	DS	3.2%	5.5%	7.1%	15.7%
2524	-$3	2-3-7-Q	S	2.8%	5.5%	6.1%	14.3%
3808	-$4	2-3-7-Q	NS	2.3%	5.5%	4.5%	12.3%
1553	-$1	2-3-7-K	DS	3.5%	5.6%	7.8%	16.9%
2185	-$2	2-3-7-K	S	3.0%	5.6%	6.6%	15.2%
3661	-$4	2-3-7-K	NS	2.4%	5.4%	4.9%	12.7%
1119	-$0	2-3-8-8	DS	4.0%	4.7%	7.8%	16.5%
1646	-$1	2-3-8-8	S	3.6%	4.6%	6.7%	14.8%
1984	-$2	2-3-8-8	NS	3.2%	4.6%	5.6%	13.4%
1510	-$1	2-3-8-9	DS	3.7%	5.5%	7.9%	17.1%
2396	-$3	2-3-8-9	S	3.6%	5.6%	6.5%	15.7%
2961	-$3	2-3-8-9	NS	3.3%	5.5%	5.9%	14.7%
1525	-$1	2-3-8-10	DS	3.7%	5.5%	7.9%	17.0%
2190	-$2	2-3-8-10	S	3.2%	5.5%	7.0%	15.7%
3171	-$4	2-3-8-10	NS	2.8%	5.5%	5.8%	14.1%
1728	-$2	2-3-8-J	DS	3.3%	5.4%	7.8%	16.5%
2442	-$3	2-3-8-J	S	3.0%	5.4%	6.7%	15.1%
3708	-$4	2-3-8-J	NS	2.4%	5.3%	5.5%	13.3%
1944	-$2	2-3-8-Q	DS	3.3%	5.3%	7.7%	16.2%
2847	-$3	2-3-8-Q	S	2.9%	5.3%	6.3%	14.6%
4059	-$5	2-3-8-Q	NS	2.3%	5.3%	5.0%	12.7%
1833	-$2	2-3-8-K	DS	3.5%	5.4%	7.7%	16.5%

OMAHA HIGH-LOW 8 OR BETTER
5,278 HANDS   9 HANDED

| HAND RANK | VALUE $4/$8 | POCKET CARDS | | HIGH % | LOW % | SCOOP % | PART OR ALL % |
		HAND	SUITED				
2592	-$3	2-3-8-K	S	3.1%	5.2%	6.5%	14.8%
4107	-$5	2-3-8-K	NS	2.4%	5.2%	4.6%	12.2%
842	$1	2-3-9-9	DS	2.8%	4.5%	8.3%	15.7%
1069	$0	2-3-9-9	S	2.2%	4.2%	6.5%	12.9%
1322	-$1	2-3-9-9	NS	1.8%	4.2%	5.6%	11.6%
1342	-$1	2-3-9-10	DS	3.7%	5.2%	8.4%	17.3%
1899	-$2	2-3-9-10	S	3.3%	5.2%	7.4%	15.8%
3041	-$3	2-3-9-10	NS	2.8%	5.2%	6.2%	14.2%
1442	-$1	2-3-9-J	DS	3.4%	5.1%	8.4%	16.9%
2283	-$3	2-3-9-J	S	2.9%	5.1%	7.2%	15.2%
3302	-$4	2-3-9-J	NS	2.3%	5.2%	6.0%	13.5%
1533	-$1	2-3-9-Q	DS	3.2%	5.0%	8.4%	16.6%
2301	-$3	2-3-9-Q	S	2.7%	5.0%	7.3%	15.0%
3660	-$4	2-3-9-Q	NS	2.1%	5.1%	5.8%	13.0%
1580	-$1	2-3-9-K	DS	3.2%	5.0%	8.6%	16.8%
2351	-$3	2-3-9-K	S	2.7%	5.0%	7.2%	14.9%
3890	-$5	2-3-9-K	NS	2.2%	5.1%	5.4%	12.7%
749	$1	2-3-10-10	DS	3.4%	5.0%	9.8%	18.3%
1043	$0	2-3-10-10	S	2.8%	4.9%	8.4%	16.1%
1327	-$1	2-3-10-10	NS	2.3%	5.0%	7.3%	14.6%
839	$1	2-3-10-J	DS	3.5%	4.5%	8.7%	16.7%
985	$0	2-3-10-J	S	3.3%	4.4%	8.7%	16.4%
2313	-$3	2-3-10-J	NS	2.2%	4.4%	6.1%	12.6%
1004	$0	2-3-10-Q	DS	3.6%	5.0%	9.6%	18.2%
1466	-$1	2-3-10-Q	S	3.1%	5.0%	8.5%	16.6%
1820	-$2	2-3-10-Q	NS	2.6%	4.3%	6.8%	13.7%
1010	$0	2-3-10-K	DS	3.6%	5.0%	9.7%	18.3%
1158	-$0	2-3-10-K	S	2.8%	4.6%	7.7%	15.1%

OMAHA HIGH-LOW 8 OR BETTER
5,278 HANDS   9 HANDED

| HAND RANK | VALUE $4/$8 | POCKET CARDS | | HIGH % | LOW % | SCOOP % | PART OR ALL % |
		HAND	SUITED				
2501	-$3	2-3-10-K	NS	2.1%	4.5%	5.2%	11.8%
665	$2	2-3-J-J	DS	3.7%	5.1%	10.7%	19.5%
920	$1	2-3-J-J	S	3.1%	5.2%	9.6%	17.9%
1294	-$1	2-3-J-J	NS	2.5%	5.2%	8.1%	15.8%
893	$1	2-3-J-Q	DS	3.7%	5.0%	10.0%	18.7%
1798	-$2	2-3-J-Q	S	2.7%	4.2%	7.2%	14.1%
2380	-$3	2-3-J-Q	NS	2.0%	4.4%	6.1%	12.6%
911	$1	2-3-J-K	DS	3.8%	5.0%	10.2%	19.0%
1440	-$1	2-3-J-K	S	2.8%	4.6%	7.4%	14.9%
2545	-$3	2-3-J-K	NS	2.1%	4.6%	5.2%	11.9%
500	$4	2-3-Q-Q	DS	4.1%	5.3%	12.8%	22.3%
735	$1	2-3-Q-Q	S	3.5%	5.4%	11.2%	20.2%
1122	-$0	2-3-Q-Q	NS	2.9%	5.5%	9.6%	17.9%
789	$1	2-3-Q-K	DS	3.6%	4.7%	9.8%	18.0%
1223	-$1	2-3-Q-K	S	2.8%	4.4%	7.8%	15.1%
1893	-$2	2-3-Q-K	NS	2.3%	4.4%	6.2%	12.9%
317	$6	2-3-K-K	DS	4.9%	5.4%	15.3%	25.7%
532	$3	2-3-K-K	S	4.3%	5.7%	13.7%	23.6%
879	$1	2-3-K-K	NS	3.4%	5.8%	12.1%	21.3%
4370	-$5	2-4-4-4	S	1.9%	4.7%	4.3%	10.8%
4638	-$6	2-4-4-4	NS	1.6%	4.7%	3.1%	9.5%
727	$1	2-4-4-5	DS	4.4%	6.0%	10.1%	20.5%
1041	$0	2-4-4-5	S	4.0%	6.0%	8.7%	18.7%
1321	-$1	2-4-4-5	NS	3.7%	6.0%	7.4%	17.2%
1008	$0	2-4-4-6	DS	4.4%	5.5%	8.7%	18.6%
1461	-$1	2-4-4-6	S	4.0%	5.6%	7.2%	16.8%
1837	-$2	2-4-4-6	NS	3.8%	5.4%	6.2%	15.4%
1608	-$1	2-4-4-7	DS	4.2%	5.1%	7.6%	16.9%

OMAHA HIGH-LOW 8 OR BETTER
5,278 HANDS   9 HANDED

HAND RANK	VALUE $4/$8	POCKET CARDS		HIGH %	LOW %	SCOOP %	PART OR ALL %
		HAND	SUITED				
2188	-$2	2-4-4-7	S	3.8%	5.0%	6.4%	15.2%
2835	-$3	2-4-4-7	NS	3.5%	5.0%	5.4%	13.9%
1844	-$2	2-4-4-8	DS	4.3%	4.8%	7.5%	16.6%
2505	-$3	2-4-4-8	S	3.9%	4.7%	6.2%	14.8%
3467	-$4	2-4-4-8	NS	3.7%	4.7%	5.0%	13.5%
2470	-$3	2-4-4-9	DS	3.8%	4.4%	7.2%	15.4%
3288	-$4	2-4-4-9	S	3.4%	4.5%	5.6%	13.5%
4011	-$5	2-4-4-9	NS	3.1%	4.5%	4.7%	12.3%
2335	-$3	2-4-4-10	DS	4.0%	4.5%	7.2%	15.7%
3255	-$4	2-4-4-10	S	3.5%	4.4%	5.8%	13.7%
4072	-$5	2-4-4-10	NS	3.1%	4.5%	4.9%	12.5%
2250	-$3	2-4-4-J	DS	4.1%	4.5%	7.4%	15.9%
3015	-$3	2-4-4-J	S	3.5%	4.5%	6.2%	14.2%
4007	-$5	2-4-4-J	NS	3.2%	4.5%	5.0%	12.7%
2123	-$2	2-4-4-Q	DS	4.1%	4.5%	7.8%	16.4%
2739	-$3	2-4-4-Q	S	3.7%	4.4%	6.6%	14.8%
3996	-$5	2-4-4-Q	NS	3.2%	4.5%	5.2%	13.0%
2010	-$2	2-4-4-K	DS	4.4%	4.5%	8.3%	17.2%
2406	-$3	2-4-4-K	S	3.9%	4.6%	7.2%	15.7%
4001	-$5	2-4-4-K	NS	3.3%	4.6%	5.5%	13.4%
765	$1	2-4-5-5	DS	4.4%	5.9%	10.1%	20.3%
998	$0	2-4-5-5	S	4.1%	5.9%	8.5%	18.6%
1391	-$1	2-4-5-5	NS	3.8%	5.8%	7.4%	17.0%
718	$2	2-4-5-6	DS	4.9%	6.5%	9.8%	21.2%
1040	$0	2-4-5-6	S	4.7%	6.6%	8.5%	19.7%
1234	-$1	2-4-5-6	NS	3.5%	5.7%	6.0%	15.1%
1023	$0	2-4-5-7	DS	4.5%	6.0%	9.1%	19.7%
1312	-$1	2-4-5-7	S	4.1%	5.8%	7.4%	17.3%

OMAHA HIGH-LOW 8 OR BETTER
5,278 HANDS 9 HANDED

| HAND RANK | VALUE $4/$8 | POCKET CARDS | | HIGH % | LOW % | SCOOP % | PART OR ALL % |
		HAND	SUITED				
1832	-$2	2-4-5-7	NS	3.2%	5.4%	5.0%	13.6%
1021	$0	2-4-5-8	DS	4.7%	5.9%	9.1%	19.7%
1361	-$1	2-4-5-8	S	3.7%	5.3%	6.7%	15.7%
1661	-$2	2-4-5-8	NS	3.3%	5.0%	5.4%	13.6%
1366	-$1	2-4-5-9	DS	3.8%	6.1%	8.8%	18.7%
1883	-$2	2-4-5-9	S	3.4%	6.0%	7.4%	16.8%
2666	-$3	2-4-5-9	NS	3.0%	6.0%	6.3%	15.3%
1382	-$1	2-4-5-10	DS	3.9%	6.1%	9.0%	18.9%
2031	-$2	2-4-5-10	S	3.4%	6.0%	7.6%	17.0%
2902	-$3	2-4-5-10	NS	3.0%	6.1%	6.4%	15.5%
1315	-$1	2-4-5-J	DS	4.0%	6.1%	9.4%	19.5%
1889	-$2	2-4-5-J	S	3.4%	6.0%	7.8%	17.3%
2877	-$3	2-4-5-J	NS	3.0%	6.0%	6.5%	15.6%
1144	-$0	2-4-5-Q	DS	4.0%	6.0%	9.8%	19.9%
1578	-$1	2-4-5-Q	S	3.7%	6.0%	8.5%	18.2%
2608	-$3	2-4-5-Q	NS	3.1%	6.1%	6.8%	16.0%
951	$0	2-4-5-K	DS	4.2%	6.1%	10.3%	20.7%
1372	-$1	2-4-5-K	S	3.8%	6.0%	9.4%	19.2%
2110	-$2	2-4-5-K	NS	2.8%	5.1%	6.2%	14.1%
946	$0	2-4-6-6	DS	4.6%	5.0%	8.6%	18.2%
1428	-$1	2-4-6-6	S	4.2%	4.9%	7.2%	16.4%
1846	-$2	2-4-6-6	NS	3.8%	4.9%	6.2%	15.0%
1226	-$1	2-4-6-7	DS	4.6%	5.7%	7.7%	18.0%
1942	-$2	2-4-6-7	S	4.3%	5.6%	6.4%	16.3%
2465	-$3	2-4-6-7	NS	4.0%	5.6%	5.3%	14.9%
1328	-$1	2-4-6-8	DS	4.7%	5.4%	7.8%	17.9%
1793	-$2	2-4-6-8	S	4.3%	5.5%	6.6%	16.4%
2607	-$3	2-4-6-8	NS	4.0%	5.4%	5.5%	14.9%

OMAHA HIGH-LOW 8 OR BETTER
5,278 HANDS   9 HANDED

| HAND RANK | VALUE $4/$8 | POCKET CARDS | | HIGH % | LOW % | SCOOP % | PART OR ALL % |
		HAND	SUITED				
1759	-$2	2-4-6-9	DS	4.1%	5.4%	7.5%	16.9%
2474	-$3	2-4-6-9	S	3.6%	5.5%	6.2%	15.3%
3503	-$4	2-4-6-9	NS	3.2%	5.3%	5.2%	13.8%
1994	-$2	2-4-6-10	DS	4.0%	5.5%	7.4%	16.9%
2553	-$3	2-4-6-10	S	3.7%	5.5%	6.4%	15.5%
3572	-$4	2-4-6-10	NS	3.2%	5.5%	5.2%	13.9%
1948	-$2	2-4-6-J	DS	3.8%	5.4%	7.5%	16.7%
2732	-$3	2-4-6-J	S	3.4%	5.4%	6.3%	15.2%
3899	-$5	2-4-6-J	NS	2.9%	5.3%	5.1%	13.3%
1847	-$2	2-4-6-Q	DS	3.9%	5.4%	7.8%	17.1%
2361	-$3	2-4-6-Q	S	3.6%	5.3%	6.9%	15.7%
3595	-$4	2-4-6-Q	NS	3.1%	5.4%	5.3%	13.8%
1416	-$1	2-4-6-K	DS	4.2%	5.5%	8.6%	18.4%
2102	-$2	2-4-6-K	S	3.8%	5.4%	7.4%	16.6%
3463	-$4	2-4-6-K	NS	3.2%	5.4%	5.6%	14.2%
1386	-$1	2-4-7-7	DS	4.4%	4.3%	7.7%	16.4%
1993	-$2	2-4-7-7	S	3.9%	4.2%	6.6%	14.7%
2499	-$3	2-4-7-7	NS	3.7%	4.1%	5.5%	13.3%
1913	-$2	2-4-7-8	DS	4.3%	4.8%	7.4%	16.6%
2475	-$3	2-4-7-8	S	4.1%	4.8%	6.5%	15.3%
3559	-$4	2-4-7-8	NS	3.7%	4.8%	5.2%	13.7%
2230	-$2	2-4-7-9	DS	3.9%	4.8%	7.1%	15.8%
2993	-$3	2-4-7-9	S	3.6%	4.8%	6.1%	14.5%
4108	-$5	2-4-7-9	NS	3.1%	4.8%	5.0%	12.9%
2207	-$2	2-4-7-10	DS	3.9%	4.8%	7.4%	16.2%
3102	-$4	2-4-7-10	S	3.6%	4.9%	6.2%	14.7%
4109	-$5	2-4-7-10	NS	3.0%	4.8%	5.2%	13.0%
2489	-$3	2-4-7-J	DS	3.7%	4.8%	7.2%	15.7%

OMAHA HIGH-LOW 8 OR BETTER
5,278 HANDS 9 HANDED

HAND RANK	VALUE $4/$8	POCKET CARDS		HIGH %	LOW %	SCOOP %	PART OR ALL %
		HAND	SUITED				
3379	-$4	2-4-7-J	S	3.3%	4.7%	6.2%	14.2%
4210	-$5	2-4-7-J	NS	2.8%	4.8%	4.9%	12.5%
2485	-$3	2-4-7-Q	DS	3.6%	4.7%	7.2%	15.5%
3452	-$4	2-4-7-Q	S	3.3%	4.7%	6.0%	14.0%
4501	-$6	2-4-7-Q	NS	2.7%	4.6%	4.7%	12.0%
2054	-$2	2-4-7-K	DS	3.9%	4.8%	7.9%	16.6%
2874	-$3	2-4-7-K	S	3.6%	4.8%	6.7%	15.1%
4241	-$5	2-4-7-K	NS	2.8%	4.7%	5.1%	12.6%
1502	-$1	2-4-8-8	DS	4.5%	4.0%	7.7%	16.1%
2093	-$2	2-4-8-8	S	4.0%	3.9%	6.7%	14.6%
2686	-$3	2-4-8-8	NS	3.7%	3.9%	5.5%	13.2%
2387	-$3	2-4-8-9	DS	4.1%	4.6%	7.6%	16.3%
3545	-$4	2-4-8-9	S	3.7%	4.6%	6.4%	14.7%
4403	-$5	2-4-8-9	NS	3.2%	4.6%	5.3%	13.2%
2074	-$2	2-4-8-10	DS	4.1%	4.6%	8.1%	16.7%
3114	-$4	2-4-8-10	S	3.7%	4.6%	6.8%	15.1%
4101	-$5	2-4-8-10	NS	3.2%	4.6%	5.9%	13.7%
2340	-$3	2-4-8-J	DS	3.8%	4.6%	7.9%	16.4%
3234	-$4	2-4-8-J	S	3.5%	4.6%	6.8%	14.9%
4396	-$5	2-4-8-J	NS	3.0%	4.6%	5.5%	13.1%
2588	-$3	2-4-8-Q	DS	3.8%	4.5%	7.7%	16.0%
3438	-$4	2-4-8-Q	S	3.3%	4.6%	6.7%	14.6%
4570	-$6	2-4-8-Q	NS	2.7%	4.6%	5.2%	12.5%
2463	-$3	2-4-8-K	DS	4.0%	4.5%	7.7%	16.2%
3424	-$4	2-4-8-K	S	3.5%	4.4%	6.7%	14.6%
4582	-$6	2-4-8-K	NS	2.8%	4.4%	4.9%	12.1%
1180	-$0	2-4-9-9	DS	3.1%	3.9%	8.6%	15.6%
1628	-$1	2-4-9-9	S	2.6%	3.9%	7.6%	14.1%

OMAHA HIGH-LOW 8 OR BETTER
5,278 HANDS   9 HANDED

HAND RANK	VALUE $4/$8	POCKET CARDS HAND	SUITED	HIGH %	LOW %	SCOOP %	PART OR ALL %
2091	-$2	2-4-9-9	NS	2.1%	3.8%	6.7%	12.6%
2121	-$2	2-4-9-10	DS	3.8%	4.1%	8.2%	16.2%
3149	-$4	2-4-9-10	S	3.3%	4.2%	7.0%	14.6%
4081	-$5	2-4-9-10	NS	2.8%	4.2%	6.0%	13.0%
2266	-$3	2-4-9-J	DS	3.4%	4.1%	8.0%	15.5%
3329	-$4	2-4-9-J	S	2.8%	4.2%	7.0%	14.0%
4356	-$5	2-4-9-J	NS	2.4%	4.2%	5.8%	12.4%
2628	-$3	2-4-9-Q	DS	3.2%	4.0%	8.1%	15.2%
3314	-$4	2-4-9-Q	S	2.7%	4.1%	7.2%	13.9%
4389	-$5	2-4-9-Q	NS	2.1%	4.0%	5.7%	11.9%
2432	-$3	2-4-9-K	DS	3.3%	4.0%	8.2%	15.5%
3226	-$4	2-4-9-K	S	2.7%	4.1%	7.3%	14.1%
4531	-$6	2-4-9-K	NS	1.9%	4.0%	5.5%	11.4%
1174	-$0	2-4-10-10	DS	3.3%	4.1%	9.3%	16.7%
1643	-$1	2-4-10-10	S	2.8%	4.0%	8.1%	15.0%
2129	-$2	2-4-10-10	NS	2.3%	4.0%	7.3%	13.6%
1404	-$1	2-4-10-J	DS	3.9%	4.0%	9.4%	17.3%
2035	-$2	2-4-10-J	S	3.3%	4.2%	8.2%	15.7%
2895	-$3	2-4-10-J	NS	2.8%	4.2%	7.3%	14.2%
1524	-$1	2-4-10-Q	DS	3.6%	4.0%	9.4%	16.9%
2166	-$2	2-4-10-Q	S	3.1%	4.1%	8.3%	15.5%
3425	-$4	2-4-10-Q	NS	2.5%	4.1%	7.1%	13.7%
1475	-$1	2-4-10-K	DS	3.7%	4.0%	9.5%	17.2%
2146	-$2	2-4-10-K	S	3.1%	4.0%	8.5%	15.7%
3855	-$4	2-4-10-K	NS	2.3%	4.1%	6.5%	12.9%
964	$0	2-4-J-J	DS	3.7%	4.2%	10.6%	18.5%
1408	-$1	2-4-J-J	S	3.1%	4.1%	9.3%	16.5%
1928	-$2	2-4-J-J	NS	2.5%	4.3%	8.1%	14.9%

OMAHA HIGH-LOW 8 OR BETTER
5,278 HANDS   9 HANDED

| HAND RANK | VALUE $4/$8 | POCKET CARDS | | HIGH % | LOW % | SCOOP % | PART OR ALL % |
		HAND	SUITED				
1339	-$1	2-4-J-Q	DS	3.7%	4.0%	9.7%	17.5%
2045	-$2	2-4-J-Q	S	3.2%	4.1%	8.5%	15.8%
3274	-$4	2-4-J-Q	NS	2.6%	4.1%	7.3%	14.0%
1310	-$1	2-4-J-K	DS	3.7%	4.0%	9.8%	17.5%
2113	-$2	2-4-J-K	S	3.2%	4.0%	8.6%	15.8%
3263	-$4	2-4-J-K	NS	2.5%	4.1%	7.3%	13.8%
831	$1	2-4-Q-Q	DS	3.8%	4.0%	11.2%	18.9%
1123	-$0	2-4-Q-Q	S	3.6%	4.4%	11.0%	18.9%
1802	-$2	2-4-Q-Q	NS	2.8%	4.5%	9.3%	16.6%
1154	-$0	2-4-Q-K	DS	4.0%	4.0%	10.4%	18.3%
1850	-$2	2-4-Q-K	S	3.4%	4.0%	9.1%	16.5%
3369	-$4	2-4-Q-K	NS	2.5%	4.1%	7.3%	13.9%
466	$4	2-4-K-K	DS	5.0%	4.5%	15.1%	24.7%
754	$1	2-4-K-K	S	4.2%	4.6%	13.4%	22.2%
1357	-$1	2-4-K-K	NS	3.2%	4.7%	11.8%	19.8%
4809	-$6	2-5-5-5	S	1.9%	2.9%	4.2%	9.0%
4947	-$7	2-5-5-5	NS	1.6%	2.8%	3.0%	7.4%
1367	-$1	2-5-5-6	DS	4.6%	4.3%	8.5%	17.3%
1664	-$2	2-5-5-6	S	4.2%	4.2%	7.3%	15.8%
2344	-$3	2-5-5-6	NS	4.0%	4.0%	6.4%	14.4%
1736	-$2	2-5-5-7	DS	4.4%	3.9%	7.8%	16.1%
2596	-$3	2-5-5-7	S	4.0%	3.7%	6.6%	14.3%
3118	-$4	2-5-5-7	NS	3.7%	3.6%	5.7%	13.1%
2168	-$2	2-5-5-8	DS	4.6%	3.6%	7.5%	15.7%
3068	-$4	2-5-5-8	S	4.1%	3.4%	6.3%	13.9%
3716	-$4	2-5-5-8	NS	3.9%	3.4%	5.5%	12.7%
3031	-$3	2-5-5-9	DS	4.3%	3.1%	7.0%	14.4%
3747	-$4	2-5-5-9	S	3.8%	3.0%	5.7%	12.5%

OMAHA HIGH-LOW 8 OR BETTER
5,278 HANDS 9 HANDED

HAND RANK	VALUE $4/$8	POCKET CARDS		HIGH %	LOW %	SCOOP %	PART OR ALL %
		HAND	SUITED				
4236	-$5	2-5-5-9	NS	3.5%	3.0%	5.0%	11.4%
3257	-$4	2-5-5-10	DS	3.9%	3.0%	6.9%	13.8%
3928	-$5	2-5-5-10	S	3.5%	2.9%	5.7%	12.1%
4461	-$5	2-5-5-10	NS	3.0%	2.9%	4.8%	10.7%
3046	-$3	2-5-5-J	DS	4.0%	3.0%	7.1%	14.1%
3814	-$4	2-5-5-J	S	3.5%	2.9%	5.9%	12.4%
4500	-$6	2-5-5-J	NS	3.1%	2.8%	5.1%	11.0%
2842	-$3	2-5-5-Q	DS	4.1%	3.0%	7.6%	14.8%
3345	-$4	2-5-5-Q	S	3.7%	2.9%	6.5%	13.1%
4345	-$5	2-5-5-Q	NS	3.2%	2.9%	5.2%	11.3%
2269	-$3	2-5-5-K	DS	4.4%	3.1%	8.1%	15.7%
3162	-$4	2-5-5-K	S			6.7%	6.7%
4415	-$5	2-5-5-K	NS	3.1%	3.0%	5.4%	11.5%
1161	-$0	2-5-6-6	DS	4.8%	4.3%	8.4%	17.6%
1588	-$1	2-5-6-6	S	4.5%	4.2%	7.3%	16.0%
2125	-$2	2-5-6-6	NS	4.2%	4.1%	6.3%	14.5%
1517	-$1	2-5-6-7	DS	5.0%	4.5%	7.7%	17.3%
2214	-$2	2-5-6-7	S	4.6%	4.5%	6.5%	15.6%
2917	-$3	2-5-6-7	NS	4.3%	4.4%	5.5%	14.2%
1585	-$1	2-5-6-8	DS	5.0%	4.3%	7.7%	17.1%
2161	-$2	2-5-6-8	S	4.8%	4.3%	6.5%	15.6%
2944	-$3	2-5-6-8	NS	4.4%	4.2%	5.6%	14.2%
1886	-$2	2-5-6-9	DS	4.6%	4.3%	7.4%	16.2%
2770	-$3	2-5-6-9	S	4.2%	4.2%	6.3%	14.7%
3494	-$4	2-5-6-9	NS	3.7%	4.1%	5.3%	13.2%
2521	-$3	2-5-6-10	DS	4.1%	4.2%	7.2%	15.5%
3248	-$4	2-5-6-10	S	3.7%	4.1%	6.2%	13.9%
4178	-$5	2-5-6-10	NS	3.2%	4.0%	5.0%	12.2%

OMAHA HIGH-LOW 8 OR BETTER
5,278 HANDS   9 HANDED

HAND RANK	VALUE $4/$8	POCKET CARDS HAND	SUITED	HIGH %	LOW %	SCOOP %	PART OR ALL %
2379	-$3	2-5-6-J	DS	4.1%	4.3%	7.4%	15.8%
3349	-$4	2-5-6-J	S	3.6%	4.1%	6.3%	14.1%
4169	-$5	2-5-6-J	NS	3.2%	4.1%	5.2%	12.5%
2192	-$2	2-5-6-Q	DS	4.2%	4.2%	7.8%	16.2%
2725	-$3	2-5-6-Q	S	3.8%	4.2%	6.8%	14.9%
4090	-$5	2-5-6-Q	NS	3.2%	4.1%	5.6%	12.9%
1753	-$2	2-5-6-K	DS	4.5%	4.2%	8.7%	17.4%
2209	-$2	2-5-6-K	S	4.1%	4.2%	7.8%	16.1%
4012	-$5	2-5-6-K	NS	3.3%	4.1%	5.8%	13.3%
1615	-$1	2-5-7-7	DS	4.7%	3.5%	7.7%	15.9%
2217	-$2	2-5-7-7	S	4.3%	3.4%	6.6%	14.4%
2921	-$3	2-5-7-7	NS	4.0%	3.3%	5.5%	12.8%
2021	-$2	2-5-7-8	DS	4.9%	3.8%	7.5%	16.2%
2843	-$3	2-5-7-8	S	4.5%	3.8%	6.5%	14.7%
3892	-$5	2-5-7-8	NS	4.1%	3.6%	5.4%	13.1%
2460	-$3	2-5-7-9	DS	4.4%	3.8%	7.1%	15.3%
3267	-$4	2-5-7-9	S	4.0%	3.6%	6.3%	13.9%
4091	-$5	2-5-7-9	NS	3.6%	3.6%	5.3%	12.5%
2983	-$3	2-5-7-10	DS	3.9%	3.6%	7.0%	14.6%
3945	-$5	2-5-7-10	S	3.6%	3.5%	5.9%	13.0%
4472	-$5	2-5-7-10	NS	3.1%	3.4%	5.1%	11.6%
3101	-$4	2-5-7-J	DS	3.9%	3.7%	7.4%	15.0%
3848	-$4	2-5-7-J	S	3.5%	3.5%	6.3%	13.3%
4484	-$5	2-5-7-J	NS	3.0%	3.5%	5.2%	11.7%
2888	-$3	2-5-7-Q	DS	4.0%	3.6%	7.3%	14.8%
3911	-$5	2-5-7-Q	S	3.5%	3.4%	6.1%	13.0%
4627	-$6	2-5-7-Q	NS	2.9%	3.4%	4.9%	11.2%
2480	-$3	2-5-7-K	DS	4.1%	3.7%	7.9%	15.7%

OMAHA HIGH-LOW 8 OR BETTER
5,278 HANDS   9 HANDED

HAND RANK	VALUE $4/$8	POCKET CARDS		HIGH %	LOW %	SCOOP %	PART OR ALL %
		HAND	SUITED				
3286	-$4	2-5-7-K	S	3.8%	3.6%	6.9%	14.3%
4478	-$5	2-5-7-K	NS	3.0%	3.5%	5.3%	11.7%
1636	-$1	2-5-8-8	DS	4.9%	3.2%	7.8%	15.9%
2179	-$2	2-5-8-8	S	4.5%	3.1%	6.7%	14.3%
3282	-$4	2-5-8-8	NS	4.1%	3.0%	5.7%	12.7%
2582	-$3	2-5-8-9	DS	4.6%	3.5%	7.7%	15.8%
3700	-$4	2-5-8-9	S	4.2%	3.5%	6.4%	14.1%
4258	-$5	2-5-8-9	NS	3.8%	3.4%	5.8%	13.0%
2710	-$3	2-5-8-10	DS	4.1%	3.5%	7.7%	15.3%
3796	-$4	2-5-8-10	S	3.7%	3.4%	6.6%	13.7%
4476	-$5	2-5-8-10	NS	3.2%	3.3%	5.7%	12.2%
2569	-$3	2-5-8-J	DS	4.2%	3.4%	8.0%	15.6%
3711	-$4	2-5-8-J	S	3.7%	3.4%	7.0%	14.0%
4454	-$5	2-5-8-J	NS	3.2%	3.3%	5.9%	12.4%
2867	-$3	2-5-8-Q	DS	4.1%	3.5%	7.8%	15.4%
3872	-$5	2-5-8-Q	S	3.7%	3.3%	6.7%	13.7%
4601	-$6	2-5-8-Q	NS	3.0%	3.2%	5.6%	11.8%
2766	-$3	2-5-8-K	DS	4.2%	3.4%	7.8%	15.4%
3679	-$4	2-5-8-K	S	3.9%	3.3%	6.6%	13.8%
4788	-$6	2-5-8-K	NS	3.0%	3.2%	5.1%	11.3%
1469	-$1	2-5-9-9	DS	3.5%	2.9%	8.5%	14.9%
1845	-$2	2-5-9-9	S	3.0%	2.8%	7.5%	13.3%
2450	-$3	2-5-9-9	NS	2.5%	2.8%	6.5%	11.8%
3026	-$3	2-5-9-10	DS	3.8%	3.0%	7.7%	14.5%
3798	-$4	2-5-9-10	S	3.3%	2.9%	6.8%	13.0%
4634	-$6	2-5-9-10	NS	2.7%	2.8%	5.7%	11.2%
3117	-$4	2-5-9-J	DS	4.0%	3.0%	7.1%	14.1%
3574	-$4	2-5-9-J	S	3.4%	2.9%	7.0%	13.2%

OMAHA HIGH-LOW 8 OR BETTER
5,278 HANDS 9 HANDED

HAND RANK	VALUE $4/$8	POCKET CARDS		HIGH %	LOW %	SCOOP %	PART OR ALL %
		HAND	SUITED				
4568	-$6	2-5-9-J	NS	2.8%	2.9%	5.9%	11.5%
2841	-$3	2-5-9-Q	DS	3.6%	2.9%	8.3%	14.8%
3631	-$4	2-5-9-Q	S	3.1%	2.9%	7.3%	13.2%
4019	-$5	2-5-9-Q	NS	3.2%	2.9%	6.9%	13.0%
2919	-$3	2-5-9-K	DS	3.6%	2.8%	8.2%	14.6%
3763	-$4	2-5-9-K	S	3.0%	2.8%	7.2%	13.0%
4683	-$6	2-5-9-K	NS	2.2%	2.7%	5.6%	10.5%
1591	-$1	2-5-10-10	DS	3.3%	2.9%	9.0%	15.2%
2048	-$2	2-5-10-10	S	2.8%	2.8%	8.0%	13.5%
2853	-$3	2-5-10-10	NS	2.2%	2.8%	6.8%	11.8%
1921	-$2	2-5-10-J	DS	3.8%	2.9%	9.0%	15.7%
2587	-$3	2-5-10-J	S	3.2%	2.9%	8.1%	14.3%
3756	-$4	2-5-10-J	NS	2.7%	2.8%	7.0%	12.5%
2105	-$2	2-5-10-Q	DS	3.6%	2.8%	8.9%	15.2%
2715	-$3	2-5-10-Q	S	3.0%	2.7%	8.1%	13.8%
4002	-$5	2-5-10-Q	NS	2.4%	2.7%	6.8%	11.9%
2038	-$2	2-5-10-K	DS	3.6%	2.8%	9.0%	15.4%
2755	-$3	2-5-10-K	S	3.0%	2.7%	8.1%	13.9%
4099	-$5	2-5-10-K	NS	2.3%	2.6%	6.6%	11.5%
1324	-$1	2-5-J-J	DS	3.6%	2.9%	10.0%	16.5%
1953	-$2	2-5-J-J	S	3.0%	2.9%	8.8%	14.7%
2665	-$3	2-5-J-J	NS	2.4%	2.9%	7.8%	13.1%
1822	-$2	2-5-J-Q	DS	3.6%	2.8%	9.4%	15.8%
2565	-$3	2-5-J-Q	S	3.2%	2.8%	8.2%	14.2%
3818	-$4	2-5-J-Q	NS	2.5%	2.7%	7.2%	12.4%
1777	-$2	2-5-J-K	DS	3.7%	2.7%	9.5%	15.9%
2554	-$3	2-5-J-K	S	3.2%	2.7%	8.5%	14.3%
4045	-$5	2-5-J-K	NS	2.3%	2.6%	6.9%	11.8%

OMAHA HIGH-LOW 8 OR BETTER
5,278 HANDS   9 HANDED

HAND RANK	VALUE $4/$8	POCKET CARDS		HIGH %	LOW %	SCOOP %	PART OR ALL %
		HAND	SUITED				
943	$1	2-5-Q-Q	DS	4.1%	3.2%	12.0%	19.3%
1562	-$1	2-5-Q-Q	S	3.4%	3.1%	10.5%	16.9%
2478	-$3	2-5-Q-Q	NS	2.8%	3.1%	9.0%	14.8%
1658	-$2	2-5-Q-K	DS	4.0%	2.8%	9.7%	16.5%
2434	-$3	2-5-Q-K	S	3.3%	2.8%	8.8%	14.8%
3782	-$4	2-5-Q-K	NS	2.4%	2.7%	7.2%	12.3%
608	$2	2-5-K-K	DS	5.0%	3.3%	14.5%	22.9%
990	$0	2-5-K-K	S	4.1%	3.3%	13.1%	20.6%
1955	-$2	2-5-K-K	NS	3.2%	2.9%	10.5%	16.6%
5084	-$8	2-6-6-6	S	1.9%	1.9%	2.8%	6.6%
5134	-$8	2-6-6-6	NS	1.6%	1.7%	1.9%	5.2%
2433	-$3	2-6-6-7	DS	4.8%	2.9%	7.1%	14.7%
3217	-$4	2-6-6-7	S	4.5%	2.7%	6.1%	13.3%
3924	-$5	2-6-6-7	NS	4.0%	2.6%	4.9%	11.5%
2443	-$3	2-6-6-8	DS	4.9%	2.7%	7.0%	14.6%
3075	-$4	2-6-6-8	S	4.7%	2.4%	6.1%	13.2%
4278	-$5	2-6-6-8	NS	4.3%	2.4%		6.6%
3585	-$4	2-6-6-9	DS	4.8%	2.2%	6.1%	13.1%
4253	-$5	2-6-6-9	S	4.2%	2.0%	5.0%	11.3%
4628	-$6	2-6-6-9	NS	3.9%	2.0%	4.1%	10.0%
3909	-$5	2-6-6-10	DS	4.3%	2.1%	6.0%	12.4%
4309	-$5	2-6-6-10	S	3.9%	2.0%	5.0%	10.9%
4787	-$6	2-6-6-10	NS	3.4%	2.0%	4.0%	9.3%
4044	-$5	2-6-6-J	DS	4.0%	2.0%	6.1%	12.1%
4508	-$6	2-6-6-J	S	3.6%	1.9%	4.9%	10.4%
4900	-$7	2-6-6-J	NS	3.1%	1.8%	3.9%	8.8%
3886	-$5	2-6-6-Q	DS	4.2%	2.1%	6.4%	12.8%
4407	-$5	2-6-6-Q	S	3.7%	2.0%	5.2%	10.9%

OMAHA HIGH-LOW 8 OR BETTER
5,278 HANDS   9 HANDED

HAND RANK	VALUE $4/$8	POCKET CARDS		HIGH %	LOW %	SCOOP %	PART OR ALL %
		HAND	SUITED				
4852	-$6	2-6-6-Q	NS	3.1%	1.8%		5.0%
3242	-$4	2-6-6-K	DS	4.5%	2.2%	7.2%	13.9%
4039	-$5	2-6-6-K	S	4.0%	2.1%	5.8%	11.9%
4839	-$6	2-6-6-K	NS	3.2%	1.9%	4.3%	9.4%
2312	-$3	2-6-7-7	DS	4.9%	2.8%	6.9%	14.7%
3084	-$4	2-6-7-7	S	4.6%	2.7%	5.9%	13.2%
4041	-$5	2-6-7-7	NS	4.1%	2.5%	4.8%	11.4%
2559	-$3	2-6-7-8	DS	5.0%	2.9%	6.8%	14.7%
3522	-$4	2-6-7-8	S	4.7%	2.7%	5.8%	13.2%
4299	-$5	2-6-7-8	NS	4.3%	2.5%	4.7%	11.6%
3335	-$4	2-6-7-9	DS	4.7%	2.7%	6.4%	13.9%
4206	-$5	2-6-7-9	S	4.3%	2.5%	5.5%	12.3%
4592	-$6	2-6-7-9	NS	3.9%	2.4%	4.5%	10.8%
3650	-$4	2-6-7-10	DS	4.2%	2.7%	6.4%	13.3%
4160	-$5	2-6-7-10	S	3.8%	2.5%	5.5%	11.8%
4673	-$6	2-6-7-10	NS	3.3%	2.4%	4.5%	10.2%
4070	-$5	2-6-7-J	DS	3.9%	2.6%	6.2%	12.7%
4546	-$6	2-6-7-J	S	3.5%	2.4%	5.2%	11.1%
4931	-$7	2-6-7-J	NS	3.0%	2.2%	4.1%	9.3%
3941	-$5	2-6-7-Q	DS	4.0%	2.7%	6.5%	13.2%
4473	-$5	2-6-7-Q	S	3.6%	2.5%	5.6%	11.7%
4966	-$7	2-6-7-Q	NS	3.0%	2.3%	4.3%	9.6%
3526	-$4	2-6-7-K	DS	4.3%	2.8%	7.0%	14.1%
4051	-$5	2-6-7-K	S	3.9%	2.6%	6.3%	12.8%
4929	-$7	2-6-7-K	NS	3.2%	2.4%	4.5%	10.1%
2182	-$2	2-6-8-8	DS	5.1%	2.4%	7.2%	14.7%
3189	-$4	2-6-8-8	S	4.6%	2.4%	6.1%	13.0%
3947	-$5	2-6-8-8	NS	4.3%	2.3%	5.0%	11.5%

OMAHA HIGH-LOW 8 OR BETTER
5,278 HANDS   9 HANDED

HAND RANK	VALUE $4/$8	POCKET CARDS		HIGH %	LOW %	SCOOP %	PART OR ALL %
		HAND	SUITED				
3168	-$4	2-6-8-9	DS	5.0%	2.5%	7.0%	14.4%
4304	-$5	2-6-8-9	S	4.5%	2.4%	5.9%	12.7%
4726	-$6	2-6-8-9	NS	4.1%	2.2%	5.0%	11.3%
3191	-$4	2-6-8-10	DS	4.5%	2.5%	7.1%	14.0%
4183	-$5	2-6-8-10	S	4.0%	2.4%	6.1%	12.6%
4637	-$6	2-6-8-10	NS	3.6%	2.3%	5.2%	11.0%
3932	-$5	2-6-8-J	DS	4.1%	2.4%	6.9%	13.4%
4418	-$5	2-6-8-J	S	3.7%	2.3%	5.9%	11.9%
4930	-$7	2-6-8-J	NS	3.1%	2.2%	4.8%	10.0%
3667	-$4	2-6-8-Q	DS	4.2%	2.5%	7.2%	13.9%
4331	-$5	2-6-8-Q	S	3.8%	2.4%	6.3%	12.4%
4903	-$7	2-6-8-Q	NS	3.2%	2.3%	5.0%	10.5%
3586	-$4	2-6-8-K	DS	4.5%	2.5%	7.2%	14.1%
4249	-$5	2-6-8-K	S	4.0%	2.4%	6.1%	12.5%
4933	-$7	2-6-8-K	NS	3.2%	2.1%	4.6%	9.9%
2014	-$2	2-6-9-9	DS	3.8%	2.1%	7.7%	13.6%
2681	-$3	2-6-9-9	S	3.2%	2.0%	6.7%	11.9%
3251	-$4	2-6-9-9	NS	2.8%	1.8%	5.9%	10.5%
3525	-$4	2-6-9-10	DS	4.3%	2.0%	6.9%	13.2%
4330	-$5	2-6-9-10	S	3.8%	1.9%	6.1%	11.8%
4727	-$6	2-6-9-10	NS	3.3%	1.9%	5.1%	10.3%
3888	-$5	2-6-9-J	DS	3.8%	2.0%	7.1%	12.8%
4553	-$6	2-6-9-J	S	3.3%	1.9%	5.9%	11.1%
4963	-$7	2-6-9-J	NS	2.7%	1.7%	4.9%	9.3%
3794	-$4	2-6-9-Q	DS	3.9%	2.0%	7.3%	13.2%
4491	-$6	2-6-9-Q	S	3.4%	1.9%	6.3%	11.6%
4928	-$7	2-6-9-Q	NS	2.7%	1.8%	5.3%	9.7%
3721	-$4	2-6-9-K	DS	3.9%	2.0%	7.4%	13.4%

OMAHA HIGH-LOW 8 OR BETTER
5,278 HANDS 9 HANDED

HAND RANK	VALUE $4/$8	POCKET CARDS		HIGH %	LOW %	SCOOP %	PART OR ALL %
		HAND	SUITED				
4288	-$5	2-6-9-K	S	3.4%	2.0%	6.6%	12.0%
4990	-$7	2-6-9-K	NS	2.5%	1.8%	4.9%	9.2%
2293	-$3	2-6-10-10	DS	3.6%	2.1%	8.0%	13.7%
2975	-$3	2-6-10-10	S	3.0%	2.0%	7.0%	11.9%
3594	-$4	2-6-10-10	NS	2.4%	1.9%	6.1%	10.4%
3090	-$4	2-6-10-J	DS	3.7%	1.9%	7.9%	13.5%
4015	-$5	2-6-10-J	S	3.2%	1.9%	6.8%	11.9%
4595	-$6	2-6-10-J	NS	2.6%	1.8%	6.0%	10.4%
2854	-$3	2-6-10-Q	DS	3.8%	2.1%	8.2%	14.1%
3931	-$5	2-6-10-Q	S	3.2%	2.0%	7.2%	12.4%
4605	-$6	2-6-10-Q	NS	2.6%	1.8%	6.1%	10.6%
2839	-$3	2-6-10-K	DS	3.9%	2.1%	8.3%	14.3%
3920	-$5	2-6-10-K	S	3.3%	2.0%	7.4%	12.7%
4713	-$6	2-6-10-K	NS	2.4%	1.8%	5.9%	10.1%
2173	-$2	2-6-J-J	DS	3.5%	2.1%	8.8%	14.4%
2956	-$3	2-6-J-J	S	2.9%	1.9%	7.7%	12.5%
3787	-$4	2-6-J-J	NS	2.3%	1.8%	6.8%	11.0%
2718	-$3	2-6-J-Q	DS	3.6%	1.9%	8.4%	13.8%
3774	-$4	2-6-J-Q	S	3.0%	1.8%	7.3%	12.1%
4599	-$6	2-6-J-Q	NS	2.4%	1.7%	5.9%	9.9%
2788	-$3	2-6-J-K	DS	3.5%	1.9%	8.4%	13.8%
3795	-$4	2-6-J-K	S	3.0%	1.9%	7.3%	12.2%
4617	-$6	2-6-J-K	NS	2.2%	1.7%	5.8%	9.7%
1511	-$1	2-6-Q-Q	DS	4.0%	2.3%	10.8%	17.1%
2626	-$3	2-6-Q-Q	S	3.3%	2.1%	9.3%	14.7%
3624	-$4	2-6-Q-Q	NS	2.5%	2.0%	8.1%	12.6%
2276	-$3	2-6-Q-K	DS	3.8%	2.0%	8.9%	14.7%
3629	-$4	2-6-Q-K	S	3.1%	1.9%	7.6%	12.6%

OMAHA HIGH-LOW 8 OR BETTER
5,278 HANDS   9 HANDED

| HAND RANK | VALUE $4/$8 | POCKET CARDS | | HIGH % | LOW % | SCOOP % | PART OR ALL % |
		HAND	SUITED				
4600	-$6	2-6-Q-K	NS	2.3%	1.7%	6.0%	10.0%
892	$1	2-6-K-K	DS	5.0%	2.5%	13.3%	20.8%
2172	-$2	2-6-K-K	S	3.9%	2.0%	11.2%	17.1%
3968	-$5	2-6-K-K	NS	2.7%	1.9%	8.8%	13.5%
5203	-$9	2-7-7-7	S	1.7%	1.1%	2.4%	5.2%
5239	-$9	2-7-7-7	NS	1.4%	0.9%	1.5%	3.8%
3142	-$4	2-7-7-8	DS	4.9%	1.9%	6.8%	13.5%
3501	-$4	2-7-7-8	S	4.5%	1.7%	5.6%	11.8%
4382	-$5	2-7-7-8	NS	4.2%	1.6%	4.9%	10.7%
4117	-$5	2-7-7-9	DS	4.8%	1.3%	5.9%	12.1%
4492	-$6	2-7-7-9	S	4.2%	1.3%	4.8%	10.3%
4862	-$6	2-7-7-9	NS	3.8%	1.2%	4.1%	9.1%
4133	-$5	2-7-7-10	DS	4.3%	1.3%	6.0%	11.6%
4499	-$6	2-7-7-10	S	3.9%	1.2%	4.9%	9.9%
4875	-$6	2-7-7-10	NS	3.4%	1.1%	4.1%	8.6%
4319	-$5	2-7-7-J	DS	4.1%	1.3%	5.9%	11.3%
4686	-$6	2-7-7-J	S	3.6%	1.2%	4.8%	9.6%
4936	-$7	2-7-7-J	NS	3.0%	1.1%	4.0%	8.1%
4381	-$5	2-7-7-Q	DS	4.1%	1.3%	6.0%	11.3%
4763	-$6	2-7-7-Q	S	3.6%	1.2%	4.7%	9.5%
4979	-$7	2-7-7-Q	NS	2.9%	1.1%	3.7%	7.7%
4130	-$5	2-7-7-K	DS	4.5%	1.5%	6.4%	12.4%
4497	-$6	2-7-7-K	S	3.9%	1.3%	5.4%	10.5%
5010	-$7	2-7-7-K	NS	3.0%	1.1%	3.9%	8.0%
2792	-$3	2-7-8-8	DS	5.0%	1.8%	7.1%	13.9%
3761	-$4	2-7-8-8	S	4.6%	1.7%	5.9%	12.1%
4350	-$5	2-7-8-8	NS	4.1%	1.5%	5.1%	10.7%
3405	-$4	2-7-8-9	DS	4.9%	1.7%	6.9%	13.5%

OMAHA HIGH-LOW 8 OR BETTER
5,278 HANDS   9 HANDED

HAND RANK	VALUE $4/$8	POCKET CARDS		HIGH %	LOW %	SCOOP %	PART OR ALL %
		HAND	SUITED				
4282	-$5	2-7-8-9	S	4.5%	1.6%	5.8%	12.0%
4693	-$6	2-7-8-9	NS	4.1%	1.5%	5.0%	10.5%
3397	-$4	2-7-8-10	DS	4.5%	1.7%	6.9%	13.1%
4111	-$5	2-7-8-10	S	4.0%	1.6%	6.1%	11.7%
4567	-$6	2-7-8-10	NS	3.6%	1.5%	5.2%	10.3%
3702	-$4	2-7-8-J	DS	4.1%	1.7%	6.9%	12.6%
4217	-$5	2-7-8-J	S	3.7%	1.6%	6.0%	11.3%
4845	-$6	2-7-8-J	NS	3.1%	1.5%	5.0%	9.6%
4055	-$5	2-7-8-Q	DS	4.1%	1.7%	6.6%	12.4%
4519	-$6	2-7-8-Q	S	3.7%	1.6%	5.8%	11.1%
4980	-$7	2-7-8-Q	NS	3.0%	1.5%	4.6%	9.1%
3832	-$4	2-7-8-K	DS	4.5%	1.7%	7.1%	13.3%
4391	-$5	2-7-8-K	S	3.9%	1.7%	6.2%	11.8%
5011	-$7	2-7-8-K	NS	3.1%	1.5%	4.6%	9.2%
2523	-$3	2-7-9-9	DS	3.7%	1.2%	7.5%	12.5%
3150	-$4	2-7-9-9	S	3.2%	1.2%	6.6%	10.9%
3793	-$4	2-7-9-9	NS	2.7%	1.1%	5.8%	9.5%
3479	-$4	2-7-9-10	DS	4.4%	1.2%	7.0%	12.6%
4151	-$5	2-7-9-10	S	3.9%	1.2%	6.1%	11.2%
4583	-$6	2-7-9-10	NS	3.4%	1.0%	5.3%	9.7%
3842	-$4	2-7-9-J	DS	3.9%	1.2%	7.0%	12.1%
4437	-$5	2-7-9-J	S	3.4%	1.1%	6.0%	10.5%
4782	-$6	2-7-9-J	NS	2.9%	1.0%	5.2%	9.2%
4128	-$5	2-7-9-Q	DS	3.7%	1.2%	6.8%	11.8%
4594	-$6	2-7-9-Q	S	3.2%	1.1%	5.9%	10.1%
5023	-$7	2-7-9-Q	NS	2.4%	1.0%	4.7%	8.1%
4113	-$5	2-7-9-K	DS	4.0%	1.3%	7.2%	12.4%
4439	-$5	2-7-9-K	S	3.4%	1.3%	6.4%	11.1%

OMAHA HIGH-LOW 8 OR BETTER
5,278 HANDS   9 HANDED

HAND RANK	VALUE $4/$8	POCKET CARDS		HIGH %	LOW %	SCOOP %	PART OR ALL %
		HAND	SUITED				
4991	-$7	2-7-9-K	NS	2.5%	1.0%	4.9%	8.5%
2533	-$3	2-7-10-10	DS	3.6%	1.2%	8.0%	12.7%
3332	-$4	2-7-10-10	S	3.0%	1.3%	7.0%	11.2%
3878	-$5	2-7-10-10	NS	2.4%	1.1%	6.1%	9.7%
2688	-$3	2-7-10-J	DS	3.9%	1.2%	7.9%	13.0%
3675	-$4	2-7-10-J	S	3.3%	1.2%	7.0%	11.5%
4399	-$5	2-7-10-J	NS	2.7%	1.1%	6.1%	10.0%
3249	-$4	2-7-10-Q	DS	3.6%	1.2%	7.6%	12.5%
4093	-$5	2-7-10-Q	S	3.2%	1.1%	6.8%	11.1%
4778	-$6	2-7-10-Q	NS	2.4%	1.0%	5.5%	9.0%
2972	-$3	2-7-10-K	DS	3.9%	1.4%	8.2%	13.5%
3596	-$4	2-7-10-K	S	3.3%	1.2%	7.4%	12.0%
4735	-$6	2-7-10-K	NS	2.5%	1.1%	5.9%	9.4%
2199	-$2	2-7-J-J	DS	3.5%	1.3%	8.9%	13.6%
3179	-$4	2-7-J-J	S	2.9%	1.2%	7.7%	11.8%
3880	-$5	2-7-J-J	NS	2.2%	1.1%	6.8%	10.1%
3385	-$4	2-7-J-Q	DS	3.4%	1.2%	7.7%	12.3%
4140	-$5	2-7-J-Q	S	2.8%	1.1%	6.7%	10.5%
4808	-$6	2-7-J-Q	NS	2.1%	1.1%	5.5%	8.7%
2957	-$3	2-7-J-K	DS	3.7%	1.2%	8.3%	13.2%
3687	-$4	2-7-J-K	S	3.1%	1.2%	7.3%	11.7%
4712	-$6	2-7-J-K	NS	2.2%	1.1%	5.8%	9.0%
2159	-$2	2-7-Q-Q	DS	3.8%	1.5%	10.0%	15.3%
3411	-$4	2-7-Q-Q	S	3.0%	1.4%	8.5%	13.0%
4276	-$5	2-7-Q-Q	NS	2.3%	1.3%	7.6%	11.1%
3061	-$4	2-7-Q-K	DS	3.7%	1.3%	8.0%	13.0%
3922	-$5	2-7-Q-K	S	3.0%	1.2%	7.1%	11.2%
4765	-$6	2-7-Q-K	NS	2.0%	1.0%	5.6%	8.6%

OMAHA HIGH-LOW 8 OR BETTER
5,278 HANDS   9 HANDED

| HAND RANK | VALUE $4/$8 | POCKET CARDS | | HIGH % | LOW % | SCOOP % | PART OR ALL % |
		HAND	SUITED				
1289	-$1	2-7-K-K	DS	5.0%	1.7%	12.6%	19.3%
2068	-$2	2-7-K-K	S	3.7%	1.6%	11.2%	16.5%
3819	-$4	2-7-K-K	NS	2.7%	1.4%	9.7%	13.8%
5246	-$9	2-8-8-8	S	1.9%	0.7%	2.4%	4.9%
5258	-$9	2-8-8-8	NS	1.5%	0.6%	1.6%	3.7%
3903	-$5	2-8-8-9	DS	5.3%	1.0%	6.5%	12.7%
4471	-$5	2-8-8-9	S	4.7%	0.9%	5.4%	11.0%
4873	-$6	2-8-8-9	NS	4.3%	0.8%	4.5%	9.6%
3528	-$4	2-8-8-10	DS	4.9%	0.9%	6.8%	12.6%
4215	-$5	2-8-8-10	S	4.3%	0.8%	5.8%	10.9%
4711	-$6	2-8-8-10	NS	3.9%	0.8%	4.9%	9.6%
4092	-$5	2-8-8-J	DS	4.6%	0.9%	6.5%	12.0%
4490	-$6	2-8-8-J	S	4.0%	0.8%	5.5%	10.3%
4859	-$6	2-8-8-J	NS	3.5%	0.8%	4.7%	9.0%
4273	-$5	2-8-8-Q	DS	4.5%	1.0%	6.4%	11.8%
4668	-$6	2-8-8-Q	S	3.9%	0.8%	5.4%	10.1%
4996	-$7	2-8-8-Q	NS	3.3%	0.8%	4.4%	8.4%
4428	-$5	2-8-8-K	DS	4.6%	1.0%	6.2%	11.9%
4669	-$6	2-8-8-K	S	4.2%	0.9%	5.2%	10.3%
5025	-$7	2-8-8-K	NS	3.3%	0.8%	4.0%	8.0%
2675	-$3	2-8-9-9	DS	4.1%	0.9%	7.7%	12.7%
3359	-$4	2-8-9-9	S	3.5%	0.8%	6.9%	11.2%
4068	-$5	2-8-9-9	NS	2.9%	0.7%	6.2%	9.8%
2891	-$3	2-8-9-10	DS	4.9%	0.9%	7.5%	13.3%
3963	-$5	2-8-9-10	S	4.2%	0.9%	6.6%	11.7%
4494	-$6	2-8-9-10	NS	3.7%	0.8%	5.8%	10.3%
3546	-$4	2-8-9-J	DS	4.4%	0.9%	7.4%	12.6%
4114	-$5	2-8-9-J	S	3.9%	0.8%	6.5%	11.2%

OMAHA HIGH-LOW 8 OR BETTER
5,278 HANDS   9 HANDED

| HAND RANK | VALUE $4/$8 | POCKET CARDS | | HIGH % | LOW % | SCOOP % | PART OR ALL % |
		HAND	SUITED				
4667	-$6	2-8-9-J	NS	3.2%	0.8%	5.8%	9.7%
3825	-$4	2-8-9-Q	DS	4.2%	0.9%	7.2%	12.3%
4416	-$5	2-8-9-Q	S	3.7%	0.8%	6.4%	10.9%
4861	-$6	2-8-9-Q	NS	2.9%	0.7%	5.4%	9.1%
4037	-$5	2-8-9-K	DS	4.3%	0.9%	7.1%	12.3%
4421	-$5	2-8-9-K	S	3.7%	0.9%	6.4%	11.0%
5015	-$7	2-8-9-K	NS	2.7%	0.7%	4.9%	8.3%
2089	-$2	2-8-10-10	DS	3.9%	0.9%	8.6%	13.4%
2795	-$3	2-8-10-10	S	3.2%	0.8%	7.8%	11.8%
3543	-$4	2-8-10-10	NS	2.6%	0.8%	6.9%	10.4%
2233	-$2	2-8-10-J	DS	4.2%	0.9%	8.6%	13.7%
2879	-$3	2-8-10-J	S	3.8%	0.8%	7.8%	12.4%
3662	-$4	2-8-10-J	NS	3.1%	0.8%	7.0%	10.9%
2543	-$3	2-8-10-Q	DS	4.2%	0.9%	8.4%	13.5%
3471	-$4	2-8-10-Q	S	3.6%	0.9%	7.5%	11.9%
4361	-$5	2-8-10-Q	NS	2.8%	0.8%	6.5%	10.1%
3123	-$4	2-8-10-K	DS	4.2%	0.9%	8.0%	13.1%
3714	-$4	2-8-10-K	S	3.6%	0.9%	7.3%	11.8%
4635	-$6	2-8-10-K	NS	2.7%	0.8%	6.0%	9.5%
2224	-$2	2-8-J-J	DS	3.7%	1.0%	9.2%	13.8%
3083	-$4	2-8-J-J	S	3.0%	0.9%	8.2%	12.1%
3775	-$4	2-8-J-J	NS	2.3%	0.8%	7.3%	10.5%
1926	-$2	2-8-J-Q	DS	3.8%	0.9%	8.5%	13.1%
3403	-$4	2-8-J-Q	S	3.1%	0.8%	7.6%	11.6%
4301	-$5	2-8-J-Q	NS	2.5%	0.8%	6.5%	9.8%
3320	-$4	2-8-J-K	DS	3.9%	0.9%	8.0%	12.9%
3898	-$5	2-8-J-K	S	3.3%	0.9%	7.3%	11.5%
4700	-$6	2-8-J-K	NS	2.3%	0.8%	6.0%	9.2%

OMAHA HIGH-LOW 8 OR BETTER
5,278 HANDS   9 HANDED

HAND RANK	VALUE $4/$8	POCKET CARDS		HIGH %	LOW %	SCOOP %	PART OR ALL %
		HAND	SUITED				
1904	-$2	2-8-Q-Q	DS	4.0%	1.1%	10.4%	15.5%
2730	-$3	2-8-Q-Q	S	3.2%	1.0%	9.3%	13.5%
3725	-$4	2-8-Q-Q	NS	2.4%	0.9%	8.2%	11.5%
3326	-$4	2-8-Q-K	DS	3.9%	0.9%	7.9%	12.6%
4147	-$5	2-8-Q-K	S	3.1%	0.9%	6.9%	10.9%
4794	-$6	2-8-Q-K	NS	2.2%	0.7%	5.7%	8.6%
1485	-$1	2-8-K-K	DS	5.0%	1.3%	12.4%	18.7%
2695	-$3	2-8-K-K	S	3.8%	1.1%	10.9%	15.8%
4097	-$5	2-8-K-K	NS	2.7%	1.0%	9.6%	13.4%
5088	-$8	2-9-9-9	S	1.2%	0.0%	2.6%	3.8%
5085	-$8	2-9-9-9	NS	0.8%	0.0%	2.1%	2.9%
2960	-$3	2-9-9-10	DS	3.9%	0.0%	7.4%	11.2%
3201	-$4	2-9-9-10	S	3.3%	0.0%	6.7%	10.0%
3881	-$5	2-9-9-10	NS	3.0%	0.0%	6.0%	9.0%
2981	-$3	2-9-9-J	DS	3.4%	0.0%	7.6%	10.9%
3389	-$4	2-9-9-J	S	2.9%	0.0%	6.8%	9.6%
3893	-$5	2-9-9-J	NS	2.4%	0.0%	6.2%	8.6%
3093	-$4	2-9-9-Q	DS	3.3%	0.0%	7.6%	10.9%
3613	-$4	2-9-9-Q	S	2.6%	0.0%	6.8%	9.4%
4271	-$5	2-9-9-Q	NS	2.0%	0.0%	5.9%	7.9%
3372	-$4	2-9-9-K	DS	3.5%	0.0%	7.5%	11.0%
4208	-$5	2-9-9-K	S	2.0%	0.0%	6.0%	8.0%
4376	-$5	2-9-9-K	NS	1.9%	0.0%	5.6%	7.5%
2726	-$3	2-9-10-10	DS	4.0%	0.0%	7.6%	11.6%
3325	-$4	2-9-10-10	S	3.4%	0.0%	7.0%	10.4%
3757	-$4	2-9-10-10	NS	3.0%	0.0%	6.4%	9.3%
2094	-$2	2-9-10-J	DS	4.4%	0.0%	8.5%	13.0%
2761	-$3	2-9-10-J	S	3.8%	0.0%	8.0%	11.8%

OMAHA HIGH-LOW 8 OR BETTER
5,278 HANDS   9 HANDED

| HAND RANK | VALUE $4/$8 | POCKET CARDS | | HIGH % | LOW % | SCOOP % | PART OR ALL % |
		HAND	SUITED				
3518	-$4	2-9-10-J	NS	3.4%	0.0%	7.3%	10.7%
2360	-$3	2-9-10-Q	DS	4.1%	0.0%	8.5%	12.6%
3055	-$4	2-9-10-Q	S	3.6%	0.0%	7.9%	11.5%
3866	-$5	2-9-10-Q	NS	2.9%	0.0%	7.1%	10.0%
2828	-$3	2-9-10-K	DS	4.3%	0.0%	8.3%	12.6%
3159	-$4	2-9-10-K	S	3.7%	0.0%	7.9%	11.7%
4246	-$5	2-9-10-K	NS	2.7%	0.0%	6.7%	9.3%
2451	-$3	2-9-J-J	DS	3.8%	0.0%	8.5%	12.3%
3210	-$4	2-9-J-J	S	3.1%	0.0%	7.8%	11.0%
3806	-$4	2-9-J-J	NS	2.7%	0.0%	7.0%	9.6%
2298	-$3	2-9-J-Q	DS	3.6%	0.0%	8.5%	12.1%
3018	-$3	2-9-J-Q	S	3.0%	0.0%	7.9%	10.9%
3605	-$4	2-9-J-Q	NS	2.5%	0.0%	7.2%	9.6%
2568	-$3	2-9-J-K	DS	4.0%	0.0%	8.6%	12.6%
3427	-$4	2-9-J-K	S	3.2%	0.0%	7.9%	11.2%
4286	-$5	2-9-J-K	NS	2.2%	0.0%	6.8%	8.9%
2210	-$2	2-9-Q-Q	DS	4.0%	0.0%	9.8%	13.8%
3028	-$3	2-9-Q-Q	S	3.2%	0.0%	8.9%	12.1%
4098	-$5	2-9-Q-Q	NS	2.5%	0.0%	7.7%	10.2%
2614	-$3	2-9-Q-K	DS	3.8%	0.0%	8.6%	12.4%
3181	-$4	2-9-Q-K	S	2.9%	0.0%	8.0%	10.9%
4153	-$5	2-9-Q-K	NS	1.9%	0.0%	6.9%	8.8%
1900	-$2	2-9-K-K	DS	5.2%	0.0%	11.6%	16.8%
2567	-$3	2-9-K-K	S	3.8%	0.0%	10.8%	14.6%
3701	-$4	2-9-K-K	NS	2.7%	0.0%	9.7%	12.5%
5116	-$8	2-10-10-10	S	1.3%	0.0%	3.0%	4.3%
5124	-$8	2-10-10-10	NS	0.9%	0.0%	2.5%	3.4%

OMAHA HIGH-LOW 8 OR BETTER
5,278 HANDS 9 HANDED

| HAND RANK | VALUE $4/$8 | POCKET CARDS | | HIGH % | LOW % | SCOOP % | PART OR ALL % |
		HAND	SUITED				
1815	-$2	2-10-10-J	DS	4.1%	0.0%	9.2%	13.2%
2424	-$3	2-10-10-J	S	3.4%	0.0%	8.3%	11.8%
3030	-$3	2-10-10-J	NS	2.9%	0.0%	7.8%	10.7%
1943	-$2	2-10-10-Q	DS	3.8%	0.0%	9.5%	13.3%
2684	-$3	2-10-10-Q	S	3.2%	0.0%	8.5%	11.7%
3491	-$4	2-10-10-Q	NS	2.5%	0.0%	7.7%	10.2%
2103	-$2	2-10-10-K	DS	4.1%	0.0%	9.3%	13.4%
2999	-$3	2-10-10-K	S	3.3%	0.0%	8.3%	11.6%
3726	-$4	2-10-10-K	NS	2.3%	0.0%	7.4%	9.8%
1674	-$2	2-10-J-J	DS	4.1%	0.0%	9.5%	13.6%
2130	-$2	2-10-J-J	S	3.6%	0.0%	8.7%	12.3%
2781	-$3	2-10-J-J	NS	3.0%	0.0%	8.1%	11.1%
1274	-$1	2-10-J-Q	DS	4.3%	0.0%	10.0%	14.4%
1654	-$2	2-10-J-Q	S	3.7%	0.0%	9.6%	13.3%
2375	-$3	2-10-J-Q	NS	3.1%	0.0%	8.7%	11.8%
1402	-$1	2-10-J-K	DS	4.6%	0.0%	10.3%	14.8%
1734	-$2	2-10-J-K	S	3.8%	0.0%	9.7%	13.6%
2498	-$3	2-10-J-K	NS	2.9%	0.0%	8.7%	11.6%
1488	-$1	2-10-Q-Q	DS	4.5%	0.0%	10.8%	15.3%
2032	-$2	2-10-Q-Q	S	3.6%	0.0%	10.1%	13.7%
2894	-$3	2-10-Q-Q	NS	2.8%	0.0%	9.0%	11.8%
1432	-$1	2-10-Q-K	DS	4.3%	0.0%	10.1%	14.4%
1858	-$2	2-10-Q-K	S	3.6%	0.0%	9.5%	13.1%
2717	-$3	2-10-Q-K	NS	2.6%	0.0%	8.5%	11.1%
1198	-$0	2-10-K-K	DS	5.6%	0.0%	12.8%	18.4%
2119	-$2	2-10-K-K	S	4.6%	0.0%	11.8%	16.4%
2786	-$3	2-10-K-K	NS	3.2%	0.0%	10.3%	13.5%
5178	-$9	2-J-J-J	S	1.6%	0.0%	3.8%	5.4%

OMAHA HIGH-LOW 8 OR BETTER
5,278 HANDS   9 HANDED

| HAND RANK | VALUE $4/$8 | POCKET CARDS | | HIGH % | LOW % | SCOOP % | PART OR ALL % |
		HAND	SUITED				
5232	-$9	2-J-J-J	NS	1.1%	0.0%	3.0%	4.1%
1755	-$2	2-J-J-Q	DS	4.2%	0.0%	10.1%	14.3%
2337	-$3	2-J-J-Q	S	3.4%	0.0%	9.4%	12.8%
3006	-$3	2-J-J-Q	NS	2.9%	0.0%	8.8%	11.7%
1912	-$2	2-J-J-K	DS	4.5%	0.0%	10.3%	14.8%
2576	-$3	2-J-J-K	S	3.6%	0.0%	9.1%	12.7%
3529	-$4	2-J-J-K	NS	2.6%	0.0%	8.6%	11.2%
1283	-$1	2-J-Q-Q	DS	4.4%	0.0%	11.2%	15.6%
2077	-$2	2-J-Q-Q	S	3.6%	0.0%	9.9%	13.5%
2903	-$3	2-J-Q-Q	NS	2.9%	0.0%	9.0%	11.8%
1333	-$1	2-J-Q-K	DS	4.5%	0.0%	10.2%	14.6%
1690	-$2	2-J-Q-K	S	3.7%	0.0%	9.7%	13.4%
2404	-$3	2-J-Q-K	NS	2.7%	0.0%	8.7%	11.4%
1107	-$0	2-J-K-K	DS	5.6%	0.0%	12.7%	18.3%
1950	-$2	2-J-K-K	S	4.2%	0.0%	10.6%	14.8%
2741	-$3	2-J-K-K	NS	3.0%	0.0%	10.5%	13.5%
5213	-$9	2-Q-Q-Q	S	2.0%	0.0%	5.1%	7.1%
5256	-$9	2-Q-Q-Q	NS	1.3%	0.0%	4.3%	5.6%
1550	-$1	2-Q-Q-K	DS	5.1%	0.0%	11.7%	16.8%
2002	-$2	2-Q-Q-K	S	4.0%	0.0%	10.8%	14.8%
2939	-$3	2-Q-Q-K	NS	2.9%	0.0%	10.1%	13.1%
1101	-$0	2-Q-K-K	DS	5.5%	0.0%	12.7%	18.2%
1640	-$1	2-Q-K-K	S	4.3%	0.0%	11.6%	15.9%
2373	-$3	2-Q-K-K	NS	3.1%	0.0%	10.6%	13.8%
5160	-$9	2-K-K-K	S	2.8%	0.0%	7.4%	10.2%
5261	-$10	2-K-K-K	NS	1.7%	0.0%	6.4%	8.1%
5138	-$8	3-3-3-3	NS	0.0%	0.0%	0.1%	0.1%
4354	-$5	3-3-3-4	S	2.1%	0.0%	4.4%	6.5%

OMAHA HIGH-LOW 8 OR BETTER
5,278 HANDS   9 HANDED

HAND RANK	VALUE $4/$8	POCKET CARDS		HIGH %	LOW %	SCOOP %	PART OR ALL %
		HAND	SUITED				
4704	-$6	3-3-3-4	NS	1.8%	0.0%	3.2%	5.0%
4633	-$6	3-3-3-5	S	2.1%	0.0%	4.3%	6.4%
4784	-$6	3-3-3-5	NS	1.9%	0.0%	3.3%	5.3%
5005	-$7	3-3-3-6	S	2.1%	0.0%	3.3%	5.4%
5050	-$8	3-3-3-6	NS	1.8%	0.0%	2.3%	4.0%
5150	-$8	3-3-3-7	S	1.9%	0.0%	2.4%	4.4%
5236	-$9	3-3-3-7	NS	1.6%	0.0%	1.4%	3.1%
5242	-$9	3-3-3-8	S	1.7%	0.0%	2.2%	3.9%
5254	-$9	3-3-3-8	NS	1.3%	0.0%	1.3%	2.6%
5118	-$8	3-3-3-9	S	1.5%	0.0%	2.0%	3.4%
5135	-$8	3-3-3-9	NS	1.1%	0.0%	1.2%	2.3%
5214	-$9	3-3-3-10	S	1.5%	0.0%	2.0%	3.5%
5129	-$8	3-3-3-10	NS	1.1%	0.0%	1.3%	2.4%
5128	-$8	3-3-3-J	S	1.6%	0.0%	2.2%	3.8%
5163	-$9	3-3-3-J	NS	1.1%	0.0%	1.4%	2.5%
5130	-$8	3-3-3-Q	S	1.7%	0.0%	2.6%	4.3%
5192	-$9	3-3-3-Q	NS	1.1%	0.0%	1.5%	2.6%
5141	-$8	3-3-3-K	S	2.0%	0.0%	3.1%	5.0%
5202	-$9	3-3-3-K	NS	1.2%	0.0%	1.7%	2.9%
1106	-$0	3-3-4-4	DS	5.4%	4.1%	9.2%	18.6%
1476	-$1	3-3-4-4	S	5.0%	4.1%	8.1%	17.2%
1855	-$2	3-3-4-4	NS	4.9%	3.9%	6.8%	15.6%
929	$1	3-3-4-5	DS	4.4%	4.3%	9.5%	18.2%
1120	-$0	3-3-4-5	S	4.2%	4.3%	8.4%	16.9%
1531	-$1	3-3-4-5	NS	3.2%	4.5%	6.1%	13.8%
1171	-$0	3-3-4-6	DS	4.5%	4.7%	8.6%	17.7%
1546	-$1	3-3-4-6	S	4.3%	4.1%	7.3%	15.7%
1856	-$2	3-3-4-6	NS	4.9%	3.9%	6.8%	15.6%

OMAHA HIGH-LOW 8 OR BETTER
5,278 HANDS   9 HANDED

HAND RANK	VALUE $4/$8	POCKET CARDS		HIGH %	LOW %	SCOOP %	PART OR ALL %
		HAND	SUITED				
1665	-$2	3-3-4-7	DS	4.5%	4.2%	7.7%	16.4%
2235	-$3	3-3-4-7	S	4.2%	4.1%	6.4%	14.7%
2893	-$3	3-3-4-7	NS	3.8%	4.0%	5.5%	13.4%
2151	-$2	3-3-4-8	DS	4.3%	3.9%	7.2%	15.5%
2825	-$3	3-3-4-8	S	3.9%	3.8%	6.1%	13.8%
3612	-$4	3-3-4-8	NS	3.6%	3.7%	5.1%	12.4%
2663	-$3	3-3-4-9	DS	4.1%	3.6%	7.1%	14.8%
3383	-$4	3-3-4-9	S	3.7%	3.5%	5.7%	13.0%
4023	-$5	3-3-4-9	NS	3.4%	3.5%	4.9%	11.7%
2539	-$3	3-3-4-10	DS	4.2%	3.7%	7.2%	15.1%
3304	-$4	3-3-4-10	S	3.9%	3.6%	6.2%	13.6%
4121	-$5	3-3-4-10	NS	3.4%	3.6%	5.0%	12.0%
2256	-$3	3-3-4-J	DS	4.3%	3.7%	7.7%	15.6%
3051	-$3	3-3-4-J	S	4.1%	3.5%	6.4%	14.1%
4027	-$5	3-3-4-J	NS	3.4%	3.6%	5.2%	12.1%
2131	-$2	3-3-4-Q	DS	4.4%	3.7%	7.9%	16.0%
3062	-$4	3-3-4-Q	S	4.1%	3.7%	6.7%	14.4%
4061	-$5	3-3-4-Q	NS	3.5%	3.6%	5.2%	12.3%
1939	-$2	3-3-4-K	DS	4.7%	3.8%	8.4%	16.8%
2374	-$3	3-3-4-K	S	4.3%	3.8%	7.5%	15.6%
3906	-$5	3-3-4-K	NS	3.6%	3.7%	5.6%	12.9%
5108	-$8	3-3-5-5	DS	5.5%	3.2%	8.9%	17.7%
1652	-$1	3-3-5-5	S	5.2%	3.2%	8.0%	16.4%
2177	-$2	3-3-5-5	NS	4.9%	3.0%	6.7%	14.7%
1260	-$1	3-3-5-6	DS	4.8%	4.2%	8.6%	17.7%
1789	-$2	3-3-5-6	S	4.5%	4.1%	7.5%	16.1%
2186	-$2	3-3-5-6	NS	4.3%	4.1%	6.4%	14.8%
1650	-$1	3-3-5-7	DS	4.8%	3.7%	8.0%	16.5%

OMAHA HIGH-LOW 8 OR BETTER
5,278 HANDS   9 HANDED

| HAND RANK | VALUE $4/$8 | POCKET CARDS | | HIGH % | LOW % | SCOOP % | PART OR ALL % |
		HAND	SUITED				
2384	-$3	3-3-5-7	S	4.5%	3.6%	6.8%	14.9%
3038	-$3	3-3-5-7	NS	4.2%	3.6%	5.7%	13.5%
2455	-$3	3-3-5-8	DS	4.7%	3.5%	7.1%	15.3%
3216	-$4	3-3-5-8	S	4.2%	3.3%	6.3%	13.8%
3706	-$4	3-3-5-8	NS	3.9%	3.2%	5.3%	12.5%
2793	-$3	3-3-5-9	DS	4.6%	3.1%	7.2%	14.9%
3472	-$4	3-3-5-9	S	4.3%	3.0%	6.1%	13.3%
4221	-$5	3-3-5-9	NS	3.8%	2.9%	4.8%	11.6%
2969	-$3	3-3-5-10	DS	4.3%	3.0%	7.1%	14.4%
3683	-$4	3-3-5-10	S	3.9%	2.9%	6.0%	12.8%
4219	-$5	3-3-5-10	NS	3.4%	2.9%	4.9%	11.2%
2817	-$3	3-3-5-J	DS	4.4%	3.0%	7.2%	14.6%
3739	-$4	3-3-5-J	S	4.0%	2.8%	6.1%	12.9%
4189	-$5	3-3-5-J	NS	3.5%	2.8%	5.3%	11.6%
2575	-$3	3-3-5-Q	DS	4.4%	3.0%	7.7%	15.2%
3279	-$4	3-3-5-Q	S	4.1%	2.9%	6.6%	13.7%
4142	-$5	3-3-5-Q	NS	3.6%	2.9%	5.4%	11.9%
2040	-$2	3-3-5-K	DS	4.7%	3.1%	8.5%	16.4%
2809	-$3	3-3-5-K	S	4.4%	3.0%	7.4%	14.8%
4227	-$5	3-3-5-K	NS	3.7%	2.9%	5.6%	12.1%
2191	-$2	3-3-6-6	DS	5.5%	2.3%	7.7%	15.5%
2693	-$3	3-3-6-6	S	5.2%	2.3%	6.7%	14.3%
3388	-$4	3-3-6-6	NS	4.9%	2.1%	5.6%	12.7%
2534	-$3	3-3-6-7	DS	5.0%	3.1%	7.1%	15.2%
3306	-$4	3-3-6-7	S	4.6%	2.9%	6.1%	13.6%
3990	-$5	3-3-6-7	NS	4.3%	2.8%	5.0%	12.1%
3175	-$4	3-3-6-8	DS	4.8%	2.8%	6.8%	14.3%
3975	-$5	3-3-6-8	S	4.4%	2.6%	5.5%	12.6%

OMAHA HIGH-LOW 8 OR BETTER
5,278 HANDS   9 HANDED

HAND RANK	VALUE $4/$8	POCKET CARDS		HIGH %	LOW %	SCOOP %	PART OR ALL %
		HAND	SUITED				
4498	-$6	3-3-6-8	NS	4.0%	2.5%	4.6%	11.1%
3857	-$4	3-3-6-9	DS	4.9%	2.4%	6.3%	13.6%
4379	-$5	3-3-6-9	S	4.4%	2.3%	5.2%	11.9%
4751	-$6	3-3-6-9	NS	4.0%	2.2%	4.2%	10.4%
4120	-$5	3-3-6-10	DS	4.5%	2.3%	6.1%	13.0%
4532	-$6	3-3-6-10	S	4.1%	2.2%	5.2%	11.5%
4860	-$6	3-3-6-10	NS	3.6%	2.1%	4.1%	9.8%
4069	-$5	3-3-6-J	DS	4.2%	2.2%	6.2%	12.6%
4573	-$6	3-3-6-J	S	3.8%	2.1%	5.3%	11.1%
4912	-$7	3-3-6-J	NS	3.4%	1.9%	4.0%	9.3%
3847	-$4	3-3-6-Q	DS	4.3%	2.2%	6.5%	13.1%
4411	-$5	3-3-6-Q	S	4.0%	2.1%	5.6%	11.7%
4893	-$7	3-3-6-Q	NS	4.0%	2.0%	4.3%	10.3%
3309	-$4	3-3-6-K	DS	4.7%	2.4%	7.2%	14.3%
4166	-$5	3-3-6-K	S	4.3%	2.3%	6.2%	12.8%
4804	-$6	3-3-6-K	NS	3.5%	2.1%	4.6%	10.1%
3243	-$4	3-3-7-7	DS	5.4%	1.6%	6.8%	13.8%
3752	-$4	3-3-7-7	S	5.1%	1.4%	5.8%	12.3%
4201	-$5	3-3-7-7	NS	4.8%	1.3%	4.9%	11.0%
4125	-$5	3-3-7-8	DS	4.7%	2.0%	6.4%	13.1%
4619	-$6	3-3-7-8	S	4.3%	1.9%	5.4%	11.5%
4906	-$7	3-3-7-8	NS	3.9%	1.7%	4.4%	10.0%
4436	-$5	3-3-7-9	DS	4.9%	1.6%	5.8%	12.4%
4844	-$6	3-3-7-9	S	4.5%	1.5%	4.9%	10.9%
4959	-$7	3-3-7-9	NS	4.0%	1.4%	4.0%	9.4%
4475	-$5	3-3-7-10	DS	4.5%	1.5%	5.9%	12.0%
4819	-$6	3-3-7-10	S	4.2%	1.5%	4.9%	10.5%
4986	-$7	3-3-7-10	NS	3.6%	1.4%	4.1%	9.1%

OMAHA HIGH-LOW 8 OR BETTER
5,278 HANDS   9 HANDED

| HAND RANK | VALUE $4/$8 | POCKET CARDS | | HIGH % | LOW % | SCOOP % | PART OR ALL % |
		HAND	SUITED				
4631	-$6	3-3-7-J	DS	4.2%	1.5%	5.8%	11.5%
4854	-$6	3-3-7-J	S	3.9%	1.4%	4.8%	10.1%
5039	-$7	3-3-7-J	NS	3.3%	1.3%	3.7%	8.3%
4523	-$6	3-3-7-Q	DS	4.3%	1.5%	5.9%	11.7%
4884	-$6	3-3-7-Q	S	3.8%	1.4%	4.7%	9.9%
5048	-$8	3-3-7-Q	NS	3.2%	1.2%	3.6%	8.0%
4284	-$5	3-3-7-K	DS	4.5%	1.7%	6.4%	12.6%
4708	-$6	3-3-7-K	S	4.1%	1.5%	5.5%	11.1%
5027	-$7	3-3-7-K	NS	3.3%	1.3%	4.0%	8.5%
3691	-$4	3-3-8-8	DS	5.3%	1.2%	6.7%	13.1%
4290	-$5	3-3-8-8	S	4.9%	1.0%	5.5%	11.4%
4558	-$6	3-3-8-8	NS	4.4%	0.9%	4.8%	10.1%
4741	-$6	3-3-8-9	DS	4.9%	1.1%	5.9%	11.9%
4982	-$7	3-3-8-9	S	4.4%	1.0%	4.9%	10.3%
5060	-$8	3-3-8-9	NS	3.8%	0.9%	4.2%	9.0%
4410	-$5	3-3-8-10	DS	4.4%	1.1%	6.3%	11.9%
4876	-$6	3-3-8-10	S	4.0%	1.0%	5.3%	10.2%
4976	-$7	3-3-8-10	NS	3.4%	0.9%	4.5%	8.9%
4514	-$6	3-3-8-J	DS	4.0%	1.0%	6.1%	11.0%
4874	-$6	3-3-8-J	S	3.7%	1.0%	5.3%	10.0%
5036	-$7	3-3-8-J	NS	3.1%	0.9%	4.3%	8.3%
4658	-$6	3-3-8-Q	DS	4.1%	1.1%	6.1%	11.3%
4964	-$7	3-3-8-Q	S	3.6%	1.0%	5.1%	9.7%
5057	-$8	3-3-8-Q	NS	2.9%	0.9%	4.1%	7.9%
4682	-$6	3-3-8-K	DS	4.3%	1.1%	6.2%	11.6%
4953	-$7	3-3-8-K	S	3.9%	1.0%	5.2%	10.1%
5089	-$8	3-3-8-K	NS	2.9%	0.8%	3.7%	7.4%
3077	-$4	3-3-9-9	DS	4.2%	0.0%	7.0%	11.2%

OMAHA HIGH-LOW 8 OR BETTER
5,278 HANDS   9 HANDED

HAND RANK	VALUE $4/$8	POCKET CARDS HAND	SUITED	HIGH %	LOW %	SCOOP %	PART OR ALL %
3322	-$4	3-3-9-9	S	3.7%	0.0%	6.3%	10.0%
3580	-$4	3-3-9-9	NS	3.2%	0.0%	5.6%	8.8%
4502	-$6	3-3-9-10	DS	4.4%	0.0%	5.8%	10.2%
4747	-$6	3-3-9-10	S	4.0%	0.0%	5.1%	9.0%
4939	-$7	3-3-9-10	NS	3.5%	0.0%	4.2%	7.7%
4458	-$5	3-3-9-J	DS	4.0%	0.0%	6.0%	10.0%
4755	-$6	3-3-9-J	S	3.5%	0.0%	5.2%	8.6%
4957	-$7	3-3-9-J	NS	3.0%	0.0%	4.4%	7.3%
4555	-$6	3-3-9-Q	DS	3.8%	0.0%	6.0%	9.8%
4837	-$6	3-3-9-Q	S	3.4%	0.0%	5.2%	8.6%
4962	-$7	3-3-9-Q	NS	2.8%	0.0%	4.3%	7.0%
4539	-$6	3-3-9-K	DS	4.1%	0.0%	6.1%	10.3%
4781	-$6	3-3-9-K	S	3.5%	0.0%	5.4%	8.9%
4994	-$7	3-3-9-K	NS	2.6%	0.0%	4.0%	6.5%
2971	-$3	3-3-10-10	DS	4.4%	0.0%	7.4%	11.8%
3414	-$4	3-3-10-10	S	4.0%	0.0%	6.7%	10.6%
3749	-$4	3-3-10-10	NS	3.4%	0.0%	6.0%	9.5%
3809	-$4	3-3-10-J	DS	4.4%	0.0%	6.9%	11.3%
4254	-$5	3-3-10-J	S	3.9%	0.0%	6.1%	10.0%
4585	-$6	3-3-10-J	NS	3.5%	0.0%	5.4%	8.9%
3835	-$4	3-3-10-Q	DS	4.2%	0.0%	7.0%	11.3%
4264	-$5	3-3-10-Q	S	3.7%	0.0%	6.3%	10.1%
4756	-$6	3-3-10-Q	NS	3.1%	0.0%	5.3%	8.4%
3952	-$5	3-3-10-K	DS	4.4%	0.0%	7.2%	11.5%
4280	-$5	3-3-10-K	S	4.0%	0.0%	6.5%	10.5%
4818	-$6	3-3-10-K	NS	3.0%	0.0%	5.0%	8.0%
2649	-$3	3-3-J-J	DS	4.7%	0.0%	8.6%	13.2%
3209	-$4	3-3-J-J	S	4.2%	0.0%	7.6%	11.8%

OMAHA HIGH-LOW 8 OR BETTER
5,278 HANDS   9 HANDED

| HAND RANK | VALUE $4/$8 | POCKET CARDS | | HIGH % | LOW % | SCOOP % | PART OR ALL % |
		HAND	SUITED				
3940	-$5	3-3-J-J	NS	3.7%	0.0%	6.7%	10.4%
3677	-$4	3-3-J-Q	DS	4.3%	0.0%	7.3%	11.6%
4154	-$5	3-3-J-Q	S	3.9%	0.0%	6.5%	10.4%
4724	-$6	3-3-J-Q	NS	3.2%	0.0%	5.4%	8.6%
3821	-$4	3-3-J-K	DS	4.5%	0.0%	7.4%	12.0%
4281	-$5	3-3-J-K	S	4.0%	0.0%	6.6%	10.6%
4801	-$6	3-3-J-K	NS	3.0%	0.0%	5.2%	8.2%
2153	-$2	3-3-Q-Q	DS	5.4%	0.0%	10.2%	15.6%
3151	-$4	3-3-Q-Q	S	4.6%	0.0%	9.1%	13.8%
3916	-$5	3-3-Q-Q	NS	4.0%	0.0%	8.1%	12.1%
1988	-$2	3-3-Q-K	DS	5.5%	0.0%	10.4%	15.9%
4197	-$5	3-3-Q-K	S	4.1%	0.0%	6.9%	11.0%
4630	-$6	3-3-Q-K	NS	3.2%	0.0%	5.7%	8.8%
1369	-$1	3-3-K-K	DS	6.7%	0.0%	13.0%	19.7%
2549	-$3	3-3-K-K	S	4.8%	0.0%	9.8%	14.6%
4141	-$5	3-3-K-K	NS	4.4%	0.0%	8.8%	13.2%
4451	-$5	3-4-4-4	S	2.1%	3.9%	4.3%	10.3%
4701	-$6	3-4-4-4	NS	1.8%	3.8%	3.3%	8.9%
907	$1	3-4-4-5	DS	4.5%	5.2%	9.6%	19.3%
1256	-$1	3-4-4-5	S	3.6%	4.2%	6.6%	14.5%
1827	-$2	3-4-4-5	NS	3.4%	4.4%	5.9%	13.7%
1074	-$0	3-4-4-6	DS	4.6%	4.7%	8.6%	17.9%
1609	-$1	3-4-4-6	S	4.3%	4.5%	7.1%	15.9%
2009	-$2	3-4-4-6	NS	4.0%	4.4%	6.4%	14.7%
1619	-$1	3-4-4-7	DS	4.5%	4.2%	7.7%	16.4%
2135	-$2	3-4-4-7	S	4.2%	4.1%	6.4%	14.7%
2882	-$3	3-4-4-7	NS	3.9%	4.0%	5.5%	13.4%
2167	-$2	3-4-4-8	DS	4.3%	3.9%	7.2%	15.3%

OMAHA HIGH-LOW 8 OR BETTER
5,278 HANDS   9 HANDED

HAND RANK	VALUE $4/$8	POCKET CARDS HAND	POCKET CARDS SUITED	HIGH %	LOW %	SCOOP %	PART OR ALL %
2940	-$3	3-4-4-8	S	3.9%	3.8%	5.9%	13.6%
3778	-$4	3-4-4-8	NS	3.6%	3.7%	4.9%	12.3%
2729	-$3	3-4-4-9	DS	4.2%	3.6%	7.0%	14.7%
3368	-$4	3-4-4-9	S	3.7%	3.4%	5.9%	13.0%
4089	-$5	3-4-4-9	NS	3.4%	3.5%	4.9%	11.7%
2723	-$3	3-4-4-10	DS	4.2%	3.7%	7.1%	15.0%
3254	-$4	3-4-4-10	S	3.8%	3.5%	6.1%	13.4%
4145	-$5	3-4-4-10	NS	3.4%	3.5%	4.9%	11.8%
2315	-$3	3-4-4-J	DS	4.2%	3.6%	7.6%	15.4%
3021	-$3	3-4-4-J	S	3.9%	3.6%	6.3%	13.7%
4143	-$5	3-4-4-J	NS	3.4%	3.5%	5.1%	12.0%
2143	-$2	3-4-4-Q	DS	4.4%	3.7%	7.8%	15.9%
2897	-$3	3-4-4-Q	S	4.0%	3.6%	6.6%	14.2%
4056	-$5	3-4-4-Q	NS	3.4%	3.5%	5.4%	12.4%
1888	-$2	3-4-4-K	DS	4.4%	3.5%	7.8%	15.7%
2264	-$3	3-4-4-K	S	4.3%	3.5%	6.2%	13.9%
4047	-$5	3-4-4-K	NS	3.6%	3.6%	5.5%	12.7%
917	$1	3-4-5-5	DS	4.7%	5.0%	9.5%	19.2%
1173	-$0	3-4-5-5	S	4.5%	5.2%	8.7%	18.3%
1617	-$1	3-4-5-5	NS	4.1%	5.0%	7.2%	16.2%
869	$1	3-4-5-6	DS	5.2%	5.5%	9.5%	20.2%
1147	-$0	3-4-5-6	S	5.0%	5.4%	8.4%	18.8%
1385	-$1	3-4-5-6	NS	3.9%	4.7%	6.3%	14.8%
1012	$0	3-4-5-7	DS	5.1%	5.1%	9.1%	19.4%
1452	-$1	3-4-5-7	S	4.8%	5.1%	7.8%	17.7%
1747	-$2	3-4-5-7	NS	3.6%	4.2%	5.4%	13.2%
1410	-$1	3-4-5-8	DS	4.6%	5.0%	8.5%	18.1%
1778	-$2	3-4-5-8	S	3.8%	4.5%	6.6%	14.9%

OMAHA HIGH-LOW 8 OR BETTER
5,278 HANDS   9 HANDED

| HAND RANK | VALUE $4/$8 | POCKET CARDS | | HIGH % | LOW % | SCOOP % | PART OR ALL % |
		HAND	SUITED				
2461	-$3	3-4-5-8	NS	3.3%	4.1%	4.8%	12.1%
1529	-$1	3-4-5-9	DS	4.3%	5.1%	8.9%	18.2%
2133	-$2	3-4-5-9	S	3.9%	4.8%	7.4%	16.1%
3187	-$4	3-4-5-9	NS	3.4%	4.9%	6.2%	14.5%
1663	-$2	3-4-5-10	DS	4.4%	5.1%	9.0%	18.5%
2267	-$3	3-4-5-10	S	3.7%	5.1%	7.6%	16.4%
3136	-$4	3-4-5-10	NS	3.4%	5.0%	6.5%	14.8%
1532	-$1	3-4-5-J	DS	4.3%	5.1%	9.4%	18.9%
1978	-$2	3-4-5-J	S	3.8%	5.1%	7.9%	16.8%
3017	-$3	3-4-5-J	NS	3.3%	5.0%	6.7%	15.1%
1298	-$1	3-4-5-Q	DS	4.5%	5.1%	9.7%	19.4%
1741	-$2	3-4-5-Q	S	4.0%	5.1%	8.4%	17.5%
2943	-$3	3-4-5-Q	NS	3.5%	5.1%	6.9%	15.4%
1083	-$0	3-4-5-K	DS	4.8%	5.3%	10.4%	20.5%
2174	-$2	3-4-5-K	S	4.4%	5.1%	8.6%	18.2%
2425	-$3	3-4-5-K	NS	2.9%	4.5%	6.3%	13.7%
1108	-$0	3-4-6-6	DS	4.8%	4.2%	8.3%	17.3%
1394	-$1	3-4-6-6	S	4.5%	4.1%	7.4%	16.0%
1885	-$2	3-4-6-6	NS	4.2%	4.0%	6.2%	14.5%
1216	-$1	3-4-6-7	DS	5.1%	4.7%	7.7%	17.5%
1668	-$2	3-4-6-7	S	5.0%	4.6%	6.6%	16.2%
2308	-$3	3-4-6-7	NS	4.6%	4.5%	5.5%	14.6%
1698	-$2	3-4-6-8	DS	4.8%	4.5%	7.3%	16.6%
2333	-$3	3-4-6-8	S	4.5%	4.5%	6.3%	15.2%
3426	-$4	3-4-6-8	NS	4.0%	4.3%	5.1%	13.4%
2239	-$3	3-4-6-9	DS	4.7%	4.4%	7.3%	16.4%
2716	-$3	3-4-6-9	S	4.1%	4.3%	6.3%	14.8%
3530	-$4	3-4-6-9	NS	3.8%	4.3%	5.4%	13.4%

OMAHA HIGH-LOW 8 OR BETTER
5,278 HANDS   9 HANDED

| HAND RANK | VALUE $4/$8 | POCKET CARDS | | HIGH % | LOW % | SCOOP % | PART OR ALL % |
		HAND	SUITED				
2067	-$2	3-4-6-10	DS	4.4%	4.5%	7.5%	16.5%
2858	-$3	3-4-6-10	S	4.0%	4.5%	6.6%	15.1%
3759	-$4	3-4-6-10	NS	3.6%	4.4%	5.5%	13.5%
2154	-$2	3-4-6-J	DS	4.1%	4.3%	7.6%	16.1%
2846	-$3	3-4-6-J	S	3.8%	4.2%	6.6%	14.6%
3950	-$5	3-4-6-J	NS	3.3%	4.1%	5.3%	12.8%
1757	-$2	3-4-6-Q	DS	4.4%	4.3%	8.1%	16.8%
2540	-$3	3-4-6-Q	S	4.0%	4.2%	7.0%	15.3%
3692	-$4	3-4-6-Q	NS	3.4%	4.1%	5.7%	13.2%
1480	-$1	3-4-6-K	DS	4.6%	4.5%	8.7%	17.8%
2079	-$2	3-4-6-K	S	4.2%	4.3%	7.6%	16.2%
3577	-$4	3-4-6-K	NS	3.5%	4.3%	5.8%	13.6%
1281	-$1	3-4-7-7	DS	4.7%	3.6%	7.8%	16.2%
1803	-$2	3-4-7-7	S	4.5%	3.5%	6.6%	14.6%
2508	-$3	3-4-7-7	NS	4.0%	3.4%	5.6%	13.0%
2169	-$2	3-4-7-8	DS	4.5%	4.0%	7.3%	15.8%
2929	-$3	3-4-7-8	S	4.2%	4.0%	6.2%	14.3%
3991	-$5	3-4-7-8	NS	3.9%	3.9%	5.0%	12.8%
2423	-$3	3-4-7-9	DS	4.4%	4.0%	7.1%	15.4%
3260	-$4	3-4-7-9	S	4.0%	3.8%	6.2%	14.0%
4115	-$5	3-4-7-9	NS	3.5%	3.8%	5.1%	12.4%
2316	-$3	3-4-7-10	DS	4.4%	4.0%	7.4%	15.9%
3092	-$4	3-4-7-10	S	4.1%	4.1%	6.3%	14.5%
4100	-$5	3-4-7-10	NS	3.5%	3.9%	5.3%	12.7%
2481	-$3	3-4-7-J	DS	4.2%	3.9%	7.4%	15.4%
3495	-$4	3-4-7-J	S	3.7%	3.9%	6.2%	13.8%
4372	-$5	3-4-7-J	NS	3.2%	3.8%	5.1%	12.1%
2519	-$3	3-4-7-Q	DS	4.0%	3.7%	7.4%	15.1%

OMAHA HIGH-LOW 8 OR BETTER
5,278 HANDS   9 HANDED

| HAND RANK | VALUE $4/$8 | POCKET CARDS | | HIGH % | LOW % | SCOOP % | PART OR ALL % |
		HAND	SUITED				
3343	-$4	3-4-7-Q	S	3.6%	3.7%	6.3%	13.6%
4419	-$5	3-4-7-Q	NS	3.1%	3.6%	4.8%	11.5%
2076	-$2	3-4-7-K	DS	4.3%	3.9%	8.0%	16.2%
2772	-$3	3-4-7-K	S	4.0%	3.7%	7.0%	14.7%
4297	-$5	3-4-7-K	NS	3.2%	3.7%	5.3%	12.2%
1725	-$2	3-4-8-8	DS	4.6%	3.3%	7.6%	15.4%
2309	-$3	3-4-8-8	S	4.1%	3.2%	6.4%	13.8%
3053	-$3	3-4-8-8	NS	3.8%	3.1%	5.4%	12.3%
3045	-$3	3-4-8-9	DS	4.1%	3.7%	7.2%	15.0%
3767	-$4	3-4-8-9	S	3.7%	3.7%	6.4%	13.8%
4564	-$6	3-4-8-9	NS	3.2%	3.6%	5.2%	12.1%
2389	-$3	3-4-8-10	DS	4.1%	3.8%	7.9%	15.8%
3328	-$4	3-4-8-10	S	3.8%	3.7%	6.8%	14.2%
4325	-$5	3-4-8-10	NS	3.2%	3.7%	5.7%	12.6%
2978	-$3	3-4-8-J	DS	3.8%	3.7%	7.6%	15.1%
3732	-$4	3-4-8-J	S	3.5%	3.5%	6.6%	13.6%
4485	-$5	3-4-8-J	NS	3.0%	3.6%	5.6%	12.1%
3002	-$3	3-4-8-Q	DS	3.7%	3.6%	7.5%	14.9%
3854	-$4	3-4-8-Q	S	3.3%	3.6%	6.4%	13.3%
4695	-$6	3-4-8-Q	NS	2.8%	3.5%	5.1%	11.3%
2642	-$3	3-4-8-K	DS	3.3%	3.1%	6.3%	12.6%
3856	-$4	3-4-8-K	S	3.5%	3.5%	6.5%	13.5%
4705	-$6	3-4-8-K	NS	2.8%	3.4%	4.9%	11.1%
1405	-$1	3-4-9-9	DS	3.3%	3.1%	8.6%	15.0%
1712	-$2	3-4-9-9	S	2.8%	3.1%	7.7%	13.6%
2245	-$3	3-4-9-9	NS	2.4%	3.0%	6.7%	12.1%
2526	-$3	3-4-9-10	DS	4.1%	3.3%	8.0%	15.5%
3395	-$4	3-4-9-10	S	3.6%	3.3%	7.0%	14.0%

OMAHA HIGH-LOW 8 OR BETTER
5,278 HANDS   9 HANDED

HAND RANK	VALUE $4/$8	POCKET CARDS		HIGH %	LOW %	SCOOP %	PART OR ALL %
		HAND	SUITED				
4256	-$5	3-4-9-10	NS	3.1%	3.3%	6.1%	12.5%
2557	-$3	3-4-9-J	DS	3.7%	3.3%	8.3%	15.2%
3591	-$4	3-4-9-J	S	3.2%	3.3%	7.1%	13.5%
4440	-$5	3-4-9-J	NS	2.7%	3.3%	6.0%	11.9%
2548	-$3	3-4-9-Q	DS	3.5%	3.3%	8.2%	15.0%
3633	-$4	3-4-9-Q	S	3.0%	3.2%	7.2%	13.4%
4556	-$6	3-4-9-Q	NS	2.3%	3.1%	5.8%	11.3%
2542	-$3	3-4-9-K	DS	3.6%	3.2%	8.3%	15.1%
3550	-$4	3-4-9-K	S	3.0%	3.1%	7.2%	13.3%
4646	-$6	3-4-9-K	NS	2.2%	3.0%	5.6%	10.8%
1387	-$1	3-4-10-10	DS	3.6%	3.3%	9.0%	15.9%
1703	-$2	3-4-10-10	S	3.1%	3.2%	8.2%	14.6%
2496	-$3	3-4-10-10	NS	2.5%	3.2%	7.1%	12.8%
1670	-$2	3-4-10-J	DS	4.2%	3.4%	9.2%	16.8%
2295	-$3	3-4-10-J	S	3.7%	3.4%	8.4%	15.4%
3509	-$4	3-4-10-J	NS	3.1%	3.4%	7.1%	13.7%
1656	-$2	3-4-10-Q	DS	4.0%	3.3%	9.5%	16.7%
2487	-$3	3-4-10-Q	S	3.4%	3.3%	8.4%	15.1%
3520	-$4	3-4-10-Q	NS	2.8%	3.3%	7.2%	13.4%
1558	-$1	3-4-10-K	DS	4.0%	3.3%	9.7%	17.0%
2420	-$3	3-4-10-K	S	3.4%	3.3%	8.5%	15.2%
3901	-$5	3-4-10-K	NS	2.6%	3.2%	6.8%	12.6%
1097	-$0	3-4-J-J	DS	4.0%	3.4%	10.5%	17.8%
1516	-$1	3-4-J-J	S	3.3%	3.3%	9.2%	15.8%
2155	-$2	3-4-J-J	NS	2.8%	3.3%	8.0%	14.1%
1504	-$1	3-4-J-Q	DS	4.0%	3.3%	9.8%	17.1%
2246	-$3	3-4-J-Q	S	3.5%	3.3%	8.6%	15.5%
3321	-$4	3-4-J-Q	NS	2.9%	3.3%	7.5%	13.7%

OMAHA HIGH-LOW 8 OR BETTER
5,278 HANDS   9 HANDED

| HAND RANK | VALUE $4/$8 | POCKET CARDS | | HIGH % | LOW % | SCOOP % | PART OR ALL % |
		HAND	SUITED				
1484	-$1	3-4-J-K	DS	4.1%	3.3%	9.8%	17.2%
2189	-$2	3-4-J-K	S	3.6%	3.3%	8.7%	15.5%
3743	-$4	3-4-J-K	NS	2.7%	3.3%	7.1%	13.1%
733	$1	3-4-Q-Q	DS	4.5%	3.5%	12.3%	20.4%
1218	-$1	3-4-Q-Q	S	3.2%	3.1%	9.2%	15.4%
2364	-$3	3-4-Q-Q	NS	2.8%	3.0%	8.0%	13.8%
1303	-$1	3-4-Q-K	DS	4.3%	3.3%	10.3%	17.8%
1992	-$2	3-4-Q-K	S	3.9%	3.3%	9.2%	16.3%
3553	-$4	3-4-Q-K	NS	2.9%	3.2%	7.4%	13.5%
519	$3	3-4-K-K	DS	5.4%	3.7%	15.0%	24.1%
787	$1	3-4-K-K	S	4.4%	3.8%	13.6%	21.9%
2018	-$2	3-4-K-K	NS	3.1%	3.4%	10.7%	17.2%
4739	-$6	3-5-5-5	S	2.3%	2.8%	4.3%	9.4%
4890	-$7	3-5-5-5	NS	2.0%	2.7%	3.4%	8.1%
1267	-$1	3-5-5-6	DS	5.0%	4.0%	8.6%	17.6%
1781	-$2	3-5-5-6	S	4.6%	3.7%	7.4%	15.8%
2341	-$3	3-5-5-6	NS	4.3%	3.7%	6.5%	14.6%
1549	-$1	3-5-5-7	DS	5.0%	3.5%	8.1%	16.6%
2291	-$3	3-5-5-7	S	4.6%	3.3%	6.7%	14.6%
2992	-$3	3-5-5-7	NS	4.3%	3.3%	5.9%	13.5%
2213	-$2	3-5-5-8	DS	4.7%	3.2%	7.6%	15.6%
3027	-$3	3-5-5-8	S	4.3%	3.2%	6.3%	13.8%
3904	-$5	3-5-5-8	NS	4.0%	3.1%	5.2%	12.3%
3022	-$3	3-5-5-9	DS	4.6%	2.8%	7.2%	14.6%
3498	-$4	3-5-5-9	S	4.2%	2.8%	6.0%	13.0%
4146	-$5	3-5-5-9	NS	3.8%	2.6%	5.3%	11.7%
3034	-$3	3-5-5-10	DS	4.3%	2.7%	7.1%	14.2%
3744	-$4	3-5-5-10	S	3.9%	2.6%	6.0%	12.5%

OMAHA HIGH-LOW 8 OR BETTER
5,278 HANDS   9 HANDED

| HAND RANK | VALUE $4/$8 | POCKET CARDS | | HIGH % | LOW % | SCOOP % | PART OR ALL % |
		HAND	SUITED				
4496	-$6	3-5-5-10	NS	3.4%	2.5%	5.0%	10.9%
3010	-$3	3-5-5-J	DS	4.4%	2.7%	7.2%	14.4%
3681	-$4	3-5-5-J	S	3.9%	2.6%	6.2%	12.7%
4480	-$5	3-5-5-J	NS	3.5%	2.6%	5.1%	11.2%
2734	-$3	3-5-5-Q	DS	4.5%	2.8%	7.7%	15.0%
3400	-$4	3-5-5-Q	S	4.1%	2.7%	6.5%	13.3%
4251	-$5	3-5-5-Q	NS	3.5%	2.7%	5.5%	11.7%
2329	-$3	3-5-5-K	DS	4.8%	2.9%	8.3%	16.0%
2926	-$3	3-5-5-K	S	4.4%	2.8%	7.1%	14.3%
4190	-$5	3-5-5-K	NS	3.6%	2.7%	5.6%	11.9%
1206	-$0	3-5-6-6	DS	5.3%	3.9%	8.4%	17.5%
1634	-$1	3-5-6-6	S	4.9%	3.8%	7.4%	16.1%
2132	-$2	3-5-6-6	NS	4.5%	3.6%	6.4%	14.6%
1346	-$1	3-5-6-7	DS	5.6%	4.1%	7.9%	17.6%
1795	-$2	3-5-6-7	S	5.4%	3.9%	6.9%	16.2%
2510	-$3	3-5-6-7	NS	4.9%	3.9%	5.8%	14.7%
1738	-$2	3-5-6-8	DS	5.2%	3.9%	7.7%	16.8%
2440	-$3	3-5-6-8	S	4.8%	3.9%	6.5%	15.2%
3303	-$4	3-5-6-8	NS	4.5%	3.8%	5.5%	13.8%
1911	-$2	3-5-6-9	DS	5.0%	3.9%	7.6%	16.6%
2624	-$3	3-5-6-9	S	4.8%	3.7%	6.6%	15.1%
3454	-$4	3-5-6-9	NS	4.3%	3.6%	5.7%	13.6%
2472	-$3	3-5-6-10	DS	4.5%	3.7%	7.4%	15.6%
3219	-$4	3-5-6-10	S	4.1%	3.7%	6.5%	14.3%
3999	-$5	3-5-6-10	NS	3.6%	3.6%	5.5%	12.7%
2334	-$3	3-5-6-J	DS	4.5%	3.8%	7.7%	16.0%
3231	-$4	3-5-6-J	S	4.1%	3.7%	6.7%	14.5%
4163	-$5	3-5-6-J	NS	3.6%	3.6%	5.5%	12.8%

OMAHA HIGH-LOW 8 OR BETTER
5,278 HANDS   9 HANDED

HAND RANK	VALUE $4/$8	POCKET CARDS		HIGH %	LOW %	SCOOP %	PART OR ALL %
		HAND	SUITED				
2073	-$2	3-5-6-Q	DS	4.7%	3.8%	8.2%	16.6%
2951	-$3	3-5-6-Q	S	4.2%	3.7%	7.0%	15.0%
3978	-$5	3-5-6-Q	NS	3.8%	3.7%	5.8%	13.3%
1671	-$2	3-5-6-K	DS	4.9%	3.9%	9.0%	17.8%
2673	-$3	3-5-6-K	S	4.3%	3.8%	7.3%	15.4%
4082	-$5	3-5-6-K	NS	3.8%	3.7%	5.9%	13.4%
1482	-$1	3-5-7-7	DS	5.3%	3.2%	7.8%	16.3%
2062	-$2	3-5-7-7	S	4.9%	3.1%	6.8%	14.7%
2668	-$3	3-5-7-7	NS	4.5%	3.0%	5.7%	13.2%
2099	-$2	3-5-7-8	DS	5.1%	3.5%	7.5%	16.1%
2826	-$3	3-5-7-8	S	4.7%	3.4%	6.6%	14.7%
3910	-$5	3-5-7-8	NS	4.3%	3.3%	5.6%	13.2%
2317	-$3	3-5-7-9	DS	5.0%	3.4%	7.5%	15.9%
3158	-$4	3-5-7-9	S	4.8%	3.2%	6.4%	14.4%
3980	-$5	3-5-7-9	NS	4.3%	3.2%	5.5%	13.0%
2824	-$3	3-5-7-10	DS	4.5%	3.3%	7.2%	15.0%
3709	-$4	3-5-7-10	S	4.1%	3.2%	6.5%	13.8%
4425	-$5	3-5-7-10	NS	3.6%	3.2%	5.2%	12.0%
2694	-$3	3-5-7-J	DS	4.5%	3.3%	7.5%	15.3%
3589	-$4	3-5-7-J	S	4.1%	3.2%	6.6%	13.8%
4441	-$5	3-5-7-J	NS	3.6%	3.2%	5.4%	12.2%
2658	-$3	3-5-7-Q	DS	4.5%	3.3%	7.4%	15.1%
3663	-$4	3-5-7-Q	S	4.0%	3.2%	6.4%	13.6%
4495	-$6	3-5-7-Q	NS	3.5%	3.0%	5.3%	11.7%
2251	-$3	3-5-7-K	DS	4.8%	3.3%	8.1%	16.2%
2851	-$3	3-5-7-K	S	4.4%	3.3%	7.3%	15.0%
4329	-$5	3-5-7-K	NS	3.6%	3.1%	5.5%	12.3%
1816	-$2	3-5-8-8	DS	5.1%	2.9%	7.7%	15.7%

OMAHA HIGH-LOW 8 OR BETTER
5,278 HANDS   9 HANDED

HAND RANK	VALUE $4/$8	POCKET CARDS		HIGH %	LOW %	SCOOP %	PART OR ALL %
		HAND	SUITED				
2319	-$3	3-5-8-8	S	4.6%	2.8%	6.7%	14.1%
3435	-$4	3-5-8-8	NS	4.1%	2.7%	5.5%	12.3%
2997	-$3	3-5-8-9	DS	4.7%	3.2%	7.4%	15.3%
3957	-$5	3-5-8-9	S	4.3%	3.0%	6.5%	13.8%
4618	-$6	3-5-8-9	NS	3.8%	2.9%	5.5%	12.2%
3065	-$4	3-5-8-10	DS	4.2%	3.1%	7.5%	14.8%
3800	-$4	3-5-8-10	S	3.8%	3.0%	6.6%	13.4%
4604	-$6	3-5-8-10	NS	3.2%	2.9%	5.6%	11.7%
2746	-$3	3-5-8-J	DS	4.3%	3.2%	7.8%	15.2%
3755	-$4	3-5-8-J	S	3.9%	3.0%	7.0%	13.8%
4560	-$6	3-5-8-J	NS	3.3%	3.0%	5.8%	12.1%
3247	-$4	3-5-8-Q	DS	4.0%	3.0%	7.7%	14.8%
2535	-$3	3-5-8-Q	S	3.5%	2.8%	6.5%	12.9%
4857	-$6	3-5-8-Q	NS	3.1%	2.8%	5.3%	11.2%
2844	-$3	3-5-8-K	DS	4.4%	3.0%	7.8%	15.2%
3762	-$4	3-5-8-K	S	3.9%	3.0%	6.8%	13.7%
4774	-$6	3-5-8-K	NS	3.1%	2.8%	5.1%	11.0%
1420	-$1	3-5-9-9	DS	3.9%	2.5%	8.6%	15.0%
1876	-$2	3-5-9-9	S	3.3%	2.5%	7.8%	13.6%
2532	-$3	3-5-9-9	NS	2.8%	2.4%	6.8%	12.0%
3059	-$4	3-5-9-10	DS	4.2%	2.6%	7.9%	14.8%
3929	-$5	3-5-9-10	S	3.7%	2.6%	7.0%	13.3%
4576	-$6	3-5-9-10	NS	3.1%	2.6%	6.0%	11.7%
3001	-$3	3-5-9-J	DS	4.2%	2.7%	8.1%	15.0%
3689	-$4	3-5-9-J	S	3.7%	2.6%	7.3%	13.7%
4586	-$6	3-5-9-J	NS	3.1%	2.6%	6.1%	11.8%
2832	-$3	3-5-9-Q	DS	4.0%	2.6%	8.4%	15.0%
3802	-$4	3-5-9-Q	S	3.5%	2.5%	7.4%	13.5%

OMAHA HIGH-LOW 8 OR BETTER
5,278 HANDS   9 HANDED

| HAND RANK | VALUE $4/$8 | POCKET CARDS | | HIGH % | LOW % | SCOOP % | PART OR ALL % |
		HAND	SUITED				
4694	-$6	3-5-9-Q	NS	2.8%	2.5%	6.1%	11.4%
3024	-$3	3-5-9-K	DS	3.9%	2.5%	8.4%	14.9%
3641	-$4	3-5-9-K	S	3.5%	2.5%	7.5%	13.5%
4744	-$6	3-5-9-K	NS	2.7%	2.4%	5.8%	10.9%
1600	-$1	3-5-10-10	DS	3.6%	2.5%	9.0%	15.2%
2052	-$2	3-5-10-10	S	3.1%	2.5%	8.1%	13.7%
2860	-$3	3-5-10-10	NS	2.6%	2.5%	7.1%	12.2%
1934	-$2	3-5-10-J	DS	4.2%	2.7%	9.1%	16.0%
2750	-$3	3-5-10-J	S	3.7%	2.6%	8.2%	14.6%
4005	-$5	3-5-10-J	NS	3.2%	2.6%	7.1%	12.9%
2065	-$2	3-5-10-Q	DS	4.0%	2.5%	9.2%	15.6%
3047	-$3	3-5-10-Q	S	3.5%	2.6%	8.2%	14.3%
4062	-$5	3-5-10-Q	NS	2.7%	2.5%	7.1%	12.4%
2034	-$2	3-5-10-K	DS	4.1%	2.5%	9.4%	16.0%
2804	-$3	3-5-10-K	S	3.5%	2.5%	8.4%	14.4%
4200	-$5	3-5-10-K	NS	2.7%	2.4%	6.8%	11.8%
1291	-$1	3-5-J-J	DS	4.0%	2.6%	10.1%	16.7%
1811	-$2	3-5-J-J	S	3.4%	2.6%	9.1%	15.0%
2635	-$3	3-5-J-J	NS	2.9%	2.6%	7.8%	13.3%
1701	-$2	3-5-J-Q	DS	4.1%	2.6%	9.6%	16.3%
2696	-$3	3-5-J-Q	S	3.4%	2.5%	8.5%	14.5%
4004	-$5	3-5-J-Q	NS	2.8%	2.5%	7.4%	12.7%
1709	-$2	3-5-J-K	DS	4.1%	2.6%	9.8%	16.4%
2861	-$3	3-5-J-K	S	3.6%	2.5%	8.5%	14.6%
4074	-$5	3-5-J-K	NS	2.8%	2.4%	7.2%	12.3%
969	$0	3-5-Q-Q	DS	4.5%	2.8%	12.1%	19.5%
1468	-$1	3-5-Q-Q	S	3.2%	2.4%	9.6%	15.1%
2593	-$3	3-5-Q-Q	NS	2.9%	2.3%	8.1%	13.3%

OMAHA HIGH-LOW 8 OR BETTER
5,278 HANDS   9 HANDED

| HAND RANK | VALUE $4/$8 | POCKET CARDS | | HIGH % | LOW % | SCOOP % | PART OR ALL % |
		HAND	SUITED				
1500	-$1	3-5-Q-K	DS	4.3%	2.6%	10.3%	17.2%
2296	-$3	3-5-Q-K	S	3.7%	2.6%	9.1%	15.3%
4075	-$5	3-5-Q-K	NS	2.8%	2.4%	7.2%	12.3%
587	$3	3-5-K-K	DS	5.4%	3.0%	14.8%	23.2%
983	$0	3-5-K-K	S	4.5%	3.0%	13.3%	20.8%
2410	-$3	3-5-K-K	NS	3.4%	2.5%	10.3%	16.2%
5045	-$7	3-6-6-6	S	2.4%	1.9%	3.1%	7.4%
5086	-$8	3-6-6-6	NS	2.0%	1.8%	2.2%	5.9%
2122	-$2	3-6-6-7	DS	5.3%	2.7%	7.2%	15.3%
2918	-$3	3-6-6-7	S	4.8%	2.6%	6.0%	13.5%
3593	-$4	3-6-6-7	NS	4.7%	2.5%	5.0%	12.2%
2849	-$3	3-6-6-8	DS	5.1%	2.5%	6.8%	14.4%
3476	-$4	3-6-6-8	S	4.7%	2.4%	5.6%	12.7%
4259	-$5	3-6-6-8	NS	4.2%	2.3%	4.7%	11.2%
3365	-$4	3-6-6-9	DS	5.3%	2.1%	6.3%	13.7%
4038	-$5	3-6-6-9	S	4.8%	2.0%	5.2%	11.9%
4611	-$6	3-6-6-9	NS	4.3%	1.9%	4.2%	10.4%
3784	-$4	3-6-6-10	DS	4.9%	2.0%	6.3%	13.2%
4316	-$5	3-6-6-10	S	4.3%	1.9%	5.2%	11.3%
4780	-$6	3-6-6-10	NS	3.9%	1.9%	4.2%	10.0%
3908	-$5	3-6-6-J	DS	4.5%	2.0%	6.3%	12.7%
4306	-$5	3-6-6-J	S	4.1%	1.8%	5.2%	11.1%
4831	-$6	3-6-6-J	NS	3.6%	1.8%	4.1%	9.4%
3745	-$4	3-6-6-Q	DS	4.7%	2.0%	6.5%	13.2%
4048	-$5	3-6-6-Q	S	4.3%	1.9%	5.5%	11.6%
4783	-$6	3-6-6-Q	NS	3.6%	1.8%	4.3%	9.7%
3220	-$4	3-6-6-K	DS	5.0%	2.1%	7.2%	14.3%
3810	-$4	3-6-6-K	S	4.5%	2.0%	6.1%	12.6%

OMAHA HIGH-LOW 8 OR BETTER
5,278 HANDS   9 HANDED

| HAND RANK | VALUE $4/$8 | POCKET CARDS | | HIGH % | LOW % | SCOOP % | PART OR ALL % |
		HAND	SUITED				
4789	-$6	3-6-6-K	NS	3.8%	1.8%	4.4%	10.0%
2137	-$2	3-6-7-7	DS	5.4%	2.6%	7.1%	15.1%
2697	-$3	3-6-7-7	S	4.9%	2.6%	6.2%	13.7%
3511	-$4	3-6-7-7	NS	4.7%	2.3%	5.1%	12.1%
2616	-$3	3-6-7-8	DS	5.2%	2.7%	6.8%	14.7%
3549	-$4	3-6-7-8	S	4.9%	2.6%	5.7%	13.2%
4255	-$5	3-6-7-8	NS	4.5%	2.4%	4.9%	11.9%
2946	-$3	3-6-7-9	DS	5.4%	2.6%	6.8%	14.8%
3606	-$4	3-6-7-9	S	5.1%	2.5%	5.8%	13.3%
4303	-$5	3-6-7-9	NS	4.6%	2.4%	4.9%	11.8%
3134	-$4	3-6-7-10	DS	4.9%	2.6%	6.7%	14.2%
4058	-$5	3-6-7-10	S	4.5%	2.4%	5.6%	12.5%
4552	-$6	3-6-7-10	NS	4.0%	2.4%	4.7%	11.1%
3823	-$4	3-6-7-J	DS	4.5%	2.5%	6.4%	13.4%
4341	-$5	3-6-7-J	S	4.1%	2.3%	5.5%	11.9%
4882	-$6	3-6-7-J	NS	3.6%	2.2%	4.3%	10.1%
3410	-$4	3-6-7-Q	DS	4.6%	2.6%	6.7%	13.9%
4187	-$5	3-6-7-Q	S	4.2%	2.5%	5.8%	12.5%
4891	-$7	3-6-7-Q	NS	3.7%	2.2%	4.5%	10.4%
2602	-$3	3-6-7-K	DS	5.1%	2.6%	7.2%	14.9%
3750	-$4	3-6-7-K	S	4.5%	2.5%	6.4%	13.5%
4805	-$6	3-6-7-K	NS	3.7%	2.3%	4.9%	10.9%
2085	-$2	3-6-8-8	DS	5.2%	2.3%	7.2%	14.7%
3112	-$4	3-6-8-8	S	4.7%	2.3%	6.0%	13.0%
3824	-$4	3-6-8-8	NS	4.4%	2.2%	5.1%	11.7%
3461	-$4	3-6-8-9	DS	5.0%	2.3%	6.9%	14.3%
3953	-$5	3-6-8-9	S	4.7%	2.2%	5.9%	12.9%
4736	-$6	3-6-8-9	NS	4.6%	2.2%	4.9%	11.7%

OMAHA HIGH-LOW 8 OR BETTER
5,278 HANDS   9 HANDED

| HAND RANK | VALUE $4/$8 | POCKET CARDS | | HIGH % | LOW % | SCOOP % | PART OR ALL % |
		HAND	SUITED				
3259	-$4	3-6-8-10	DS	4.6%	2.3%	7.1%	14.1%
4119	-$5	3-6-8-10	S	4.1%	2.2%	6.2%	12.5%
4565	-$6	3-6-8-10	NS	3.7%	2.1%	5.2%	11.1%
3841	-$4	3-6-8-J	DS	4.3%	2.2%	6.9%	13.4%
4435	-$5	3-6-8-J	S	3.7%	2.2%	5.8%	11.7%
4924	-$7	3-6-8-J	NS	3.3%	2.1%	4.7%	10.1%
3640	-$4	3-6-8-Q	DS	4.4%	2.4%	7.2%	13.9%
4368	-$5	3-6-8-Q	S	3.9%	2.3%	6.2%	12.4%
4926	-$7	3-6-8-Q	NS	3.2%	2.1%	5.0%	10.3%
3514	-$4	3-6-8-K	DS	4.6%	2.3%	7.1%	14.1%
4152	-$5	3-6-8-K	S	4.1%	2.3%	6.3%	12.6%
4988	-$7	3-6-8-K	NS	3.2%	2.0%	4.6%	9.8%
2015	-$2	3-6-9-9	DS	4.1%	2.0%	7.8%	13.9%
2531	-$3	3-6-9-9	S	3.6%	1.9%	6.9%	12.4%
3250	-$4	3-6-9-9	NS	3.1%	1.8%	5.9%	10.8%
3363	-$4	3-6-9-10	DS	4.8%	2.0%	7.2%	14.0%
4159	-$5	3-6-9-10	S	4.3%	1.9%	6.3%	12.5%
4800	-$6	3-6-9-10	NS	3.7%	1.7%	5.3%	10.7%
3998	-$5	3-6-9-J	DS	4.2%	1.9%	7.1%	13.2%
4445	-$5	3-6-9-J	S	3.7%	1.8%	6.2%	11.8%
4904	-$7	3-6-9-J	NS	3.1%	1.7%	5.2%	10.0%
3645	-$4	3-6-9-Q	DS	4.4%	1.9%	7.5%	13.7%
4315	-$5	3-6-9-Q	S	3.8%	1.9%	6.6%	12.3%
4920	-$7	3-6-9-Q	NS	3.1%	1.7%	5.4%	10.3%
3671	-$4	3-6-9-K	DS	4.4%	1.9%	7.7%	13.9%
4229	-$5	3-6-9-K	S	3.9%	1.9%	6.7%	12.5%
4948	-$7	3-6-9-K	NS	3.0%	1.7%	5.2%	9.9%
2004	-$2	3-6-10-10	DS	4.0%	2.0%	8.3%	14.2%

OMAHA HIGH-LOW 8 OR BETTER
5,278 HANDS   9 HANDED

HAND RANK	VALUE $4/$8	POCKET CARDS		HIGH %	LOW %	SCOOP %	PART OR ALL %
		HAND	SUITED				
2822	-$3	3-6-10-10	S	3.4%	1.9%	7.2%	12.5%
3604	-$4	3-6-10-10	NS	2.8%	1.8%	6.3%	10.9%
2967	-$3	3-6-10-J	DS	4.1%	1.9%	8.0%	14.1%
3948	-$5	3-6-10-J	S	3.7%	1.8%	7.1%	12.6%
4545	-$6	3-6-10-J	NS	3.0%	1.8%	6.2%	11.1%
2829	-$3	3-6-10-Q	DS	4.3%	2.0%	8.4%	14.7%
3532	-$4	3-6-10-Q	S	3.8%	1.9%	7.6%	13.3%
4541	-$6	3-6-10-Q	NS	3.1%	1.9%	6.4%	11.3%
2402	-$3	3-6-10-K	DS	4.4%	2.0%	8.7%	15.1%
3453	-$4	3-6-10-K	S	3.8%	2.0%	7.8%	13.7%
4672	-$6	3-6-10-K	NS	2.9%	1.8%	6.2%	10.9%
1938	-$2	3-6-J-J	DS	3.9%	2.0%	9.1%	15.0%
2745	-$3	3-6-J-J	S	3.2%	1.9%	8.1%	13.3%
3897	-$5	3-6-J-J	NS	2.7%	1.8%	6.7%	11.3%
2528	-$3	3-6-J-Q	DS	4.1%	1.9%	8.5%	14.4%
3724	-$4	3-6-J-Q	S	3.4%	1.8%	7.4%	12.7%
4521	-$6	3-6-J-Q	NS	2.8%	1.7%	6.3%	10.9%
2818	-$3	3-6-J-K	DS	4.1%	1.9%	8.5%	14.5%
3651	-$4	3-6-J-K	S	3.5%	1.8%	7.6%	12.9%
4717	-$6	3-6-J-K	NS	2.6%	1.7%	6.0%	10.3%
806	$1	3-6-Q-Q	DS	4.4%	2.1%	10.9%	17.4%
2181	-$2	3-6-Q-Q	S	3.5%	2.0%	9.7%	15.2%
3512	-$4	3-6-Q-Q	NS	3.0%	1.9%	8.2%	13.2%
2194	-$2	3-6-Q-K	DS	4.3%	1.9%	9.0%	15.2%
3367	-$4	3-6-Q-K	S	3.6%	1.8%	7.8%	13.3%
4467	-$5	3-6-Q-K	NS	2.8%	1.7%	6.5%	11.0%
798	$1	3-6-K-K	DS	5.5%	2.4%	13.7%	21.5%
2005	-$2	3-6-K-K	S	4.5%	2.0%	11.5%	18.0%

246

		POCKET CARDS					
HAND RANK	VALUE $4/$8	HAND	SUITED	HIGH %	LOW %	SCOOP %	PART OR ALL %
2864	-$3	3-6-K-K	NS	3.4%	2.0%	9.1%	14.5%
5173	-$9	3-7-7-7	S	2.1%	1.1%	2.5%	5.7%
5234	-$9	3-7-7-7	NS	1.8%	1.0%	1.6%	4.3%
3280	-$4	3-7-7-8	DS	5.0%	1.8%	6.6%	13.4%
3962	-$5	3-7-7-8	S	4.6%	1.6%	5.6%	11.8%
4457	-$5	3-7-7-8	NS	4.3%	1.5%	4.8%	10.6%
3852	-$4	3-7-7-9	DS	5.5%	1.4%	5.9%	12.8%
4307	-$5	3-7-7-9	S	4.9%	1.2%	5.0%	11.2%
4663	-$6	3-7-7-9	NS	4.4%	1.2%	4.3%	9.9%
4071	-$5	3-7-7-10	DS	5.0%	1.4%	5.9%	12.2%
4430	-$5	3-7-7-10	S	4.4%	1.2%	4.9%	10.6%
4888	-$6	3-7-7-10	NS	4.0%	1.1%	4.1%	9.2%
4077	-$5	3-7-7-J	DS	4.6%	1.3%	6.1%	11.9%
4632	-$6	3-7-7-J	S	4.1%	1.2%	4.8%	10.1%
4916	-$7	3-7-7-J	NS	3.5%	1.1%	4.0%	8.7%
4321	-$5	3-7-7-Q	DS	4.5%	1.3%	5.9%	11.8%
4547	-$6	3-7-7-Q	S	4.0%	1.2%	4.9%	10.1%
4989	-$7	3-7-7-Q	NS	3.4%	1.0%	3.8%	8.2%
3862	-$4	3-7-7-K	DS	4.9%	1.4%	5.6%	11.9%
4383	-$5	3-7-7-K	S	4.3%	1.3%	5.4%	11.0%
4949	-$7	3-7-7-K	NS	3.6%	1.1%	3.9%	8.6%
2744	-$3	3-7-8-8	DS	5.0%	1.8%	7.0%	13.7%
3801	-$4	3-7-8-8	S	4.6%	1.6%	5.9%	12.1%
4367	-$5	3-7-8-8	NS	4.2%	1.5%	5.1%	10.8%
3402	-$4	3-7-8-9	DS	5.0%	1.7%	6.8%	13.4%
4196	-$5	3-7-8-9	S	4.5%	1.6%	5.9%	12.0%
4733	-$6	3-7-8-9	NS	4.1%	1.4%	5.0%	10.5%
3488	-$4	3-7-8-10	DS	4.5%	1.6%	7.0%	13.0%

OMAHA HIGH-LOW 8 OR BETTER
5,278 HANDS   9 HANDED

OMAHA HIGH-LOW 8 OR BETTER
5,278 HANDS   9 HANDED

HAND RANK	VALUE $4/$8	POCKET CARDS		HIGH %	LOW %	SCOOP %	PART OR ALL %
		HAND	SUITED				
4118	-$5	3-7-8-10	S	4.1%	1.5%	6.1%	11.7%
4621	-$6	3-7-8-10	NS	3.6%	1.4%	5.2%	10.2%
3864	-$4	3-7-8-J	DS	4.1%	1.6%	6.8%	12.5%
4347	-$5	3-7-8-J	S	3.8%	1.4%	5.9%	11.1%
4867	-$6	3-7-8-J	NS	3.2%	1.4%	4.9%	9.5%
4155	-$5	3-7-8-Q	DS	4.1%	1.6%	6.6%	12.3%
4687	-$6	3-7-8-Q	S	3.7%	1.5%	5.6%	10.8%
5033	-$7	3-7-8-Q	NS	3.0%	1.4%	4.4%	8.8%
4102	-$5	3-7-8-K	DS	4.4%	1.7%	6.9%	13.0%
4450	-$5	3-7-8-K	S	4.1%	1.6%	6.1%	11.8%
4998	-$7	3-7-8-K	NS	3.1%	1.4%	4.8%	9.2%
2299	-$3	3-7-9-9	DS	4.2%	1.2%	7.6%	13.1%
3029	-$3	3-7-9-9	S	3.7%	1.2%	6.7%	11.6%
3703	-$4	3-7-9-9	NS	3.1%	1.1%	5.9%	10.2%
3477	-$4	3-7-9-10	DS	4.9%	1.2%	7.1%	13.3%
4320	-$5	3-7-9-10	S	4.4%	1.2%	6.2%	11.8%
4654	-$6	3-7-9-10	NS	3.9%	1.1%	5.4%	10.4%
3781	-$4	3-7-9-J	DS	4.5%	1.3%	7.0%	12.8%
4413	-$5	3-7-9-J	S	3.9%	1.2%	6.3%	11.4%
4901	-$7	3-7-9-J	NS	3.3%	1.1%	5.2%	9.6%
4310	-$5	3-7-9-Q	DS	4.2%	1.2%	6.7%	12.1%
4685	-$6	3-7-9-Q	S	3.6%	1.1%	6.0%	10.7%
5002	-$7	3-7-9-Q	NS	2.9%	1.0%	4.9%	8.8%
3771	-$4	3-7-9-K	DS	4.5%	1.3%	7.5%	13.3%
4474	-$5	3-7-9-K	S	4.0%	1.2%	6.6%	11.7%
5014	-$7	3-7-9-K	NS	3.0%	1.0%	5.0%	9.0%
2243	-$3	3-7-10-10	DS	4.0%	1.3%	8.1%	13.3%
3122	-$4	3-7-10-10	S	3.4%	1.2%	7.1%	11.7%

OMAHA HIGH-LOW 8 OR BETTER
5,278 HANDS   9 HANDED

HAND RANK	VALUE $4/$8	POCKET CARDS HAND	SUITED	HIGH %	LOW %	SCOOP %	PART OR ALL %
3887	-$5	3-7-10-10	NS	2.8%	1.1%	6.2%	10.2%
2722	-$3	3-7-10-J	DS	4.4%	1.3%	8.0%	13.7%
3769	-$4	3-7-10-J	S	3.8%	1.2%	7.1%	12.1%
4460	-$5	3-7-10-J	NS	3.2%	1.1%	6.3%	10.6%
3440	-$4	3-7-10-Q	DS	4.1%	1.3%	7.8%	13.1%
4139	-$5	3-7-10-Q	S	3.6%	1.2%	6.8%	11.6%
4752	-$6	3-7-10-Q	NS	2.9%	1.1%	5.9%	9.9%
2737	-$3	3-7-10-K	DS	4.4%	1.3%	8.6%	14.3%
3960	-$5	3-7-10-K	S	3.8%	1.3%	7.4%	12.5%
4753	-$6	3-7-10-K	NS	2.9%	1.1%	6.1%	10.1%
2307	-$3	3-7-J-J	DS	3.8%	1.3%	8.7%	13.9%
3040	-$3	3-7-J-J	S	3.2%	1.2%	7.8%	12.3%
3986	-$5	3-7-J-J	NS	2.7%	1.2%	6.7%	10.5%
3205	-$4	3-7-J-Q	DS	3.9%	1.2%	7.8%	12.9%
4204	-$5	3-7-J-Q	S	3.2%	1.2%	6.9%	11.3%
4855	-$6	3-7-J-Q	NS	2.5%	1.1%	5.7%	9.2%
3070	-$4	3-7-J-K	DS	4.2%	1.3%	8.4%	13.8%
3902	-$5	3-7-J-K	S	3.5%	1.3%	7.4%	12.2%
4677	-$6	3-7-J-K	NS	2.5%	1.1%	6.2%	9.8%
2024	-$2	3-7-Q-Q	DS	4.2%	1.5%	10.1%	15.8%
3182	-$4	3-7-Q-Q	S	3.4%	1.4%	8.9%	13.6%
4212	-$5	3-7-Q-Q	NS	2.8%	1.3%	7.6%	11.6%
2862	-$3	3-7-Q-K	DS	4.2%	1.3%	8.3%	13.7%
3949	-$5	3-7-Q-K	S	3.4%	1.2%	7.2%	11.8%
4843	-$6	3-7-Q-K	NS	2.5%	1.0%	5.8%	9.3%
1130	-$0	3-7-K-K	DS	5.3%	1.7%	12.8%	19.8%
2049	-$2	3-7-K-K	S	4.2%	1.5%	11.3%	17.0%
3736	-$4	3-7-K-K	NS	3.2%	1.5%	9.6%	14.2%

OMAHA HIGH-LOW 8 OR BETTER
5,278 HANDS 9 HANDED

| HAND RANK | VALUE $4/$8 | POCKET CARDS | | HIGH % | LOW % | SCOOP % | PART OR ALL % |
		HAND	SUITED				
5238	-$9	3-8-8-8	S	2.0%	0.7%	2.3%	5.0%
5263	-$10	3-8-8-8	NS	1.6%	0.6%	1.5%	3.7%
4085	-$5	3-8-8-9	DS	5.3%	0.9%	6.3%	12.5%
4477	-$5	3-8-8-9	S	4.8%	0.9%	5.2%	10.9%
4865	-$6	3-8-8-9	NS	4.4%	0.8%	4.6%	9.8%
3976	-$5	3-8-8-10	DS	4.9%	0.9%	6.4%	12.3%
4346	-$5	3-8-8-10	S	4.3%	0.9%	5.6%	10.8%
4681	-$6	3-8-8-10	NS	3.9%	0.9%	4.9%	9.7%
3946	-$5	3-8-8-J	DS	4.6%	0.9%	6.7%	12.2%
4569	-$6	3-8-8-J	S	4.1%	0.8%	5.4%	10.3%
4872	-$6	3-8-8-J	NS	3.5%	0.8%	4.7%	9.0%
4267	-$5	3-8-8-Q	DS	4.5%	1.0%	6.4%	11.9%
4616	-$6	3-8-8-Q	S	4.0%	0.9%	5.3%	10.1%
4958	-$7	3-8-8-Q	NS	3.4%	0.8%	4.4%	8.5%
4408	-$5	3-8-8-K	DS	4.8%	1.0%	6.2%	12.0%
4577	-$6	3-8-8-K	S	4.2%	0.9%	5.4%	10.5%
5003	-$7	3-8-8-K	NS	3.4%	0.8%	3.9%	8.1%
2796	-$3	3-8-9-9	DS	4.0%	0.9%	7.8%	12.6%
3597	-$4	3-8-9-9	S	3.6%	0.7%	6.7%	11.0%
3958	-$5	3-8-9-9	NS	3.0%	0.7%	6.2%	9.9%
3299	-$4	3-8-9-10	DS	4.8%	0.9%	7.4%	13.0%
4161	-$5	3-8-9-10	S	3.8%	0.8%	6.7%	11.3%
4438	-$5	3-8-9-10	NS	3.7%	0.8%	6.0%	10.5%
3493	-$4	3-8-9-J	DS	4.4%	0.9%	7.4%	12.7%
3938	-$5	3-8-9-J	S	4.3%	0.8%	6.7%	11.8%
4676	-$6	3-8-9-J	NS	3.2%	0.7%	5.8%	9.7%
3944	-$5	3-8-9-Q	DS	4.2%	0.9%	7.3%	12.4%
4453	-$5	3-8-9-Q	S	3.6%	0.8%	6.4%	10.8%

OMAHA HIGH-LOW 8 OR BETTER
5,278 HANDS   9 HANDED

HAND RANK	VALUE $4/$8	POCKET CARDS		HIGH %	LOW %	SCOOP %	PART OR ALL %
		HAND	SUITED				
4914	-$7	3-8-9-Q	NS	2.9%	0.7%	5.3%	8.9%
4148	-$5	3-8-9-K	DS	4.3%	0.9%	7.0%	12.2%
4591	-$6	3-8-9-K	S	3.8%	0.8%	6.1%	10.7%
5008	-$7	3-8-9-K	NS	2.8%	0.7%	5.0%	8.5%
2343	-$3	3-8-10-10	DS	3.9%	0.9%	8.5%	13.2%
3098	-$4	3-8-10-10	S	3.2%	0.9%	7.7%	11.8%
3609	-$4	3-8-10-10	NS	2.6%	0.8%	6.9%	10.3%
2277	-$3	3-8-10-J	DS	4.3%	0.9%	8.4%	13.6%
2941	-$3	3-8-10-J	S	3.7%	0.8%	7.7%	12.2%
3780	-$4	3-8-10-J	NS	3.1%	0.8%	7.0%	10.9%
2632	-$3	3-8-10-Q	DS	4.2%	0.9%	8.3%	13.3%
3401	-$4	3-8-10-Q	S	3.5%	0.8%	7.6%	12.0%
4231	-$5	3-8-10-Q	NS	2.9%	0.8%	6.6%	10.3%
3127	-$4	3-8-10-K	DS	4.3%	0.9%	8.1%	13.2%
3715	-$4	3-8-10-K	S	3.7%	0.9%	7.4%	11.9%
4745	-$6	3-8-10-K	NS	2.7%	0.8%	5.9%	9.4%
2100	-$2	3-8-J-J	DS	3.7%	0.9%	9.3%	13.9%
3019	-$3	3-8-J-J	S	3.1%	0.9%	8.2%	12.2%
3720	-$4	3-8-J-J	NS	2.5%	0.8%	7.4%	10.6%
2806	-$3	3-8-J-Q	DS	3.8%	0.9%	8.3%	13.0%
3450	-$4	3-8-J-Q	S	3.3%	0.8%	7.6%	11.6%
4287	-$5	3-8-J-Q	NS	2.5%	0.8%	6.5%	9.8%
3230	-$4	3-8-J-K	DS	3.9%	0.9%	8.1%	12.9%
4020	-$5	3-8-J-K	S	3.3%	0.9%	7.2%	11.3%
4722	-$6	3-8-J-K	NS	2.4%	0.7%	6.1%	9.2%
2000	-$2	3-8-Q-Q	DS	4.0%	1.1%	10.3%	15.4%
2613	-$3	3-8-Q-Q	S	3.2%	1.0%	9.4%	13.6%
3610	-$4	3-8-Q-Q	NS	2.4%	0.9%	8.3%	11.6%

OMAHA HIGH-LOW 8 OR BETTER
5,278 HANDS 9 HANDED

HAND RANK	VALUE $4/$8	POCKET CARDS		HIGH %	LOW %	SCOOP %	PART OR ALL %
		HAND	SUITED				
3317	-$4	3-8-Q-K	DS	3.9%	0.9%	7.9%	12.7%
4203	-$5	3-8-Q-K	S	3.1%	0.8%	6.9%	10.9%
4816	-$6	3-8-Q-K	NS	2.3%	0.7%	5.7%	8.7%
1584	-$1	3-8-K-K	DS	5.0%	1.3%	12.2%	18.4%
2589	-$3	3-8-K-K	S	3.4%	1.1%	10.4%	14.9%
3992	-$5	3-8-K-K	NS	2.8%	1.0%	9.7%	13.5%
5074	-$8	3-9-9-9	S	1.2%	0.0%	2.7%	3.9%
5100	-$8	3-9-9-9	NS	0.8%	0.0%	2.0%	2.8%
2812	-$3	3-9-9-10	DS	3.9%	0.0%	7.5%	11.4%
3311	-$4	3-9-9-10	S	3.3%	0.0%	6.7%	10.1%
3785	-$4	3-9-9-10	NS	2.8%	0.0%	6.3%	9.1%
2690	-$3	3-9-9-J	DS	3.9%	0.0%	7.4%	11.4%
3346	-$4	3-9-9-J	S	2.8%	0.0%	6.9%	9.7%
4116	-$5	3-9-9-J	NS	2.3%	0.0%	6.1%	8.5%
3327	-$4	3-9-9-Q	DS	3.2%	0.0%	7.5%	10.7%
3628	-$4	3-9-9-Q	S	2.6%	0.0%	6.7%	9.4%
4223	-$5	3-9-9-Q	NS	2.0%	0.0%	6.0%	8.0%
3261	-$4	3-9-9-K	DS	3.5%	0.0%	7.5%	11.1%
3632	-$4	3-9-9-K	S	2.9%	0.0%	6.8%	9.7%
4362	-$5	3-9-9-K	NS	1.9%	0.0%	5.7%	7.6%
2714	-$3	3-9-10-10	DS	4.0%	0.0%	7.7%	11.6%
3333	-$4	3-9-10-10	S	3.5%	0.0%	7.0%	10.5%
3987	-$5	3-9-10-10	NS	2.9%	0.0%	6.2%	9.2%
2081	-$2	3-9-10-J	DS	4.5%	0.0%	8.5%	12.9%
2904	-$3	3-9-10-J	S	3.9%	0.0%	7.8%	11.7%
3569	-$4	3-9-10-J	NS	3.4%	0.0%	7.2%	10.7%
2370	-$3	3-9-10-Q	DS	4.1%	0.0%	8.6%	12.7%
2958	-$3	3-9-10-Q	S	3.6%	0.0%	8.0%	11.6%

OMAHA HIGH-LOW 8 OR BETTER
5,278 HANDS   9 HANDED

HAND RANK	VALUE $4/$8	POCKET CARDS		HIGH %	LOW %	SCOOP %	PART OR ALL %
		HAND	SUITED				
3885	-$5	3-9-10-Q	NS	2.9%	0.0%	7.0%	10.0%
2640	-$3	3-9-10-K	DS	4.3%	0.0%	8.5%	12.8%
3208	-$4	3-9-10-K	S	3.7%	0.0%	7.9%	11.7%
4335	-$5	3-9-10-K	NS	2.6%	0.0%	6.7%	9.3%
2447	-$3	3-9-J-J	DS	3.7%	0.0%	8.4%	12.1%
3087	-$4	3-9-J-J	S	3.2%	0.0%	7.9%	11.1%
3772	-$4	3-9-J-J	NS	2.6%	0.0%	7.0%	9.6%
2289	-$3	3-9-J-Q	DS	3.6%	0.0%	8.6%	12.2%
3081	-$4	3-9-J-Q	S	3.1%	0.0%	8.0%	11.1%
3690	-$4	3-9-J-Q	NS	2.5%	0.0%	7.1%	9.6%
2692	-$3	3-9-J-K	DS	3.9%	0.0%	8.5%	12.4%
3163	-$4	3-9-J-K	S	3.2%	0.0%	8.2%	11.4%
4188	-$5	3-9-J-K	NS	2.2%	0.0%	6.7%	8.9%
2218	-$2	3-9-Q-Q	DS	4.1%	0.0%	9.7%	13.8%
2916	-$3	3-9-Q-Q	S	3.3%	0.0%	8.9%	12.2%
3925	-$5	3-9-Q-Q	NS	2.6%	0.0%	7.8%	10.4%
2689	-$3	3-9-Q-K	DS	3.7%	0.0%	8.7%	12.4%
3284	-$4	3-9-Q-K	S	2.9%	0.0%	8.1%	11.0%
4222	-$5	3-9-Q-K	NS	1.8%	0.0%	6.8%	8.7%
1613	-$1	3-9-K-K	DS	5.2%	0.0%	11.8%	17.0%
2367	-$3	3-9-K-K	S	3.8%	0.0%	10.9%	14.7%
3630	-$4	3-9-K-K	NS	2.8%	0.0%	9.7%	12.5%
5106	-$8	3-10-10-10	S	1.4%	0.0%	3.0%	4.3%
5155	-$8	3-10-10-10	NS	0.9%	0.0%	2.4%	3.3%
1945	-$2	3-10-10-J	DS	4.0%	0.0%	9.0%	13.0%
2347	-$3	3-10-10-J	S	3.4%	0.0%	8.3%	11.7%
3126	-$4	3-10-10-J	NS	3.0%	0.0%	7.8%	10.8%

OMAHA HIGH-LOW 8 OR BETTER
5,278 HANDS   9 HANDED

| HAND RANK | VALUE $4/$8 | POCKET CARDS | | HIGH % | LOW % | SCOOP % | PART OR ALL % |
		HAND	SUITED				
1985	-$2	3-10-10-Q	DS	3.8%	0.0%	9.3%	13.2%
2671	-$3	3-10-10-Q	S	3.1%	0.0%	8.5%	11.6%
3422	-$4	3-10-10-Q	NS	2.6%	0.0%	7.8%	10.4%
2144	-$2	3-10-10-K	DS	4.1%	0.0%	9.3%	13.4%
2859	-$3	3-10-10-K	S	3.3%	0.0%	8.5%	11.8%
3997	-$5	3-10-10-K	NS	2.4%	0.0%	7.1%	9.6%
1764	-$2	3-10-J-J	DS	4.1%	0.0%	9.3%	13.4%
2175	-$2	3-10-J-J	S	3.6%	0.0%	8.7%	12.3%
2901	-$3	3-10-J-J	NS	3.0%	0.0%	8.1%	11.1%
1249	-$1	3-10-J-Q	DS	4.3%	0.0%	10.2%	14.5%
1607	-$1	3-10-J-Q	S	3.7%	0.0%	9.6%	13.4%
2292	-$3	3-10-J-Q	NS	3.1%	0.0%	8.8%	11.9%
1431	-$1	3-10-J-K	DS	4.5%	0.0%	10.0%	14.5%
1730	-$2	3-10-J-K	S	3.9%	0.0%	9.6%	13.5%
2525	-$3	3-10-J-K	NS	2.9%	0.0%	8.7%	11.6%
1462	-$1	3-10-Q-Q	DS	4.3%	0.0%	10.7%	15.1%
1977	-$2	3-10-Q-Q	S	3.6%	0.0%	10.0%	13.6%
3009	-$3	3-10-Q-Q	NS	2.9%	0.0%	8.9%	11.8%
1348	-$1	3-10-Q-K	DS	4.5%	0.0%	10.3%	14.8%
1761	-$2	3-10-Q-K	S	3.6%	0.0%	9.7%	13.3%
2579	-$3	3-10-Q-K	NS	2.7%	0.0%	8.6%	11.2%
1189	-$0	3-10-K-K	DS	5.6%	0.0%	12.5%	18.1%
1745	-$2	3-10-K-K	S	4.2%	0.0%	11.6%	15.8%
2757	-$3	3-10-K-K	NS	3.1%	0.0%	10.5%	13.7%
5188	-$9	3-J-J-J	S	1.5%	0.0%	3.7%	5.3%
5220	-$9	3-J-J-J	NS	1.1%	0.0%	3.1%	4.1%
1681	-$2	3-J-J-Q	DS	4.2%	0.0%	10.3%	14.6%
2390	-$3	3-J-J-Q	S	3.5%	0.0%	9.2%	12.7%

OMAHA HIGH-LOW 8 OR BETTER
5,278 HANDS   9 HANDED

HAND RANK	VALUE $4/$8	POCKET CARDS		HIGH %	LOW %	SCOOP %	PART OR ALL %
		HAND	SUITED				
2985	-$3	3-J-J-Q	NS	2.9%	0.0%	8.8%	11.7%
2348	-$3	3-J-J-K	DS	4.4%	0.0%	10.4%	14.8%
2454	-$3	3-J-J-K	S	3.6%	0.0%	9.6%	13.3%
3737	-$4	3-J-J-K	NS	2.6%	0.0%	8.5%	11.1%
1444	-$1	3-J-Q-Q	DS	4.4%	0.0%	11.0%	15.4%
1922	-$2	3-J-Q-Q	S	3.6%	0.0%	10.0%	13.6%
2868	-$3	3-J-Q-Q	NS	2.9%	0.0%	9.0%	11.9%
1233	-$1	3-J-Q-K	DS	4.5%	0.0%	10.3%	14.8%
1570	-$1	3-J-Q-K	S	3.7%	0.0%	9.8%	13.5%
2415	-$3	3-J-Q-K	NS	2.7%	0.0%	8.6%	11.3%
1125	-$0	3-J-K-K	DS	5.7%	0.0%	12.6%	18.4%
1638	-$1	3-J-K-K	S	4.2%	0.0%	11.6%	15.8%
2504	-$3	3-J-K-K	NS	3.1%	0.0%	10.6%	13.7%
5211	-$9	3-Q-Q-Q	S	2.1%	0.0%	5.3%	7.3%
5257	-$9	3-Q-Q-Q	NS	1.3%	0.0%	4.3%	5.6%
1490	-$1	3-Q-Q-K	DS	5.0%	0.0%	11.5%	16.5%
2008	-$2	3-Q-Q-K	S	3.5%	0.0%	10.5%	13.9%
3156	-$4	3-Q-Q-K	NS	3.0%	0.0%	10.0%	13.0%
1162	-$0	3-Q-K-K	DS	5.6%	0.0%	12.5%	18.1%
1842	-$2	3-Q-K-K	S	4.9%	0.0%	11.7%	16.5%
2427	-$3	3-Q-K-K	NS	3.1%	0.0%	10.6%	13.7%
5194	-$9	3-K-K-K	S	2.7%	0.0%	7.4%	10.2%
5262	-$10	3-K-K-K	NS	1.6%	0.0%	6.4%	8.0%
5185	-$9	4-4-4-4	NS	0.0%	0.0%	0.1%	0.1%
4665	-$6	4-4-4-5	S	2.5%	2.9%	4.6%	10.0%
4937	-$7	4-4-4-5	NS	2.1%	2.7%	3.3%	8.1%
4970	-$7	4-4-4-6	S	2.5%	2.4%	3.6%	8.5%
5054	-$8	4-4-4-6	NS	2.2%	2.2%	2.7%	7.1%

OMAHA HIGH-LOW 8 OR BETTER
5,278 HANDS   9 HANDED

| HAND RANK | VALUE $4/$8 | POCKET CARDS | | HIGH % | LOW % | SCOOP % | PART OR ALL % |
		HAND	SUITED				
5119	-$8	4-4-4-7	S	2.4%	1.6%	2.7%	6.8%
5209	-$9	4-4-4-7	NS	2.0%	1.4%	1.8%	5.2%
5237	-$9	4-4-4-8	S	2.1%	1.1%	2.4%	5.5%
5255	-$9	4-4-4-8	NS	1.7%	0.9%	1.5%	4.1%
5148	-$8	4-4-4-9	S	1.5%	0.0%	2.0%	3.4%
5165	-$9	4-4-4-9	NS	1.1%	0.0%	1.2%	2.3%
5146	-$8	4-4-4-10	S	1.5%	0.0%	2.1%	3.6%
5193	-$9	4-4-4-10	NS	1.1%	0.0%	1.3%	2.4%
5175	-$9	4-4-4-J	S	1.5%	0.0%	2.1%	3.6%
5222	-$9	4-4-4-J	NS	1.1%	0.0%	1.3%	2.3%
5145	-$8	4-4-4-Q	S	1.7%	0.0%	2.6%	4.2%
5216	-$9	4-4-4-Q	NS	1.2%	0.0%	1.5%	2.6%
5143	-$8	4-4-4-K	S	2.0%	0.0%	3.2%	5.2%
5206	-$9	4-4-4-K	NS	1.2%	0.0%	1.7%	3.0%
1141	-$0	4-4-5-5	DS	6.1%	3.0%	9.2%	18.3%
1598	-$1	4-4-5-5	S	5.7%	2.9%	7.9%	16.5%
2059	-$2	4-4-5-5	NS	5.4%	2.8%	7.0%	15.2%
1296	-$1	4-4-5-6	DS	5.4%	3.8%	8.7%	17.9%
1817	-$2	4-4-5-6	S	4.9%	3.7%	7.6%	16.2%
2323	-$3	4-4-5-6	NS	4.6%	3.6%	6.6%	14.8%
1739	-$2	4-4-5-7	DS	5.3%	3.3%	8.0%	16.6%
2261	-$3	4-4-5-7	S	5.0%	3.3%	6.9%	15.1%
3105	-$4	4-4-5-7	NS	4.6%	3.2%	5.8%	13.6%
2047	-$2	4-4-5-8	DS	5.2%	3.1%	7.5%	15.8%
3048	-$3	4-4-5-8	S	4.9%	3.0%	6.3%	14.1%
3652	-$4	4-4-5-8	NS	4.5%	2.8%	5.4%	12.7%
3008	-$3	4-4-5-9	DS	4.8%	2.6%	7.1%	14.4%
3539	-$4	4-4-5-9	S	4.4%	2.5%	6.1%	13.1%

OMAHA HIGH-LOW 8 OR BETTER
5,278 HANDS   9 HANDED

| HAND RANK | VALUE $4/$8 | POCKET CARDS | | HIGH % | LOW % | SCOOP % | PART OR ALL % |
		HAND	SUITED				
4207	-$5	4-4-5-9	NS	3.9%	2.4%	5.1%	11.4%
2949	-$3	4-4-5-10	DS	4.7%	2.7%	7.4%	14.8%
3621	-$4	4-4-5-10	S	4.4%	2.6%	6.3%	13.2%
4318	-$5	4-4-5-10	NS	3.9%	2.5%	5.3%	11.7%
3091	-$4	4-4-5-J	DS	4.8%	2.7%	7.3%	14.8%
3626	-$4	4-4-5-J	S	4.5%	2.5%	6.4%	13.4%
4369	-$5	4-4-5-J	NS	3.9%	2.5%	5.3%	11.7%
2621	-$3	4-4-5-Q	DS	5.0%	2.7%	7.7%	15.4%
3484	-$4	4-4-5-Q	S	4.5%	2.6%	6.9%	14.0%
4338	-$5	4-4-5-Q	NS	4.0%	2.6%	5.5%	12.0%
2126	-$2	4-4-5-K	DS	5.3%	2.8%	8.5%	16.5%
3035	-$3	4-4-5-K	S	4.8%	2.7%	7.5%	15.0%
4248	-$5	4-4-5-K	NS	4.1%	2.7%	5.7%	12.5%
1605	-$1	4-4-6-6	DS	6.1%	2.4%	8.1%	16.6%
2302	-$3	4-4-6-6	S	5.7%	2.3%	7.0%	15.0%
2915	-$3	4-4-6-6	NS	5.4%	2.1%	5.9%	13.5%
2253	-$3	4-4-6-7	DS	5.5%	2.8%	7.2%	15.6%
2911	-$3	4-4-6-7	S	5.2%	2.8%	6.3%	14.2%
3653	-$4	4-4-6-7	NS	4.9%	2.6%	5.3%	12.7%
2803	-$3	4-4-6-8	DS	5.3%	2.6%	6.9%	14.8%
3600	-$4	4-4-6-8	S	5.1%	2.5%	5.7%	13.3%
4270	-$5	4-4-6-8	NS	4.7%	2.3%	4.8%	11.8%
3558	-$4	4-4-6-9	DS	5.0%	2.2%	6.5%	13.7%
4279	-$5	4-4-6-9	S	4.6%	2.1%	5.4%	12.1%
4716	-$6	4-4-6-9	NS	4.2%	1.9%	4.4%	10.4%
3758	-$4	4-4-6-10	DS	5.0%	2.2%	6.5%	13.8%
4420	-$5	4-4-6-10	S	4.6%	2.1%	5.5%	12.2%
4754	-$6	4-4-6-10	NS	4.1%	2.1%	4.4%	10.6%

OMAHA HIGH-LOW 8 OR BETTER
5,278 HANDS   9 HANDED

HAND RANK	VALUE $4/$8	POCKET CARDS		HIGH %	LOW %	SCOOP %	PART OR ALL %
		HAND	SUITED				
3777	-$4	4-4-6-J	DS	4.8%	2.1%	6.5%	13.4%
4414	-$5	4-4-6-J	S	4.4%	2.0%	5.5%	11.9%
4834	-$6	4-4-6-J	N	3.8%	2.0%	4.3%	10.0%
3618	-$4	4-4-6-Q	DS	4.9%	2.2%	6.8%	13.9%
4214	-$5	4-4-6-Q	S	4.5%	2.1%	5.8%	12.5%
4836	-$6	4-4-6-Q	NS	3.9%	1.9%	4.5%	10.3%
3131	-$4	4-4-6-K	DS	5.1%	2.3%	7.4%	14.8%
4112	-$5	4-4-6-K	S	4.8%	2.1%	6.5%	13.5%
4806	-$6	4-4-6-K	NS	4.0%	2.0%	4.6%	10.6%
2421	-$3	4-4-7-7	DS	6.1%	1.6%	7.0%	14.7%
3376	-$4	4-4-7-7	S	5.7%	1.4%	6.0%	13.1%
3955	-$5	4-4-7-7	NS	5.4%	1.3%	5.0%	11.7%
3575	-$4	4-4-7-8	DS	5.3%	2.0%	6.5%	13.8%
4234	-$5	4-4-7-8	S	5.0%	1.8%	5.6%	12.3%
4662	-$6	4-4-7-8	NS	4.6%	1.7%	4.5%	10.8%
4349	-$5	4-4-7-9	DS	5.1%	1.6%	5.9%	12.6%
4771	-$6	4-4-7-9	S	4.7%	1.4%	4.9%	11.1%
4971	-$7	4-4-7-9	NS	4.2%	1.4%	3.9%	9.4%
4220	-$5	4-4-7-10	DS	5.2%	1.5%	6.2%	12.9%
4760	-$6	4-4-7-10	S	4.7%	1.4%	5.1%	11.2%
4945	-$7	4-4-7-10	NS	4.2%	1.4%	4.3%	9.8%
4427	-$5	4-4-7-J	DS	4.8%	1.5%	6.0%	12.3%
4840	-$6	4-4-7-J	S	4.3%	1.4%	5.0%	10.8%
5007	-$7	4-4-7-J	NS	3.8%	1.3%	4.0%	9.2%
4456	-$5	4-4-7-Q	DS	4.8%	1.5%	6.0%	12.3%
4768	-$6	4-4-7-Q	S	4.4%	1.4%	5.1%	10.9%
5029	-$7	4-4-7-Q	NS	3.7%	1.2%	3.8%	8.7%
4156	-$5	4-4-7-K	DS	5.1%	1.6%	6.6%	13.4%

OMAHA HIGH-LOW 8 OR BETTER
5,278 HANDS   9 HANDED

| HAND RANK | VALUE $4/$8 | POCKET CARDS | | HIGH % | LOW % | SCOOP % | PART OR ALL % |
		HAND	SUITED				
4641	-$6	4-4-7-K	S	4.7%	1.5%	5.6%	11.7%
5019	-$7	4-4-7-K	NS	3.7%	1.3%	4.1%	9.1%
3331	-$4	4-4-8-8	DS	5.9%	1.1%	6.6%	13.6%
3966	-$5	4-4-8-8	S	5.5%	1.0%	5.7%	12.1%
4358	-$5	4-4-8-8	NS	5.1%	0.9%	4.7%	10.6%
4706	-$6	4-4-8-9	DS	4.9%	1.1%	6.0%	11.9%
4956	-$7	4-4-8-9	S	4.5%	1.0%	4.8%	10.3%
5047	-$8	4-4-8-9	NS	3.9%	0.9%	4.2%	9.0%
4365	-$5	4-4-8-10	DS	5.0%	1.1%	6.5%	12.5%
4680	-$6	4-4-8-10	S	4.5%	1.0%	5.6%	11.1%
4978	-$7	4-4-8-10	NS	4.0%	1.0%	4.5%	9.4%
4444	-$5	4-4-8-J	DS	4.7%	1.0%	6.4%	12.1%
4892	-$7	4-4-8-J	S	4.2%	0.9%	5.3%	10.5%
5040	-$7	4-4-8-J	NS	3.5%	0.9%	4.5%	8.9%
4696	-$6	4-4-8-Q	DS	4.5%	1.1%	6.1%	11.8%
4887	-$6	4-4-8-Q	S	4.1%	1.0%	5.2%	10.3%
5070	-$8	4-4-8-Q	NS	3.4%	0.9%	4.0%	8.3%
4671	-$6	4-4-8-K	DS	4.8%	1.1%	6.1%	12.0%
4866	-$6	4-4-8-K	S	4.5%	1.1%	5.3%	10.8%
5063	-$8	4-4-8-K	NS	3.4%	0.8%	3.9%	8.2%
2883	-$3	4-4-9-9	DS	4.2%	0.0%	7.1%	11.3%
3277	-$4	4-4-9-9	S	3.6%	0.0%	6.3%	9.9%
3603	-$4	4-4-9-9	NS	3.2%	0.0%	5.5%	8.6%
4551	-$6	4-4-9-10	DS	4.3%	0.0%	5.8%	10.1%
4885	-$6	4-4-9-10	S	3.8%	0.0%	4.9%	8.8%
4977	-$7	4-4-9-10	NS	3.4%	0.0%	4.3%	7.7%
4487	-$5	4-4-9-J	DS	4.0%	0.0%	6.0%	10.0%
4770	-$6	4-4-9-J	S	3.5%	0.0%	5.1%	8.6%

OMAHA HIGH-LOW 8 OR BETTER
5,278 HANDS   9 HANDED

| HAND RANK | VALUE $4/$8 | POCKET CARDS | | HIGH % | LOW % | SCOOP % | PART OR ALL % |
		HAND	SUITED				
4981	-$7	4-4-9-J	NS	3.0%	0.0%	4.2%	7.3%
4533	-$6	4-4-9-Q	DS	3.8%	0.0%	6.1%	9.9%
4791	-$6	4-4-9-Q	S	3.4%	0.0%	5.2%	8.6%
4987	-$7	4-4-9-Q	NS	2.7%	0.0%	4.3%	7.0%
4509	-$6	4-4-9-K	DS	4.1%	0.0%	6.3%	10.4%
4842	-$6	4-4-9-K	S	3.5%	0.0%	5.4%	8.9%
4973	-$7	4-4-9-K	NS	2.6%	0.0%	4.2%	6.7%
3071	-$4	4-4-10-10	DS	4.5%	0.0%	7.3%	11.8%
3139	-$4	4-4-10-10	S	3.9%	0.0%	6.8%	10.7%
3933	-$5	4-4-10-10	NS	3.5%	0.0%	5.8%	9.4%
3773	-$4	4-4-10-J	DS	4.3%	0.0%	6.9%	11.2%
4182	-$5	4-4-10-J	S	3.9%	0.0%	6.3%	10.2%
4659	-$6	4-4-10-J	NS	3.4%	0.0%	5.4%	8.8%
3634	-$4	4-4-10-Q	DS	4.2%	0.0%	7.1%	11.4%
4339	-$5	4-4-10-Q	S	3.8%	0.0%	6.2%	10.0%
4697	-$6	4-4-10-Q	NS	3.2%	0.0%	5.3%	8.5%
3984	-$5	4-4-10-K	DS	4.4%	0.0%	7.2%	11.6%
4175	-$5	4-4-10-K	S	4.0%	0.0%	6.6%	10.5%
4803	-$6	4-4-10-K	NS	2.9%	0.0%	5.0%	7.9%
2709	-$3	4-4-J-J	DS	4.8%	0.0%	8.4%	13.2%
3253	-$4	4-4-J-J	S	4.3%	0.0%	7.5%	11.8%
3707	-$4	4-4-J-J	NS	3.8%	0.0%	6.7%	10.4%
3562	-$4	4-4-J-Q	DS	4.3%	0.0%	7.3%	11.6%
4247	-$5	4-4-J-Q	S	3.8%	0.0%	6.5%	10.3%
4748	-$6	4-4-J-Q	NS	3.1%	0.0%	5.5%	8.6%
3753	-$4	4-4-J-K	DS	4.6%	0.0%	7.5%	12.0%
4422	-$5	4-4-J-K	S	4.0%	0.0%	6.6%	10.6%
4758	-$6	4-4-J-K	NS	3.0%	0.0%	5.3%	8.3%

OMAHA HIGH-LOW 8 OR BETTER
5,278 HANDS   9 HANDED

HAND RANK	VALUE $4/$8	POCKET CARDS		HIGH %	LOW %	SCOOP %	PART OR ALL %
		HAND	SUITED				
1771	-$2	4-4-Q-Q	DS	5.5%	0.0%	10.5%	16.1%
2833	-$3	4-4-Q-Q	S	4.8%	0.0%	9.2%	14.0%
3655	-$4	4-4-Q-Q	NS	4.0%	0.0%	8.0%	12.1%
3357	-$4	4-4-Q-K	DS	4.8%	0.0%	8.0%	12.8%
4064	-$5	4-4-Q-K	S	4.1%	0.0%	7.0%	11.1%
4572	-$6	4-4-Q-K	NS	3.1%	0.0%	5.7%	8.8%
1168	-$0	4-4-K-K	DS	6.8%	0.0%	13.0%	19.7%
1882	-$2	4-4-K-K	S	5.7%	0.0%	11.7%	17.4%
3049	-$3	4-4-K-K	NS	4.6%	0.0%	10.4%	15.0%
4723	-$6	4-5-5-5	S	2.6%	2.7%	4.4%	9.7%
4925	-$7	4-5-5-5	NS	2.3%	2.7%	3.4%	8.4%
1244	-$1	4-5-5-6	DS	5.4%	3.8%	8.7%	17.8%
2141	-$2	4-5-5-6	S	4.2%	2.4%	5.7%	12.3%
2513	-$3	4-5-5-6	NS	3.8%	2.5%	5.4%	11.6%
1691	-$2	4-5-5-7	DS	5.4%	3.2%	7.8%	16.5%
2249	-$3	4-5-5-7	S	5.0%	3.2%	6.7%	14.8%
2869	-$3	4-5-5-7	NS	4.8%	3.1%	5.9%	13.7%
2142	-$2	4-5-5-8	DS	5.3%	3.0%	7.3%	15.7%
2865	-$3	4-5-5-8	S	4.8%	2.9%	6.4%	14.2%
3731	-$4	4-5-5-8	NS	4.5%	2.8%	5.3%	12.7%
3107	-$4	4-5-5-9	DS	4.7%	2.6%	7.0%	14.3%
3694	-$4	4-5-5-9	S	4.3%	2.4%	5.8%	12.6%
4344	-$5	4-5-5-9	NS	4.0%	2.4%	5.0%	11.3%
3079	-$4	4-5-5-10	DS	4.8%	2.6%	7.1%	14.4%
3754	-$4	4-5-5-10	S	4.3%	2.5%	6.0%	12.8%
4385	-$5	4-5-5-10	NS	3.9%	2.4%	5.1%	11.5%
2964	-$3	4-5-5-J	DS	4.9%	2.5%	7.4%	14.8%
3680	-$4	4-5-5-J	S	4.3%	2.5%	6.1%	12.9%

OMAHA HIGH-LOW 8 OR BETTER
5,278 HANDS   9 HANDED

| HAND RANK | VALUE $4/$8 | POCKET CARDS | | HIGH % | LOW % | SCOOP % | PART OR ALL % |
		HAND	SUITED				
4357	-$5	4-5-5-J	NS	4.0%	2.4%	5.3%	11.7%
2779	-$3	4-5-5-Q	DS	5.0%	2.6%	7.8%	15.4%
3319	-$4	4-5-5-Q	S	4.6%	2.5%	6.6%	13.7%
4442	-$5	4-5-5-Q	NS	3.8%	2.5%	5.5%	11.8%
2280	-$3	4-5-5-K	DS	5.2%	2.7%	8.4%	16.2%
2937	-$3	4-5-5-K	S	4.8%	2.6%	7.2%	14.6%
4317	-$5	4-5-5-K	NS	4.0%	2.5%	5.6%	12.1%
1224	-$1	4-5-6-6	DS	5.6%	3.6%	8.6%	17.8%
1692	-$2	4-5-6-6	S	5.2%	3.6%	7.4%	16.2%
2165	-$2	4-5-6-6	NS	5.0%	3.4%	6.3%	14.8%
1301	-$1	4-5-6-7	DS	6.1%	3.6%	7.9%	17.6%
1779	-$2	4-5-6-7	S	5.8%	3.6%	6.7%	16.1%
2350	-$3	4-5-6-7	NS	5.5%	2.9%	4.3%	12.7%
1499	-$1	4-5-6-8	DS	5.9%	3.6%	7.7%	17.2%
2083	-$2	4-5-6-8	S	5.6%	3.5%	6.6%	15.7%
2925	-$3	4-5-6-8	NS	5.1%	3.4%	5.6%	14.1%
2756	-$3	4-5-6-9	DS	4.8%	3.4%	6.6%	14.8%
2962	-$3	4-5-6-9	S	4.6%	3.3%	6.5%	14.3%
3627	-$4	4-5-6-9	NS	4.3%	3.2%	5.5%	13.0%
2220	-$2	4-5-6-10	DS	5.2%	3.5%	7.6%	16.3%
3111	-$4	4-5-6-10	S	4.7%	3.4%	6.6%	14.6%
3861	-$4	4-5-6-10	NS	4.2%	3.2%	5.6%	13.1%
2238	-$3	4-5-6-J	DS	5.1%	3.6%	7.7%	16.4%
3103	-$4	4-5-6-J	S	4.6%	3.4%	6.9%	14.9%
4084	-$5	4-5-6-J	NS	4.1%	3.3%	5.7%	13.1%
2156	-$2	4-5-6-Q	DS	5.0%	3.6%	8.1%	16.7%
2759	-$3	4-5-6-Q	S	4.8%	3.4%	7.3%	15.4%
3973	-$5	4-5-6-Q	NS	4.2%	3.3%	5.9%	13.5%

OMAHA HIGH-LOW 8 OR BETTER
5,278 HANDS   9 HANDED

HAND RANK	VALUE $4/$8	POCKET CARDS		HIGH %	LOW %	SCOOP %	PART OR ALL %
		HAND	SUITED				
1639	-$1	4-5-6-K	DS	5.4%	3.7%	9.1%	18.2%
2128	-$2	4-5-6-K	S	5.0%	3.5%	8.0%	16.6%
3914	-$5	4-5-6-K	NS	4.4%	3.3%	6.2%	13.9%
1401	-$1	4-5-7-7	DS	5.8%	3.0%	8.0%	16.8%
1986	-$2	4-5-7-7	S	5.4%	2.8%	6.8%	14.9%
2721	-$3	4-5-7-7	NS	5.0%	2.8%	5.6%	13.4%
1813	-$2	4-5-7-8	DS	5.7%	3.0%	7.2%	16.0%
2285	-$3	4-5-7-8	S	5.4%	2.9%	6.4%	14.7%
3374	-$4	4-5-7-8	NS	5.1%	2.9%	5.2%	13.2%
2328	-$3	4-5-7-9	DS	5.1%	3.0%	7.2%	15.2%
3233	-$4	4-5-7-9	S	4.7%	2.8%	6.1%	13.6%
4042	-$5	4-5-7-9	NS	4.3%	2.8%	5.1%	12.2%
2606	-$3	4-5-7-10	DS	5.0%	3.0%	7.2%	15.1%
3466	-$4	4-5-7-10	S	4.6%	2.9%	6.1%	13.6%
4179	-$5	4-5-7-10	NS	4.1%	2.8%	5.1%	12.1%
2586	-$3	4-5-7-J	DS	5.0%	3.1%	7.3%	15.3%
3420	-$4	4-5-7-J	S	4.6%	2.9%	6.4%	13.9%
4426	-$5	4-5-7-J	NS	4.0%	2.8%	5.3%	12.2%
2551	-$3	4-5-7-Q	DS	5.0%	2.9%	7.2%	15.2%
3448	-$4	4-5-7-Q	S	4.5%	2.8%	6.3%	13.7%
4366	-$5	4-5-7-Q	NS	4.0%	2.7%	5.0%	11.7%
1983	-$2	4-5-7-K	DS	5.2%	3.0%	8.1%	16.3%
2706	-$3	4-5-7-K	S	4.8%	2.9%	7.1%	14.8%
4326	-$5	4-5-7-K	NS	4.0%	2.7%	5.5%	12.2%
1624	-$1	4-5-8-8	DS	5.4%	2.6%	7.4%	15.4%
2282	-$3	4-5-8-8	S	5.1%	2.5%	6.3%	13.8%
2970	-$3	4-5-8-8	NS	4.5%	2.4%	5.4%	12.3%
3012	-$3	4-5-8-9	DS	4.9%	2.6%	7.1%	14.6%

		POCKET CARDS					
HAND RANK	VALUE $4/$8	HAND	SUITED	HIGH %	LOW %	SCOOP %	PART OR ALL %
3956	-$5	4-5-8-9	S	4.4%	2.6%	6.2%	13.2%
4540	-$6	4-5-8-9	NS	3.9%	2.7%	5.2%	11.8%
2863	-$3	4-5-8-10	DS	4.9%	2.7%	7.0%	14.5%
3765	-$4	4-5-8-10	S	4.3%	2.7%	6.5%	13.5%
4359	-$5	4-5-8-10	NS	3.8%	2.6%	5.7%	12.0%
2644	-$3	4-5-8-J	DS	4.8%	2.8%	7.7%	15.2%
3620	-$4	4-5-8-J	S	4.4%	2.6%	6.8%	13.8%
4463	-$5	4-5-8-J	NS	3.8%	2.6%	5.7%	12.1%
2719	-$3	4-5-8-Q	DS	4.6%	2.7%	7.7%	15.0%
3643	-$4	4-5-8-Q	S	4.2%	2.6%	6.6%	13.4%
4640	-$6	4-5-8-Q	NS	3.6%	2.5%	5.3%	11.4%
2791	-$3	4-5-8-K	DS	5.0%	2.6%	7.2%	14.9%
3353	-$4	4-5-8-K	S	4.5%	2.6%	6.6%	13.8%
4610	-$6	4-5-8-K	NS	3.7%	2.5%	5.0%	11.2%
1559	-$1	4-5-9-9	DS	3.9%	2.3%	8.4%	14.6%
2092	-$2	4-5-9-9	S	3.4%	2.2%	7.6%	13.2%
2326	-$3	4-5-9-9	NS	2.8%	2.1%	6.6%	11.5%
3106	-$4	4-5-9-10	DS	4.2%	2.3%	7.6%	14.0%
4009	-$5	4-5-9-10	S	3.7%	2.2%	6.6%	12.4%
4566	-$6	4-5-9-10	NS	3.1%	2.1%	5.6%	10.9%
2906	-$3	4-5-9-J	DS	4.3%	2.3%	7.8%	14.4%
3635	-$4	4-5-9-J	S	3.7%	2.2%	7.1%	13.0%
4526	-$6	4-5-9-J	NS	3.1%	2.1%	5.9%	11.2%
2995	-$3	4-5-9-Q	DS	4.0%	2.2%	8.1%	14.3%
3982	-$5	4-5-9-Q	S	3.5%	2.2%	6.9%	12.6%
4691	-$6	4-5-9-Q	NS	2.8%	2.0%	5.8%	10.6%
2989	-$3	4-5-9-K	DS	4.0%	2.2%	8.1%	14.3%
3768	-$4	4-5-9-K	S	3.5%	2.1%	7.1%	12.7%

OMAHA HIGH-LOW 8 OR BETTER
5,278 HANDS   9 HANDED

OMAHA HIGH-LOW 8 OR BETTER
5,278 HANDS   9 HANDED

| HAND RANK | VALUE $4/$8 | POCKET CARDS | | HIGH % | LOW % | SCOOP % | PART OR ALL % |
		HAND	SUITED				
4703	-$6	4-5-9-K	NS	2.6%	2.0%	5.9%	10.4%
1583	-$1	4-5-10-10	DS	4.1%	2.4%	9.2%	15.7%
2203	-$2	4-5-10-10	S	3.3%	2.2%	7.8%	13.3%
2687	-$3	4-5-10-10	NS	2.8%	2.2%	7.0%	12.1%
1884	-$2	4-5-10-J	DS	4.5%	2.4%	9.0%	15.9%
2595	-$3	4-5-10-J	S	4.2%	2.3%	8.1%	14.6%
3926	-$5	4-5-10-J	NS	3.5%	2.3%	7.1%	12.9%
1935	-$2	4-5-10-Q	DS	4.3%	2.3%	9.2%	15.8%
2942	-$3	4-5-10-Q	S	3.8%	2.3%	8.2%	14.3%
3954	-$5	4-5-10-Q	NS	3.2%	2.2%	7.1%	12.6%
1851	-$2	4-5-10-K	DS	4.4%	2.3%	9.4%	16.0%
2518	-$3	4-5-10-K	S	3.8%	2.2%	8.6%	14.6%
4235	-$5	4-5-10-K	NS	3.0%	2.1%	6.8%	11.9%
1454	-$1	4-5-J-J	DS	4.3%	2.4%	10.0%	16.7%
1991	-$2	4-5-J-J	S	3.8%	2.4%	9.0%	15.2%
2493	-$3	4-5-J-J	NS	3.1%	2.3%	7.8%	13.2%
1731	-$2	4-5-J-Q	DS	4.5%	2.3%	9.5%	16.3%
2514	-$3	4-5-J-Q	S	3.9%	2.3%	8.7%	14.8%
3934	-$5	4-5-J-Q	NS	3.2%	2.3%	7.3%	12.8%
1715	-$2	4-5-J-K	DS	4.5%	2.2%	9.7%	16.4%
2564	-$3	4-5-J-K	S	3.8%	2.3%	8.7%	14.8%
4289	-$5	4-5-J-K	NS	3.0%	2.2%	6.8%	12.0%
968	$0	4-5-Q-Q	DS	4.8%	2.6%	11.9%	19.2%
1594	-$1	4-5-Q-Q	S	4.1%	2.5%	10.3%	16.8%
2452	-$3	4-5-Q-Q	NS	3.3%	2.4%	9.1%	14.9%
1456	-$1	4-5-Q-K	DS	4.7%	2.4%	10.1%	17.2%
2305	-$3	4-5-Q-K	S	3.9%	2.3%	9.1%	15.3%
3817	-$4	4-5-Q-K	NS	3.1%	2.2%	7.5%	12.9%

OMAHA HIGH-LOW 8 OR BETTER
5,278 HANDS 9 HANDED

| HAND RANK | VALUE $4/$8 | POCKET CARDS | | HIGH % | LOW % | SCOOP % | PART OR ALL % |
		HAND	SUITED				
569	$3	4-5-K-K	DS	5.7%	2.7%	14.5%	22.9%
1014	$0	4-5-K-K	S	4.9%	2.7%	12.9%	20.5%
2114	-$2	4-5-K-K	NS	3.8%	2.6%	11.3%	17.7%
5000	-$7	4-6-6-6	S	2.7%	1.9%	3.3%	7.8%
5059	-$8	4-6-6-6	NS	2.3%	1.7%	2.3%	6.3%
1774	-$2	4-6-6-7	DS	5.7%	2.6%	7.2%	15.5%
2541	-$3	4-6-6-7	S	5.3%	2.5%	6.0%	13.7%
3264	-$4	4-6-6-7	NS	5.0%	2.3%	5.2%	12.5%
2482	-$3	4-6-6-8	DS	5.5%	2.4%	6.5%	14.4%
3096	-$4	4-6-6-8	S	5.1%	2.2%	5.6%	12.9%
3789	-$4	4-6-6-8	NS	4.9%	2.1%	4.7%	11.7%
3350	-$4	4-6-6-9	DS	5.3%	1.9%	6.0%	13.1%
3971	-$5	4-6-6-9	S	4.8%	1.8%	4.9%	11.4%
4536	-$6	4-6-6-9	NS	4.4%	1.7%	4.1%	10.2%
3456	-$4	4-6-6-10	DS	5.2%	2.0%	6.1%	13.3%
4010	-$5	4-6-6-10	S	4.7%	1.9%	5.1%	11.7%
4518	-$6	4-6-6-10	NS	4.2%	1.8%	4.3%	10.3%
3560	-$4	4-6-6-J	DS	4.9%	1.9%	6.2%	13.0%
4110	-$5	4-6-6-J	S	4.5%	1.8%	5.1%	11.4%
4612	-$6	4-6-6-J	NS	4.0%	1.8%	4.1%	9.9%
3381	-$4	4-6-6-Q	DS	5.0%	1.9%	6.6%	13.5%
3917	-$5	4-6-6-Q	S	4.6%	1.8%	5.4%	11.9%
4575	-$6	4-6-6-Q	NS	4.1%	1.8%	4.4%	10.3%
2654	-$3	4-6-6-K	DS	5.4%	2.0%	7.4%	14.7%
3517	-$4	4-6-6-K	S	5.0%	1.9%	6.0%	12.9%
4603	-$6	4-6-6-K	NS	4.1%	1.8%	4.5%	10.4%
1874	-$2	4-6-7-7	DS	5.8%	2.4%	7.0%	15.2%
2456	-$3	4-6-7-7	S	5.5%	2.3%	6.0%	13.8%

OMAHA HIGH-LOW 8 OR BETTER
5,278 HANDS   9 HANDED

HAND RANK	VALUE $4/$8	POCKET CARDS		HIGH %	LOW %	SCOOP %	PART OR ALL %
		HAND	SUITED				
3193	-$4	4-6-7-7	NS	5.1%	2.2%	5.1%	12.3%
2087	-$2	4-6-7-8	DS	6.0%	2.5%	6.7%	15.1%
2899	-$3	4-6-7-8	S	5.6%	2.2%	5.7%	13.5%
3536	-$4	4-6-7-8	NS	5.3%	2.2%	4.8%	12.3%
2701	-$3	4-6-7-9	DS	5.5%	2.4%	6.5%	14.4%
3638	-$4	4-6-7-9	S	5.0%	2.2%	5.6%	12.8%
4395	-$5	4-6-7-9	NS	4.6%	2.1%	4.5%	11.2%
2742	-$3	4-6-7-10	DS	5.5%	2.3%	6.8%	14.6%
3415	-$4	4-6-7-10	S	5.0%	2.2%	5.8%	13.1%
4238	-$5	4-6-7-10	NS	4.5%	2.1%	4.9%	11.5%
3377	-$4	4-6-7-J	DS	5.0%	2.4%	6.4%	13.7%
3969	-$5	4-6-7-J	S	4.7%	2.2%	5.5%	12.3%
4636	-$6	4-6-7-J	NS	4.0%	2.0%	4.5%	10.5%
3166	-$4	4-6-7-Q	DS	5.1%	2.4%	6.8%	14.4%
3869	-$5	4-6-7-Q	S	4.8%	2.2%	5.8%	12.9%
4718	-$6	4-6-7-Q	NS	4.2%	2.0%	4.5%	10.7%
2683	-$3	4-6-7-K	DS	5.5%	2.4%	7.4%	15.3%
3281	-$4	4-6-7-K	S	5.1%	2.4%	6.5%	14.0%
4653	-$6	4-6-7-K	NS	4.2%	2.1%	4.7%	11.1%
1979	-$2	4-6-8-8	DS	5.7%	2.2%	7.0%	14.8%
2619	-$3	4-6-8-8	S	5.2%	2.0%	6.0%	13.2%
3534	-$4	4-6-8-8	NS	4.8%	2.0%	4.9%	11.7%
3266	-$4	4-6-8-9	DS	5.2%	2.2%	6.8%	14.2%
4104	-$5	4-6-8-9	S	4.8%	2.0%	5.8%	12.6%
4730	-$6	4-6-8-9	NS	4.4%	1.9%	4.7%	11.0%
2816	-$3	4-6-8-10	DS	5.3%	2.2%	7.1%	14.5%
3674	-$4	4-6-8-10	S	4.9%	2.0%	6.2%	13.2%
4530	-$6	4-6-8-10	NS	4.3%	2.0%	5.1%	11.3%

OMAHA HIGH-LOW 8 OR BETTER
5,278 HANDS   9 HANDED

| HAND RANK | VALUE $4/$8 | POCKET CARDS | | HIGH % | LOW % | SCOOP % | PART OR ALL % |
		HAND	SUITED				
3390	-$4	4-6-8-J	DS	4.8%	2.1%	6.9%	13.8%
4305	-$5	4-6-8-J	S	4.4%	1.9%	5.7%	12.1%
4761	-$6	4-6-8-J	NS	3.8%	1.9%	4.9%	10.6%
3223	-$4	4-6-8-Q	DS	4.9%	2.2%	7.3%	14.4%
4157	-$5	4-6-8-Q	S	4.5%	2.1%	6.1%	12.7%
4849	-$6	4-6-8-Q	NS	3.8%	1.9%	4.9%	10.6%
3085	-$4	4-6-8-K	DS	5.1%	2.2%	7.1%	14.4%
4000	-$5	4-6-8-K	S	4.7%	2.1%	6.1%	12.9%
4858	-$6	4-6-8-K	NS	3.8%	1.9%	4.7%	10.3%
1908	-$2	4-6-9-9	DS	4.1%	1.7%	7.7%	13.5%
2369	-$3	4-6-9-9	S	3.6%	1.7%	6.8%	12.0%
3073	-$4	4-6-9-9	NS	3.1%	1.6%	5.9%	10.5%
3185	-$4	4-6-9-10	DS	4.8%	1.7%	7.1%	13.7%
4134	-$5	4-6-9-10	S	4.3%	1.7%	6.1%	12.0%
4652	-$6	4-6-9-10	NS	3.8%	1.6%	5.1%	10.4%
3895	-$5	4-6-9-J	DS	4.2%	1.7%	6.8%	12.7%
4274	-$5	4-6-9-J	S	3.7%	1.6%	6.1%	11.4%
4883	-$6	4-6-9-J	NS	3.1%	1.5%	5.0%	9.5%
3587	-$4	4-6-9-Q	DS	4.3%	1.7%	7.4%	13.4%
4252	-$5	4-6-9-Q	S	3.8%	1.6%	6.4%	11.8%
4856	-$6	4-6-9-Q	NS	3.1%	1.5%	5.3%	9.9%
3601	-$4	4-6-9-K	DS	4.3%	1.8%	7.4%	13.4%
4168	-$5	4-6-9-K	S	3.8%	1.6%	6.5%	12.0%
4902	-$7	4-6-9-K	NS	2.9%	1.5%	5.1%	9.5%
2046	-$2	4-6-10-10	DS	4.5%	1.9%	8.3%	14.7%
2502	-$3	4-6-10-10	S	3.7%	1.8%	7.2%	12.7%
3184	-$4	4-6-10-10	NS	3.2%	1.7%	6.5%	11.4%
2646	-$3	4-6-10-J	DS	4.6%	1.8%	8.1%	14.5%

OMAHA HIGH-LOW 8 OR BETTER
5,278 HANDS   9 HANDED

HAND RANK	VALUE $4/$8	POCKET CARDS HAND	SUITED	HIGH %	LOW %	SCOOP %	PART OR ALL %
3705	-$4	4-6-10-J	S	4.1%	1.8%	7.0%	12.9%
4512	-$6	4-6-10-J	NS	3.5%	1.7%	6.1%	11.3%
2462	-$3	4-6-10-Q	DS	4.7%	1.9%	8.4%	15.0%
3305	-$4	4-6-10-Q	S	4.1%	1.8%	7.6%	13.6%
4363	-$5	4-6-10-Q	NS	3.5%	1.7%	6.5%	11.7%
2248	-$3	4-6-10-K	DS	4.8%	1.9%	8.6%	15.3%
3145	-$4	4-6-10-K	S	4.3%	1.8%	7.8%	13.8%
4643	-$6	4-6-10-K	NS	3.4%	1.6%	6.1%	11.0%
1834	-$2	4-6-J-J	DS	4.2%	1.9%	9.0%	15.1%
2457	-$3	4-6-J-J	S	3.6%	1.8%	8.0%	13.4%
3489	-$4	4-6-J-J	NS	3.0%	1.8%	6.9%	11.7%
2490	-$3	4-6-J-Q	DS	4.5%	1.8%	8.4%	14.7%
3338	-$4	4-6-J-Q	S	3.8%	1.7%	7.7%	13.3%
4400	-$5	4-6-J-Q	NS	3.2%	1.7%	6.4%	11.3%
2435	-$3	4-6-J-K	DS	4.5%	1.8%	8.5%	14.8%
3432	-$4	4-6-J-K	S	4.0%	1.7%	7.5%	13.2%
4598	-$6	4-6-J-K	NS	3.0%	1.6%	6.0%	10.6%
1338	-$1	4-6-Q-Q	DS	4.6%	2.0%	10.9%	17.5%
2028	-$2	4-6-Q-Q	S	4.1%	1.9%	9.4%	15.4%
3235	-$4	4-6-Q-Q	NS	3.3%	1.8%	8.3%	13.4%
2050	-$2	4-6-Q-K	DS	4.7%	1.8%	9.1%	15.6%
3202	-$4	4-6-Q-K	S	4.0%	1.7%	7.8%	13.5%
4529	-$6	4-6-Q-K	NS	3.1%	1.6%	6.3%	11.0%
779	$1	4-6-K-K	DS	5.9%	2.0%	13.5%	21.3%
1489	-$1	4-6-K-K	S	4.8%	2.1%	11.9%	18.8%
2811	-$3	4-6-K-K	NS	3.8%	2.0%	10.3%	16.1%
5102	-$8	4-7-7-7	S	2.6%	1.1%	2.5%	6.2%
5161	-$9	4-7-7-7	NS	2.3%	0.9%	1.6%	4.8%

OMAHA HIGH-LOW 8 OR BETTER
5,278 HANDS 9 HANDED

| HAND RANK | VALUE $4/$8 | POCKET CARDS | | HIGH % | LOW % | SCOOP % | PART OR ALL % |
		HAND	SUITED				
2590	-$3	4-7-7-8	DS	5.5%	1.6%	6.6%	13.7%
3439	-$4	4-7-7-8	S	5.1%	1.5%	5.5%	12.1%
4124	-$5	4-7-7-8	NS	4.7%	1.4%	4.6%	10.8%
3519	-$4	4-7-7-9	DS	5.3%	1.3%	5.9%	12.5%
4211	-$5	4-7-7-9	S	4.8%	1.2%	4.8%	10.8%
4620	-$6	4-7-7-9	NS	4.4%	1.1%	4.1%	9.6%
3563	-$4	4-7-7-10	DS	5.4%	1.3%	6.0%	12.7%
4198	-$5	4-7-7-10	S	4.9%	1.2%	4.9%	11.0%
4655	-$6	4-7-7-10	NS	4.5%	1.2%	4.0%	9.7%
4016	-$5	4-7-7-J	DS	5.1%	1.2%	5.8%	12.1%
4285	-$5	4-7-7-J	S	4.6%	1.1%	4.9%	10.7%
4870	-$6	4-7-7-J	NS	4.0%	1.1%	4.0%	9.0%
4029	-$5	4-7-7-Q	DS	5.0%	1.3%	5.8%	12.1%
4449	-$5	4-7-7-Q	S	4.4%	1.1%	4.8%	10.4%
4877	-$6	4-7-7-Q	NS	3.8%	1.0%	3.8%	8.7%
3458	-$4	4-7-7-K	DS	5.7%	1.4%	7.0%	14.1%
4186	-$5	4-7-7-K	S	4.7%	1.3%	5.3%	11.3%
4841	-$6	4-7-7-K	NS	4.0%	1.0%	4.0%	9.1%
2594	-$3	4-7-8-8	DS	5.5%	1.6%	6.7%	13.8%
3334	-$4	4-7-8-8	S	5.1%	1.5%	5.8%	12.4%
4021	-$5	4-7-8-8	NS	4.6%	1.4%	4.9%	10.9%
3392	-$4	4-7-8-9	DS	5.2%	1.5%	6.5%	13.2%
4199	-$5	4-7-8-9	S	4.8%	1.4%	5.5%	11.7%
4593	-$6	4-7-8-9	NS	4.3%	1.3%	4.9%	10.5%
2653	-$3	4-7-8-10	DS	5.3%	1.5%	6.9%	13.7%
3639	-$4	4-7-8-10	S	4.8%	1.5%	5.9%	12.2%
4364	-$5	4-7-8-10	NS	4.3%	1.4%	5.2%	10.9%
3161	-$4	4-7-8-J	DS	4.9%	1.5%	6.7%	13.1%

OMAHA HIGH-LOW 8 OR BETTER
5,278 HANDS   9 HANDED

HAND RANK	VALUE $4/$8	POCKET CARDS		HIGH %	LOW %	SCOOP %	PART OR ALL %
		HAND	SUITED				
3994	-$5	4-7-8-J	S	4.3%	1.4%	5.9%	11.6%
4355	-$5	4-7-8-J	NS	4.2%	1.3%	5.1%	10.7%
3590	-$4	4-7-8-Q	DS	4.8%	1.5%	6.5%	12.8%
4228	-$5	4-7-8-Q	S	4.3%	1.4%	5.7%	11.4%
4898	-$7	4-7-8-Q	NS	3.6%	1.3%	4.4%	9.3%
3312	-$4	4-7-8-K	DS	5.0%	1.7%	7.0%	13.7%
4030	-$5	4-7-8-K	S	4.7%	1.5%	6.1%	12.3%
4897	-$7	4-7-8-K	NS	3.7%	1.3%	4.7%	9.8%
2306	-$3	4-7-9-9	DS	4.2%	1.2%	7.3%	12.7%
3036	-$3	4-7-9-9	S	3.6%	1.1%	6.4%	11.1%
3535	-$4	4-7-9-9	NS	3.1%	1.0%	5.7%	9.8%
3291	-$4	4-7-9-10	DS	4.9%	1.2%	6.8%	12.9%
4106	-$5	4-7-9-10	S	4.4%	1.1%	6.0%	11.5%
4678	-$6	4-7-9-10	NS	3.8%	1.0%	5.2%	10.0%
3654	-$4	4-7-9-J	DS	4.5%	1.1%	6.8%	12.4%
4443	-$5	4-7-9-J	S	3.9%	1.0%	5.8%	10.7%
4838	-$6	4-7-9-J	NS	3.3%	1.0%	5.0%	9.3%
4066	-$5	4-7-9-Q	DS	4.2%	1.1%	6.6%	11.9%
4542	-$6	4-7-9-Q	S	3.6%	1.0%	5.8%	10.4%
4954	-$7	4-7-9-Q	NS	2.9%	0.9%	4.6%	8.5%
3826	-$4	4-7-9-K	DS	4.4%	1.2%	7.1%	12.8%
4250	-$5	4-7-9-K	S	4.0%	1.1%	6.5%	11.5%
4941	-$7	4-7-9-K	NS	2.9%	1.0%	5.0%	8.9%
2226	-$2	4-7-10-10	DS	4.3%	1.2%	8.0%	13.5%
2637	-$3	4-7-10-10	S	3.8%	1.2%	7.3%	12.3%
3538	-$4	4-7-10-10	NS	3.2%	1.1%	6.3%	10.6%
2550	-$3	4-7-10-J	DS	4.8%	1.2%	7.9%	14.0%
3271	-$4	4-7-10-J	S	4.3%	1.1%	7.2%	12.6%

OMAHA HIGH-LOW 8 OR BETTER
5,278 HANDS   9 HANDED

HAND RANK	VALUE $4/$8	POCKET CARDS		HIGH %	LOW %	SCOOP %	PART OR ALL %
		HAND	SUITED				
4294	-$5	4-7-10-J	NS	3.7%	1.1%	6.2%	11.1%
3135	-$4	4-7-10-Q	DS	4.5%	1.2%	7.7%	13.5%
3900	-$5	4-7-10-Q	S	4.0%	1.2%	6.8%	12.0%
4596	-$6	4-7-10-Q	NS	3.3%	1.0%	5.9%	10.2%
2419	-$3	4-7-10-K	DS	4.9%	1.3%	8.4%	14.6%
3297	-$4	4-7-10-K	S	4.4%	1.2%	7.5%	13.1%
4607	-$6	4-7-10-K	NS	3.4%	1.1%	6.1%	10.5%
1973	-$2	4-7-J-J	DS	4.3%	1.3%	8.7%	14.3%
2783	-$3	4-7-J-J	S	3.7%	1.2%	7.7%	12.6%
3446	-$4	4-7-J-J	NS	3.1%	1.1%	6.9%	11.1%
3147	-$4	4-7-J-Q	DS	4.3%	1.2%	7.8%	13.2%
4013	-$5	4-7-J-Q	S	3.7%	1.1%	6.8%	11.6%
4698	-$6	4-7-J-Q	NS	3.0%	1.0%	5.8%	9.8%
2627	-$3	4-7-J-K	DS	4.6%	1.2%	8.5%	14.3%
3552	-$4	4-7-J-K	S	3.9%	1.2%	7.5%	12.7%
4657	-$6	4-7-J-K	NS	3.0%	1.1%	6.1%	10.2%
1818	-$2	4-7-Q-Q	DS	4.5%	1.4%	10.1%	15.9%
2720	-$3	4-7-Q-Q	S	3.8%	1.3%	8.8%	13.8%
3965	-$5	4-7-Q-Q	NS	3.1%	1.2%	7.6%	11.9%
2610	-$3	4-7-Q-K	DS	4.5%	1.2%	8.4%	14.1%
3555	-$4	4-7-Q-K	S	3.9%	1.1%	7.3%	12.3%
4689	-$6	4-7-Q-K	NS	2.9%	1.0%	5.8%	9.7%
909	$1	4-7-K-K	DS	5.6%	1.6%	12.8%	20.1%
1903	-$2	4-7-K-K	S	4.5%	1.4%	11.3%	17.2%
3373	-$4	4-7-K-K	NS	3.5%	1.4%	9.8%	14.7%
5199	-$9	4-8-8-8	S	2.3%	0.7%	2.3%	5.3%
5247	-$9	4-8-8-8	NS	1.9%	0.6%	1.4%	4.0%
3882	-$5	4-8-8-9	DS	5.4%	0.9%	6.0%	12.3%

OMAHA HIGH-LOW 8 OR BETTER
5,278 HANDS   9 HANDED

| HAND RANK | VALUE $4/$8 | POCKET CARDS | | HIGH % | LOW % | SCOOP % | PART OR ALL % |
		HAND	SUITED				
4511	-$6	4-8-8-9	S	4.8%	0.8%	5.1%	10.6%
4773	-$6	4-8-8-9	NS	4.3%	0.7%	4.4%	9.4%
3352	-$4	4-8-8-10	DS	5.4%	0.9%	6.5%	12.9%
4094	-$5	4-8-8-10	S	4.9%	0.8%	5.5%	11.2%
4470	-$5	4-8-8-10	NS	4.4%	0.8%	4.8%	10.0%
3791	-$4	4-8-8-J	DS	5.0%	0.9%	6.4%	12.3%
4194	-$5	4-8-8-J	S	4.6%	0.8%	5.5%	10.8%
4767	-$6	4-8-8-J	NS	4.0%	0.8%	4.6%	9.3%
3849	-$4	4-8-8-Q	DS	4.9%	0.9%	6.4%	12.2%
4507	-$6	4-8-8-Q	S	4.4%	0.9%	5.2%	10.4%
4915	-$7	4-8-8-Q	NS	3.7%	0.7%	4.2%	8.6%
3983	-$5	4-8-8-K	DS	5.2%	1.0%	6.3%	12.4%
4384	-$5	4-8-8-K	S	4.6%	0.9%	5.2%	10.7%
4950	-$7	4-8-8-K	NS	3.7%	0.7%	3.8%	8.3%
2578	-$3	4-8-9-9	DS	3.9%	0.8%	7.6%	12.4%
3356	-$4	4-8-9-9	S	3.4%	0.8%	6.7%	10.9%
3894	-$5	4-8-9-9	NS	2.9%	0.7%	6.0%	9.6%
3318	-$4	4-8-9-10	DS	4.9%	0.8%	7.4%	13.1%
4033	-$5	4-8-9-10	S	4.3%	0.8%	6.6%	11.7%
4481	-$5	4-8-9-10	NS	3.5%	0.7%	5.7%	9.9%
3417	-$4	4-8-9-J	DS	4.3%	0.7%	7.2%	12.2%
4193	-$5	4-8-9-J	S	3.8%	0.8%	6.7%	11.3%
4740	-$6	4-8-9-J	NS	3.2%	0.7%	5.7%	9.7%
3735	-$4	4-8-9-Q	DS	4.2%	0.8%	7.3%	12.3%
4386	-$5	4-8-9-Q	S	3.6%	0.8%	6.4%	10.9%
4907	-$7	4-8-9-Q	NS	2.9%	0.7%	5.4%	9.0%
4230	-$5	4-8-9-K	DS	4.3%	0.9%	6.9%	12.1%
4642	-$6	4-8-9-K	S	3.8%	0.8%	6.3%	10.9%

OMAHA HIGH-LOW 8 OR BETTER
5,278 HANDS   9 HANDED

| HAND RANK | VALUE $4/$8 | POCKET CARDS | | | | | |
		HAND	SUITED	HIGH %	LOW %	SCOOP %	PART OR ALL %
5022	-$7	4-8-9-K	NS	2.8%	0.7%	4.9%	8.4%
2106	-$2	4-8-10-10	DS	4.3%	0.9%	8.6%	13.9%
3056	-$4	4-8-10-10	S	3.7%	0.8%	7.6%	12.2%
3480	-$4	4-8-10-10	NS	3.2%	0.8%	7.0%	11.0%
2366	-$3	4-8-10-J	DS	4.8%	0.9%	8.6%	14.2%
3128	-$4	4-8-10-J	S	4.2%	0.9%	7.7%	12.8%
4032	-$5	4-8-10-J	NS	3.7%	0.8%	7.0%	11.4%
2467	-$3	4-8-10-Q	DS	4.7%	0.9%	8.5%	14.1%
3433	-$4	4-8-10-Q	S	3.9%	0.9%	7.7%	12.5%
4398	-$5	4-8-10-Q	NS	3.3%	0.8%	6.8%	10.8%
3094	-$4	4-8-10-K	DS	4.8%	0.9%	8.0%	13.8%
3961	-$5	4-8-10-K	S	4.1%	0.9%	7.3%	12.3%
4815	-$6	4-8-10-K	NS	3.1%	0.8%	6.0%	9.9%
1828	-$2	4-8-J-J	DS	4.2%	0.9%	9.3%	14.5%
2738	-$3	4-8-J-J	S	3.5%	0.9%	8.3%	12.7%
3521	-$4	4-8-J-J	NS	2.9%	0.8%	7.4%	11.2%
2650	-$3	4-8-J-Q	DS	4.3%	0.9%	8.4%	13.7%
3727	-$4	4-8-J-Q	S	3.7%	0.8%	7.5%	12.0%
4375	-$5	4-8-J-Q	NS	3.0%	0.8%	6.7%	10.4%
3108	-$4	4-8-J-K	DS	4.5%	0.9%	8.1%	13.5%
4022	-$5	4-8-J-K	S	3.8%	0.9%	7.3%	12.0%
4814	-$6	4-8-J-K	NS	2.8%	0.8%	6.1%	9.6%
1752	-$2	4-8-Q-Q	DS	4.4%	1.0%	10.5%	15.9%
2711	-$3	4-8-Q-Q	S	3.6%	1.0%	9.2%	13.8%
3820	-$4	4-8-Q-Q	NS	2.9%	0.9%	8.1%	11.9%
3172	-$4	4-8-Q-K	DS	4.4%	0.9%	8.2%	13.4%
4177	-$5	4-8-Q-K	S	3.6%	0.8%	7.1%	11.5%
4863	-$6	4-8-Q-K	NS	2.6%	0.7%	5.8%	9.2%

OMAHA HIGH-LOW 8 OR BETTER
5,278 HANDS   9 HANDED

HAND RANK	VALUE $4/$8	POCKET CARDS		HIGH %	LOW %	SCOOP %	PART OR ALL %
		HAND	SUITED				
1377	-$1	4-8-K-K	DS	5.6%	1.3%	12.0%	18.8%
2537	-$3	4-8-K-K	S	4.3%	1.1%	10.9%	16.3%
4073	-$5	4-8-K-K	NS	3.3%	1.0%	9.6%	13.9%
5075	-$8	4-9-9-9	S	1.2%	0.0%	2.7%	3.9%
5094	-$8	4-9-9-9	NS	0.8%	0.0%	2.1%	2.9%
2936	-$3	4-9-9-10	DS	3.9%	0.0%	7.3%	11.2%
3052	-$3	4-9-9-10	S	3.3%	0.0%	6.8%	10.1%
3828	-$4	4-9-9-10	NS	2.9%	0.0%	6.1%	9.0%
2856	-$3	4-9-9-J	DS	3.4%	0.0%	7.7%	11.1%
3445	-$4	4-9-9-J	S	2.8%	0.0%	6.8%	9.7%
3967	-$5	4-9-9-J	NS	2.4%	0.0%	6.3%	8.6%
3164	-$4	4-9-9-Q	DS	3.3%	0.0%	7.5%	10.8%
3656	-$4	4-9-9-Q	S	2.7%	0.0%	6.8%	9.5%
4311	-$5	4-9-9-Q	NS	2.1%	0.0%	5.9%	8.0%
3273	-$4	4-9-9-K	DS	3.5%	0.0%	7.6%	11.1%
3717	-$4	4-9-9-K	S	2.8%	0.0%	6.7%	9.5%
4390	-$5	4-9-9-K	NS	1.9%	0.0%	5.7%	7.6%
2407	-$3	4-9-10-10	DS	4.0%	0.0%	7.8%	11.7%
3229	-$4	4-9-10-10	S	3.4%	0.0%	7.1%	10.5%
3871	-$5	4-9-10-10	NS	2.9%	0.0%	6.3%	9.2%
2033	-$2	4-9-10-J	DS	4.4%	0.0%	8.5%	13.0%
2623	-$3	4-9-10-J	S	3.9%	0.0%	8.0%	11.8%
3478	-$4	4-9-10-J	NS	3.4%	0.0%	7.4%	10.8%
2471	-$3	4-9-10-Q	DS	4.1%	0.0%	8.5%	12.6%
3141	-$4	4-9-10-Q	S	3.6%	0.0%	8.0%	11.5%
3836	-$4	4-9-10-Q	NS	2.8%	0.0%	7.3%	10.1%
2634	-$3	4-9-10-K	DS	4.4%	0.0%	8.5%	12.8%
3275	-$4	4-9-10-K	S	3.7%	0.0%	7.8%	11.5%

OMAHA HIGH-LOW 8 OR BETTER
5,278 HANDS   9 HANDED

| HAND RANK | VALUE $4/$8 | POCKET CARDS | | HIGH % | LOW % | SCOOP % | PART OR ALL % |
		HAND	SUITED				
4394	-$5	4-9-10-K	NS	2.6%	0.0%	6.6%	9.3%
2260	-$3	4-9-J-J	DS	3.8%	0.0%	8.6%	12.5%
3124	-$4	4-9-J-J	S	3.2%	0.0%	7.8%	11.0%
3766	-$4	4-9-J-J	NS	2.7%	0.0%	7.0%	9.7%
2187	-$2	4-9-J-Q	DS	3.6%	0.0%	8.6%	12.2%
2819	-$3	4-9-J-Q	S	3.1%	0.0%	8.1%	11.2%
3859	-$4	4-9-J-Q	NS	2.4%	0.0%	7.0%	9.4%
2422	-$3	4-9-J-K	DS	3.9%	0.0%	8.7%	12.6%
3307	-$4	4-9-J-K	S	3.3%	0.0%	8.0%	11.2%
4067	-$5	4-9-J-K	NS	2.3%	0.0%	7.0%	9.3%
2287	-$3	4-9-Q-Q	DS	4.0%	0.0%	9.8%	13.8%
2872	-$3	4-9-Q-Q	S	3.2%	0.0%	9.0%	12.2%
3853	-$4	4-9-Q-Q	NS	2.6%	0.0%	7.8%	10.4%
2807	-$3	4-9-Q-K	DS	3.8%	0.0%	8.5%	12.3%
3330	-$4	4-9-Q-K	S	3.0%	0.0%	8.0%	11.0%
4268	-$5	4-9-Q-K	NS	1.9%	0.0%	6.8%	8.7%
1610	-$1	4-9-K-K	DS	5.2%	0.0%	11.9%	17.1%
2469	-$3	4-9-K-K	S	3.9%	0.0%	10.8%	14.6%
3429	-$4	4-9-K-K	NS	2.8%	0.0%	9.8%	12.6%
5140	-$8	4-10-10-10	S	1.4%	0.0%	3.0%	4.4%
5151	-$8	4-10-10-10	NS	0.9%	0.0%	2.5%	3.4%
1765	-$2	4-10-10-J	DS	4.0%	0.0%	9.2%	13.2%
2275	-$3	4-10-10-J	S	3.5%	0.0%	8.4%	11.8%
2920	-$3	4-10-10-J	NS	2.9%	0.0%	7.8%	10.8%
2019	-$2	4-10-10-Q	DS	3.8%	0.0%	9.3%	13.1%
2563	-$3	4-10-10-Q	S	3.1%	0.0%	8.6%	11.8%
3361	-$4	4-10-10-Q	NS	2.6%	0.0%	7.9%	10.5%

OMAHA HIGH-LOW 8 OR BETTER
5,278 HANDS   9 HANDED

| HAND RANK | VALUE $4/$8 | POCKET CARDS | | HIGH % | LOW % | SCOOP % | PART OR ALL % |
		HAND	SUITED				
2265	-$3	4-10-10-K	DS	4.1%	0.0%	9.1%	13.2%
2932	-$3	4-10-10-K	S	3.3%	0.0%	8.4%	11.7%
3930	-$5	4-10-10-K	NS	2.4%	0.0%	7.2%	9.6%
1556	-$1	4-10-J-J	DS	4.1%	0.0%	9.6%	13.7%
2221	-$2	4-10-J-J	S	3.5%	0.0%	8.8%	12.3%
2876	-$3	4-10-J-J	NS	3.1%	0.0%	8.0%	11.0%
1264	-$1	4-10-J-Q	DS	4.2%	0.0%	10.1%	14.3%
1633	-$1	4-10-J-Q	S	3.7%	0.0%	9.7%	13.4%
2356	-$3	4-10-J-Q	NS	3.1%	0.0%	8.8%	12.0%
1438	-$1	4-10-J-K	DS	4.6%	0.0%	10.0%	14.6%
1873	-$2	4-10-J-K	S	4.1%	0.0%	9.5%	13.6%
2517	-$3	4-10-J-K	NS	2.9%	0.0%	8.7%	11.6%
1464	-$1	4-10-Q-Q	DS	4.5%	0.0%	10.7%	15.2%
2025	-$2	4-10-Q-Q	S	3.5%	0.0%	10.0%	13.6%
2840	-$3	4-10-Q-Q	NS	2.9%	0.0%	9.1%	12.0%
1318	-$1	4-10-Q-K	DS	4.5%	0.0%	10.1%	14.6%
1763	-$2	4-10-Q-K	S	3.6%	0.0%	9.5%	13.1%
2667	-$3	4-10-Q-K	NS	2.5%	0.0%	8.7%	11.2%
1030	$0	4-10-K-K	DS	5.6%	0.0%	12.7%	18.3%
1675	-$2	4-10-K-K	S	4.2%	0.0%	11.6%	15.8%
2636	-$3	4-10-K-K	NS	3.1%	0.0%	10.5%	13.6%
5149	-$8	4-J-J-J	S	1.6%	0.0%	3.8%	5.4%
5244	-$9	4-J-J-J	NS	1.1%	0.0%	3.0%	4.1%
1641	-$1	4-J-J-Q	DS	4.1%	0.0%	10.4%	14.6%
2107	-$2	4-J-J-Q	S	3.6%	0.0%	9.5%	13.0%
2913	-$3	4-J-J-Q	NS	2.8%	0.0%	8.7%	11.6%
1840	-$2	4-J-J-K	DS	4.4%	0.0%	10.4%	14.8%
2538	-$3	4-J-J-K	S	3.6%	0.0%	9.6%	13.2%

OMAHA HIGH-LOW 8 OR BETTER
5,278 HANDS   9 HANDED

| HAND RANK | VALUE $4/$8 | POCKET CARDS | | HIGH % | LOW % | SCOOP % | PART OR ALL % |
		HAND	SUITED				
3469	-$4	4-J-J-K	NS	2.7%	0.0%	8.6%	11.2%
1341	-$1	4-J-Q-Q	DS	4.5%	0.0%	11.1%	15.5%
1814	-$2	4-J-Q-Q	S	3.7%	0.0%	10.0%	13.7%
2631	-$3	4-J-Q-Q	NS	2.9%	0.0%	9.0%	11.9%
1177	-$0	4-J-Q-K	DS	4.5%	0.0%	10.5%	15.0%
1649	-$1	4-J-Q-K	S	3.6%	0.0%	9.8%	13.4%
2556	-$3	4-J-Q-K	NS	2.6%	0.0%	8.6%	11.3%
1188	-$0	4-J-K-K	DS	5.6%	0.0%	12.4%	18.0%
1760	-$2	4-J-K-K	S	4.6%	0.0%	12.0%	16.6%
2500	-$3	4-J-K-K	NS	3.2%	0.0%	10.7%	13.8%
5217	-$9	4-Q-Q-Q	S	2.0%	0.0%	5.2%	7.2%
5268	-$10	4-Q-Q-Q	NS	1.3%	0.0%	4.2%	5.5%
1375	-$1	4-Q-Q-K	DS	5.1%	0.0%	12.0%	17.1%
1831	-$2	4-Q-Q-K	S	4.9%	0.0%	11.8%	16.6%
3082	-$4	4-Q-Q-K	NS	3.0%	0.0%	10.0%	13.0%
1197	-$0	4-Q-K-K	DS	5.8%	0.0%	12.2%	18.0%
1868	-$2	4-Q-K-K	S	4.7%	0.0%	11.6%	16.2%
2512	-$3	4-Q-K-K	NS	3.2%	0.0%	10.5%	13.7%
5157	-$9	4-K-K-K	S	2.7%	0.0%	7.6%	10.3%
5267	-$10	4-K-K-K	NS	1.7%	0.0%	6.4%	8.0%
5219	-$9	5-5-5-5	NS	0.0%	0.0%	0.1%	0.1%
4965	-$7	5-5-5-6	S	2.9%	2.2%	3.8%	8.9%
5076	-$8	5-5-5-6	NS	2.6%	2.1%	2.7%	7.4%
5095	-$8	5-5-5-7	S	2.8%	1.6%	3.1%	7.5%
5184	-$9	5-5-5-7	NS	2.4%	1.4%	2.1%	5.9%
5225	-$9	5-5-5-8	S	2.5%	1.0%	2.6%	6.1%
5265	-$10	5-5-5-8	NS	2.1%	0.9%	1.6%	4.5%
5180	-$9	5-5-5-9	S	1.6%	0.0%	2.0%	3.6%

OMAHA HIGH-LOW 8 OR BETTER
5,278 HANDS   9 HANDED

| HAND RANK | VALUE $4/$8 | POCKET CARDS | | HIGH % | LOW % | SCOOP % | PART OR ALL % |
		HAND	SUITED				
5204	-$9	5-5-5-9	NS	1.3%	0.0%	1.3%	2.6%
5172	-$9	5-5-5-10	S	1.4%	0.0%	2.1%	3.5%
5197	-$9	5-5-5-10	NS	1.1%	0.0%	1.3%	2.4%
5159	-$9	5-5-5-J	S	1.6%	0.0%	2.3%	3.8%
5208	-$9	5-5-5-J	NS	1.2%	0.0%	1.4%	2.6%
5167	-$9	5-5-5-Q	S	1.7%	0.0%	2.6%	4.3%
5218	-$9	5-5-5-Q	NS	1.2%	0.0%	1.5%	2.7%
5156	-$9	5-5-5-K	S	2.1%	0.0%	3.1%	5.2%
5230	-$9	5-5-5-K	NS	1.2%	0.0%	1.7%	2.9%
1421	-$1	5-5-6-6	DS	6.6%	2.3%	8.3%	17.2%
2022	-$2	5-5-6-6	S	6.2%	2.2%	7.0%	15.4%
2768	-$3	5-5-6-6	NS	5.9%	2.0%	6.0%	14.0%
1952	-$2	5-5-6-7	DS	6.0%	2.7%	7.6%	16.2%
2652	-$3	5-5-6-7	S	5.7%	2.5%	6.4%	14.6%
3696	-$4	5-5-6-7	NS	5.2%	2.4%	5.3%	12.9%
2428	-$3	5-5-6-8	DS	5.9%	2.4%	7.0%	15.4%
3278	-$4	5-5-6-8	S	5.5%	2.3%	6.0%	13.8%
4122	-$5	5-5-6-8	NS	5.1%	2.2%	4.9%	12.2%
3441	-$4	5-5-6-9	DS	5.6%	2.1%	6.4%	14.0%
4087	-$5	5-5-6-9	S	5.2%	1.9%	5.4%	12.5%
4587	-$6	5-5-6-9	NS	4.7%	1.9%	4.5%	11.0%
3695	-$4	5-5-6-10	DS	5.2%	2.0%	6.4%	13.6%
4434	-$5	5-5-6-10	S	4.8%	1.9%	5.4%	12.1%
4799	-$6	5-5-6-10	NS	4.3%	1.8%	4.5%	10.5%
3576	-$4	5-5-6-J	DS	5.3%	2.0%	6.7%	13.9%
4242	-$5	5-5-6-J	S	4.8%	1.9%	5.7%	12.4%
4825	-$6	5-5-6-J	NS	4.2%	1.8%	4.5%	10.5%
3611	-$4	5-5-6-Q	DS	5.4%	2.1%	6.8%	14.4%

OMAHA HIGH-LOW 8 OR BETTER
5,278 HANDS   9 HANDED

HAND RANK	VALUE $4/$8	POCKET CARDS HAND	SUITED	HIGH %	LOW %	SCOOP %	PART OR ALL %
4296	-$5	5-5-6-Q	S	5.0%	1.9%	5.8%	12.7%
4829	-$6	5-5-6-Q	NS	4.3%	1.9%	4.7%	10.9%
2857	-$3	5-5-6-K	DS	5.7%	2.2%	7.7%	15.5%
3704	-$4	5-5-6-K	S	5.2%	2.1%	6.7%	14.1%
4833	-$6	5-5-6-K	NS	4.3%	1.9%	5.0%	11.2%
2051	-$2	5-5-7-7	DS	6.6%	1.5%	7.3%	15.4%
2754	-$3	5-5-7-7	S	6.2%	1.4%	6.2%	13.8%
3308	-$4	5-5-7-7	NS	5.8%	1.3%	5.4%	12.5%
3020	-$3	5-5-7-8	DS	5.8%	1.8%	6.8%	14.5%
3838	-$4	5-5-7-8	S	5.4%	1.7%	5.9%	13.0%
4340	-$5	5-5-7-8	NS	5.1%	1.7%	4.8%	11.6%
3937	-$5	5-5-7-9	DS	5.7%	1.5%	6.1%	13.3%
4404	-$5	5-5-7-9	S	5.3%	1.4%	5.3%	11.9%
4881	-$6	5-5-7-9	NS	4.7%	1.3%	4.2%	10.2%
4083	-$5	5-5-7-10	DS	5.3%	1.4%	6.1%	12.9%
4602	-$6	5-5-7-10	S	4.9%	1.4%	5.2%	11.4%
4911	-$7	5-5-7-10	NS	4.3%	1.3%	4.2%	9.7%
4035	-$5	5-5-7-J	DS	5.3%	1.5%	6.5%	13.2%
4465	-$5	5-5-7-J	S	4.9%	1.4%	5.5%	11.7%
4955	-$7	5-5-7-J	NS	4.2%	1.3%	4.3%	9.8%
4171	-$5	5-5-7-Q	DS	5.2%	1.5%	6.3%	13.0%
4597	-$6	5-5-7-Q	S	4.8%	1.4%	5.4%	11.5%
4999	-$7	5-5-7-Q	NS	4.1%	1.3%	4.0%	9.4%
3699	-$4	5-5-7-K	DS	5.5%	1.6%	7.1%	14.1%
4397	-$5	5-5-7-K	S	5.1%	1.5%	5.9%	12.5%
4993	-$7	5-5-7-K	NS	4.1%	1.3%	4.4%	9.8%
2560	-$3	5-5-8-8	DS	6.5%	1.0%	6.8%	14.4%
3416	-$4	5-5-8-8	S	5.9%	1.0%	5.9%	12.8%

		POCKET CARDS					
HAND RANK	VALUE $4/$8	HAND	SUITED	HIGH %	LOW %	SCOOP %	PART OR ALL %
3985	-$5	5-5-8-8	NS	5.6%	0.9%	5.0%	11.4%
4371	-$5	5-5-8-9	DS	5.5%	1.0%	6.2%	12.7%
4769	-$6	5-5-8-9	S	5.0%	0.9%	5.4%	11.3%
4951	-$7	5-5-8-9	NS	4.5%	0.9%	4.5%	9.9%
4263	-$5	5-5-8-10	DS	5.1%	1.0%	6.3%	12.4%
4675	-$6	5-5-8-10	S	4.6%	0.9%	5.4%	10.9%
4972	-$7	5-5-8-10	NS	4.0%	0.9%	4.6%	9.5%
4086	-$5	5-5-8-J	DS	5.1%	1.0%	6.7%	12.9%
4702	-$6	5-5-8-J	S	4.7%	1.0%	5.7%	11.3%
4992	-$7	5-5-8-J	NS	4.1%	0.9%	4.7%	9.7%
4275	-$5	5-5-8-Q	DS	5.1%	1.1%	6.7%	12.8%
4798	-$6	5-5-8-Q	S	4.6%	1.0%	5.6%	11.2%
5043	-$7	5-5-8-Q	NS	3.9%	0.9%	4.3%	9.1%
4417	-$5	5-5-8-K	DS	5.3%	1.1%	6.5%	12.9%
4720	-$6	5-5-8-K	S	4.8%	1.1%	5.5%	11.4%
5041	-$7	5-5-8-K	NS	3.9%	0.9%	4.1%	8.8%
2752	-$3	5-5-9-9	DS	4.5%	0.0%	6.9%	11.4%
3170	-$4	5-5-9-9	S	4.1%	0.0%	6.2%	10.3%
3238	-$4	5-5-9-9	NS	3.6%	0.0%	5.6%	9.2%
4455	-$5	5-5-9-10	DS	4.5%	0.0%	5.9%	10.4%
4812	-$6	5-5-9-10	S	3.9%	0.0%	5.0%	8.9%
4974	-$7	5-5-9-10	NS	3.5%	0.0%	4.2%	7.7%
4524	-$6	5-5-9-J	DS	4.4%	0.0%	6.0%	10.4%
4707	-$6	5-5-9-J	S	4.1%	0.0%	5.0%	9.1%
4935	-$7	5-5-9-J	NS	3.4%	0.0%	4.6%	8.0%
4412	-$5	5-5-9-Q	DS	4.2%	0.0%	6.3%	10.5%
4679	-$6	5-5-9-Q	S	3.8%	0.0%	5.5%	9.3%
4983	-$7	5-5-9-Q	NS	3.0%	0.0%	4.5%	7.5%

OMAHA HIGH-LOW 8 OR BETTER
5,278 HANDS   9 HANDED

OMAHA HIGH-LOW 8 OR BETTER
5,278 HANDS   9 HANDED

| HAND RANK | VALUE $4/$8 | POCKET CARDS | | HIGH % | LOW % | SCOOP % | PART OR ALL % |
		HAND	SUITED				
4348	-$5	5-5-9-K	DS	4.4%	0.0%	6.4%	10.8%
4732	-$6	5-5-9-K	S	3.9%	0.0%	5.7%	9.6%
5001	-$7	5-5-9-K	NS	2.9%	0.0%	4.1%	6.9%
2928	-$3	5-5-10-10	DS	4.5%	0.0%	7.5%	11.9%
3398	-$4	5-5-10-10	S	3.9%	0.0%	6.6%	10.5%
3803	-$4	5-5-10-10	NS	3.5%	0.0%	5.9%	9.3%
3648	-$4	5-5-10-J	DS	4.4%	0.0%	7.0%	11.4%
4261	-$5	5-5-10-J	S	4.0%	0.0%	6.1%	10.1%
4714	-$6	5-5-10-J	NS	3.4%	0.0%	5.3%	8.8%
3845	-$4	5-5-10-Q	DS	4.2%	0.0%	7.0%	11.3%
4405	-$5	5-5-10-Q	S	3.8%	0.0%	6.2%	10.0%
4715	-$6	5-5-10-Q	NS	3.2%	0.0%	5.3%	8.4%
3734	-$4	5-5-10-K	DS	4.5%	0.0%	7.3%	11.8%
4300	-$5	5-5-10-K	S	4.0%	0.0%	6.4%	10.4%
4810	-$6	5-5-10-K	NS	3.0%	0.0%	5.0%	8.0%
2477	-$3	5-5-J-J	DS	4.8%	0.0%	8.5%	13.3%
2996	-$3	5-5-J-J	S	4.3%	0.0%	7.7%	12.0%
3850	-$4	5-5-J-J	NS	3.7%	0.0%	6.7%	10.4%
3507	-$4	5-5-J-Q	DS	4.3%	0.0%	7.4%	11.7%
4060	-$5	5-5-J-Q	S	3.8%	0.0%	6.8%	10.6%
4746	-$6	5-5-J-Q	NS	3.2%	0.0%	5.5%	8.7%
3647	-$4	5-5-J-K	DS	4.6%	0.0%	7.5%	12.0%
4167	-$5	5-5-J-K	S	4.1%	0.0%	6.7%	10.8%
4827	-$6	5-5-J-K	NS	3.0%	0.0%	5.2%	8.2%
1830	-$2	5-5-Q-Q	DS	5.6%	0.0%	10.5%	16.1%
2900	-$3	5-5-Q-Q	S	4.8%	0.0%	8.9%	13.7%
3657	-$4	5-5-Q-Q	NS	4.0%	0.0%	8.1%	12.1%
3100	-$4	5-5-Q-K	DS	4.8%	0.0%	8.2%	13.0%

OMAHA HIGH-LOW 8 OR BETTER
5,278 HANDS   9 HANDED

| HAND RANK | VALUE $4/$8 | POCKET CARDS | | HIGH % | LOW % | SCOOP % | PART OR ALL % |
		HAND	SUITED				
4164	-$5	5-5-Q-K	S	4.1%	0.0%	6.9%	11.0%
4766	-$6	5-5-Q-K	NS	3.1%	0.0%	5.6%	8.7%
1093	-$0	5-5-K-K	DS	6.8%	0.0%	12.9%	19.8%
1901	-$2	5-5-K-K	S	5.8%	0.0%	11.6%	17.4%
3058	-$4	5-5-K-K	NS	4.6%	0.0%	10.3%	14.8%
4995	-$7	5-6-6-6	S	3.1%	2.0%	3.6%	8.7%
5055	-$8	5-6-6-6	NS	2.8%	1.9%	2.6%	7.4%
1724	-$2	5-6-6-7	DS	6.1%	2.7%	7.5%	16.3%
2388	-$3	5-6-6-7	S	5.8%	2.5%	6.3%	14.6%
3310	-$4	5-6-6-7	NS	5.4%	2.3%	5.3%	13.0%
2215	-$2	5-6-6-8	DS	6.2%	2.3%	6.9%	15.4%
2959	-$3	5-6-6-8	S	5.7%	2.2%	5.8%	13.7%
4008	-$5	5-6-6-8	NS	5.3%	2.1%	4.7%	12.1%
2935	-$3	5-6-6-9	DS	5.9%	1.9%	6.4%	14.3%
3617	-$4	5-6-6-9	S	5.5%	1.8%	5.3%	12.6%
4239	-$5	5-6-6-9	NS	5.1%	1.7%	4.5%	11.3%
3460	-$4	5-6-6-10	DS	5.6%	1.9%	6.2%	13.7%
4105	-$5	5-6-6-10	S	5.0%	1.8%	5.2%	12.0%
4517	-$6	5-6-6-10	NS	4.5%	1.8%	4.3%	10.6%
3449	-$4	5-6-6-J	DS	5.5%	1.9%	6.5%	13.9%
4080	-$5	5-6-6-J	S	5.0%	1.8%	5.4%	12.2%
4557	-$6	5-6-6-J	NS	4.5%	1.8%	4.6%	10.9%
3060	-$4	5-6-6-Q	DS	5.6%	2.0%	7.0%	14.5%
3729	-$4	5-6-6-Q	S	5.1%	1.9%	5.9%	12.9%
4674	-$6	5-6-6-Q	NS	4.4%	1.8%	4.7%	10.9%
2611	-$3	5-6-6-K	DS	5.9%	2.1%	7.7%	15.7%
3355	-$4	5-6-6-K	S	5.4%	2.0%	6.4%	13.7%
4550	-$6	5-6-6-K	NS	4.6%	1.8%	5.0%	11.4%

OMAHA HIGH-LOW 8 OR BETTER
5,278 HANDS   9 HANDED

HAND RANK	VALUE $4/$8	POCKET CARDS HAND	POCKET CARDS SUITED	HIGH %	LOW %	SCOOP %	PART OR ALL %
1720	-$2	5-6-7-7	DS	6.3%	2.4%	7.3%	16.0%
2441	-$3	5-6-7-7	S	5.8%	2.3%	6.2%	14.4%
3044	-$3	5-6-7-7	NS	5.6%	2.2%	5.3%	13.1%
1812	-$2	5-6-7-8	DS	6.5%	2.3%	7.0%	15.9%
2376	-$3	5-6-7-8	S	6.2%	2.2%	6.1%	14.5%
3366	-$4	5-6-7-8	NS	5.8%	2.0%	5.1%	12.9%
2163	-$2	5-6-7-9	DS	6.3%	2.3%	6.8%	15.4%
3188	-$4	5-6-7-9	S	5.8%	2.2%	5.8%	13.8%
3936	-$5	5-6-7-9	NS	5.4%	2.0%	4.8%	12.3%
2852	-$3	5-6-7-10	DS	5.6%	2.3%	6.8%	14.7%
3642	-$4	5-6-7-10	S	5.4%	2.2%	5.8%	13.4%
4462	-$5	5-6-7-10	NS	4.8%	2.0%	4.9%	11.7%
3005	-$3	5-6-7-J	DS	5.6%	2.2%	7.0%	14.9%
3867	-$5	5-6-7-J	S	5.2%	2.2%	5.9%	13.3%
4581	-$6	5-6-7-J	NS	4.7%	2.0%	4.9%	11.6%
2782	-$3	5-6-7-Q	DS	5.8%	2.3%	7.3%	15.4%
3913	-$5	5-6-7-Q	S	5.4%	2.2%	6.1%	13.7%
4563	-$6	5-6-7-Q	NS	4.7%	2.1%	5.1%	12.0%
2603	-$3	5-6-7-K	DS	6.1%	2.4%	7.6%	16.0%
3236	-$4	5-6-7-K	S	5.6%	2.3%	6.8%	14.7%
4535	-$6	5-6-7-K	NS	4.8%	2.1%	5.3%	12.3%
1932	-$2	5-6-8-8	DS	6.2%	2.1%	7.1%	15.4%
2483	-$3	5-6-8-8	S	5.8%	2.0%	6.1%	13.9%
3336	-$4	5-6-8-8	NS	5.4%	1.9%	5.2%	12.5%
2771	-$3	5-6-8-9	DS	6.1%	2.1%	6.8%	15.0%
3451	-$4	5-6-8-9	S	5.8%	1.9%	6.1%	13.8%
4165	-$5	5-6-8-9	NS	5.3%	1.8%	5.2%	12.4%
2736	-$3	5-6-8-10	DS	5.6%	2.1%	7.3%	15.0%

OMAHA HIGH-LOW 8 OR BETTER
5,278 HANDS   9 HANDED

| HAND RANK | VALUE $4/$8 | POCKET CARDS | | HIGH % | LOW % | SCOOP % | PART OR ALL % |
		HAND	SUITED				
3779	-$4	5-6-8-10	S	5.2%	2.0%	6.2%	13.4%
4554	-$6	5-6-8-10	NS	4.6%	1.9%	5.3%	11.8%
3129	-$4	5-6-8-J	DS	5.5%	2.1%	7.1%	14.7%
3974	-$5	5-6-8-J	S	5.1%	2.0%	6.2%	13.2%
4650	-$6	5-6-8-J	NS	4.5%	1.9%	5.2%	11.7%
2954	-$3	5-6-8-Q	DS	5.6%	2.1%	7.6%	15.4%
3874	-$5	5-6-8-Q	S	5.3%	2.0%	6.5%	13.8%
4779	-$6	5-6-8-Q	NS	4.5%	1.9%	5.4%	11.7%
3016	-$3	5-6-8-K	DS	5.9%	2.1%	7.3%	15.3%
3923	-$5	5-6-8-K	S	5.4%	2.1%	6.3%	13.7%
4690	-$6	5-6-8-K	NS	4.6%	1.8%	5.0%	11.4%
1877	-$2	5-6-9-9	DS	4.8%	1.7%	7.8%	14.3%
2372	-$3	5-6-9-9	S	4.3%	1.6%	7.0%	12.9%
3144	-$4	5-6-9-9	NS	3.8%	1.5%	6.0%	11.3%
3380	-$4	5-6-9-10	DS	5.1%	1.7%	7.2%	14.1%
4245	-$5	5-6-9-10	S	4.6%	1.6%	6.3%	12.5%
4792	-$6	5-6-9-10	NS	4.1%	1.5%	5.3%	10.9%
3516	-$4	5-6-9-J	DS	5.1%	1.7%	7.2%	14.0%
4269	-$5	5-6-9-J	S	4.5%	1.6%	6.4%	12.5%
4830	-$6	5-6-9-J	NS	3.9%	1.6%	5.4%	10.9%
3464	-$4	5-6-9-Q	DS	5.0%	1.7%	7.6%	14.4%
4162	-$5	5-6-9-Q	S	4.6%	1.7%	6.8%	13.1%
4823	-$6	5-6-9-Q	NS	4.0%	1.5%	5.6%	11.1%
3042	-$3	5-6-9-K	DS	5.2%	1.7%	8.0%	14.9%
3843	-$4	5-6-9-K	S	4.7%	1.6%	7.0%	13.4%
4905	-$7	5-6-9-K	NS	3.7%	1.5%	5.3%	10.5%
1982	-$2	5-6-10-10	DS	4.6%	1.8%	8.3%	14.6%
2764	-$3	5-6-10-10	S	4.0%	1.6%	7.2%	12.9%

OMAHA HIGH-LOW 8 OR BETTER
5,278 HANDS   9 HANDED

HAND RANK	VALUE $4/$8	POCKET CARDS		HIGH %	LOW %	SCOOP %	PART OR ALL %
		HAND	SUITED				
3265	-$4	5-6-10-10	NS	3.4%	1.6%	6.6%	11.7%
2705	-$3	5-6-10-J	DS	4.9%	1.7%	8.2%	14.8%
3673	-$4	5-6-10-J	S	4.4%	1.7%	7.3%	13.4%
4510	-$6	5-6-10-J	NS	3.7%	1.6%	6.3%	11.6%
2412	-$3	5-6-10-Q	DS	5.0%	1.8%	8.6%	15.4%
3351	-$4	5-6-10-Q	S	4.5%	1.7%	7.7%	13.9%
4493	-$6	5-6-10-Q	NS	3.7%	1.6%	6.6%	11.9%
2445	-$3	5-6-10-K	DS	5.1%	1.8%	8.6%	15.4%
3588	-$4	5-6-10-K	S	4.5%	1.7%	7.7%	13.9%
4613	-$6	5-6-10-K	NS	3.5%	1.6%	6.4%	11.5%
1864	-$2	5-6-J-J	DS	4.7%	1.8%	9.2%	15.7%
2398	-$3	5-6-J-J	S	4.1%	1.7%	8.4%	14.2%
3504	-$4	5-6-J-J	NS	3.5%	1.7%	7.1%	12.3%
2278	-$3	5-6-J-Q	DS	5.0%	1.8%	8.9%	15.8%
3459	-$4	5-6-J-Q	S	4.4%	1.7%	8.0%	14.1%
4446	-$5	5-6-J-Q	NS	3.7%	1.6%	6.9%	12.2%
2339	-$3	5-6-J-K	DS	5.1%	1.8%	9.0%	16.0%
3316	-$4	5-6-J-K	S	4.4%	1.8%	8.1%	14.3%
4661	-$6	5-6-J-K	NS	3.5%	1.6%	6.6%	11.8%
1210	-$0	5-6-Q-Q	DS	5.3%	2.0%	11.3%	18.6%
2084	-$2	5-6-Q-Q	S	4.5%	1.9%	9.7%	16.1%
3214	-$4	5-6-Q-Q	NS	3.8%	1.9%	8.6%	14.2%
1907	-$2	5-6-Q-K	DS	5.2%	1.8%	9.5%	16.5%
3132	-$4	5-6-Q-K	S	4.6%	1.8%	8.3%	14.6%
4527	-$6	5-6-Q-K	NS	3.7%	1.7%	7.0%	12.3%
707	$2	5-6-K-K	DS	6.3%	2.2%	13.5%	22.0%
1373	-$1	5-6-K-K	S	5.4%	2.1%	12.1%	19.6%
2630	-$3	5-6-K-K	NS	4.3%	2.0%	10.6%	16.9%

OMAHA HIGH-LOW 8 OR BETTER
5,278 HANDS   9 HANDED

| HAND RANK | VALUE $4/$8 | POCKET CARDS | | HIGH % | LOW % | SCOOP % | PART OR ALL % |
		HAND	SUITED				
5087	-$8	5-7-7-7	S	3.1%	1.2%	2.9%	7.2%
5152	-$8	5-7-7-7	NS	2.7%	1.1%	2.1%	5.9%
2322	-$3	5-7-7-8	DS	6.1%	1.7%	6.9%	14.7%
2912	-$3	5-7-7-8	S	5.7%	1.6%	6.0%	13.3%
3977	-$5	5-7-7-8	NS	5.4%	1.5%	5.0%	11.9%
3119	-$4	5-7-7-9	DS	6.0%	1.3%	6.3%	13.7%
4063	-$5	5-7-7-9	S	5.6%	1.2%	5.0%	11.8%
4423	-$5	5-7-7-9	NS	5.1%	1.2%	4.4%	10.7%
3447	-$4	5-7-7-10	DS	5.6%	1.3%	6.2%	13.1%
4034	-$5	5-7-7-10	S	5.1%	1.2%	5.1%	11.5%
4656	-$6	5-7-7-10	NS	4.7%	1.2%	4.2%	10.1%
3637	-$4	5-7-7-J	DS	5.6%	1.4%	6.4%	13.3%
4185	-$5	5-7-7-J	S	5.1%	1.2%	5.4%	11.6%
4795	-$6	5-7-7-J	NS	4.5%	1.1%	4.3%	10.0%
3584	-$4	5-7-7-Q	DS	5.5%	1.3%	6.3%	13.2%
4132	-$5	5-7-7-Q	S	5.0%	1.3%	5.3%	11.6%
4817	-$6	5-7-7-Q	NS	4.4%	1.1%	4.2%	9.8%
3160	-$4	5-7-7-K	DS	5.9%	1.4%	6.9%	14.2%
3863	-$4	5-7-7-K	S	5.3%	1.3%	5.8%	12.4%
4846	-$6	5-7-7-K	NS	4.5%	1.2%	4.3%	10.0%
2229	-$2	5-7-8-8	DS	6.1%	1.6%	7.1%	14.8%
2982	-$3	5-7-8-8	S	5.6%	1.5%	6.3%	13.4%
3571	-$4	5-7-8-8	NS	5.3%	1.4%	5.3%	12.0%
2629	-$3	5-7-8-9	DS	6.2%	1.5%	6.9%	14.5%
3537	-$4	5-7-8-9	S	5.7%	1.5%	5.8%	13.0%
4131	-$5	5-7-8-9	NS	5.3%	1.3%	5.1%	11.8%
2712	-$3	5-7-8-10	DS	5.6%	1.5%	7.2%	14.3%
3666	-$4	5-7-8-10	S	5.1%	1.4%	6.2%	12.7%

OMAHA HIGH-LOW 8 OR BETTER
5,278 HANDS 9 HANDED

| HAND RANK | VALUE $4/$8 | POCKET CARDS | | HIGH % | LOW % | SCOOP % | PART OR ALL % |
		HAND	SUITED				
4184	-$5	5-7-8-10	NS	4.6%	1.4%	5.5%	11.5%
2713	-$3	5-7-8-J	DS	5.5%	1.6%	7.3%	14.4%
3544	-$4	5-7-8-J	S	5.1%	1.4%	6.5%	13.0%
4337	-$5	5-7-8-J	NS	4.6%	1.4%	5.5%	11.4%
3375	-$4	5-7-8-Q	DS	5.4%	1.6%	6.9%	13.9%
4078	-$5	5-7-8-Q	S	5.0%	1.5%	6.1%	12.6%
4728	-$6	5-7-8-Q	NS	4.3%	1.3%	5.0%	10.6%
3014	-$3	5-7-8-K	DS	5.8%	1.6%	7.3%	14.7%
3875	-$5	5-7-8-K	S	5.3%	1.5%	6.5%	13.3%
4738	-$6	5-7-8-K	NS	4.5%	1.3%	5.1%	10.9%
2080	-$2	5-7-9-9	DS	4.9%	1.2%	7.7%	13.8%
2620	-$3	5-7-9-9	S	4.4%	1.1%	6.8%	12.3%
3430	-$4	5-7-9-9	NS	3.8%	1.0%	6.0%	10.8%
3492	-$4	5-7-9-10	DS	5.3%	1.2%	6.9%	13.5%
4233	-$5	5-7-9-10	S	4.8%	1.1%	6.2%	12.1%
4579	-$6	5-7-9-10	NS	4.2%	1.0%	5.6%	10.9%
3221	-$4	5-7-9-J	DS	5.4%	1.2%	7.4%	13.9%
4040	-$5	5-7-9-J	S	4.8%	1.1%	6.5%	12.4%
4544	-$6	5-7-9-J	NS	4.2%	1.0%	5.6%	10.9%
3730	-$4	5-7-9-Q	DS	4.9%	1.2%	7.1%	13.3%
4313	-$5	5-7-9-Q	S	4.4%	1.1%	6.3%	11.8%
4880	-$6	5-7-9-Q	NS	3.8%	1.0%	5.1%	9.9%
3499	-$4	5-7-9-K	DS	5.3%	1.2%	7.6%	14.1%
4103	-$5	5-7-9-K	S	4.8%	1.2%	6.8%	12.7%
4850	-$6	5-7-9-K	NS	3.8%	1.1%	5.5%	10.4%
2178	-$2	5-7-10-10	DS	4.6%	1.3%	8.1%	14.0%
2648	-$3	5-7-10-10	S	4.0%	1.2%	7.3%	12.5%
3564	-$4	5-7-10-10	NS	3.4%	1.1%	6.4%	11.0%

HAND RANK	VALUE $4/$8	POCKET CARDS		HIGH %	LOW %	SCOOP %	PART OR ALL %
		HAND	SUITED				
2566	-$3	5-7-10-J	DS	5.0%	1.3%	8.2%	14.5%
3421	-$4	5-7-10-J	S	4.5%	1.2%	7.5%	13.1%
4378	-$5	5-7-10-J	NS	3.8%	1.1%	6.3%	11.3%
3148	-$4	5-7-10-Q	DS	4.7%	1.2%	7.9%	13.8%
3815	-$4	5-7-10-Q	S	4.2%	1.2%	7.2%	12.6%
4684	-$6	5-7-10-Q	NS	3.5%	1.1%	6.0%	10.6%
2707	-$3	5-7-10-K	DS	5.0%	1.3%	8.4%	14.7%
3524	-$4	5-7-10-K	S	4.5%	1.2%	7.7%	13.4%
4516	-$6	5-7-10-K	NS	3.6%	1.1%	6.4%	11.1%
1794	-$2	5-7-J-J	DS	4.7%	1.3%	9.3%	15.3%
2664	-$3	5-7-J-J	S	4.2%	1.2%	8.1%	13.5%
3354	-$4	5-7-J-J	NS	3.6%	1.2%	7.3%	12.1%
2907	-$3	5-7-J-Q	DS	4.9%	1.2%	8.3%	14.4%
3912	-$5	5-7-J-Q	S	4.2%	1.2%	7.4%	12.8%
4629	-$6	5-7-J-Q	NS	3.5%	1.1%	6.3%	10.8%
2386	-$3	5-7-J-K	DS	5.1%	1.3%	8.8%	15.2%
3340	-$4	5-7-J-K	S	4.5%	1.2%	8.0%	13.7%
4625	-$6	5-7-J-K	NS	3.5%	1.2%	6.6%	11.2%
1875	-$2	5-7-Q-Q	DS	5.0%	1.4%	10.2%	16.6%
2680	-$3	5-7-Q-Q	S	4.4%	1.3%	9.1%	14.8%
3905	-$5	5-7-Q-Q	NS	3.5%	1.3%	8.1%	12.8%
2395	-$3	5-7-Q-K	DS	5.0%	1.3%	8.9%	15.2%
3625	-$4	5-7-Q-K	S	4.3%	1.2%	7.8%	13.4%
4645	-$6	5-7-Q-K	NS	3.4%	1.1%	6.6%	11.1%
926	$1	5-7-K-K	DS	6.1%	1.6%	12.9%	20.6%
1716	-$2	5-7-K-K	S	5.0%	1.5%	11.5%	18.0%
3133	-$4	5-7-K-K	NS	4.1%	1.4%	10.1%	15.6%
5191	-$9	5-8-8-8	S	2.8%	0.8%	2.6%	6.2%

OMAHA HIGH-LOW 8 OR BETTER
5,278 HANDS   9 HANDED

OMAHA HIGH-LOW 8 OR BETTER
5,278 HANDS   9 HANDED

| HAND RANK | VALUE $4/$8 | POCKET CARDS | | HIGH % | LOW % | SCOOP % | PART OR ALL % |
		HAND	SUITED				
5243	-$9	5-8-8-8	NS	2.3%	0.7%	1.8%	4.8%
3408	-$4	5-8-8-9	DS	6.0%	0.9%	6.4%	13.3%
4046	-$5	5-8-8-9	S	5.5%	0.9%	5.4%	11.8%
4609	-$6	5-8-8-9	NS	5.0%	0.8%	4.6%	10.5%
3434	-$4	5-8-8-10	DS	5.6%	0.9%	6.6%	13.0%
4054	-$5	5-8-8-10	S	4.9%	0.8%	5.7%	11.4%
4606	-$6	5-8-8-10	NS	4.5%	0.8%	4.9%	10.2%
3206	-$4	5-8-8-J	DS	5.7%	0.9%	6.9%	13.5%
3989	-$5	5-8-8-J	S	5.1%	0.9%	5.9%	11.8%
4574	-$6	5-8-8-J	NS	4.5%	0.8%	5.1%	10.5%
3831	-$4	5-8-8-Q	DS	5.4%	1.0%	6.7%	13.0%
4373	-$5	5-8-8-Q	S	4.9%	0.9%	5.6%	11.4%
4821	-$6	5-8-8-Q	NS	4.3%	0.8%	4.7%	9.8%
3915	-$5	5-8-8-K	DS	5.8%	1.0%	6.4%	13.2%
4327	-$5	5-8-8-K	S	5.1%	0.9%	5.6%	11.6%
4944	-$7	5-8-8-K	NS	4.2%	0.8%	4.2%	9.2%
2314	-$3	5-8-9-9	DS	4.8%	0.8%	7.8%	13.4%
3211	-$4	5-8-9-9	S	4.1%	0.8%	7.0%	11.8%
3659	-$4	5-8-9-9	NS	3.7%	0.7%	6.2%	10.6%
3080	-$4	5-8-9-10	DS	5.2%	0.8%	7.5%	13.5%
3883	-$5	5-8-9-10	S	4.6%	0.8%	6.8%	12.2%
4561	-$6	5-8-9-10	NS	4.0%	0.7%	5.8%	10.5%
2998	-$3	5-8-9-J	DS	5.2%	0.8%	7.6%	13.7%
3770	-$4	5-8-9-J	S	4.6%	0.8%	6.8%	12.2%
4409	-$5	5-8-9-J	NS	4.1%	0.7%	6.1%	10.9%
3486	-$4	5-8-9-Q	DS	4.9%	0.8%	7.5%	13.2%
4049	-$5	5-8-9-Q	S	4.4%	0.8%	6.7%	11.8%
4737	-$6	5-8-9-Q	NS	3.6%	0.7%	5.7%	10.0%

HAND RANK	VALUE $4/$8	POCKET CARDS		HIGH %	LOW %	SCOOP %	PART OR ALL %
		HAND	SUITED				
3602	-$4	5-8-9-K	DS	5.0%	0.8%	7.2%	13.1%
4260	-$5	5-8-9-K	S	4.5%	0.8%	6.5%	11.8%
4943	-$7	5-8-9-K	NS	3.5%	0.7%	5.0%	9.2%
1974	-$2	5-8-10-10	DS	4.5%	0.9%	8.5%	13.9%
2762	-$3	5-8-10-10	S	3.8%	0.8%	7.7%	12.3%
3542	-$4	5-8-10-10	NS	3.2%	0.8%	6.9%	10.9%
2255	-$3	5-8-10-J	DS	4.9%	0.8%	8.4%	14.2%
3032	-$3	5-8-10-J	S	4.4%	0.8%	7.7%	12.9%
3918	-$5	5-8-10-J	NS	3.8%	0.8%	7.0%	11.6%
2605	-$3	5-8-10-Q	DS	4.7%	0.9%	8.3%	13.9%
3298	-$4	5-8-10-Q	S	4.2%	0.8%	7.7%	12.7%
4374	-$5	5-8-10-Q	NS	3.4%	0.8%	6.7%	10.9%
3154	-$4	5-8-10-K	DS	4.8%	0.9%	8.0%	13.6%
4053	-$5	5-8-10-K	S	4.2%	0.8%	7.2%	12.3%
4608	-$6	5-8-10-K	NS	3.3%	0.7%	6.1%	10.1%
1861	-$2	5-8-J-J	DS	4.6%	0.9%	9.4%	14.9%
2660	-$3	5-8-J-J	S	3.9%	0.8%	8.4%	13.2%
3462	-$4	5-8-J-J	NS	3.3%	0.8%	7.7%	11.8%
2411	-$3	5-8-J-Q	DS	4.8%	0.9%	8.6%	14.3%
3115	-$4	5-8-J-Q	S	4.1%	0.8%	8.1%	13.0%
4298	-$5	5-8-J-Q	NS	3.4%	0.8%	6.9%	11.1%
2790	-$3	5-8-J-K	DS	5.0%	0.9%	8.4%	14.2%
3566	-$4	5-8-J-K	S	4.2%	0.9%	7.8%	12.9%
4651	-$6	5-8-J-K	NS	3.3%	0.8%	6.4%	10.4%
1568	-$1	5-8-Q-Q	DS	4.8%	1.0%	10.6%	16.5%
2284	-$3	5-8-Q-Q	S	4.1%	0.9%	9.7%	14.7%
3428	-$4	5-8-Q-Q	NS	3.3%	0.9%	8.5%	12.7%
3109	-$4	5-8-Q-K	DS	4.8%	0.9%	8.2%	14.0%

Table title: OMAHA HIGH-LOW 8 OR BETTER — 5,278 HANDS   9 HANDED

OMAHA HIGH-LOW 8 OR BETTER
5,278 HANDS   9 HANDED

| HAND RANK | VALUE $4/$8 | POCKET CARDS | | HIGH % | LOW % | SCOOP % | PART OR ALL % |
		HAND	SUITED				
3964	-$5	5-8-Q-K	S	4.0%	0.8%	7.4%	12.3%
4797	-$6	5-8-Q-K	NS	3.1%	0.8%	6.2%	10.1%
1186	-$0	5-8-K-K	DS	6.0%	1.2%	12.2%	19.4%
2222	-$2	5-8-K-K	S	4.8%	1.1%	11.1%	16.9%
3496	-$4	5-8-K-K	NS	3.8%	1.0%	10.0%	14.7%
5073	-$8	5-9-9-9	S	1.5%	0.0%	2.7%	4.2%
5091	-$8	5-9-9-9	NS	1.1%	0.0%	2.1%	3.2%
2774	-$3	5-9-9-10	DS	3.8%	0.0%	7.6%	11.4%
3199	-$4	5-9-9-10	S	3.3%	0.0%	6.8%	10.1%
3760	-$4	5-9-9-10	NS	2.9%	0.0%	6.3%	9.2%
2731	-$3	5-9-9-J	DS	4.0%	0.0%	7.6%	11.6%
3258	-$4	5-9-9-J	S	3.4%	0.0%	6.9%	10.3%
3858	-$4	5-9-9-J	NS	2.8%	0.0%	6.3%	9.1%
3023	-$3	5-9-9-Q	DS	3.6%	0.0%	7.7%	11.3%
3487	-$4	5-9-9-Q	S	3.0%	0.0%	7.0%	10.0%
4172	-$5	5-9-9-Q	NS	2.5%	0.0%	6.0%	8.5%
3064	-$4	5-9-9-K	DS	3.8%	0.0%	7.7%	11.6%
3473	-$4	5-9-9-K	S	3.2%	0.0%	6.9%	10.1%
4312	-$5	5-9-9-K	NS	2.2%	0.0%	5.8%	8.0%
2656	-$3	5-9-10-10	DS	4.0%	0.0%	7.7%	11.7%
3169	-$4	5-9-10-10	S	3.4%	0.0%	7.0%	10.4%
3805	-$4	5-9-10-10	NS	2.9%	0.0%	6.3%	9.2%
2030	-$2	5-9-10-J	DS	4.4%	0.0%	8.7%	13.1%
2815	-$3	5-9-10-J	S	3.9%	0.0%	7.8%	11.7%
3567	-$4	5-9-10-J	NS	3.5%	0.0%	7.2%	10.7%
2198	-$2	5-9-10-Q	DS	4.1%	0.0%	8.6%	12.7%
3097	-$4	5-9-10-Q	S	3.6%	0.0%	7.9%	11.5%
3799	-$4	5-9-10-Q	NS	3.0%	0.0%	7.1%	10.1%

OMAHA HIGH-LOW 8 OR BETTER
5,278 HANDS   9 HANDED

HAND RANK	VALUE $4/$8	POCKET CARDS		HIGH %	LOW %	SCOOP %	PART OR ALL %
		HAND	SUITED				
2797	-$3	5-9-10-K	DS	4.3%	0.0%	8.3%	12.6%
3296	-$4	5-9-10-K	S	3.8%	0.0%	7.9%	11.6%
4324	-$5	5-9-10-K	NS	2.6%	0.0%	6.7%	9.3%
2158	-$2	5-9-J-J	DS	4.3%	0.0%	8.7%	13.1%
2679	-$3	5-9-J-J	S	3.7%	0.0%	8.0%	11.7%
3740	-$4	5-9-J-J	NS	3.1%	0.0%	7.1%	10.2%
2149	-$2	5-9-J-Q	DS	4.2%	0.0%	8.7%	12.9%
2910	-$3	5-9-J-Q	S	3.6%	0.0%	7.9%	11.6%
3829	-$4	5-9-J-Q	NS	3.0%	0.0%	7.2%	10.1%
2747	-$3	5-9-J-K	DS	4.4%	0.0%	8.5%	12.9%
3195	-$4	5-9-J-K	S	3.7%	0.0%	8.0%	11.7%
4137	-$5	5-9-J-K	NS	2.6%	0.0%	7.0%	9.6%
2617	-$3	5-9-Q-Q	DS	3.6%	0.0%	9.2%	12.8%
3227	-$4	5-9-Q-Q	S	3.3%	0.0%	8.1%	11.4%
3622	-$4	5-9-Q-Q	NS	3.0%	0.0%	8.0%	10.9%
2622	-$3	5-9-Q-K	DS	4.1%	0.0%	8.6%	12.7%
3224	-$4	5-9-Q-K	S	3.3%	0.0%	8.0%	11.4%
4180	-$5	5-9-Q-K	NS	2.2%	0.0%	7.1%	9.2%
1467	-$1	5-9-K-K	DS	5.4%	0.0%	12.0%	17.4%
2227	-$2	5-9-K-K	S	4.1%	0.0%	10.9%	15.0%
3360	-$4	5-9-K-K	NS	3.0%	0.0%	9.8%	12.9%
5133	-$8	5-10-10-10	S	1.3%	0.0%	3.0%	4.3%
5166	-$9	5-10-10-10	NS	0.9%	0.0%	2.4%	3.3%
1796	-$2	5-10-10-J	DS	4.0%	0.0%	9.0%	13.1%
2355	-$3	5-10-10-J	S	3.4%	0.0%	8.3%	11.8%
3140	-$4	5-10-10-J	NS	2.9%	0.0%	7.8%	10.8%
2078	-$2	5-10-10-Q	DS	3.8%	0.0%	9.2%	13.0%

OMAHA HIGH-LOW 8 OR BETTER
5,278 HANDS   9 HANDED

| HAND RANK | VALUE $4/$8 | POCKET CARDS | | HIGH % | LOW % | SCOOP % | PART OR ALL % |
		HAND	SUITED				
2509	-$3	5-10-10-Q	S	3.2%	0.0%	8.6%	11.8%
3270	-$4	5-10-10-Q	NS	2.6%	0.0%	7.8%	10.4%
2353	-$3	5-10-10-K	DS	4.1%	0.0%	9.0%	13.1%
2984	-$3	5-10-10-K	S	3.4%	0.0%	8.4%	11.7%
3840	-$4	5-10-10-K	NS	2.3%	0.0%	7.3%	9.6%
1688	-$2	5-10-J-J	DS	4.1%	0.0%	9.4%	13.5%
2136	-$2	5-10-J-J	S	3.6%	0.0%	8.7%	12.3%
2884	-$3	5-10-J-J	NS	3.0%	0.0%	8.0%	11.0%
1250	-$1	5-10-J-Q	DS	4.3%	0.0%	10.1%	14.4%
1631	-$1	5-10-J-Q	S	3.6%	0.0%	9.7%	13.4%
2268	-$3	5-10-J-Q	NS	3.2%	0.0%	8.8%	12.0%
1463	-$1	5-10-J-K	DS	4.5%	0.0%	9.9%	14.4%
1857	-$2	5-10-J-K	S	4.0%	0.0%	9.5%	13.5%
2571	-$3	5-10-J-K	NS	2.9%	0.0%	8.8%	11.6%
1326	-$1	5-10-Q-Q	DS	4.5%	0.0%	10.8%	15.3%
2120	-$2	5-10-Q-Q	S	3.6%	0.0%	9.8%	13.4%
2814	-$3	5-10-Q-Q	NS	2.9%	0.0%	9.0%	11.8%
1353	-$1	5-10-Q-K	DS	4.4%	0.0%	10.2%	14.6%
1776	-$2	5-10-Q-K	S	3.7%	0.0%	9.6%	13.2%
2643	-$3	5-10-Q-K	NS	2.6%	0.0%	8.5%	11.1%
1075	-$0	5-10-K-K	DS	5.6%	0.0%	12.5%	18.1%
1683	-$2	5-10-K-K	S	4.2%	0.0%	11.6%	15.7%
2659	-$3	5-10-K-K	NS	3.1%	0.0%	10.3%	13.4%
5171	-$9	5-J-J-J	S	1.6%	0.0%	3.8%	5.4%
5233	-$9	5-J-J-J	NS	1.1%	0.0%	3.0%	4.1%
1783	-$2	5-J-J-Q	DS	4.1%	0.0%	10.2%	14.3%
2216	-$2	5-J-J-Q	S	3.5%	0.0%	9.5%	13.0%
3000	-$3	5-J-J-Q	NS	2.8%	0.0%	8.7%	11.5%

OMAHA HIGH-LOW 8 OR BETTER
5,278 HANDS   9 HANDED

| HAND RANK | VALUE $4/$8 | POCKET CARDS | | HIGH % | LOW % | SCOOP % | PART OR ALL % |
		HAND	SUITED				
1910	-$2	5-J-J-K	DS	4.4%	0.0%	10.1%	14.6%
2449	-$3	5-J-J-K	S	3.6%	0.0%	9.6%	13.2%
3437	-$4	5-J-J-K	NS	2.6%	0.0%	8.7%	11.3%
1393	-$1	5-J-Q-Q	DS	4.5%	0.0%	10.8%	15.3%
1892	-$2	5-J-Q-Q	S	3.6%	0.0%	10.0%	13.6%
2678	-$3	5-J-Q-Q	NS	2.9%	0.0%	9.0%	12.0%
1254	-$1	5-J-Q-K	DS	4.5%	0.0%	10.4%	14.9%
1592	-$1	5-J-Q-K	S	3.7%	0.0%	9.7%	13.4%
2399	-$3	5-J-Q-K	NS	2.7%	0.0%	8.8%	11.5%
988	$0	5-J-K-K	DS	5.5%	0.0%	12.5%	18.0%
1599	-$1	5-J-K-K	S	4.2%	0.0%	11.7%	15.9%
2468	-$3	5-J-K-K	NS	3.1%	0.0%	10.6%	13.6%
5205	-$9	5-Q-Q-Q	S	2.0%	0.0%	5.3%	7.3%
5260	-$10	5-Q-Q-Q	NS	1.3%	0.0%	4.2%	5.5%
1262	-$1	5-Q-Q-K	DS	5.1%	0.0%	12.0%	17.1%
1894	-$2	5-Q-Q-K	S	4.1%	0.0%	11.0%	15.1%
3033	-$3	5-Q-Q-K	NS	3.0%	0.0%	10.0%	13.0%
972	$0	5-Q-K-K	DS	5.6%	0.0%	12.6%	18.2%
1503	-$1	5-Q-K-K	S	4.3%	0.0%	11.8%	16.1%
2273	-$3	5-Q-K-K	NS	3.2%	0.0%	10.7%	13.9%
5136	-$8	5-K-K-K	S	2.8%	0.0%	7.4%	10.2%
5266	-$10	5-K-K-K	NS	1.7%	0.0%	6.3%	8.0%
5250	-$9	6-6-6-6	NS	0.0%	0.0%	0.1%	0.1%
5065	-$8	6-6-6-7	S	3.1%	1.4%	3.5%	8.0%
5177	-$9	6-6-6-7	NS	2.7%	1.3%	2.4%	6.4%
5144	-$8	6-6-6-8	S	2.9%	0.9%	3.1%	6.9%
5240	-$9	6-6-6-8	NS	2.5%	0.8%	2.1%	5.4%
5154	-$8	6-6-6-9	S	2.2%	0.0%	2.2%	4.4%

OMAHA HIGH-LOW 8 OR BETTER
5,278 HANDS   9 HANDED

| HAND RANK | VALUE $4/$8 | POCKET CARDS | | HIGH % | LOW % | SCOOP % | PART OR ALL % |
		HAND	SUITED				
5215	-$9	6-6-6-9	NS	1.8%	0.0%	1.4%	3.3%
5169	-$9	6-6-6-10	S	1.8%	0.0%	2.3%	4.1%
5198	-$9	6-6-6-10	NS	1.5%	0.0%	1.5%	2.9%
5196	-$9	6-6-6-J	S	1.7%	0.0%	2.2%	3.9%
5210	-$9	6-6-6-J	NS	1.3%	0.0%	1.5%	2.8%
5182	-$9	6-6-6-Q	S	1.9%	0.0%	2.5%	4.4%
5226	-$9	6-6-6-Q	NS	1.3%	0.0%	1.5%	2.8%
5183	-$9	6-6-6-K	S	2.2%	0.0%	3.1%	5.3%
5235	-$9	6-6-6-K	NS	1.4%	0.0%	1.8%	3.1%
1493	-$1	6-6-7-7	DS	7.1%	1.5%	7.6%	16.2%
2070	-$2	6-6-7-7	S	6.7%	1.4%	6.6%	14.6%
2801	-$3	6-6-7-7	NS	6.3%	1.2%	5.6%	13.1%
2371	-$3	6-6-7-8	DS	6.3%	1.6%	7.0%	15.0%
3245	-$4	6-6-7-8	S	5.9%	1.5%	5.9%	13.4%
3981	-$5	6-6-7-8	NS	5.6%	1.5%	5.2%	12.2%
3285	-$4	6-6-7-9	DS	6.2%	1.4%	6.4%	14.0%
3741	-$4	6-6-7-9	S	5.9%	1.3%	5.4%	12.6%
4393	-$5	6-6-7-9	NS	5.4%	1.2%	4.6%	11.1%
2938	-$3	6-6-7-10	DS	6.0%	1.3%	6.6%	13.9%
3797	-$4	6-6-7-10	S	5.5%	1.3%	5.6%	12.3%
4571	-$6	6-6-7-10	NS	4.9%	1.2%	4.6%	10.6%
3599	-$4	6-6-7-J	DS	5.6%	1.3%	6.4%	13.3%
4224	-$5	6-6-7-J	S	5.2%	1.2%	5.4%	11.8%
4851	-$6	6-6-7-J	NS	4.6%	1.2%	4.2%	9.9%
3391	-$4	6-6-7-Q	DS	5.8%	1.4%	6.6%	13.8%
4170	-$5	6-6-7-Q	S	5.3%	1.3%	5.7%	12.3%
4820	-$6	6-6-7-Q	NS	4.6%	1.2%	4.5%	10.3%
3037	-$3	6-6-7-K	DS	6.0%	1.5%	7.2%	14.7%

OMAHA HIGH-LOW 8 OR BETTER
5,278 HANDS   9 HANDED

HAND RANK	VALUE $4/$8	POCKET CARDS		HIGH %	LOW %	SCOOP %	PART OR ALL %
		HAND	SUITED				
3877	-$5	6-6-7-K	S	5.6%	1.4%	6.4%	13.4%
4759	-$6	6-6-7-K	NS	4.6%	1.2%	4.9%	10.7%
1879	-$2	6-6-8-8	DS	6.9%	1.0%	7.4%	15.2%
2466	-$3	6-6-8-8	S	6.5%	0.9%	6.3%	13.7%
3300	-$4	6-6-8-8	NS	5.9%	0.8%	5.4%	12.2%
3573	-$4	6-6-8-9	DS	6.1%	0.9%	6.7%	13.7%
4283	-$5	6-6-8-9	S	5.7%	0.9%	5.7%	12.2%
4757	-$6	6-6-8-9	NS	5.1%	0.8%	4.8%	10.7%
3190	-$4	6-6-8-10	DS	5.8%	0.9%	6.9%	13.6%
4017	-$5	6-6-8-10	S	5.3%	0.8%	6.0%	12.1%
4670	-$6	6-6-8-10	NS	4.7%	0.8%	4.9%	10.4%
3646	-$4	6-6-8-J	DS	5.5%	0.9%	6.7%	13.0%
4380	-$5	6-6-8-J	S	5.0%	0.9%	5.8%	11.7%
4796	-$6	6-6-8-J	NS	4.4%	0.8%	4.8%	10.0%
3830	-$4	6-6-8-Q	DS	5.6%	1.0%	6.9%	13.5%
4277	-$5	6-6-8-Q	S	5.1%	0.9%	6.1%	12.2%
4889	-$6	6-6-8-Q	NS	4.4%	0.9%	4.9%	10.1%
3619	-$4	6-6-8-K	DS	5.8%	1.0%	6.9%	13.8%
4237	-$5	6-6-8-K	S	5.5%	0.9%	6.0%	12.4%
4969	-$7	6-6-8-K	NS	4.3%	0.8%	4.4%	9.6%
1956	-$2	6-6-9-9	DS	5.2%	0.0%	7.3%	12.6%
2346	-$3	6-6-9-9	S	4.8%	0.0%	6.4%	11.2%
2810	-$3	6-6-9-9	NS	4.2%	0.0%	5.8%	10.0%
3783	-$4	6-6-9-10	DS	5.3%	0.0%	6.2%	11.4%
4226	-$5	6-6-9-10	S	4.8%	0.0%	5.3%	10.1%
4589	-$6	6-6-9-10	NS	4.4%	0.0%	4.6%	8.9%
4213	-$5	6-6-9-J	DS	4.7%	0.0%	6.1%	10.8%
4522	-$6	6-6-9-J	S	4.3%	0.0%	5.3%	9.6%

OMAHA HIGH-LOW 8 OR BETTER
5,278 HANDS   9 HANDED

| HAND RANK | VALUE $4/$8 | POCKET CARDS | | HIGH % | LOW % | SCOOP % | PART OR ALL % |
		HAND	SUITED				
4879	-$6	6-6-9-J	NS	3.9%	0.0%	4.4%	8.3%
4028	-$5	6-6-9-Q	DS	5.0%	0.0%	6.4%	11.5%
4479	-$5	6-6-9-Q	S	4.6%	0.0%	5.7%	10.2%
4871	-$6	6-6-9-Q	NS	3.8%	0.0%	4.8%	8.6%
4057	-$5	6-6-9-K	DS	5.2%	0.0%	6.6%	11.8%
4392	-$5	6-6-9-K	S	4.7%	0.0%	6.0%	10.7%
4913	-$7	6-6-9-K	NS	3.6%	0.0%	4.5%	8.1%
2117	-$2	6-6-10-10	DS	4.9%	0.0%	7.7%	12.6%
2597	-$3	6-6-10-10	S	4.4%	0.0%	6.8%	11.3%
3125	-$4	6-6-10-10	NS	3.9%	0.0%	6.1%	10.0%
3396	-$4	6-6-10-J	DS	4.6%	0.0%	6.9%	11.5%
3972	-$5	6-6-10-J	S	4.2%	0.0%	6.2%	10.4%
4466	-$5	6-6-10-J	NS	3.8%	0.0%	5.4%	9.2%
3089	-$4	6-6-10-Q	DS	4.9%	0.0%	7.5%	12.4%
3891	-$5	6-6-10-Q	S	4.4%	0.0%	6.5%	10.9%
4433	-$5	6-6-10-Q	NS	3.8%	0.0%	5.6%	9.4%
3167	-$4	6-6-10-K	DS	5.1%	0.0%	7.5%	12.6%
3837	-$4	6-6-10-K	S	4.5%	0.0%	6.8%	11.4%
4639	-$6	6-6-10-K	NS	3.5%	0.0%	5.4%	8.9%
2232	-$2	6-6-J-J	DS	4.9%	0.0%	8.4%	13.3%
2677	-$3	6-6-J-J	S	4.5%	0.0%	7.6%	12.1%
3423	-$4	6-6-J-J	NS	3.9%	0.0%	6.7%	10.6%
3323	-$4	6-6-J-Q	DS	4.7%	0.0%	7.4%	12.1%
4036	-$5	6-6-J-Q	S	4.1%	0.0%	6.5%	10.7%
4559	-$6	6-6-J-Q	NS	3.4%	0.0%	5.6%	9.1%
3137	-$4	6-6-J-K	DS	4.9%	0.0%	7.6%	12.5%
4043	-$5	6-6-J-K	S	4.3%	0.0%	6.7%	11.0%
4580	-$6	6-6-J-K	NS	3.3%	0.0%	5.4%	8.7%

OMAHA HIGH-LOW 8 OR BETTER
5,278 HANDS   9 HANDED

HAND RANK	VALUE $4/$8	POCKET CARDS		HIGH %	LOW %	SCOOP %	PART OR ALL %
		HAND	SUITED				
1487	-$1	6-6-Q-Q	DS	5.8%	0.0%	10.5%	16.3%
2429	-$3	6-6-Q-Q	S	4.9%	0.0%	9.1%	14.0%
3078	-$4	6-6-Q-Q	NS	4.3%	0.0%	8.1%	12.4%
2753	-$3	6-6-Q-K	DS	5.1%	0.0%	8.1%	13.2%
3649	-$4	6-6-Q-K	S	4.3%	0.0%	7.1%	11.4%
4468	-$5	6-6-Q-K	NS	3.4%	0.0%	5.8%	9.2%
925	$1	6-6-K-K	DS	7.0%	0.0%	13.0%	19.9%
1659	-$2	6-6-K-K	S	5.8%	0.0%	11.7%	17.5%
2383	-$3	6-6-K-K	NS	4.8%	0.0%	10.5%	15.3%
5066	-$8	6-7-7-7	S	3.2%	1.2%	3.3%	7.7%
5137	-$8	6-7-7-7	NS	2.8%	1.1%	2.5%	6.4%
2043	-$2	6-7-7-8	DS	6.3%	1.6%	7.2%	15.1%
2787	-$3	6-7-7-8	S	5.8%	1.5%	6.1%	13.4%
3583	-$4	6-7-7-8	NS	5.7%	1.4%	5.2%	12.3%
2639	-$3	6-7-7-9	DS	6.4%	1.3%	6.6%	14.2%
3578	-$4	6-7-7-9	S	5.9%	1.2%	5.4%	12.4%
4342	-$5	6-7-7-9	NS	5.5%	1.1%	4.5%	11.1%
2914	-$3	6-7-7-10	DS	6.1%	1.3%	6.4%	13.7%
3623	-$4	6-7-7-10	S	5.5%	1.2%	5.5%	12.2%
4336	-$5	6-7-7-10	NS	5.0%	1.1%	4.7%	10.7%
3110	-$4	6-7-7-J	DS	5.7%	1.3%	6.5%	13.4%
4126	-$5	6-7-7-J	S	5.1%	1.1%	5.3%	11.6%
4644	-$6	6-7-7-J	NS	4.6%	1.1%	4.5%	10.2%
3347	-$4	6-7-7-Q	DS	5.7%	1.3%	6.7%	13.7%
4076	-$5	6-7-7-Q	S	5.2%	1.2%	5.5%	11.9%
4785	-$6	6-7-7-Q	NS	4.7%	1.2%	4.5%	10.4%
2776	-$3	6-7-7-K	DS	6.1%	1.4%	7.3%	14.8%
3811	-$4	6-7-7-K	S	5.5%	1.4%	6.0%	12.9%

OMAHA HIGH-LOW 8 OR BETTER
5,278 HANDS   9 HANDED

HAND RANK	VALUE $4/$8	POCKET CARDS		HIGH %	LOW %	SCOOP %	PART OR ALL %
		HAND	SUITED				
4666	-$6	6-7-7-K	NS	4.7%	1.2%	4.9%	10.8%
1713	-$2	6-7-8-8	DS	6.3%	1.5%	7.5%	15.4%
2258	-$3	6-7-8-8	S	6.1%	1.4%	6.5%	14.0%
3237	-$4	6-7-8-8	NS	5.6%	1.3%	5.6%	12.5%
2090	-$2	6-7-8-9	DS	6.6%	1.4%	6.8%	14.9%
2991	-$3	6-7-8-9	S	6.1%	1.3%	6.0%	13.4%
3686	-$4	6-7-8-9	NS	5.6%	1.2%	5.2%	12.0%
1936	-$2	6-7-8-10	DS	6.2%	1.4%	7.3%	14.9%
2749	-$3	6-7-8-10	S	5.7%	1.4%	6.4%	13.5%
3474	-$4	6-7-8-10	NS	5.2%	1.3%	5.6%	12.1%
2438	-$3	6-7-8-J	DS	5.8%	1.4%	7.2%	14.4%
3465	-$4	6-7-8-J	S	5.3%	1.3%	6.2%	12.8%
4195	-$5	6-7-8-J	NS	4.7%	1.2%	5.5%	11.4%
2735	-$3	6-7-8-Q	DS	5.9%	1.5%	7.3%	14.6%
3581	-$4	6-7-8-Q	S	5.4%	1.3%	6.3%	13.1%
4515	-$6	6-7-8-Q	NS	4.7%	1.2%	5.3%	11.2%
2426	-$3	6-7-8-K	DS	6.1%	1.6%	7.6%	15.3%
3386	-$4	6-7-8-K	S	5.7%	1.4%	6.8%	13.9%
4647	-$6	6-7-8-K	NS	4.8%	1.3%	5.4%	11.5%
1775	-$2	6-7-9-9	DS	5.4%	1.1%	7.8%	14.3%
2446	-$3	6-7-9-9	S	4.8%	1.0%	7.0%	12.8%
3104	-$4	6-7-9-9	NS	4.2%	1.0%	6.2%	11.4%
2362	-$3	6-7-9-10	DS	6.1%	1.1%	7.3%	14.6%
3197	-$4	6-7-9-10	S	5.6%	1.0%	6.5%	13.1%
4096	-$5	6-7-9-10	NS	5.0%	1.0%	5.6%	11.6%
3011	-$3	6-7-9-J	DS	5.6%	1.1%	7.4%	14.1%
3788	-$4	6-7-9-J	S	5.1%	1.0%	6.6%	12.7%
4743	-$6	6-7-9-J	NS	4.3%	1.0%	5.5%	10.8%

OMAHA HIGH-LOW 8 OR BETTER
5,278 HANDS   9 HANDED

| HAND RANK | VALUE $4/$8 | POCKET CARDS | | HIGH % | LOW % | SCOOP % | PART OR ALL % |
		HAND	SUITED				
3244	-$4	6-7-9-Q	DS	5.5%	1.1%	7.5%	14.2%
4025	-$5	6-7-9-Q	S	5.1%	1.1%	6.5%	12.6%
4811	-$6	6-7-9-Q	NS	4.4%	0.9%	5.3%	10.7%
2885	-$3	6-7-9-K	DS	5.9%	1.2%	8.0%	15.0%
4006	-$5	6-7-9-K	S	5.3%	1.1%	7.0%	13.4%
4775	-$6	6-7-9-K	NS	4.4%	1.0%	5.7%	11.1%
1722	-$2	6-7-10-10	DS	5.0%	1.2%	8.5%	14.7%
2196	-$2	6-7-10-10	S	4.5%	1.1%	7.5%	13.1%
3099	-$4	6-7-10-10	NS	3.9%	1.0%	6.6%	11.6%
2359	-$3	6-7-10-J	DS	5.2%	1.1%	8.4%	14.8%
3406	-$4	6-7-10-J	S	4.8%	1.1%	7.3%	13.2%
4323	-$5	6-7-10-J	NS	4.1%	1.0%	6.5%	11.7%
2270	-$3	6-7-10-Q	DS	5.4%	1.2%	8.4%	15.0%
3533	-$4	6-7-10-Q	S	4.8%	1.1%	7.5%	13.4%
4353	-$5	6-7-10-Q	NS	4.1%	1.1%	6.5%	11.7%
1909	-$2	6-7-10-K	DS	5.7%	1.2%	9.1%	16.0%
2950	-$3	6-7-10-K	S	5.1%	1.2%	8.3%	14.6%
4272	-$5	6-7-10-K	NS	4.1%	1.1%	6.9%	12.1%
1626	-$1	6-7-J-J	DS	4.9%	1.2%	9.2%	15.3%
2368	-$3	6-7-J-J	S	4.2%	1.2%	8.1%	13.5%
3215	-$4	6-7-J-J	NS	3.6%	1.1%	7.3%	12.0%
2674	-$3	6-7-J-Q	DS	4.9%	1.2%	8.3%	14.4%
3738	-$4	6-7-J-Q	S	4.3%	1.1%	7.4%	12.9%
4537	-$6	6-7-J-Q	NS	3.6%	1.0%	6.4%	11.0%
2393	-$3	6-7-J-K	DS	5.2%	1.2%	8.9%	15.3%
3252	-$4	6-7-J-K	S	4.6%	1.2%	8.0%	13.8%
4578	-$6	6-7-J-K	NS	3.7%	1.1%	6.6%	11.4%
1340	-$1	6-7-Q-Q	DS	5.4%	1.4%	10.7%	17.5%

		OMAHA HIGH-LOW 8 OR BETTER 5,278 HANDS 9 HANDED					
		POCKET CARDS					
HAND RANK	VALUE $4/$8	HAND	SUITED	HIGH %	LOW %	SCOOP %	PART OR ALL %
2236	-$3	6-7-Q-Q	S	4.5%	1.3%	9.5%	15.2%
3177	-$4	6-7-Q-Q	NS	3.9%	1.2%	8.4%	13.5%
2118	-$2	6-7-Q-K	DS	5.4%	1.2%	9.2%	15.8%
3113	-$4	6-7-Q-K	S	4.6%	1.2%	8.3%	14.1%
4464	-$5	6-7-Q-K	NS	3.8%	1.1%	6.9%	11.8%
776	$1	6-7-K-K	DS	6.5%	1.6%	13.2%	21.3%
1623	-$1	6-7-K-K	S	5.3%	1.4%	11.6%	18.4%
2798	-$3	6-7-K-K	NS	4.3%	1.3%	10.5%	16.1%
5117	-$8	6-8-8-8	S	2.9%	0.8%	3.2%	6.8%
5207	-$9	6-8-8-8	NS	2.6%	0.7%	2.2%	5.5%
2845	-$3	6-8-8-9	DS	6.3%	0.9%	6.8%	14.0%
3827	-$4	6-8-8-9	S	5.8%	0.8%	5.6%	12.3%
4387	-$5	6-8-8-9	NS	5.3%	0.8%	5.0%	11.1%
2763	-$3	6-8-8-10	DS	5.9%	0.9%	7.0%	13.8%
3668	-$4	6-8-8-10	S	5.5%	0.8%	5.9%	12.2%
4209	-$5	6-8-8-10	NS	4.9%	0.8%	5.3%	11.0%
3143	-$4	6-8-8-J	DS	5.6%	0.9%	6.8%	13.3%
4149	-$5	6-8-8-J	S	5.2%	0.8%	5.6%	11.6%
4623	-$6	6-8-8-J	NS	4.6%	0.8%	5.0%	10.3%
3290	-$4	6-8-8-Q	DS	5.7%	0.9%	7.2%	13.8%
3844	-$4	6-8-8-Q	S	5.2%	0.9%	6.2%	12.3%
4664	-$6	6-8-8-Q	NS	4.5%	0.8%	5.2%	10.5%
3295	-$4	6-8-8-K	DS	6.0%	1.0%	7.0%	13.9%
3860	-$4	6-8-8-K	S	5.5%	0.9%	5.9%	12.3%
4848	-$6	6-8-8-K	NS	4.5%	0.8%	4.7%	10.0%
2075	-$2	6-8-9-9	DS	5.2%	0.7%	7.9%	13.9%
2604	-$3	6-8-9-9	S	4.7%	0.7%	7.1%	12.6%
3547	-$4	6-8-9-9	NS	4.1%	0.7%	6.4%	11.1%

OMAHA HIGH-LOW 8 OR BETTER
5,278 HANDS 9 HANDED

HAND RANK	VALUE $4/$8	POCKET CARDS		HIGH %	LOW %	SCOOP %	PART OR ALL %
		HAND	SUITED				
2197	-$2	6-8-9-10	DS	5.9%	0.8%	7.6%	14.2%
3173	-$4	6-8-9-10	S	5.3%	0.7%	6.8%	12.9%
3813	-$4	6-8-9-10	NS	4.7%	0.7%	6.1%	11.5%
3003	-$3	6-8-9-J	DS	5.5%	0.7%	7.4%	13.6%
3614	-$4	6-8-9-J	S	4.9%	0.7%	6.8%	12.4%
4244	-$5	6-8-9-J	NS	4.3%	0.7%	6.1%	11.1%
2909	-$3	6-8-9-Q	DS	5.5%	0.8%	7.9%	14.1%
3457	-$4	6-8-9-Q	S	4.9%	0.7%	7.3%	12.9%
4483	-$5	6-8-9-Q	NS	4.4%	0.7%	6.1%	11.1%
3155	-$4	6-8-9-K	DS	5.7%	0.8%	7.5%	14.0%
3939	-$5	6-8-9-K	S	5.0%	0.8%	6.8%	12.6%
4790	-$6	6-8-9-K	NS	4.1%	0.7%	5.6%	10.3%
1685	-$2	6-8-10-10	DS	4.9%	0.8%	8.7%	14.4%
2331	-$3	6-8-10-10	S	4.3%	0.8%	7.9%	13.0%
2871	-$3	6-8-10-10	NS	3.7%	0.7%	7.4%	11.8%
2055	-$2	6-8-10-J	DS	5.2%	0.8%	8.6%	14.6%
2924	-$3	6-8-10-J	S	4.6%	0.8%	7.8%	13.2%
3713	-$4	6-8-10-J	NS	4.0%	0.7%	7.1%	11.9%
1981	-$2	6-8-10-Q	DS	5.4%	0.8%	8.8%	15.0%
2562	-$3	6-8-10-Q	S	4.8%	0.8%	8.2%	13.8%
3733	-$4	6-8-10-Q	NS	4.0%	0.7%	7.2%	12.0%
2300	-$3	6-8-10-K	DS	5.4%	0.9%	8.6%	14.9%
3204	-$4	6-8-10-K	S	4.9%	0.8%	7.9%	13.6%
4343	-$5	6-8-10-K	NS	3.9%	0.8%	6.7%	11.3%
1719	-$2	6-8-J-J	DS	4.7%	0.9%	9.4%	15.0%
2430	-$3	6-8-J-J	S	4.0%	0.8%	8.4%	13.3%
3341	-$4	6-8-J-J	NS	3.4%	0.7%	7.8%	11.8%
2403	-$3	6-8-J-Q	DS	5.0%	0.8%	8.6%	14.3%

OMAHA HIGH-LOW 8 OR BETTER
5,278 HANDS   9 HANDED

HAND RANK	VALUE $4/$8	POCKET CARDS		HIGH %	LOW %	SCOOP %	PART OR ALL %
		HAND	SUITED				
3292	-$4	6-8-J-Q	S	4.2%	0.7%	7.9%	12.8%
4173	-$5	6-8-J-Q	NS	3.5%	0.7%	7.0%	11.3%
2784	-$3	6-8-J-K	DS	5.0%	0.8%	8.4%	14.2%
3523	-$4	6-8-J-K	S	4.5%	0.8%	7.6%	12.8%
4588	-$6	6-8-J-K	NS	3.4%	0.7%	6.4%	10.5%
1229	-$1	6-8-Q-Q	DS	5.2%	1.0%	10.9%	17.0%
2061	-$2	6-8-Q-Q	S	4.3%	0.9%	9.8%	15.0%
3180	-$4	6-8-Q-Q	NS	3.5%	0.9%	8.7%	13.1%
2392	-$3	6-8-Q-K	DS	5.2%	0.9%	8.7%	14.9%
3644	-$4	6-8-Q-K	S	4.5%	0.8%	7.8%	13.1%
4649	-$6	6-8-Q-K	NS	3.4%	0.7%	6.6%	10.8%
1062	$0	6-8-K-K	DS	6.1%	1.2%	12.5%	19.7%
1791	-$2	6-8-K-K	S	5.0%	1.0%	11.3%	17.4%
3218	-$4	6-8-K-K	NS	4.0%	1.0%	10.0%	15.0%
5069	-$8	6-9-9-9	S	1.9%	0.0%	2.8%	4.7%
5072	-$8	6-9-9-9	NS	1.5%	0.0%	2.4%	3.9%
2200	-$2	6-9-9-10	DS	4.5%	0.0%	7.7%	12.2%
2702	-$3	6-9-9-10	S	3.9%	0.0%	6.9%	10.8%
3442	-$4	6-9-9-10	NS	3.4%	0.0%	6.2%	9.6%
2536	-$3	6-9-9-J	DS	4.0%	0.0%	7.7%	11.8%
3222	-$4	6-9-9-J	S	3.4%	0.0%	6.9%	10.4%
3907	-$5	6-9-9-J	NS	2.9%	0.0%	6.2%	9.1%
2529	-$3	6-9-9-Q	DS	4.1%	0.0%	8.0%	12.1%
3076	-$4	6-9-9-Q	S	3.6%	0.0%	7.4%	11.0%
3919	-$5	6-9-9-Q	NS	2.9%	0.0%	6.5%	9.4%
2655	-$3	6-9-9-K	DS	4.4%	0.0%	8.0%	12.3%
3404	-$4	6-9-9-K	S	3.6%	0.0%	7.2%	10.8%
4257	-$5	6-9-9-K	NS	2.7%	0.0%	6.0%	8.7%

OMAHA HIGH-LOW 8 OR BETTER
5,278 HANDS   9 HANDED

HAND RANK	VALUE $4/$8	POCKET CARDS		HIGH %	LOW %	SCOOP %	PART OR ALL %
		HAND	SUITED				
2098	-$2	6-9-10-10	DS	4.5%	0.0%	7.9%	12.4%
2760	-$3	6-9-10-10	S	3.9%	0.0%	7.2%	11.1%
3371	-$4	6-9-10-10	NS	3.5%	0.0%	6.6%	10.0%
1989	-$2	6-9-10-J	DS	4.7%	0.0%	8.6%	13.2%
2572	-$3	6-9-10-J	S	4.1%	0.0%	8.1%	12.2%
3436	-$4	6-9-10-J	NS	3.6%	0.0%	7.2%	10.9%
1854	-$2	6-9-10-Q	DS	4.8%	0.0%	8.8%	13.7%
2345	-$3	6-9-10-Q	S	4.3%	0.0%	8.3%	12.6%
3232	-$4	6-9-10-Q	NS	3.6%	0.0%	7.4%	11.1%
2342	-$3	6-9-10-K	DS	4.9%	0.0%	8.5%	13.4%
2661	-$3	6-9-10-K	S	4.4%	0.0%	8.3%	12.6%
3682	-$4	6-9-10-K	NS	3.3%	0.0%	7.2%	10.5%
2148	-$2	6-9-J-J	DS	4.3%	0.0%	8.6%	12.9%
2708	-$3	6-9-J-J	S	3.8%	0.0%	8.0%	11.7%
3541	-$4	6-9-J-J	NS	3.2%	0.0%	7.2%	10.4%
2184	-$2	6-9-J-Q	DS	4.2%	0.0%	8.7%	12.9%
2728	-$3	6-9-J-Q	S	3.7%	0.0%	7.9%	11.5%
3698	-$4	6-9-J-Q	NS	3.0%	0.0%	7.2%	10.2%
2547	-$3	6-9-J-K	DS	4.5%	0.0%	8.6%	13.0%
3066	-$4	6-9-J-K	S	3.8%	0.0%	8.2%	12.0%
4129	-$5	6-9-J-K	NS	2.8%	0.0%	7.0%	9.7%
1829	-$2	6-9-Q-Q	DS	4.9%	0.0%	10.0%	14.9%
2583	-$3	6-9-Q-Q	S	4.1%	0.0%	9.1%	13.2%
3497	-$4	6-9-Q-Q	NS	3.4%	0.0%	8.1%	11.5%
2247	-$3	6-9-Q-K	DS	4.6%	0.0%	9.0%	13.6%
2923	-$3	6-9-Q-K	S	3.8%	0.0%	8.5%	12.4%
4123	-$5	6-9-Q-K	NS	2.8%	0.0%	7.2%	10.0%
1397	-$1	6-9-K-K	DS	6.0%	0.0%	11.8%	17.8%

OMAHA HIGH-LOW 8 OR BETTER
5,278 HANDS   9 HANDED

| HAND RANK | VALUE $4/$8 | POCKET CARDS | | HIGH % | LOW % | SCOOP % | PART OR ALL % |
		HAND	SUITED				
1997	-$2	6-9-K-K	S	4.6%	0.0%	11.0%	15.7%
3072	-$4	6-9-K-K	NS	3.5%	0.0%	10.0%	13.5%
5092	-$8	6-10-10-10	S	1.6%	0.0%	3.3%	4.9%
5158	-$9	6-10-10-10	NS	1.2%	0.0%	2.5%	3.7%
1721	-$2	6-10-10-J	DS	4.1%	0.0%	9.1%	13.2%
2183	-$2	6-10-10-J	S	3.4%	0.0%	8.5%	11.9%
3069	-$4	6-10-10-J	NS	2.9%	0.0%	7.7%	10.7%
1769	-$2	6-10-10-Q	DS	4.3%	0.0%	9.5%	13.8%
2140	-$2	6-10-10-Q	S	3.6%	0.0%	8.9%	12.4%
2963	-$3	6-10-10-Q	NS	3.0%	0.0%	8.0%	11.0%
1925	-$2	6-10-10-K	DS	4.4%	0.0%	9.3%	13.7%
2458	-$3	6-10-10-K	S	3.7%	0.0%	8.7%	12.3%
3598	-$4	6-10-10-K	NS	2.7%	0.0%	7.6%	10.3%
1708	-$2	6-10-J-J	DS	4.1%	0.0%	9.4%	13.5%
2058	-$2	6-10-J-J	S	3.5%	0.0%	8.9%	12.4%
2850	-$3	6-10-J-J	NS	3.0%	0.0%	8.0%	11.0%
1287	-$1	6-10-J-Q	DS	4.3%	0.0%	10.0%	14.3%
1527	-$1	6-10-J-Q	S	3.8%	0.0%	9.7%	13.5%
2231	-$2	6-10-J-Q	NS	3.2%	0.0%	8.8%	12.0%
1403	-$1	6-10-J-K	DS	4.6%	0.0%	10.1%	14.7%
1821	-$2	6-10-J-K	S	3.9%	0.0%	9.6%	13.5%
2780	-$3	6-10-J-K	NS	2.9%	0.0%	8.5%	11.4%
1337	-$1	6-10-Q-Q	DS	4.7%	0.0%	10.8%	15.6%
1711	-$2	6-10-Q-Q	S	4.0%	0.0%	10.3%	14.2%
2581	-$3	6-10-Q-Q	NS	3.2%	0.0%	9.2%	12.4%
1273	-$1	6-10-Q-K	DS	4.8%	0.0%	10.3%	15.2%
1596	-$1	6-10-Q-K	S	4.0%	0.0%	9.9%	13.8%

OMAHA HIGH-LOW 8 OR BETTER
5,278 HANDS 9 HANDED

| HAND RANK | VALUE $4/$8 | POCKET CARDS | | HIGH % | LOW % | SCOOP % | PART OR ALL % |
		HAND	SUITED				
2647	-$3	6-10-Q-K	NS	3.0%	0.0%	8.7%	11.7%
878	$1	6-10-K-K	DS	5.8%	0.0%	12.8%	18.6%
1412	-$1	6-10-K-K	S	4.5%	0.0%	11.7%	16.2%
2211	-$2	6-10-K-K	NS	3.4%	0.0%	10.7%	14.2%
5170	-$9	6-J-J-J	S	1.6%	0.0%	3.8%	5.4%
5241	-$9	6-J-J-J	NS	1.1%	0.0%	3.1%	4.1%
1547	-$1	6-J-J-Q	DS	4.1%	0.0%	10.4%	14.6%
1975	-$2	6-J-J-Q	S	3.4%	0.0%	9.7%	13.1%
3192	-$4	6-J-J-Q	NS	2.8%	0.0%	8.7%	11.4%
1772	-$2	6-J-J-K	DS	4.4%	0.0%	10.3%	14.7%
2170	-$2	6-J-J-K	S	3.7%	0.0%	9.7%	13.4%
3431	-$4	6-J-J-K	NS	2.6%	0.0%	8.7%	11.4%
1383	-$1	6-J-Q-Q	DS	4.5%	0.0%	10.8%	15.3%
1954	-$2	6-J-Q-Q	S	3.6%	0.0%	10.0%	13.5%
2685	-$3	6-J-Q-Q	NS	3.0%	0.0%	9.0%	11.9%
1297	-$1	6-J-Q-K	DS	4.5%	0.0%	10.2%	14.7%
1542	-$1	6-J-Q-K	S	3.8%	0.0%	9.8%	13.6%
2418	-$3	6-J-Q-K	NS	2.7%	0.0%	8.7%	11.5%
1038	$0	6-J-K-K	DS	5.6%	0.0%	12.6%	18.1%
1536	-$1	6-J-K-K	S	4.2%	0.0%	11.6%	15.9%
2416	-$3	6-J-K-K	NS	3.1%	0.0%	10.6%	13.7%
5227	-$9	6-Q-Q-Q	S	2.0%	0.0%	5.2%	7.2%
5269	-$10	6-Q-Q-Q	NS	1.3%	0.0%	4.2%	5.5%
1238	-$1	6-Q-Q-K	DS	5.2%	0.0%	12.0%	17.1%
1749	-$2	6-Q-Q-K	S	4.0%	0.0%	11.1%	15.2%
3152	-$4	6-Q-Q-K	NS	2.9%	0.0%	9.9%	12.9%
992	$0	6-Q-K-K	DS	5.6%	0.0%	12.6%	18.2%
1565	-$1	6-Q-K-K	S	4.3%	0.0%	11.6%	15.9%

		POCKET CARDS					
HAND RANK	VALUE $4/$8	HAND	SUITED	HIGH %	LOW %	SCOOP %	PART OR ALL %
2336	-$3	6-Q-K-K	NS	3.2%	0.0%	10.6%	13.7%
5164	-$9	6-K-K-K	S	2.8%	0.0%	7.4%	10.1%
5264	-$10	6-K-K-K	NS	1.6%	0.0%	6.5%	8.1%
5271	-$10	7-7-7-7	NS	0.0%	0.0%	0.1%	0.2%
5103	-$8	7-7-7-8	S	3.0%	0.8%	3.6%	7.4%
5228	-$9	7-7-7-8	NS	2.6%	0.7%	2.8%	6.1%
5132	-$8	7-7-7-9	S	2.6%	0.0%	2.6%	5.2%
5189	-$9	7-7-7-9	NS	2.2%	0.0%	1.9%	4.1%
5113	-$8	7-7-7-10	S	2.1%	0.0%	2.7%	4.9%
5195	-$9	7-7-7-10	NS	1.7%	0.0%	1.9%	3.6%
5126	-$8	7-7-7-J	S	2.1%	0.0%	2.7%	4.8%
5231	-$9	7-7-7-J	NS	1.4%	0.0%	1.9%	3.3%
5181	-$9	7-7-7-Q	S	1.9%	0.0%	2.6%	4.5%
5245	-$9	7-7-7-Q	NS	1.4%	0.0%	1.6%	3.0%
5174	-$9	7-7-7-K	S	2.3%	0.0%	3.0%	5.3%
5249	-$9	7-7-7-K	NS	1.4%	0.0%	1.8%	3.2%
1345	-$1	7-7-8-8	DS	7.1%	0.9%	7.9%	15.9%
1743	-$2	7-7-8-8	S	6.7%	0.8%	7.0%	14.5%
2584	-$3	7-7-8-8	NS	6.4%	0.7%	5.9%	13.1%
2837	-$3	7-7-8-9	DS	6.5%	0.8%	7.0%	14.2%
3658	-$4	7-7-8-9	S	6.0%	0.8%	6.1%	12.8%
4328	-$5	7-7-8-9	NS	5.5%	0.7%	5.2%	11.4%
2520	-$3	7-7-8-10	DS	6.1%	0.8%	7.2%	14.2%
3240	-$4	7-7-8-10	S	5.5%	0.8%	6.4%	12.7%
4291	-$5	7-7-8-10	NS	5.0%	0.7%	5.4%	11.2%
2751	-$3	7-7-8-J	DS	5.8%	0.8%	7.2%	13.8%
3568	-$4	7-7-8-J	S	5.3%	0.8%	6.3%	12.3%
4308	-$5	7-7-8-J	NS	4.8%	0.7%	5.4%	11.0%

OMAHA HIGH-LOW 8 OR BETTER
5,278 HANDS   9 HANDED

OMAHA HIGH-LOW 8 OR BETTER
5,278 HANDS   9 HANDED

HAND RANK	VALUE $4/$8	POCKET CARDS HAND	SUITED	HIGH %	LOW %	SCOOP %	PART OR ALL %
3358	-$4	7-7-8-Q	DS	5.7%	0.8%	7.0%	13.5%
4026	-$5	7-7-8-Q	S	5.3%	0.8%	6.1%	12.2%
4699	-$6	7-7-8-Q	NS	4.5%	0.7%	5.0%	10.2%
2933	-$3	7-7-8-K	DS	6.1%	0.9%	7.4%	14.4%
3870	-$5	7-7-8-K	S	5.6%	0.9%	6.5%	13.0%
4742	-$6	7-7-8-K	NS	4.6%	0.8%	5.2%	10.6%
1474	-$1	7-7-9-9	DS	5.6%	0.0%	7.7%	13.4%
1853	-$2	7-7-9-9	S	5.1%	0.0%	6.9%	12.0%
2240	-$3	7-7-9-9	NS	4.6%	0.0%	6.2%	10.8%
2948	-$3	7-7-9-10	DS	5.7%	0.0%	6.6%	12.3%
3531	-$4	7-7-9-10	S	5.1%	0.0%	5.9%	11.1%
4031	-$5	7-7-9-10	NS	4.7%	0.0%	5.2%	9.9%
2965	-$3	7-7-9-J	DS	5.4%	0.0%	6.7%	12.1%
3669	-$4	7-7-9-J	S	4.9%	0.0%	6.0%	10.9%
4486	-$5	7-7-9-J	NS	4.3%	0.0%	5.0%	9.3%
3527	-$4	7-7-9-Q	DS	5.2%	0.0%	6.6%	11.9%
4150	-$5	7-7-9-Q	S	4.8%	0.0%	5.9%	10.6%
4725	-$6	7-7-9-Q	NS	4.0%	0.0%	4.7%	8.7%
3482	-$4	7-7-9-K	DS	5.6%	0.0%	7.1%	12.7%
3935	-$5	7-7-9-K	S	5.1%	0.0%	6.5%	11.5%
4729	-$6	7-7-9-K	NS	4.1%	0.0%	4.9%	9.0%
1479	-$1	7-7-10-10	DS	5.2%	0.0%	8.3%	13.5%
1810	-$2	7-7-10-10	S	4.7%	0.0%	7.4%	12.1%
2279	-$3	7-7-10-10	NS	4.3%	0.0%	6.7%	10.9%
2138	-$2	7-7-10-J	DS	5.1%	0.0%	7.7%	12.9%
2976	-$3	7-7-10-J	S	4.6%	0.0%	6.9%	11.5%
3548	-$4	7-7-10-J	NS	4.2%	0.0%	6.1%	10.3%
2821	-$3	7-7-10-Q	DS	5.0%	0.0%	7.3%	12.4%

OMAHA HIGH-LOW 8 OR BETTER
5,278 HANDS   9 HANDED

HAND RANK	VALUE $4/$8	POCKET CARDS HAND	SUITED	HIGH %	LOW %	SCOOP %	PART OR ALL %
3362	-$4	7-7-10-Q	S	4.6%	0.0%	6.8%	11.4%
4216	-$5	7-7-10-Q	NS	3.9%	0.0%	5.7%	9.6%
2464	-$3	7-7-10-K	DS	5.5%	0.0%	8.0%	13.5%
3225	-$4	7-7-10-K	S	5.0%	0.0%	7.3%	12.3%
4232	-$5	7-7-10-K	NS	4.0%	0.0%	5.9%	9.9%
1422	-$1	7-7-J-J	DS	5.3%	0.0%	8.9%	14.2%
1895	-$2	7-7-J-J	S	4.7%	0.0%	8.2%	12.8%
2530	-$3	7-7-J-J	NS	4.1%	0.0%	7.2%	11.3%
2808	-$3	7-7-J-Q	DS	4.9%	0.0%	7.5%	12.4%
3592	-$4	7-7-J-Q	S	4.3%	0.0%	6.8%	11.0%
4352	-$5	7-7-J-Q	NS	3.7%	0.0%	5.7%	9.4%
2511	-$3	7-7-J-K	DS	5.3%	0.0%	8.1%	13.4%
3241	-$4	7-7-J-K	S	4.7%	0.0%	7.3%	12.0%
4292	-$5	7-7-J-K	NS	3.7%	0.0%	5.9%	9.6%
1417	-$1	7-7-Q-Q	DS	5.8%	0.0%	10.4%	16.2%
2082	-$2	7-7-Q-Q	S	4.9%	0.0%	9.3%	14.2%
3200	-$4	7-7-Q-Q	NS	4.2%	0.0%	8.1%	12.3%
2625	-$3	7-7-Q-K	DS	5.2%	0.0%	8.2%	13.4%
3561	-$4	7-7-Q-K	S	4.6%	0.0%	7.0%	11.6%
4505	-$6	7-7-Q-K	NS	3.4%	0.0%	5.8%	9.2%
855	$1	7-7-K-K	DS	6.9%	0.0%	13.0%	19.9%
1354	-$1	7-7-K-K	S	5.8%	0.0%	11.7%	17.5%
2201	-$2	7-7-K-K	NS	4.8%	0.0%	10.4%	15.2%
5082	-$8	7-8-8-8	S	3.0%	0.8%	3.7%	7.6%
5190	-$9	7-8-8-8	NS	2.6%	0.7%	2.9%	6.2%
2570	-$3	7-8-8-9	DS	6.5%	0.9%	7.0%	14.4%
3339	-$4	7-8-8-9	S	6.0%	0.8%	6.2%	13.0%
4205	-$5	7-8-8-9	NS	5.4%	0.7%	5.4%	11.6%

OMAHA HIGH-LOW 8 OR BETTER
5,278 HANDS   9 HANDED

HAND RANK	VALUE $4/$8	POCKET CARDS HAND	SUITED	HIGH %	LOW %	SCOOP %	PART OR ALL %
2115	-$2	7-8-8-10	DS	6.2%	0.8%	7.4%	14.5%
2980	-$3	7-8-8-10	S	5.6%	0.8%	6.4%	12.8%
3927	-$5	7-8-8-10	NS	5.1%	0.7%	5.7%	11.5%
2378	-$3	7-8-8-J	DS	5.9%	0.8%	7.4%	14.1%
3413	-$4	7-8-8-J	S	5.3%	0.7%	6.3%	12.4%
4065	-$5	7-8-8-J	NS	4.8%	0.7%	5.7%	11.2%
2875	-$3	7-8-8-Q	DS	5.8%	0.9%	7.2%	13.9%
3678	-$4	7-8-8-Q	S	5.2%	0.8%	6.2%	12.2%
4538	-$6	7-8-8-Q	NS	4.5%	0.7%	5.2%	10.5%
2743	-$3	7-8-8-K	DS	6.1%	0.9%	7.5%	14.5%
3607	-$4	7-8-8-K	S	5.5%	0.9%	6.6%	12.9%
4710	-$6	7-8-8-K	NS	4.6%	0.8%	5.2%	10.6%
2013	-$2	7-8-9-9	DS	5.4%	0.7%	8.1%	14.2%
2561	-$3	7-8-9-9	S	5.0%	0.6%	7.3%	13.0%
3165	-$4	7-8-9-9	NS	4.4%	0.6%	6.7%	11.7%
1714	-$2	7-8-9-10	DS	6.2%	0.7%	7.9%	14.7%
2223	-$2	7-8-9-10	S	5.6%	0.6%	7.1%	13.4%
3063	-$4	7-8-9-10	NS	5.0%	0.6%	6.5%	12.1%
2027	-$2	7-8-9-J	DS	5.9%	0.7%	7.9%	14.5%
2748	-$3	7-8-9-J	S	5.3%	0.6%	7.1%	13.0%
3579	-$4	7-8-9-J	NS	4.6%	0.6%	6.5%	11.6%
2527	-$3	7-8-9-Q	DS	5.7%	0.7%	7.8%	14.3%
3212	-$4	7-8-9-Q	S	5.1%	0.6%	7.1%	12.9%
4334	-$5	7-8-9-Q	NS	4.4%	0.6%	6.1%	11.1%
2497	-$3	7-8-9-K	DS	6.0%	0.8%	8.0%	14.7%
3272	-$4	7-8-9-K	S	5.4%	0.7%	7.3%	13.4%
4469	-$5	7-8-9-K	NS	4.4%	0.6%	6.1%	11.1%
1419	-$1	7-8-10-10	DS	5.2%	0.8%	9.0%	15.0%

OMAHA HIGH-LOW 8 OR BETTER
5,278 HANDS   9 HANDED

HAND RANK	VALUE $4/$8	POCKET CARDS HAND	SUITED	HIGH %	LOW %	SCOOP %	PART OR ALL %
1918	-$2	7-8-10-10	S	4.6%	0.7%	8.3%	13.6%
2600	-$3	7-8-10-10	NS	3.9%	0.7%	7.6%	12.2%
1436	-$1	7-8-10-J	DS	5.7%	0.7%	8.9%	15.4%
1788	-$2	7-8-10-J	S	5.1%	0.7%	8.3%	14.1%
2651	-$3	7-8-10-J	NS	4.5%	0.7%	7.7%	12.8%
1787	-$2	7-8-10-Q	DS	5.6%	0.8%	8.8%	15.2%
2413	-$3	7-8-10-Q	S	4.9%	0.7%	8.3%	13.9%
3443	-$4	7-8-10-Q	NS	4.2%	0.7%	7.5%	12.3%
1735	-$2	7-8-10-K	DS	6.0%	0.8%	9.0%	15.8%
2352	-$3	7-8-10-K	S	5.4%	0.8%	8.3%	14.4%
4003	-$5	7-8-10-K	NS	4.3%	0.7%	7.0%	12.1%
1365	-$1	7-8-J-J	DS	4.9%	0.8%	9.7%	15.4%
2064	-$2	7-8-J-J	S	4.3%	0.8%	8.8%	13.8%
2777	-$3	7-8-J-J	NS	3.6%	0.7%	8.1%	12.4%
2111	-$2	7-8-J-Q	DS	5.2%	0.7%	8.7%	14.6%
2890	-$3	7-8-J-Q	S	4.5%	0.7%	8.2%	13.5%
3993	-$5	7-8-J-Q	NS	3.8%	0.6%	7.2%	11.6%
2056	-$2	7-8-J-K	DS	5.5%	0.8%	9.0%	15.3%
2778	-$3	7-8-J-K	S	4.8%	0.8%	8.3%	13.9%
4127	-$5	7-8-J-K	NS	3.8%	0.7%	7.3%	11.7%
1265	-$1	7-8-Q-Q	DS	5.2%	0.9%	10.9%	16.9%
1905	-$2	7-8-Q-Q	S	4.3%	0.9%	9.9%	15.1%
2823	-$3	7-8-Q-Q	NS	3.5%	0.8%	8.9%	13.2%
2397	-$3	7-8-Q-K	DS	5.4%	0.8%	8.7%	14.8%
3153	-$4	7-8-Q-K	S	4.7%	0.8%	8.0%	13.4%
4447	-$5	7-8-Q-K	NS	3.6%	0.7%	6.7%	11.0%
775	$1	7-8-K-K	DS	6.2%	1.1%	13.0%	20.3%
1418	-$1	7-8-K-K	S	5.2%	1.0%	11.8%	17.9%

OMAHA HIGH-LOW 8 OR BETTER
5,278 HANDS   9 HANDED

| HAND RANK | VALUE $4/$8 | POCKET CARDS | | HIGH % | LOW % | SCOOP % | PART OR ALL % |
		HAND	SUITED				
2522	-$3	7-8-K-K	NS	4.0%	0.9%	10.7%	15.7%
5018	-$7	7-9-9-9	S	2.2%	0.0%	3.3%	5.5%
5052	-$8	7-9-9-9	NS	1.8%	0.0%	2.8%	4.5%
1797	-$2	7-9-9-10	DS	4.8%	0.0%	8.0%	12.8%
2145	-$2	7-9-9-10	S	4.2%	0.0%	7.3%	11.5%
3183	-$4	7-9-9-10	NS	3.6%	0.0%	6.6%	10.3%
1976	-$2	7-9-9-J	DS	4.4%	0.0%	8.2%	12.5%
2580	-$3	7-9-9-J	S	3.8%	0.0%	7.3%	11.1%
3196	-$4	7-9-9-J	NS	3.3%	0.0%	6.7%	10.0%
2414	-$3	7-9-9-Q	DS	4.2%	0.0%	8.0%	12.3%
2966	-$3	7-9-9-Q	S	3.7%	0.0%	7.2%	10.9%
3719	-$4	7-9-9-Q	NS	2.9%	0.0%	6.6%	9.5%
2116	-$2	7-9-9-K	DS	4.7%	0.0%	8.4%	13.1%
2834	-$3	7-9-9-K	S	4.0%	0.0%	7.7%	11.7%
3776	-$4	7-9-9-K	NS	3.0%	0.0%	6.7%	9.7%
1662	-$2	7-9-10-10	DS	4.9%	0.0%	8.4%	13.2%
1987	-$2	7-9-10-10	S	4.3%	0.0%	7.6%	12.0%
2794	-$3	7-9-10-10	NS	3.8%	0.0%	6.9%	10.7%
1270	-$1	7-9-10-J	DS	5.4%	0.0%	8.9%	14.3%
1660	-$2	7-9-10-J	S	4.8%	0.0%	8.4%	13.3%
2321	-$3	7-9-10-J	NS	4.4%	0.0%	7.6%	12.1%
1700	-$2	7-9-10-Q	DS	5.2%	0.0%	8.8%	14.0%
2112	-$2	7-9-10-Q	S	4.7%	0.0%	8.4%	13.1%
3256	-$4	7-9-10-Q	NS	3.9%	0.0%	7.4%	11.3%
1684	-$2	7-9-10-K	DS	5.5%	0.0%	9.2%	14.7%
1980	-$2	7-9-10-K	S	4.9%	0.0%	8.9%	13.8%
3157	-$4	7-9-10-K	NS	3.9%	0.0%	7.5%	11.5%
1635	-$1	7-9-J-J	DS	4.7%	0.0%	8.9%	13.6%

OMAHA HIGH-LOW 8 OR BETTER
5,278 HANDS   9 HANDED

HAND RANK	VALUE $4/$8	POCKET CARDS		HIGH %	LOW %	SCOOP %	PART OR ALL %
		HAND	SUITED				
2053	-$2	7-9-J-J	S	4.1%	0.0%	8.5%	12.6%
3138	-$4	7-9-J-J	NS	3.6%	0.0%	7.4%	11.0%
1967	-$2	7-9-J-Q	DS	4.5%	0.0%	8.8%	13.4%
2459	-$3	7-9-J-Q	S	4.0%	0.0%	8.3%	12.3%
3268	-$4	7-9-J-Q	NS	3.3%	0.0%	7.6%	10.9%
1657	-$2	7-9-J-K	DS	5.0%	0.0%	9.2%	14.3%
2259	-$3	7-9-J-K	S	4.4%	0.0%	8.9%	13.2%
3364	-$4	7-9-J-K	NS	3.3%	0.0%	7.7%	11.0%
1707	-$2	7-9-Q-Q	DS	4.9%	0.0%	10.0%	15.0%
2297	-$3	7-9-Q-Q	S	4.1%	0.0%	9.3%	13.4%
3228	-$4	7-9-Q-Q	NS	3.5%	0.0%	8.3%	11.7%
1995	-$2	7-9-Q-K	DS	4.8%	0.0%	9.2%	14.0%
2691	-$3	7-9-Q-K	S	4.1%	0.0%	8.3%	12.4%
3884	-$5	7-9-Q-K	NS	2.9%	0.0%	7.3%	10.2%
1098	-$0	7-9-K-K	DS	6.2%	0.0%	12.1%	18.4%
1718	-$2	7-9-K-K	S	4.9%	0.0%	11.2%	16.1%
2953	-$3	7-9-K-K	NS	3.8%	0.0%	9.9%	13.8%
5030	-$7	7-10-10-10	S	1.9%	0.0%	3.8%	5.7%
5083	-$8	7-10-10-10	NS	1.4%	0.0%	3.0%	4.4%
1325	-$1	7-10-10-J	DS	4.4%	0.0%	9.5%	13.8%
1564	-$1	7-10-10-J	S	3.8%	0.0%	8.9%	12.7%
2244	-$3	7-10-10-J	NS	3.3%	0.0%	8.3%	11.6%
1637	-$1	7-10-10-Q	DS	4.3%	0.0%	9.4%	13.7%
2057	-$2	7-10-10-Q	S	3.7%	0.0%	8.7%	12.4%
2896	-$3	7-10-10-Q	NS	3.0%	0.0%	8.1%	11.1%
1447	-$1	7-10-10-K	DS	4.7%	0.0%	10.0%	14.8%
1823	-$2	7-10-10-K	S	4.0%	0.0%	9.3%	13.4%

OMAHA HIGH-LOW 8 OR BETTER
5,278 HANDS   9 HANDED

| HAND RANK | VALUE $4/$8 | POCKET CARDS | | HIGH % | LOW % | SCOOP % | PART OR ALL % |
		HAND	SUITED				
2990	-$3	7-10-10-K	NS	3.0%	0.0%	8.2%	11.2%
1235	-$1	7-10-J-J	DS	4.4%	0.0%	9.8%	14.1%
1589	-$1	7-10-J-J	S	3.8%	0.0%	9.2%	13.0%
1930	-$2	7-10-J-J	NS	3.4%	0.0%	8.6%	12.0%
1185	-$0	7-10-J-Q	DS	4.5%	0.0%	10.1%	14.6%
1569	-$1	7-10-J-Q	S	4.0%	0.0%	9.6%	13.6%
1933	-$2	7-10-J-Q	NS	3.4%	0.0%	9.1%	12.5%
1022	$0	7-10-J-K	DS	5.1%	0.0%	10.5%	15.6%
1409	-$1	7-10-J-K	S	4.4%	0.0%	10.1%	14.5%
1940	-$2	7-10-J-K	NS	3.5%	0.0%	9.3%	12.7%
1205	-$0	7-10-Q-Q	DS	4.9%	0.0%	10.8%	15.7%
1603	-$1	7-10-Q-Q	S	4.0%	0.0%	10.3%	14.3%
2394	-$3	7-10-Q-Q	NS	3.2%	0.0%	9.4%	12.6%
1181	-$0	7-10-Q-K	DS	4.9%	0.0%	10.3%	15.2%
1513	-$1	7-10-Q-K	S	4.2%	0.0%	9.8%	14.0%
2219	-$2	7-10-Q-K	NS	3.1%	0.0%	9.0%	12.1%
783	$1	7-10-K-K	DS	6.1%	0.0%	13.3%	19.5%
1179	-$0	7-10-K-K	S	4.8%	0.0%	12.3%	17.0%
2036	-$2	7-10-K-K	NS	3.6%	0.0%	11.0%	14.6%
5064	-$8	7-J-J-J	S	1.7%	0.0%	4.4%	6.1%
5120	-$8	7-J-J-J	NS	1.2%	0.0%	3.6%	4.9%
1563	-$1	7-J-J-Q	DS	4.1%	0.0%	10.3%	14.4%
2171	-$2	7-J-J-Q	S	3.4%	0.0%	9.4%	12.8%
2889	-$3	7-J-J-Q	NS	2.9%	0.0%	8.7%	11.6%
1506	-$1	7-J-J-K	DS	4.6%	0.0%	10.6%	15.2%
1927	-$2	7-J-J-K	S	3.9%	0.0%	10.0%	13.9%
2968	-$3	7-J-J-K	NS	2.8%	0.0%	8.9%	11.7%
1293	-$1	7-J-Q-Q	DS	4.5%	0.0%	10.9%	15.3%

OMAHA HIGH-LOW 8 OR BETTER
5,278 HANDS   9 HANDED

| HAND RANK | VALUE $4/$8 | POCKET CARDS | | HIGH % | LOW % | SCOOP % | PART OR ALL % |
		HAND	SUITED				
1843	-$2	7-J-Q-Q	S	3.6%	0.0%	10.0%	13.6%
2700	-$3	7-J-Q-Q	NS	2.9%	0.0%	9.1%	12.0%
1213	-$1	7-J-Q-K	DS	4.6%	0.0%	10.3%	14.9%
1526	-$1	7-J-Q-K	S	3.8%	0.0%	10.0%	13.8%
2263	-$3	7-J-Q-K	NS	2.9%	0.0%	8.8%	11.6%
872	$1	7-J-K-K	DS	5.8%	0.0%	12.8%	18.6%
1501	-$1	7-J-K-K	S	4.4%	0.0%	11.7%	16.2%
1916	-$2	7-J-K-K	NS	3.2%	0.0%	11.1%	14.3%
5224	-$9	7-Q-Q-Q	S	2.0%	0.0%	5.1%	7.1%
5253	-$9	7-Q-Q-Q	NS	1.2%	0.0%	4.4%	5.6%
1331	-$1	7-Q-Q-K	DS	5.2%	0.0%	11.8%	16.9%
1972	-$2	7-Q-Q-K	S	4.0%	0.0%	10.7%	14.8%
2930	-$3	7-Q-Q-K	NS	2.9%	0.0%	10.0%	12.9%
976	$0	7-Q-K-K	DS	5.6%	0.0%	12.6%	18.1%
1433	-$1	7-Q-K-K	S	4.3%	0.0%	11.7%	16.0%
2208	-$2	7-Q-K-K	NS	3.0%	0.0%	10.8%	13.8%
5187	-$9	7-K-K-K	S	2.6%	0.0%	7.4%	10.0%
5270	-$10	7-K-K-K	NS	1.6%	0.0%	6.3%	7.9%
5274	-$10	8-8-8-8	NS	0.0%	0.0%	0.2%	0.2%
5110	-$8	8-8-8-9	S	2.9%	0.0%	3.2%	6.1%
5212	-$9	8-8-8-9	NS	2.4%	0.0%	2.5%	4.9%
5062	-$8	8-8-8-10	S	2.4%	0.0%	3.6%	6.0%
5142	-$8	8-8-8-10	NS	2.0%	0.0%	2.8%	4.7%
5099	-$8	8-8-8-J	S	2.1%	0.0%	3.4%	5.5%
5201	-$9	8-8-8-J	NS	1.6%	0.0%	2.5%	4.2%
5179	-$9	8-8-8-Q	S	2.1%	0.0%	3.2%	5.4%
5248	-$9	8-8-8-Q	NS	1.5%	0.0%	2.1%	3.7%
5200	-$9	8-8-8-K	S	2.4%	0.0%	3.1%	5.6%

OMAHA HIGH-LOW 8 OR BETTER
5,278 HANDS 9 HANDED

HAND RANK	VALUE $4/$8	POCKET CARDS HAND	SUITED	HIGH %	LOW %	SCOOP %	PART OR ALL %
5252	-$9	8-8-8-K	NS	1.5%	0.0%	1.9%	3.4%
1209	-$0	8-8-9-9	DS	5.8%	0.0%	8.3%	14.1%
1455	-$1	8-8-9-9	S	5.4%	0.0%	7.7%	13.0%
1809	-$2	8-8-9-9	NS	4.9%	0.0%	6.9%	11.8%
1999	-$2	8-8-9-10	DS	5.9%	0.0%	7.7%	13.5%
2699	-$3	8-8-9-10	S	5.5%	0.0%	6.9%	12.3%
3475	-$4	8-8-9-10	NS	5.0%	0.0%	6.0%	11.0%
2311	-$3	8-8-9-J	DS	5.6%	0.0%	7.5%	13.2%
2838	-$3	8-8-9-J	S	5.1%	0.0%	6.8%	11.9%
4052	-$5	8-8-9-J	NS	4.6%	0.0%	5.8%	10.4%
2599	-$3	8-8-9-Q	DS	5.7%	0.0%	7.4%	13.1%
3130	-$4	8-8-9-Q	S	5.0%	0.0%	6.7%	11.8%
4136	-$5	8-8-9-Q	NS	4.4%	0.0%	5.6%	10.0%
3067	-$4	8-8-9-K	DS	5.9%	0.0%	7.2%	13.1%
3718	-$4	8-8-9-K	S	5.4%	0.0%	6.6%	11.9%
4534	-$6	8-8-9-K	NS	4.4%	0.0%	5.2%	9.6%
1061	$0	8-8-10-10	DS	5.6%	0.0%	9.1%	14.7%
1214	-$1	8-8-10-10	S	5.1%	0.0%	8.3%	13.4%
1687	-$2	8-8-10-10	NS	4.6%	0.0%	7.5%	12.1%
1566	-$1	8-8-10-J	DS	5.4%	0.0%	8.6%	14.0%
1966	-$2	8-8-10-J	S	5.0%	0.0%	7.8%	12.9%
2724	-$3	8-8-10-J	NS	4.5%	0.0%	7.0%	11.5%
1920	-$2	8-8-10-Q	DS	5.5%	0.0%	8.3%	13.9%
2272	-$3	8-8-10-Q	S	5.0%	0.0%	7.7%	12.8%
3508	-$4	8-8-10-Q	NS	4.4%	0.0%	6.6%	11.0%
1960	-$2	8-8-10-K	DS	5.8%	0.0%	8.4%	14.1%
2886	-$3	8-8-10-K	S	5.3%	0.0%	7.6%	12.9%
3970	-$5	8-8-10-K	NS	4.3%	0.0%	6.2%	10.6%

OMAHA HIGH-LOW 8 OR BETTER
5,278 HANDS   9 HANDED

HAND RANK	VALUE $4/$8	POCKET CARDS HAND	SUITED	HIGH %	LOW %	SCOOP %	PART OR ALL %
1054	$0	8-8-J-J	DS	5.4%	0.0%	9.8%	15.2%
1336	-$1	8-8-J-J	S	4.9%	0.0%	8.8%	13.7%
1723	-$2	8-8-J-J	NS	4.3%	0.0%	8.0%	12.4%
1891	-$2	8-8-J-Q	DS	5.2%	0.0%	8.5%	13.7%
2585	-$3	8-8-J-Q	S	4.7%	0.0%	7.6%	12.3%
3728	-$4	8-8-J-Q	NS	3.9%	0.0%	6.6%	10.5%
2310	-$3	8-8-J-K	DS	5.5%	0.0%	8.3%	13.8%
3315	-$4	8-8-J-K	S	4.8%	0.0%	7.4%	12.2%
4202	-$5	8-8-J-K	NS	3.9%	0.0%	6.2%	10.1%
930	$1	8-8-Q-Q	DS	5.9%	0.0%	11.3%	17.2%
1344	-$1	8-8-Q-Q	S	5.0%	0.0%	10.2%	15.2%
1836	-$2	8-8-Q-Q	NS	4.4%	0.0%	9.0%	13.4%
2494	-$3	8-8-Q-K	DS	5.5%	0.0%	8.2%	13.6%
3665	-$4	8-8-Q-K	S	4.9%	0.0%	7.0%	11.9%
4432	-$5	8-8-Q-K	NS	3.8%	0.0%	5.9%	9.7%
771	$1	8-8-K-K	DS	7.0%	0.0%	13.0%	20.1%
1237	-$1	8-8-K-K	S	5.8%	0.0%	12.1%	17.9%
2212	-$2	8-8-K-K	NS	4.8%	0.0%	10.6%	15.4%
4997	-$7	8-9-9-9	S	2.3%	0.0%	4.0%	6.3%
5077	-$8	8-9-9-9	NS	1.9%	0.0%	3.1%	5.0%
1606	-$1	8-9-9-10	DS	5.0%	0.0%	8.5%	13.4%
2041	-$2	8-9-9-10	S	4.3%	0.0%	7.7%	12.0%
2439	-$3	8-9-9-10	NS	3.9%	0.0%	7.2%	11.1%
1746	-$2	8-9-9-J	DS	4.5%	0.0%	8.5%	13.0%
2237	-$3	8-9-9-J	S	3.9%	0.0%	7.8%	11.6%
2669	-$3	8-9-9-J	NS	3.5%	0.0%	7.2%	10.6%
1824	-$2	8-9-9-Q	DS	4.5%	0.0%	8.6%	13.1%
2325	-$3	8-9-9-Q	S	3.8%	0.0%	7.8%	11.7%

OMAHA HIGH-LOW 8 OR BETTER
5,278 HANDS 9 HANDED

| HAND RANK | VALUE $4/$8 | POCKET CARDS | | HIGH % | LOW % | SCOOP % | PART OR ALL % |
		HAND	SUITED				
3004	-$3	8-9-9-Q	NS	3.2%	0.0%	7.1%	10.3%
1998	-$2	8-9-9-K	DS	4.8%	0.0%	8.5%	13.3%
2473	-$3	8-9-9-K	S	4.1%	0.0%	7.8%	11.9%
3804	-$4	8-9-9-K	NS	3.0%	0.0%	6.5%	9.6%
1286	-$1	8-9-10-10	DS	5.0%	0.0%	8.9%	14.0%
1790	-$2	8-9-10-10	S	4.4%	0.0%	8.1%	12.5%
2385	-$3	8-9-10-10	NS	3.9%	0.0%	7.4%	11.4%
1031	$0	8-9-10-J	DS	5.4%	0.0%	9.3%	14.7%
1220	-$1	8-9-10-J	S	5.0%	0.0%	9.0%	13.9%
1737	-$2	8-9-10-J	NS	4.4%	0.0%	8.1%	12.5%
1049	$0	8-9-10-Q	DS	5.5%	0.0%	9.5%	15.0%
1560	-$1	8-9-10-Q	S	4.9%	0.0%	8.7%	13.6%
1961	-$2	8-9-10-Q	NS	4.2%	0.0%	8.0%	12.3%
1478	-$1	8-9-10-K	DS	5.8%	0.0%	9.2%	14.9%
1880	-$2	8-9-10-K	S	5.2%	0.0%	8.7%	13.8%
2645	-$3	8-9-10-K	NS	4.2%	0.0%	7.9%	12.0%
1443	-$1	8-9-J-J	DS	4.9%	0.0%	9.4%	14.3%
1710	-$2	8-9-J-J	S	4.2%	0.0%	8.9%	13.1%
2354	-$3	8-9-J-J	NS	3.6%	0.0%	8.2%	11.8%
1257	-$1	8-9-J-Q	DS	4.9%	0.0%	9.4%	14.3%
1744	-$2	8-9-J-Q	S	4.4%	0.0%	8.7%	13.1%
2202	-$2	8-9-J-Q	NS	3.6%	0.0%	8.1%	11.7%
1642	-$1	8-9-J-K	DS	5.4%	0.0%	9.2%	14.6%
2020	-$2	8-9-J-K	S	4.5%	0.0%	8.8%	13.3%
3121	-$4	8-9-J-K	NS	3.7%	0.0%	7.6%	11.3%
1196	-$0	8-9-Q-Q	DS	5.2%	0.0%	10.6%	15.8%
1620	-$1	8-9-Q-Q	S	4.4%	0.0%	9.9%	14.3%
2495	-$3	8-9-Q-Q	NS	3.6%	0.0%	8.8%	12.4%

OMAHA HIGH-LOW 8 OR BETTER
5,278 HANDS   9 HANDED

| HAND RANK | VALUE $4/$8 | POCKET CARDS | | HIGH % | LOW % | SCOOP % | PART OR ALL % |
		HAND	SUITED				
1826	-$2	8-9-Q-K	DS	5.1%	0.0%	9.3%	14.4%
2234	-$3	8-9-Q-K	S	4.2%	0.0%	8.8%	13.0%
3722	-$4	8-9-Q-K	NS	3.2%	0.0%	7.5%	10.7%
978	$0	8-9-K-K	DS	6.3%	0.0%	12.1%	18.5%
1441	-$1	8-9-K-K	S	5.1%	0.0%	11.4%	16.4%
2401	-$3	8-9-K-K	NS	3.9%	0.0%	10.3%	14.2%
4918	-$7	8-10-10-10	S	2.0%	0.0%	4.7%	6.7%
5020	-$7	8-10-10-10	NS	1.5%	0.0%	4.0%	5.5%
1073	-$0	8-10-10-J	DS	4.5%	0.0%	10.0%	14.5%
1259	-$1	8-10-10-J	S	4.0%	0.0%	9.5%	13.5%
1786	-$2	8-10-10-J	NS	3.5%	0.0%	8.9%	12.4%
1057	$0	8-10-10-Q	DS	4.6%	0.0%	10.4%	15.0%
1437	-$1	8-10-10-Q	S	3.9%	0.0%	9.6%	13.5%
1963	-$2	8-10-10-Q	NS	3.3%	0.0%	8.9%	12.2%
1282	-$1	8-10-10-K	DS	4.9%	0.0%	10.0%	14.9%
1807	-$2	8-10-10-K	S	4.1%	0.0%	9.3%	13.4%
2515	-$3	8-10-10-K	NS	3.2%	0.0%	8.4%	11.6%
1007	$0	8-10-J-J	DS	4.7%	0.0%	10.3%	15.0%
1251	-$1	8-10-J-J	S	4.1%	0.0%	9.6%	13.7%
1597	-$1	8-10-J-J	NS	3.6%	0.0%	9.1%	12.7%
794	$1	8-10-J-Q	DS	5.0%	0.0%	10.8%	15.8%
1000	$0	8-10-J-Q	S	4.5%	0.0%	10.3%	14.8%
1413	-$1	8-10-J-Q	NS	3.8%	0.0%	9.5%	13.3%
921	$1	8-10-J-K	DS	5.4%	0.0%	10.8%	16.2%
1175	-$0	8-10-J-K	S	4.7%	0.0%	10.3%	15.0%
1732	-$2	8-10-J-K	NS	3.7%	0.0%	9.4%	13.1%
922	$1	8-10-Q-Q	DS	5.1%	0.0%	11.8%	16.8%

OMAHA HIGH-LOW 8 OR BETTER
5,278 HANDS 9 HANDED

HAND RANK	VALUE $4/$8	POCKET CARDS		HIGH %	LOW %	SCOOP %	PART OR ALL %
		HAND	SUITED				
1204	-$0	8-10-Q-Q	S	4.2%	0.0%	10.9%	15.1%
1601	-$1	8-10-Q-Q	NS	3.5%	0.0%	10.0%	13.5%
975	$0	8-10-Q-K	DS	5.3%	0.0%	10.8%	16.1%
1378	-$1	8-10-Q-K	S	4.5%	0.0%	10.1%	14.6%
1439	-$1	8-10-Q-K	NS	4.2%	0.0%	10.0%	14.1%
743	$1	8-10-K-K	DS	6.2%	0.0%	13.0%	19.2%
1199	-$0	8-10-K-K	S	5.0%	0.0%	12.0%	17.0%
1751	-$2	8-10-K-K	NS	3.7%	0.0%	11.2%	14.9%
5009	-$7	8-J-J-J	S	1.8%	0.0%	5.0%	6.7%
5079	-$8	8-J-J-J	NS	1.3%	0.0%	4.2%	5.5%
1060	$0	8-J-J-Q	DS	4.4%	0.0%	11.1%	15.5%
1621	-$1	8-J-J-Q	S	3.6%	0.0%	10.0%	13.6%
1896	-$2	8-J-J-Q	NS	3.0%	0.0%	9.7%	12.7%
1308	-$1	8-J-J-K	DS	4.8%	0.0%	10.8%	15.7%
1838	-$2	8-J-J-K	S	4.0%	0.0%	10.0%	14.0%
2799	-$3	8-J-J-K	NS	2.9%	0.0%	9.0%	11.9%
949	$0	8-J-Q-Q	DS	4.7%	0.0%	11.4%	16.1%
1400	-$1	8-J-Q-Q	S	3.9%	0.0%	10.4%	14.3%
1773	-$2	8-J-Q-Q	NS	3.1%	0.0%	9.8%	12.9%
1009	$0	8-J-Q-K	DS	4.9%	0.0%	10.7%	15.7%
1458	-$1	8-J-Q-K	S	4.1%	0.0%	10.1%	14.2%
2069	-$2	8-J-Q-K	NS	3.1%	0.0%	9.1%	12.2%
858	$1	8-J-K-K	DS	5.8%	0.0%	12.9%	18.7%
1228	-$1	8-J-K-K	S	4.4%	0.0%	12.2%	16.6%
1962	-$2	8-J-K-K	NS	3.3%	0.0%	11.1%	14.4%
5053	-$8	8-Q-Q-Q	S	2.0%	0.0%	6.1%	8.1%
5131	-$8	8-Q-Q-Q	NS	1.3%	0.0%	5.2%	6.5%
1302	-$1	8-Q-Q-K	DS	5.0%	0.0%	11.7%	16.8%

OMAHA HIGH-LOW 8 OR BETTER
5,278 HANDS 9 HANDED

HAND RANK	VALUE $4/$8	POCKET CARDS HAND	POCKET CARDS SUITED	HIGH %	LOW %	SCOOP %	PART OR ALL %
1727	-$2	8-Q-Q-K	S	4.0%	0.0%	10.9%	14.9%
2866	-$3	8-Q-Q-K	NS	3.0%	0.0%	10.0%	13.0%
923	$1	8-Q-K-K	DS	5.5%	0.0%	12.8%	18.3%
1457	-$1	8-Q-K-K	S	4.3%	0.0%	11.8%	16.0%
2417	-$3	8-Q-K-K	NS	3.1%	0.0%	10.6%	13.7%
5139	-$8	8-K-K-K	S	2.7%	0.0%	7.5%	10.2%
5259	-$9	8-K-K-K	NS	1.6%	0.0%	6.5%	8.1%
5273	-$10	9-9-9-9	NS	0.1%	0.0%	0.1%	0.2%
5028	-$7	9-9-9-10	S	2.5%	0.0%	4.0%	6.5%
5114	-$8	9-9-9-10	NS	1.1%	0.0%	3.5%	4.6%
5046	-$7	9-9-9-J	S	2.0%	0.0%	4.1%	6.2%
5090	-$8	9-9-9-J	NS	1.4%	0.0%	3.6%	5.0%
5058	-$8	9-9-9-Q	S	1.9%	0.0%	4.2%	6.1%
5123	-$8	9-9-9-Q	NS	1.1%	0.0%	3.4%	4.5%
5104	-$8	9-9-9-K	S	2.1%	0.0%	4.1%	6.2%
5176	-$9	9-9-9-K	NS	1.0%	0.0%	3.1%	4.1%
820	$1	9-9-10-10	DS	5.2%	0.0%	9.7%	15.0%
944	$1	9-9-10-10	S	4.7%	0.0%	9.2%	13.9%
1133	-$0	9-9-10-10	NS	4.2%	0.0%	8.7%	12.8%
1136	-$0	9-9-10-J	DS	5.2%	0.0%	9.4%	14.6%
1446	-$1	9-9-10-J	S	4.7%	0.0%	8.9%	13.5%
1869	-$2	9-9-10-J	NS	4.1%	0.0%	8.3%	12.4%
1211	-$0	9-9-10-Q	DS	5.1%	0.0%	9.4%	14.5%
1586	-$1	9-9-10-Q	S	4.5%	0.0%	8.9%	13.5%
2124	-$2	9-9-10-Q	NS	3.7%	0.0%	8.2%	11.9%
1311	-$1	9-9-10-K	DS	5.3%	0.0%	9.5%	14.8%
1676	-$2	9-9-10-K	S	4.7%	0.0%	8.9%	13.7%
2437	-$3	9-9-10-K	NS	3.5%	0.0%	8.0%	11.5%

OMAHA HIGH-LOW 8 OR BETTER
5,278 HANDS   9 HANDED

HAND RANK	VALUE $4/$8	POCKET CARDS HAND	SUITED	HIGH %	LOW %	SCOOP %	PART OR ALL %
822	$1	9-9-J-J	DS	5.1%	0.0%	10.6%	15.7%
956	$0	9-9-J-J	S	4.4%	0.0%	9.9%	14.4%
1152	-$0	9-9-J-J	NS	3.9%	0.0%	9.3%	13.1%
1300	-$1	9-9-J-Q	DS	4.6%	0.0%	9.6%	14.2%
1622	-$1	9-9-J-Q	S	3.9%	0.0%	9.0%	12.9%
2228	-$2	9-9-J-Q	NS	3.1%	0.0%	8.2%	11.3%
1406	-$1	9-9-J-K	DS	4.8%	0.0%	9.6%	14.4%
1766	-$2	9-9-J-K	S	4.2%	0.0%	9.1%	13.3%
2552	-$3	9-9-J-K	NS	3.0%	0.0%	8.1%	11.1%
732	$1	9-9-Q-Q	DS	5.4%	0.0%	11.7%	17.1%
919	$1	9-9-Q-Q	S	4.5%	0.0%	11.0%	15.5%
1169	-$0	9-9-Q-Q	NS	3.6%	0.0%	10.1%	13.7%
1481	-$1	9-9-Q-K	DS	4.7%	0.0%	9.8%	14.5%
1890	-$2	9-9-Q-K	S	3.8%	0.0%	9.1%	13.0%
2657	-$3	9-9-Q-K	NS	2.6%	0.0%	8.2%	10.8%
578	$3	9-9-K-K	DS	6.5%	0.0%	13.4%	19.9%
781	$1	9-9-K-K	S	5.2%	0.0%	12.6%	17.8%
1082	-$0	9-9-K-K	NS	3.8%	0.0%	11.9%	15.7%
4934	-$7	9-10-10-10	S	2.6%	0.0%	4.4%	7.1%
5032	-$7	9-10-10-10	NS	2.1%	0.0%	3.9%	6.0%
1028	$0	9-10-10-J	DS	5.3%	0.0%	9.8%	15.0%
1299	-$1	9-10-10-J	S	4.6%	0.0%	9.2%	13.8%
1686	-$2	9-10-10-J	NS	4.1%	0.0%	8.8%	12.8%
1066	$0	9-10-10-Q	DS	5.1%	0.0%	10.0%	15.1%
1384	-$1	9-10-10-Q	S	4.5%	0.0%	9.3%	13.8%
1859	-$2	9-10-10-Q	NS	3.7%	0.0%	8.7%	12.4%
1190	-$0	9-10-10-K	DS	5.4%	0.0%	9.9%	15.2%

OMAHA HIGH-LOW 8 OR BETTER
5,278 HANDS   9 HANDED

HAND RANK	VALUE $4/$8	POCKET CARDS		HIGH %	LOW %	SCOOP %	PART OR ALL %
		HAND	SUITED				
1555	-$1	9-10-10-K	S	4.7%	0.0%	9.2%	13.9%
2205	-$2	9-10-10-K	NS	3.5%	0.0%	8.4%	12.0%
1005	$0	9-10-J-J	DS	5.4%	0.0%	10.1%	15.5%
1225	-$1	9-10-J-J	S	4.7%	0.0%	9.5%	14.2%
1627	-$1	9-10-J-J	NS	4.1%	0.0%	8.9%	13.0%
700	$2	9-10-J-Q	DS	5.5%	0.0%	10.8%	16.2%
877	$1	9-10-J-Q	S	4.9%	0.0%	10.2%	15.1%
1079	-$0	9-10-J-Q	NS	4.2%	0.0%	9.8%	14.0%
731	$1	9-10-J-K	DS	5.9%	0.0%	10.8%	16.7%
933	$1	9-10-J-K	S	5.3%	0.0%	10.4%	15.7%
1222	-$1	9-10-J-K	NS	4.1%	0.0%	9.7%	13.8%
908	$1	9-10-Q-Q	DS	5.8%	0.0%	11.1%	16.9%
1202	-$0	9-10-Q-Q	S	4.9%	0.0%	10.3%	15.2%
1651	-$1	9-10-Q-Q	NS	4.1%	0.0%	9.6%	13.7%
818	$1	9-10-Q-K	DS	5.6%	0.0%	11.0%	16.5%
1026	$0	9-10-Q-K	S	4.8%	0.0%	10.4%	15.2%
1371	-$1	9-10-Q-K	NS	3.6%	0.0%	9.8%	13.4%
708	$2	9-10-K-K	DS	6.9%	0.0%	12.4%	19.3%
1042	$0	9-10-K-K	S	5.6%	0.0%	11.8%	17.4%
1544	-$1	9-10-K-K	NS	4.3%	0.0%	11.0%	15.2%
4967	-$7	9-J-J-J	S	2.4%	0.0%	5.1%	7.4%
5044	-$7	9-J-J-J	NS	1.7%	0.0%	4.6%	6.4%
1058	$0	9-J-J-Q	DS	4.9%	0.0%	10.7%	15.7%
1323	-$1	9-J-J-Q	S	4.2%	0.0%	10.0%	14.2%
1839	-$2	9-J-J-Q	NS	3.5%	0.0%	9.3%	12.7%
1139	-$0	9-J-J-K	DS	5.2%	0.0%	10.8%	16.0%
1509	-$1	9-J-J-K	S	4.4%	0.0%	10.0%	14.4%
2109	-$2	9-J-J-K	NS	3.3%	0.0%	9.3%	12.6%

OMAHA HIGH-LOW 8 OR BETTER
5,278 HANDS   9 HANDED

| HAND RANK | VALUE $4/$8 | POCKET CARDS | | HIGH % | LOW % | SCOOP % | PART OR ALL % |
		HAND	SUITED				
945	$0	9-J-Q-Q	DS	5.2%	0.0%	11.1%	16.4%
1275	-$1	9-J-Q-Q	S	4.4%	0.0%	10.3%	14.7%
1697	-$2	9-J-Q-Q	NS	3.5%	0.0%	9.5%	13.1%
827	$1	9-J-Q-K	DS	5.1%	0.0%	11.0%	16.1%
1013	$0	9-J-Q-K	S	4.3%	0.0%	10.5%	14.8%
1335	-$1	9-J-Q-K	NS	3.1%	0.0%	9.8%	12.9%
745	$1	9-J-K-K	DS	6.4%	0.0%	12.5%	18.9%
1095	-$0	9-J-K-K	S	5.1%	0.0%	11.8%	16.8%
1557	-$1	9-J-K-K	NS	3.7%	0.0%	11.0%	14.7%
5016	-$7	9-Q-Q-Q	S	2.3%	0.0%	6.2%	8.5%
5101	-$8	9-Q-Q-Q	NS	1.5%	0.0%	5.2%	6.7%
974	$0	9-Q-Q-K	DS	5.4%	0.0%	12.0%	17.3%
1425	-$1	9-Q-Q-K	S	4.4%	0.0%	11.1%	15.5%
1937	-$2	9-Q-Q-K	NS	3.2%	0.0%	10.5%	13.6%
838	$1	9-Q-K-K	DS	6.0%	0.0%	12.5%	18.4%
1142	-$0	9-Q-K-K	S	4.7%	0.0%	11.7%	16.4%
1682	-$2	9-Q-K-K	NS	3.3%	0.0%	10.9%	14.2%
5034	-$7	9-K-K-K	S	2.8%	0.0%	6.8%	9.6%
5147	-$8	9-K-K-K	NS	1.6%	0.0%	6.9%	8.6%
5275	-$11	10-10-10-10	NS	0.2%	0.0%	0.4%	0.5%
4828	-$6	10-10-10-J	S	2.5%	0.0%	5.7%	8.2%
4984	-$7	10-10-10-J	NS	1.9%	0.0%	5.1%	7.0%
4910	-$7	10-10-10-Q	S	2.4%	0.0%	5.8%	8.1%
5051	-$8	10-10-10-Q	NS	1.5%	0.0%	5.0%	6.5%
4909	-$7	10-10-10-K	S	2.1%	0.0%	4.6%	6.7%

OMAHA HIGH-LOW 8 OR BETTER
5,278 HANDS   9 HANDED

| HAND RANK | VALUE $4/$8 | POCKET CARDS | | HIGH % | LOW % | SCOOP % | PART OR ALL % |
		HAND	SUITED				
5115	-$8	10-10-10-K	NS	1.3%	0.0%	4.6%	5.9%
525	$3	10-10-J-J	DS	5.4%	0.0%	11.7%	17.1%
634	$2	10-10-J-J	S	4.9%	0.0%	11.1%	16.0%
728	$1	10-10-J-J	NS	4.3%	0.0%	10.6%	14.8%
734	$1	10-10-J-Q	DS	5.3%	0.0%	11.5%	16.8%
957	$0	10-10-J-Q	S	4.6%	0.0%	11.1%	15.7%
1221	-$1	10-10-J-Q	NS	3.8%	0.0%	10.5%	14.3%
741	$1	10-10-J-K	DS	5.6%	0.0%	11.8%	17.4%
1033	$0	10-10-J-K	S	5.0%	0.0%	11.1%	16.0%
1424	-$1	10-10-J-K	NS	3.7%	0.0%	10.3%	14.0%
486	$4	10-10-Q-Q	DS	5.8%	0.0%	12.8%	18.7%
595	$3	10-10-Q-Q	S	5.8%	0.0%	12.9%	18.7%
768	$1	10-10-Q-Q	NS	4.1%	0.0%	11.5%	15.6%
804	$1	10-10-Q-K	DS	5.5%	0.0%	11.8%	17.2%
1103	-$0	10-10-Q-K	S	4.6%	0.0%	11.1%	15.7%
1497	-$1	10-10-Q-K	NS	3.3%	0.0%	10.3%	13.6%
372	$5	10-10-K-K	DS	6.9%	0.0%	14.3%	21.2%
387	$5	10-10-K-K	S	6.8%	0.0%	14.3%	21.0%
791	$1	10-10-K-K	NS	3.6%	0.0%	11.0%	14.6%
4731	-$6	10-J-J-J	S	2.6%	0.0%	5.8%	8.5%
4908	-$7	10-J-J-J	NS	1.9%	0.0%	5.4%	7.3%
836	$1	10-J-J-Q	DS	5.6%	0.0%	11.9%	17.5%
967	$0	10-J-J-Q	S	4.7%	0.0%	11.2%	15.8%
1170	-$0	10-J-J-Q	NS	3.9%	0.0%	10.6%	14.5%
742	$1	10-J-J-K	DS	5.7%	0.0%	11.8%	17.5%
970	$0	10-J-J-K	S	4.9%	0.0%	11.3%	16.2%
1343	-$1	10-J-J-K	NS	3.7%	0.0%	10.5%	14.2%
736	$1	10-J-Q-Q	DS	5.1%	0.0%	11.9%	17.0%

OMAHA HIGH-LOW 8 OR BETTER
5,278 HANDS   9 HANDED

HAND RANK	VALUE $4/$8	POCKET CARDS		HIGH %	LOW %	SCOOP %	PART OR ALL %
		HAND	SUITED				
885	$1	10-J-Q-Q	S	4.8%	0.0%	11.5%	16.3%
1132	-$0	10-J-Q-Q	NS	3.9%	0.0%	10.8%	14.8%
540	$3	10-J-Q-K	DS	5.7%	0.0%	11.9%	17.6%
642	$2	10-J-Q-K	S	5.0%	0.0%	11.5%	16.5%
830	$1	10-J-Q-K	NS	3.8%	0.0%	10.8%	14.6%
553	$3	10-J-K-K	DS	6.8%	0.0%	13.4%	20.1%
810	$1	10-J-K-K	S	5.1%	0.0%	12.7%	17.7%
1064	$0	10-J-K-K	NS	4.2%	0.0%	12.0%	16.3%
4772	-$6	10-Q-Q-Q	S	2.7%	0.0%	6.9%	9.6%
5026	-$7	10-Q-Q-Q	NS	1.8%	0.0%	6.1%	7.9%
627	$2	10-Q-Q-K	DS	5.9%	0.0%	13.0%	18.9%
954	$0	10-Q-Q-K	S	4.9%	0.0%	12.0%	16.9%
1295	-$1	10-Q-Q-K	NS	3.7%	0.0%	11.5%	15.2%
564	$3	10-Q-K-K	DS	6.4%	0.0%	13.2%	19.7%
812	$1	10-Q-K-K	S	5.1%	0.0%	12.6%	17.7%
1150	-$0	10-Q-K-K	NS	3.8%	0.0%	11.9%	15.7%
4793	-$6	10-K-K-K	S	3.3%	0.0%	8.6%	11.9%
5037	-$7	10-K-K-K	NS	1.9%	0.0%	7.8%	9.7%
5276	-$12	J-J-J-J	NS	0.3%	0.0%	0.9%	1.1%
4886	-$6	J-J-J-Q	S	2.6%	0.0%	6.6%	9.2%
5042	-$7	J-J-J-Q	NS	1.7%	0.0%	5.9%	7.6%
5021	-$7	J-J-J-K	S	2.8%	0.0%	6.6%	9.3%
5121	-$8	J-J-J-K	NS	1.6%	0.0%	5.6%	7.2%
435	$4	J-J-Q-Q	DS	5.9%	0.0%	13.1%	19.0%
579	$3	J-J-Q-Q	S	5.1%	0.0%	12.4%	17.4%
769	$1	J-J-Q-Q	NS	3.5%	0.0%	9.9%	13.3%
753	$1	J-J-Q-K	DS	5.8%	0.0%	12.4%	18.2%
941	$1	J-J-Q-K	S	4.9%	0.0%	12.0%	17.0%

OMAHA HIGH-LOW 8 OR BETTER
5,278 HANDS   9 HANDED

| HAND RANK | VALUE $4/$8 | POCKET CARDS | | HIGH % | LOW % | SCOOP % | PART OR ALL % |
		HAND	SUITED				
1363	-$1	J-J-Q-K	NS	3.6%	0.0%	11.2%	14.8%
353	$5	J-J-K-K	DS	6.9%	0.0%	14.4%	21.3%
497	$4	J-J-K-K	S	5.7%	0.0%	13.6%	19.3%
761	$1	J-J-K-K	NS	3.6%	0.0%	11.0%	14.6%
4813	-$6	J-Q-Q-Q	S	2.6%	0.0%	7.0%	9.6%
5017	-$7	J-Q-Q-Q	NS	1.8%	0.0%	6.3%	8.1%
628	$2	J-Q-Q-K	DS	5.9%	0.0%	13.0%	18.9%
889	$1	J-Q-Q-K	S	4.9%	0.0%	12.2%	17.1%
1215	-$1	J-Q-Q-K	NS	3.7%	0.0%	11.7%	15.4%
562	$3	J-Q-K-K	DS	6.5%	0.0%	13.2%	19.6%
777	$1	J-Q-K-K	S	5.1%	0.0%	12.6%	17.8%
1072	-$0	J-Q-K-K	NS	3.8%	0.0%	12.0%	15.9%
4894	-$7	J-K-K-K	S	3.1%	0.0%	8.4%	11.5%
5006	-$7	J-K-K-K	NS	1.9%	0.0%	7.8%	9.7%
5277	-$13	Q-Q-Q-Q	NS	0.4%	0.0%	1.9%	2.3%
4960	-$7	Q-Q-Q-K	S	3.1%	0.0%	7.9%	11.0%
5071	-$8	Q-Q-Q-K	NS	1.8%	0.0%	7.2%	9.0%
329	$6	Q-Q-K-K	DS	7.0%	0.0%	14.5%	21.5%
423	$4	Q-Q-K-K	S	5.7%	0.0%	13.9%	19.6%
602	$2	Q-Q-K-K	NS	4.4%	0.0%	13.1%	17.5%
4721	-$6	Q-K-K-K	S	3.2%	0.0%	8.5%	11.7%
5031	-$7	Q-K-K-K	NS	2.0%	0.0%	7.6%	9.6%
5278	-$14	K-K-K-K	NS	0.8%	0.0%	3.8%	4.6%

❖ 15 ❖

CONCLUSION

More than any other type of poker, Omaha high-low is driven by hand value. This means that selecting the right hands to play is the most important decision you can make. I've tried to make it easy for you to choose good hands preflop so that you can increase your profit potential in this exciting and fast-paced brand of poker.

In contrast to my first stats book, the statistics in the charts in this book are based on the play of an average, aggressive, low-limit player who is consistently successful at Omaha high-low.

I'd like to think that you are a lot like this player—you love the game, you like the camaraderie, you savor the adventure and the challenge it adds to your daily routine. Most of all, you enjoy making a profit playing a game that enriches your life.

Using the strategies and the statistics in this book, you'll be playing with the odds in your favor every time you sit down in an Omaha high-low game. And who knows? I may be the guy sitting on your left in the next cardroom or online game you play. It would indeed be my pleasure!

GREAT CARDOZA POKER BOOKS

ADD THESE TO YOUR LIBRARY - ORDER NOW!

DANIEL NEGREANU'S POWER HOLD'EM STRATEGY *by Daniel Negreanu.* This power-packed book on beating no-limit hold'em is one of the three most influential poker books ever written. Negreanu headlines a collection of young great players—Todd Brunson, David Williams. Erick Lindgren, Evelyn Ng and Paul Wasicka—who share their insider professional moves and winning secrets. You'll learn about short-handed and heads-up play, high-limit cash games, a powerful beginner's strategy to neutralize professional players, and how to mix up your play and bluff and win big pots. The centerpiece, however, is Negreanu's powerful and revolutionary small ball strategy. You'll learn how to play hold'em with cards you never would have played before—and with fantastic results. The preflop, flop, turn and river will never look the same again. A must-have! 520 pages, $34.95.

HOLD'EM WISDOM FOR ALL PLAYERS *By Daniel Negreanu.* Superstar poker player Daniel Negreanu provides 50 easy-to-read and right-to-the-point hold'em strategy nuggets that will immediately make you a better player at cash games and tournaments. His wit and wisdom makes for great reading; even better, it makes for killer winning advice. Conversational, straightforward, and educational, this book covers topics as diverse as the top 10 rookie mistakes to bullying bullies and exploiting your table image. 176 pages, $14.95.

POKER WIZARDS *by Warwick Dunnett.* In the tradition of Super System, an exclusive collection of champions and superstars have been brought together to share their strategies, insights, and tactics for winning big money at poker, specifically no-limit hold'em tournaments. This is priceless advice from players who individually have each made millions of dollars in tournaments, and collectively, have won more than 20 WSOP bracelets, two WSOP main events, 100 major tournaments and $50 million in tournament winnings! Featuring Daniel Negreanu, Dan Harrington, Marcel Luske, Kathy Liebert, Mike Sexton, Mel Judah, Marc Salem, T.J. Cloutier and Chris "Jesus" Ferguson. This must-read book is a goldmine for serious players, aspiring pros, and future champions! 352 pgs, $19.95.

MILLION DOLLAR HOLD'EM: Winning Big in Limit Cash Games *by Johnny Chan and Mark Karowe.* Learn how to win money consistently at limit hold'em, poker's most popular cash game, from one of poker's living legends. You'll get a rare opportunity to get into the mind of the man who has won ten World Series of Poker titles—tied for the most ever with Doyle Brunson—as Johnny picks out illustrative hands and shows how he thinks his way through the betting and the bluffing. No book so thoroughly details the thought process of how a hand is played, the alternative ways it could have been played, and the best way to win session after session. *Essential* reading for cash players. 400 pages, $29.95.

TOURNAMENT TIPS FROM THE POKER PROS *by Shane Smith.* Essential advice from poker theorists, authors, and tournament winners on the best strategies for winning the big prizes at low-limit rebuy tournaments. Learn proven strategies for each of the four stages of play—opening, middle, late and final—how to avoid 26 potential traps, advice on rebuys, aggressive play, clock-watching, inside moves, top 20 tips for winning tournaments, more. Advice from Brunson, McEvoy, Cloutier, Caro, Malmuth, others. 160 pages, $14.95.

NO-LIMIT TEXAS HOLD'EM: The New Player's Guide to Winning Poker's Biggest Game *by Brad Daugherty & Tom McEvoy.* For experienced limit players who want to play no-limit or rookies who has never played before, two world champions show readers how to evaluate the strength of a hand, determine the amount to bet, understand opponents' play, plus how to bluff and when to do it. Seventy-four game scenarios, unique betting charts for tournament play, and sections on essential principles and strategies show you how to get to the winner's circle. Special section on beating online tournaments. 288 pages, $24.95.

Order now at 1-800-577-WINS or go online to: www.cardozabooks.com

GREAT CARDOZA POKER BOOKS
ADD THESE TO YOUR LIBRARY - ORDER NOW!

CARO'S MOST PROFITABLE HOLD'EM ADVICE *by Mike Caro.* When Mike Caro writes a book on winning, all poker players take notice. And they should: The "Mad Genius of Poker" has influenced just about every professional player and world champion alive. You'll journey far beyond the traditional tactical tools offered in most poker books and for the first time, have access to the entire missing arsenal of strategies left out of everything you've ever seen or experienced. Caro's first major work in two decades is packed with hundreds of powerful ideas, concepts, and strategies, many of which will be new to you— they have never been made available to the general public. This book represents Caro's lifelong research into beating the game of hold em. 408 pages, $24.95

CARO'S BOOK OF POKER TELLS *by Mike Caro.* One of the ten greatest books written on poker, this must-have book should be in every player's library. If you're serious about winning, you'll realize that most of the profit comes from being able to read your opponents. Caro reveals the the secrets of interpreting *tells*—physical reactions that reveal information about a player's cards—such as shrugs, sighs, shaky hands, eye contact, and many more. Learn when opponents are bluffing, when they aren't and why—based solely on their mannerisms. Over 170 photos of players in action and play-by-play examples show the actual tells. These powerful ideas will give you the decisive edge. 320 pages, $24.95.

HOW TO BEAT SIT-AND-GO POKER TOURNAMENTS by Neil Timothy. There is a lot of dead money up for grabs in the lower limit sit-and-gos and Neil Timothy shows you how to go and get it. The author, a professional player, shows you how to reach the last six places of lower limit sit-and-go tournaments four out of five times and then how to get in the money 25-35 percent of the time using his powerful, proven strategies. This book can turn a losing sit-and-go player into a winner, and a winner into a bigger winner. Also effective for the early and middle stages of one-table satellites.176 pages, $14.95.

CHAMPIONSHIP NO-LIMIT & POT-LIMIT HOLD'EM *by T. J. Cloutier & Tom McEvoy.* The bible for winning pot-limit and no-limit hold'em tournaments gives you all the answers to your most important questions: How do you get inside your opponents' heads and learn how to beat them at their own game? How can you tell how much to bet, raise, and reraise in no-limit hold'em? When can you bluff? How do you set up your opponents in pot-limit hold'em so that you can win a monster pot? What are the best strategies for winning no-limit and pot-limit tournaments, satellites, and supersatellites? Inspired advice you can bank on from two of the most recognizable figures in poker. 304 pages, $29.95.

CHAMPIONSHIP HOLD'EM *by T. J. Cloutier & Tom McEvoy.* Hard-hitting hold'em the way it's played *today* in both limit cash games and tournaments. Get killer advice on how to win more money in rammin'-jammin' games, kill-pot, jackpot, shorthanded, and full table cash games. You'll learn the thinking process for preflop, flop, turn, and river play with specific suggestions for what to do when good or bad things happen. Includes play-by-play analyses, advice on how to maximize profits against rocks in tight games, weaklings in loose games, experts in solid games, plus tournament strategies for small buy-in, big buy-in, rebuy, add-on, satellite and major tournaments. Wow! 392 pages, $29.95.

CHAMPIONSHIP OMAHA (Omaha High-Low, Pot-limit Omaha, Limit High Omaha) *by Tom McEvoy & T.J. Cloutier.* Clearly-written strategies and powerful advice from Cloutier and McEvoy who have won four World Series of Poker Omaha titles. You'll learn how to beat low-limit and high-stakes games, play against loose and tight opponents, and the differing strategies for rebuy and freezeout tournaments. Learn the best starting hands, when slowplaying a big hand is dangerous, what danglers are (and why winners don't play them), why you sometimes fold the nuts on the flop and would be correct in doing so, and overall, how you can win a lot of money at Omaha! 296 pages, illustrations, $29.95.

POWERFUL WINNING POKER SIMULATIONS
A MUST FOR SERIOUS PLAYERS WITH A COMPUTER!
IBM compatible CD ROM Win 95, 98, 2000, NT, ME, XP

These incredible full color poker simulations are the best method to improve your game. Computer opponents play like real players. All games let you set the limits and rake and have fully programmable players, plus stat tracking, and Hand Analyzer for starting hands. Mike Caro, the world's foremost poker theoretician says, "Amazing... a steal for under $500... get it, it's great." Includes free phone support. "Smart Advisor" gives expert advice for every play!

1. TURBO TEXAS HOLD'EM FOR WINDOWS - $59.95. Choose which players, and how many (2-10) you want to play, create loose/tight games, and control check-raising, bluffing, position, sensitivity to pot odds, and more! Also, instant replay, pop-up odds, Professional Advisor keeps track of play statistics. Free bonus: Hold'em Hand Analyzer analyzes all 169 pocket hands in detail and their win rates under any conditions you set. Caro says this "hold'em software is the most powerful ever created." Great product!

2. TURBO SEVEN-CARD STUD FOR WINDOWS - $59.95. Create any conditions of play; choose number of players (2-8), bet amounts, fixed or spread limit, bring-in method, tight/loose conditions, position, reaction to board, number of dead cards, and stack deck to create special conditions. Features instant replay. Terrific stat reporting includes analysis of starting cards, 3-D bar charts, and graphs. Play interactively and run high speed simulation to test strategies. Hand Analyzer analyzes starting hands in detail. Wow!

3. TURBO OMAHA HIGH-LOW SPLIT FOR WINDOWS - $59.95. Specify any playing conditions; betting limits, number of raises, blind structures, button position, aggressiveness/passiveness of opponents, number of players (2-10), types of hands dealt, blinds, position, board reaction, and specify flop, turn, and river cards! Choose opponents and use provided point count or create your own. Statistical reporting, instant replay, pop-up odds high speed simulation to test strategies, amazing Hand Analyzer, and much more!

4. TURBO OMAHA HIGH FOR WINDOWS - $59.95. Same features as above, but tailored for Omaha High only. Caro says program is "an electrifying research tool...it can clearly be worth thousands of dollars to any serious player." A must for Omaha High players.

5. TURBO 7 STUD 8 OR BETTER - $59.95. Brand new with all the features you expect from the Wilson Turbo products: the latest artificial intelligence, instant advice and exact odds, play versus 2-7 opponents, enhanced data charts that can be exported or printed, the ability to fold out of turn and immediately go to the next hand, ability to peek at opponents hand, optional warning mode that warns you if a play disagrees with the advisor, and automatic mode that runs up to 50 tests unattended. Tough computer players vary their styles for a great game.

---

6. TOURNAMENT TEXAS HOLD'EM - $39.95

Set-up for tournament practice and play, this realistic simulation pits you against celebrity look-alikes. Tons of options let you control tournament size with 10 to 300 entrants, select limits, ante, rake, blind structures, freezeouts, number of rebuys and competition level of opponents. Pop-up status report shows how you're doing vs. the competition. Save tournaments in progress to play again later. Additional feature allows quick folds on finished hands.

Order now at 1-800-577-WINS or go online to: www.cardozabooks.com

FREE BOOK!
TAKE ADVANTAGE OF THIS OFFER NOW!

The book is **free**; the shipping is **free**. Truly, no obligation. Oops, we forgot. You also get a **free** catalog. **And a $10 off coupon!!** Mail in coupon below to get your free book or go to **www.cardozabooks.com** and click on the red OFFER button.

WHY ARE WE GIVING YOU THIS BOOK?

Why not? No, seriously, after more than 27 years as the world's foremost publisher of gaming books, we really appreciate your business. Take this **free** book as our thank you for being our customer; we're sure we'll see more of you!

THIS OFFER GETS EVEN BETTER & BETTER!

You'll get a **FREE** catalog of all our products—over 200 to choose from—and get this: you'll also get a **$10 FREE** coupon good for purchase of <u>any</u> product in our catalog! Our offer is pretty simple. Let me sum it up for you:

1. Order your **FREE** book
2. Shipping of your book is **FREE!***
3. Get a **FREE** catalog (over 200 items—and more on the web)
4. You <u>also</u> get a **$10 OFF** coupon good for anything we sell
5. Enjoy your free book and **WIN**!

CHOOSE YOUR FREE BOOK

Choose one book from any in the Basics of Winning Series (15 choices): Baccarat, Bingo, Blackjack, Bridge, Caribbean Stud Poker and Let it Ride, Chess, Craps, Hold'em, Horseracing, Keno, Lotto/Lottery, Poker, Roulette, Slots, Sports Betting, Video Poker.

Or choose one book from here: Internet Hold'em Poker, Crash Course in Beating Texas Hold'em, Poker Talk, Poker Tournament Tips from the Pros, or any other title listed.

When you order your free book by Internet, enter the coupon code **KWTHE2**.

HURRY! GET YOUR FREE BOOK NOW!
USE THIS COUPON OR GO TO OUR WEBSITE!

YES! Send me my **FREE** book! I understand there is no obligation! Send coupon to: Cardoza Publishing, P.O. Box 98115, Las Vegas, NV 89193. <u>No</u> phone calls please.

Free book by website: www.cardozabooks.com (click on red OFFER button)

*Shipping is FREE to U.S. (Sorry, due to very high ship costs, we cannot offer this outside the U.S. However, we still have good news for foreign customers: Spend $25 or more with us and we'll include that free book for you anyway!)

WRITE IN FREE BOOK HERE _____

Name _____

Address_____

City _____ State _____ Zip _____

Email Address* _____ Coupon Code: <u>BOSTON2</u>

*Get our FREE newsletter and special offers when you provide your email. Your information is <u>protected</u> by our privacy guarantee: We've been in business 27 years and do NOT and never have sold customer info. One coupon per address or per person only. Offer subject to cancellation at any time.
